W9-CGT-047

Partnerships and Collaborations in Public Library Communities:

Resources and Solutions

Karen Ellis
Taylor Public Library, USA

Managing Director:	Lindsay Johnston
Senior Editorial Director:	Heather Probst
Book Production Manager:	Sean Woznicki
Development Manager:	Joel Gamon
Development Editor:	Joel Gamon
Acquisitions Editor:	Erika Gallagher
Typesetter:	Mackenzie Snader
Cover Design:	Nick Newcomer, Greg Snader

Published in the United States of America by
Information Science Reference (an imprint of IGI Global)
701 E. Chocolate Avenue
Hershey PA 17033
Tel: 717-533-8845
Fax: 717-533-8661
E-mail: cust@igi-global.com
Web site: http://www.igi-global.com

Library of Congress Cataloging-in-Publication Data

Partnerships and collaborations in public library communities : resources and solutions / Karen Ellis, editor.
      pages cm
  Summary: "This book shows how partnerships can be cultivated through projects, programming, funding, and extending the library's presence through unique avenues, offering librarians a better understanding of what might be possible for their situational requirements and limitations"--Provided by publisher.
  Includes bibliographical references and index.
  ISBN 978-1-61350-387-4 (hardcover) -- ISBN 978-1-61350-388-1 (ebook) (print) -- ISBN 978-1-61350-389-8 (print & perpetual access) (print) 1. Libraries and community--Case studies. I. Ellis, Karen, 1961- editor of compilation.
  Z716.4.P37 2012
  021.2--dc23
                                                2011046566

British Cataloguing in Publication Data
A Cataloguing in Publication record for this book is available from the British Library.

All work contributed to this book is new, previously-unpublished material. The views expressed in this book are those of the authors, but not necessarily of the publisher.

List of Reviewers

Barbara Brattin, *Wilkinson Public Library, USA*
Barbara Hathaway, *Bee Cave Public Library, USA*
Carolyn T. Manning, *Wimberley Village Library, USA*
Hillary Dodge, *Clearview Library District, USA*
Holly Gordon, *Texas Department of Health and Human Services Commission, USA*
Katelyn Patterson, *Central Texas Library System, USA*
Kathleen Houlihan, *Austin Public Library, USA*
Kim Kroll, *Lena Armstrong Public Library, USA*
Kimber Fender, *The Public Library of Cincinnati and Hamilton County, USA*
Laura Perna, *Central Texas Library System, Inc., USA*
Laurie Mahaffey, *Central Texas Library System, Inc., USA*
Lindsy D. Serrano, *New York Public Library, Muhlenberg Library, USA*
Margaret Handrow, *Copperas Cove Public Library, USA*
Mary L. Hall, *Bedford Public Library, USA*
Morgan McMillian, *Lake Travis Community Library, USA*
Mrs. Montserrat Alvarez-Massó, *Barcelona Provincial Council Servei de Biblioteques, Spain*
Nkem Ekene Osuigwe, *Anambra State Library Board, Nigeria*
Paolo Melillo, *Orange County Library System, USA*
Peggy Thrasher, *Dover Public Library, USA*
Sol M. Hirsch, *Alachua County Library District, USA*
Sue Soy, *Austin Public Library, USA*
Suzan Nyfeler, *Austin Public Library, USA*

List of Contributors

Table of Contents

Detailed Table of Contents

Section 1

Included are chapters that have collaborations or partnerships that tie the public library better to the community, or use of social service agencies in partnership, or use those community resources to better serve an at-risk population.

The Library Partnership is a jointly operated facility that offers area residents full public library services and access to approximately thirty (30) social service agencies. The collaboration provides a unique environment for clients to receive counseling and advice from social service agencies and the resources, assistance, and services to address their needs from the public library all in one location . Clients are often referred to the library for a variety of eGovernment and other services. The presence of a public library allows potential and scheduled clients to come to the facility without the stigma often attached to entering a social service assistance center.

With competition for customers, funding, and success at a premium these days, libraries must find ways to throw in their lot with neighboring organizations and businesses in order to best serve their shared constituencies. This chapter examines success stories born from collaborations showing that all libraries can share in this type of success—no matter how big or little their community may be—and partner with local companies, businesses, social, and non-profits groups in ways that are not only cost-effective, but can also result in innovative revenue streams for all parties involved.

Chapter 3

The partnerships of the El Dorado County Library system (EDC Libraries) with the First 5 El Dorado
Children and Families Commission (First 5 El Dorado) and other public and private organizations have
created a unique web of collaborations to enhance the pre-literacy competency and confidence of young
children, newborn to five years old, and their families and caregivers in their communities. In recent
years, the EDC Libraries have exponentially increased the number of library-based educational services
for these young and their families. In 2010, 43,000 young children, their parents, and caregivers participated successfully in the pre-literacy-based programs with EDC Libraries and their collaborative partners.

Chapter 4

This chapter describes various readership promotion activities undertaken by a Nigerian State Public
Library in partnership with schools, churches, and the state owned television house. Massive failures in
O' level national and regional examinations and the entrance examinations into the tertiary institutions
have brought up the fact that the education sector in Nigeria is facing monumental challenges. This
combined with a noticeable decline in user statistics, especially amongst school age children in Onitsha
Public Library in South East Nigeria. This decline has long been associated with the school-boy drop-
out syndrome. The State Public Library Board collaborated with agencies in its community to introduce
intervention strategies to halt the trend. These were expected to increase usage of the public and school
libraries, make reading attractive to children of school age, support school curriculum, and help students
make better grades in examinations.

Section 2

*Partnerships in this section are very specific to a particular purpose, such as a unique program, focus on
a specific population or need, such computer skills for re-employment, financial education, responsible
living, science education and film festivals.*

Chapter 5

Providing public library services to a resort community whose members range from service industry
workers to Hollywood moguls positions Wilkinson Public Library in Telluride, CO, as an institution
bridging economic disparities. Community partnerships form the foundation for free library-based film
series hosted by international festivals, including the acclaimed Telluride Film Festival and eclectic Mountainfilm. Both festivals enjoy a long history of birth and nurturing in this remote western ski town, and
as a result of their national success, risk being disconnected from the average local. Through year-long
partnerships with the public library, both festivals are strengthening ties with their home base. In turn,

the library is fulfilling its role as the great equalizer and enhancing its facility through the benevolence of the festival organizations.

Chapter 6

The Mamie Doud Eisenhower Public Library is a single site, medium sized, municipal library in Broomfield, CO. After receiving an initial matched grant of $50,000 from the Sandoz US Foundation ten years ago to build the Sandoz Science and Education Center located on the first floor of the library, the continued partnership with Sandoz Pharmaceuticals, Inc. has evolved into the development of a Science Task Force composed of scientists in the community willing to volunteer their time to bring science programming to the library. This chapter details the initial development and subsequent growth of these partnerships as well as how the evolution of this collaboration has impacted the Young Adult Department science programming and education services. The chapter also focuses on developing collaborations with local companies as well as finding volunteers in the community. Procedural information regarding the recruiting and retaining of volunteers as well as key points in program planning, executing, and evaluating are also shared.

Chapter 7

With fewer staff resources, collaborations and partnerships have become even more important in today's economic environment to help deliver a quality service to library customers. The working partnership established between Malahide Library and the local post-primary school delivers mutual benefits to both. It has enabled the library to meet its customers' needs through sources of volunteers who assist in the delivery of technology-based classes within the library. The cross-generational approach of the partnership has enabled the students to fulfill their school requirements of engaging in social responsibility and developing life skills. The partnership has assisted in enhancing the role of the library within the community and fostering good relationships with its future customers.

Chapter 8

This chapter describes the Orange County Library System's financial literacy workshops and highlights the partnerships that made them a success. While the library system received a grant that helped get the project started, its partners brought expertise and a connection with the target audience that the library alone could not have provided. This project illustrates how community partnerships are a mutually beneficial way for public libraries to establish themselves as a resource for unbiased and reliable information. In addition to the describing the partnerships, this chapter will also focus on the ingredients believed to be the keys to success. The authors hope the experience can serve as a motivator and template for public libraries everywhere wanting to further establish themselves as information resources with community partnership assistance.

Chapter 9

In 2008, the Hampstead Public Library partnered with the New Hampshire Carbon Challenge to encourage Hampstead residents to reduce their carbon emissions. The multi-faceted month-long initiative included programs, services, and resources designed to educate people and motivate them to take the Carbon Challenge and help the environment. The project provided activity and publicity, which helped the library position itself as an information resource in the community. The partnership provided fresh ideas and enthusiasm to both the library and the Carbon Challenge. The Hampstead Public Library pioneered some best practices for future Carbon Challenges in other locations, and leveraged the knowledgebase of the Carbon Challenge to provide a meaningful and memorable experience for its patrons. The Hampstead Carbon Challenge was a lot of fun for everyone.

Section 3

Public libraries can extend services to incarcerated populations, complimenting or enhancing existing education initiatives in those institutions.

Chapter 10

This chapter describes the history of the Second Chance Books Program, a partnership between the Austin Public Library and the Gardner Betts Juvenile Justice Center. It covers the initiation of the partnership in 2002, through the early days and challenges, the growth of the partnership in 2007, and the maturation of the program in 2010. The focus is on the challenges encountered by a maturing community partnership and the resolution of those challenges. Topics include coordination of administrative tasks, transitional leadership, maintaining partnerships through staffing changes, strengthening partner buy-in, and funding concerns for long-term partnerships. The goal of the chapter is to help librarians with established or budding long-term partnerships strategize ways to prepare for and resolve problems encountered along the way.

Chapter 11

In New York City, over five thousand young adults are taken in to custody by the city's department of juvenile justice. (Fenster-Sparber, 2008). While in detention, they do not have easy access to books, and literacy is not always a priority. Although attempts have been made to incorporate library sites throughout New York City's juvenile correctional facilities, students there have limited access to educational materials. Research shows that a higher literacy rate in such facilities can play a vital role in an incarcerated teen's rehabilitation process. The New York Public Library (NYPL) saw an opportunity to reach students who might otherwise not be able to get access to information and build a long-lasting outreach program with Passages Academy, a multi-site correctional school run by New York City's Department of Education and the Department of Juvenile Justice. This case study describes New York Public Library's mission at Passages Academy, which started shortly after Passages was established in 1998 and continues to be a strong community partner today. The author, who also participated in the project, interviewed NYPL librarians and Passages Academy librarians and educators to gain a better understanding of their challenges.

Section 4

Public libraries and schools are common partners, though a good relationship must first be established, and then a myriad of collaborations and partnerships are possible, from small and specific, to larger and ongoing.

Chapter 12

Hillary Dodge, Clearview Library District, USA
Erica Rose, Clearview Library District, USA

The purpose of this chapter is to provide an example of a productive working relationship between a public library and a public school district. For years the Clearview Library District (CLD) struggled with an estranged relationship with the Weld Re-4 School District. Various contributing factors made it difficult for staff to proactively connect with educators and school administration. In 2008, CLD made a commitment to reassessing its role in the community and began exploring ways to better serve more members of the community. CLD selected schools as a priority because they presented a tremendous opportunity to touch a large percentage of the population. This new relationship became a major focus for the Youth Services and Outreach Departments of the Clearview Library District, who worked together to develop a plan to bridge the divide.

Chapter 13

Mary L. Hall, Bedford Public Library, USA

This case study describes the partnership between the Bedford Public Library and an elementary school. This partnership consists of a program designed to assist grade school children with literacy skills. Third grade students read aloud to a Pet Partners team made up of a therapy dog and a handler who is a professional public librarian. The team visits the school weekly with books selected from the public library's collection to provide animal assisted therapy. School staff and teachers collect and provide assessment data on students to create goals and track progress for the students. The librarian, teachers, and school staff work together to create new methods of assessing progress attributed to reading to the dog. During the summer months, the Pet Partners team visits a local Summer Meals site to help address the problem of summer reading loss. Children of all ages are invited to read aloud to the team to participate in animal assisted activities.

This case study illustrates two partnerships between the Taylor Public Library and two area schools, first with the Taylor Independent School District for facility use, and second with the Temple College satellite campus at Taylor for their use of the public library facilities in exchange for a free student worker. The partnership with the local school district was specifically during 2002 through 2006 to continue providing programming during the summer. The Taylor Public Library lost its old facility, and while temporarily located elsewhere, had no venue for summer programs. The library and the school district partnered to hold the summer events on local campuses until the new public library building opened in 2007. The partnership between the Taylor Public Library and Temple College consisted of use of library space to house the college's nursing and medical collections, allow access to these holdings to enrolled college students, and grant students public library cards. For this use, the Taylor Public Library acts as supervisor for a qualifying student worker, funded by Temple College.

Preface

PARTNERSHIPS DEFINED

A partnership or collaboration as described in these chapters has two important aspects. One party has a need, and another can help fill that need while likewise seeing some benefit. A true partnership has to be two-sided. Both parties have to put forth some sort of effort or expertise, or else it is merely outreach. Now, public libraries are very experienced at outreach, selflessly venturing out providing all the work and asking no assistance outside of their own institution. While valiant, this is no longer viable. This book contains many examples of library work beyond traditional roles and services, opening the front door to new collaborations as well as enhancing old stand-bys. Partnerships cannot be judged by duration, as some illustrated here are quite specific and temporary. Long term collaborations are marked by changing parameters and flexibility on behalf of the partners. While many of the creative and innovative collaborations are dependent upon the opportunity for the right partners, there are many lessons illustrated as to what might or might not work for another library.

An article on youth programming between the Denver Public Schools and the City of Denver Parks & Recreation Department (Byrne & Hansberry, 2007) postulated a list of needed factors for a successful collaboration between different partners:

- Shared priorities
- Combined resources
- Institutional support and political will
- Shared clarity of expectations

The benefits included added value to each partner, via the attraction of the public to added services or programs. Also, each partner can enjoy improved reputation in public opinion, and better branding or recognition for the partner. As each partnership is a learning experience, it allows each organization to further build on the skills and knowledge needed to go forth and explore other partnerships or merely to strengthen existing relationships.

Of course, there are also harsher lessons learned as well. Partners are not always compatible, either through organizational imperatives or simply at the staff level. Each collaboration must be manageable by all involved—if not, this resulting poor experience will have long term impact on any future aspirations between the partners. While not everyone "plays well with others," it could also just be a matter of different points of view between management. Or maybe it's just bad timing. It is worth re-approaching past partners who fall into this definition in the future, as climate and personalities may have changed.

Make no mistake—all partnerships or collaborations will have some problems. This is pointed out in the following case studies. The first hint of a problem is not a reason to stop by any means. However, there are some times when partnerships need to dissolve. Part of knowing when to call it quits is as important as all other aspects of a partnership (Byrne & Hansberry, 2007, p. 82).

Why do Public Libraries Need Partners?

In this era of economic downturn, both the public and the publicly supported libraries feel the pinch. In such challenging times, the public has gone back to the library—to use the computers or wireless access, to seek assistance in finding a job, enjoying entertainment such as popular literature, programming, or movies. And public libraries, great service institutions that they are, attempt to rise to the need. Libraries struggle to give instruction to those who are just now returning to a changed workplace. Many of these individuals don't know how to use online applications or how to register to use jobsites, let alone how to sign up for an e-mail account. People can no longer afford to pay for their internet access or fix their broken printer and come to use free Wi-Fi and low rate printing fees at their community library. Summer vacations are conducted at home rather than more exotic locations, so more sign up for summer programs and other library events. Checking out books and movies newly released to DVD are within restricted family entertainment budgets.

Public libraries and their staff are friendly, welcoming, and helpful. It doesn't matter that the patrons need help with computers, or need to hit the how-to books rather than paying a service company, or come to get free assistance when taxes are due. All these great services are free, without an upfront fee or billing. Sadly, very few library patrons actually know how the library is funded (De Rosa & Johnson, 2008). That funding is not increasing, though the demand and need for these library services have dramatically grown. Budgets for public institutions have been relatively flat, if not reduced. The local governing agencies for these public libraries, be they cities, districts, counties, et cetera, face budgeting restrictions of their own. Likewise, state and federal budgets fail to meet these needs as well.

Of course, public libraries are not the only tax funded local service—police, fire, and infrastructure are hard competitors for these reduced tax dollars. When it comes to a levy or tax or bond issue, how can the voters really decide between books or firefighters, librarians, or cops? Governmental decision makers, too, are forced to make hard decisions between what services to fund and which to cut or reduce. And yet government leaders are also required to look towards the future needs of the community, and which investments to make to encourage economic growth.

The public library needs money. Sorry, those new computers and nifty programs aren't free. Staff doesn't just volunteer their time, and the power bill isn't waived by the provider. Librarians have always been very inventive in finding funding. While not trained grant writers, plenty of librarians have written numerous grant applications. The funding sources—private foundations, businesses, or government grants—all have more competition. The basic grant application for more children's books may pale when compared to a complex project with sophisticated planning and measurable outcomes. So, libraries have to look around, see commonalities, and find potential partners. Maybe a partner has access to funding not otherwise available to a library alone. The public library has to be flexible in provision of services. This translates into both traditional and nontraditional partners. A public library must also stay vital to a changing population. In order to fund a directional change in programming and services, a library needs partners.

Why do Potential Partners Need Public Libraries?

Public libraries have a long reputation as a helpful and loved institution. Everyone has a fond library memory, about the library as a place or an interaction with staff. The library is a refuge from the world, an escape from personal woes, and inspiration for future achievements. Because of the mission of public libraries and their abilities to be inclusive and adventurous in services and programs, this is a platform for positional partners to use as well. The library can offer a comfortable locale for other services, and can include the mission of similar service institutions. Other governmental social services, assistance organizations, can be more approachable via the local community library. New and different educational opportunities are likewise more appealing when offered in the neutral environment of the library.

The public library has much to offer its community. With a mission of continuing education, self-enrichment, and improvement, public libraries are integral, providing services that no one else does as well. Frequently, libraries are on the cutting edge of technology. Family friendly library programming and materials are often a draw for potential residences and businesses alike. This is all about quality of life, meeting specific needs for citizens and industry.

The Urban Libraries Council's report *Partners for the Future* urges local governments to take advantage of the public library's programming and services that contribute to community sustainability and growth. (p. 7) Not only that, but the report asserts that public libraries are well positioned to attract corporate partners to further sustainability goals, as in the case of insurance provider Aflac and Columbus, Georgia. (p. 8). Aflac was a strong supporter of Chattahoochee Valley Libraries' summer reading program, allowing the library to reach a much larger audience (p. 13). The goals of the community library and community government often mesh.

Somewhat astonishing for many public librarians is the public's conception that their library is somehow intertwined with many governmental agencies and social organizations. While this is also tied to the misunderstanding of how the library is funded, it is also tied to the encompassing services and programs offered by the library. The public assumes that the library is connected—why not actually make those connections and make them work for the library?

Educational institutions and public libraries share a mission and often the same clientele. This has often resulted in collaboration with programming and facilities. Librarians often venture into area schools, but some schools remain insular, missing out on potential partnerships. As schools are increasingly accountable to state and federal agencies through standardized testing, the public library can be an untapped resource to enhance curriculum or reinforce student skills. Likewise, colleges and universities need to connect with potential students and paying parents, and collaboration with a community library can be a gateway.

Libraries provide literacy skills from early childhood to senior, with pre-literacy, sustained reading, to English as a second language, to digital and technology literacy. (ULC, p. 12). Businesses and industries can invest in their current and future workforce by partnering with libraries. Programming that focuses on the skill sets these potential employers need is an excellent avenue for both the library and the industry to see benefit. Such training initiatives may be a long term investment, but there are additional, more immediate benefits. Whether a world-wide corporation or local corner shop, every business needs a good public perception. Supporting a community via support for programming or collaboration with a community library has the potential to cultivate public good will or make the business more recognizable.

OBJECTIVES AND MISSION

The purpose of this collection of case studies is not to give a "how-to" on forming partnerships, but to give a series of examples of actual partnerships. The commonality is that all of these are based on public libraries coming into partnership with a community entity, educational institution, business, or other organization. Some of these examples are large and complex, others are smaller and simpler. These case studies have been grouped into some very general categories, but they are by no means exhaustive. The partnerships between public libraries and other institutions can be established in myriad ways and through varying levels of commitment.

Perhaps someone will see a project that matches their needs and requirements explicitly. Maybe there are elements of an illustrated partnership that can be borrowed or recreated by another. There may even be cautionary tales or a red flag for someone investigating a potential collaboration. Library administrators can discover possible partnerships that could push forward their institution's mission or services. On the other hand, businesses, schools, and service organizations can see the potential benefits of partnering with a library, and realize the rewards that such successful partnerships can bring. Library students can clearly see the pros and cons of these example partnerships and be better prepared to apply these to their professional career.

These examples of library partnerships are carefully examined for benefits and/or drawbacks. It is much less painful to learn from the mistakes of others. It is too easy to paint a rosy picture of partnerships, and harder to reveal the less desirable examples. Part of what the contributors were asked to point out was an honest examination of the partnerships or collaborations. The aim is to analyze how libraries can best partner with other institutions in their communities with beneficial results. While especially relevant and useful to current library managers, the book may also prove useful to new librarians entering the profession and interested in aggressively reaching out to their communities.

Government and Social Services Agencies

In the first section of chapters, partnerships and collaborations illustrate community partnerships utilizing government and social service agencies.

Sol M. Hirsch, retired director of the Alachua County Library District in Florida, USA, has provided a good example of a more complex partnership and collaboration. Alachua County Library District, located in north central Florida, has provided traditional library services to its quarter of a million citizens. However, the library's focus has shifted to improving the community it serves. Indeed, to remain vital in this economy, the focus on what citizens need to make their lives better is a key mission. This shift in philosophy allowed for the opportunity for new partnerships with organizations or agencies that shared that goal. A coincidence of needs for new facilities, both with the library district planning for a branch, and the social service agencies looking for a location in an at risk neighborhood, led to a match. Both library and agencies had much to learn from each other before they could truly complement each other. Clients found coming to a library that just happened to house other social services they might need much more approachable. This unique meld of missions and facility is a great example of what is possible between a public library and social service agencies.

While there are several examples in this book of large projects, collaborations with big educational institutions, state and county agencies, et cetera, this is not the only way to approach partnerships. Catherine Hakala-Ausperk, of the Northeast Ohio Regional Library System, Warren, Ohio, relays some these smaller successes. Cleveland Heights–University Heights Library in Ohio instead took a more narrow focus. The library instead saw great success with smaller business partnerships in the community. This also took a reexamination of the library's role in the community. The library felt that support of all aspects of the community would make the library more vital to their users. This included partnerships with grocery stores, restaurants, caterers, camera and toy shops, food vendors, art groups, as well as literacy and parenting groups. The library reinvented itself as a real cultural and social gathering location and opened up their meeting room to all manner of meetings, parties, and the like. Too many times public libraries shy away from commercial partners such as small and local business. Cleveland Heights–University Heights Library chose to embrace these partners and realized that the business' success was the library's success.

With another example of collaborating with social services and agencies to advance a shared mission, Carolyn Brooks of the El Dorado Hills Branch Library in California, offers this case study. To the east of Sacramento, California, is El Dorado County. This county library system has the challenge of providing services to a diverse population of 181,058—from suburban to small rural communities. Funding cuts did not lessen the need to address early childhood literacy. A natural partnership evolved between El Dorado County Library and First 5 of El Dorado. In 1998, through passage of a state tax on cigarettes, the First 5 of California was created to address the needs of the state's youth, from newborn to age five. Funding is then disseminated to the counties to address issues early childhood health, education, and childcare. Tied to this initiative are a multitude of state, county, and other local groups. The El Dorado County Library partnered with some of these organizations and institutions, including the national store chain, Target, to implement several programs to address early childhood literacy, as well as some parental education on the side. This chapter represents a collection of smaller projects all tied into the mission of the First 5 program. This assortment can be taken as a whole, or as individual projects that could replicated elsewhere. Flexibility is the key when working with such a variety of partners, but finding common ground within the initiative of betterment of young children allowed for some creative solutions.

Such partnerships and collaborations to achieve a shared goal are also illustrated by Nkem Ekene Osuigwe of the Onisha Public Library in the Nigerian State of Anambra. In this African state, there are quite a few hurtles to advance literacy. Local students would stop going to school and instead apprentice at the big area markets. With this high student drop-out rate, the Anambra State Library Board crafted some clever programs to attract these students to learning and reading. The Onitsha Public Library worked with area schools to incorporate reading into the local schools by way of a spelling competition. The teachers were involved, and the students were keen to compete. The public library in Anambra also re-established bookmobile services as a way to continually provide books to these students. The library staff also recognized the power of the church ladies—mothers, grandmothers, and other relatives of these potential drop-out students. Pulling all these partners together, and including the state television station, the spelling competitions led to great publicity and generated excitement about the library and learning. There were some hard lessons learned, but the Anambra State Library Board has established connections, partners and programs that will enable them to continue to lure at-risk students back to reading and education.

Targeted Programming and Populations

Partnerships can be very specific, with either a certain population or program in mind. This can encompass teaching needed skills to a specific population, focusing on a unique program, and further enhancing the library's community in new ways. This section features such case studies.

Sometimes a successful partnership is all about location. Barbara Brattin, Director of the Wilkinson Public Library in Telluride, Colorado, was able to meet the needs of local film festivals as well as enhancing programming to the community. Telluride, Colorado, besides its fantastic ski resorts and vacation destination, also has two film festivals that see national acclaim, hosting Hollywood directors and movie stars. So, this small historic mining town swells to double its population during festivals and ski season with more affluent seasonal visitors. The library's district serves almost 6,000 residents, a mix of service industry employees and more affluent people who were drawn to the location and could afford the high cost of housing. Seasonal visitors and tourists may have little inclination to use the library, with assumptions that it won't meet high expectations. So, Wilkinson Public Library has the challenge of serving two very different populations, but with the healthy tax base could provide a wide variety of services to all its patrons. So, when the Telluride Film Festival sought to find a good location to expand its screen of free films, they approached the Wilkinson Public Library. With details, exceptions, and other issues hammered out between the festival organizers and library administration, the effort was successful and much appreciated by festival goers and local community members. A second film festival, Mountainfilm, was at first not as smooth. Library policies were revised, and the Mountainfilm management funded a third of the costs to renovate the library's meeting room into a film-friendly space. Successes with the two film festivals led to additional partnerships enhancing the library's other programming and also becoming a more flexible venue for other community events.

A 2006 study produced by the National Science Board (NSB, 2006) indicated a strong need for improvement in student science and math, showing a downward trend for achievement since 1995. One way to bring the United States back into international standing is to address science and math education in young students. Erica Seagraves of the Mamie Doud Eisenhower Public Library illustrates a very successful example of a targeted partnership. The Mamie Doud Eisenhower Public Library, located in Broomfield, Colorado was built with emphasis on science education, using a grant from Sandoz US Foundation to create a science center in the library. Sandoz is an international pharmaceutical company with a manufacturing and product development facility in Broomfield, a suburb of Denver, Colorado. Science programming was the basis for a strong partnership between Sandoz and Mamie Doud Eisenhower Public Library. The construction of the Sandoz Science and Education Center in the library was the first step to addressing science education for youth. A Science Task Force at the library was created, and efforts led to further grants to fund science programming. This also led to programming supported by Sandoz, with their chemists providing several hands-on chemistry workshops for youth. More community experts volunteered their time and expertise to other science related programs, from genetics to botany. The library's dedication to science education made them open to big and smaller collaborations and partnerships, some that could be easily replicated by other libraries who may not have a large pharmaceutical company in town.

Can teenagers and seniors get along at the library? They can if they are both embarked on education. Susan Lovatt of Malahide Library, Fingal County Libraries in Ireland, provides a study of a specific partnership utilizing local teenage students. This chapter introduces American readers to the Irish school system, were there is a break in the middle of secondary education called Transition Year, with an emphasis on personal development, learning life skills and social responsibility. The Malahide Library is seeing growing demand in community use, especially for those needing to return to the workforce or those needing to learn new technology. These tend to be a population over 55 years old, who did not need such skills when they first entered the workforce. And while Malahide Library does offer computer courses, the demand far outstrips the availability. This is a very familiar issue. However, Malahide Library partnered up with the local community school to use those Transitional Year (TY) students and their more savvy technology skills. By volunteering as teachers for technology classes, the TY students were indeed meeting some of the requirements for school. But there were challenges, due to different learning styles and maturity of the student teachers. The challenges overcome still serve as an example of what might be possible at any location, using high school age students as class instructors, particularly pertaining to computers and current technology.

Orange County Library System in Central Florida serves almost a million citizens and growing. The Hispanic population makes up more than a quarter of that figure, and is equally fast growing. Paolo Melillo of the Orange County Library System and staff saw the need for specific programming and needed a partner to provide programming. Many of this Hispanic population are more comfortable with Spanish than with English, a fact that the Orange County Library System recognized as a barrier to existing programming. Language also created an impediment to financial skills, such as banking, budgeting, investing, and related matters. The library was able to obtain a Smart Investing @ Your Library grant from the American Library Association and the Financial Industry Regulatory Authority (FINRA) Investor Education Foundation in 2007. The library saw the need to customize financial education for their Hispanic population and found a partner in the Crummer Graduate School of Business at Rollins College, just north of Orlando. The nationally renowned business school certainly had the expertise and Hispanic Spanish-speaking MBA students. The library coordinated, the MBA students taught, and everyone benefited. This potentially opened the door for more targeting programming with other partners. In many US communities, minority populations are growing. Concerns and planning presented in this chapter are translatable to elsewhere to help local libraries engage these new community members.

Can a public library train the community to live more green? Peggy Thrasher, now of the Dover Public Library, Dover, New Hampshire, presents this unique collaboration. Being environmentally responsible is a growing priority for many people. When the staff at Hampstead Public Library in New Hampshire brainstormed ideas for revitalizing the library and addressing current issues of interest to their adult patrons, saving the planet through green choices and responsible use of resources was a priority. The library partnered with staff of the University of New Hampshire to promote the New Hampshire Carbon Challenge. The Challenge, now the New England Carbon Challenge, was the impetus for a series of programs on reducing a person's carbon footprint. This also led to recruiting other community partners for assistance with programming and the theme. The Hampstead Public Library also set an example, undergoing an energy audit, incorporating additional programs such as battery recycling. Even library staff took the challenge and personally engaged in discussion with patrons to encourage more participation. This program can certainly replicated, in part or in whole, especially with the online tools set up by the New England Carbon Challenge.

Incarcerated Populations

For some libraries, their service population extends into detention centers and correctional facilities. Eventually, these incarcerated individuals will return to the community. There is certainly value in serving these individuals before they are released and giving them skills and training to make their transition back to the community a little better.

Teenagers are a challenging audience, let alone teenagers who are in detention or incarcerated for committing a crime. Establishing library services in collaboration with the detention centers and the assigned school teachers was not a program for the timid. Convincing library administration and the Travis County Juvenile Board that programming for the detention center youth was a worthy cause during economic shortfalls was challenging. Kathleen Houlihan, Austin Public Library, Texas, presents this case study. This is a venture into a service model that is not well explored—how to address the needs of these detained youth. The Gardner Betts Juvenile Justice Center had two facilities—one for short term detention of youth awaiting trial, and another for long-term housing unit called the Leadership Academy. The Austin Public Library established two satellite libraries in both the short term and long term facilities at Gardner Betts. Working with facility staff, teachers from the Austin Independent School District assigned to the facility, and assistance from publishers, the satellite libraries shaped up to be collections of interest to this underserved population of youth. There were many issues that had to be addressed, from coordination to staff training. From scandals about youth correctional centers in Texas to more budget cuts and commitment issues from partners, this eye opening chapter lays out this complex project.

Also addressing the need of incarcerated youth, the New York Public Library has long standing initiative of providing services to inmates, as described by Lindsy D. Serrano of the New York Public Library, New York. While earlier focus for the library's programming had traditionally been on adult inmates, detained or incarcerated youth had been long overlooked. The prison system had adult librarians and facilities, but was unable to sustain services to the youth facilities due to funding cuts. New York City's Board of Education worked with the Department of Juvenile Justice to create a regular educational program within the youth system called Passages Academy. This was a great advance, but more could be done. The Passages Academy called upon the NYPL librarians, and they collaborated with Passages staff to encourage love of reading among the young inmates. There were many successful programs and equally as many challenges. NYPL librarians worked with two different agencies—the Department of Juvenile Justice and the Board of Education. This population cannot be ignored, as they will eventually return to their communities. The efforts of Passages Academy teachers and NYPL librarians serve as a positive influence on this population.

Educational Partners

Public libraries and schools are common partners; though a good relationship must first be established, a myriad of collaborations and partnerships are possible, from small and specific, to larger and ongoing.

Whether or not a partnership appears logical and potentially rich with possibilities, nothing will work if your partner doesn't want to play. While some chapters in this collection are working off a great partnership due to common goals, great short term or long term relationships or other motivations, how do you woo a partner who is uninterested or even antagonistic? This was the dilemma described by Hillary Dodge and Erica Rose of the Clearview Library District in Colorado. Of course, it made perfect sense to establish collaborative programs with the local school district, but past partnering between the library and the schools had a checkered past. With some fresh enthusiasm from newer library staff, and with the purpose of becoming more proactive in the relationship, Clearview Library District had to rebuild a foundation for a partnership. A foothold in this process was meeting with school officials and securing the support for library/school collaborations. This also progressed into some flexibility with library policy and procedures. With the goal of getting the public library to the schools and the schools to the public library, it took steady effort to establish the partnership. The dedicated staff of the Clearview Library District is an excellent example of how to approach and reestablish a good partner in their community, something that any other public library could tailor to meet their own needs. Collaborative projects with community partners are important, but first you must either find or mold a willing partner.

You may have heard about using therapy dogs to encourage children to read. And what an endearing program, to have child reading to nonjudgmental dog. Is it worth the effort to set up such a program? And where would you ever begin? How would you make such a program work? Reading with a therapy dog has been recognized in the past decade as having more than just health benefits. Some therapy dogs have made the transition to reading coaches at Bedford Public Library, in Bedford, Indiana, USA. The point of view in this chapter is unique in that the author, Mary Hall, the Adult Services and Circulation Manager, is also a service dog trainer. With good preexisting working relationship between Bedford Public Library and the local school district, grounds for a focused partnership program were already laid. Indiana state standardized tests revealed poor reading comprehension in 4th graders, and in improvement plan was drawn up by the Indiana Department of Education. To focus on third grade students at most risk, the school and the library worked together through the reading therapy dog program. Not just an outreach program, the school teachers and administrators are fully invested in the reading dog program, and with that cooperation, the program was extended into the summer. An additional partner joined the reading dog program, funding the purchase of books given to participating students.

Education is the common ground that brings schools and public libraries together. The two examples of school collaborations or partnerships in this chapter are quite specific, as described by Karen Ellis, Library Director of the Taylor Public Library, Taylor, Texas. The Taylor Public Library partnered with the local school district for facility use when the public library lost its building due to an accumulation of water damage. Until a new public library could be built, the library was squeezed into a much smaller space at the city hall. That proposed a problem for summer reading events that were very well attended. The local school district, with whom the library had an excellent and well established relationship, assisted with this need for programming space, and the school students got treated to programming not otherwise available to them. The second example involved the local junior college campus in town and their need for library space. The public library offered shelving for college materials, and became a site for library instruction and services. In turn, the college supplied the library what they most needed: a free worker. These two school partnerships saw gains on both sides of the relationships, which is what really makes a partnership work.

Karen Ellis
Taylor Public Library, Texas, USA

REFERENCES

Byrne, A., & Hansberry, J. (2007). Collaboration: Leveraging resources and expertise. *New Directions for Youth Development*, (114): 75–84. doi:10.1002/yd.214

De Rosa, C., & Johnson, J. (2008). *From awareness to funding: A study of library support in America: A report to the OCLC Membership.* Retrieved from http://www.oclc.org/reports/funding/default.htm

National Science Board. (January 2006). *America's pressing challenge-Building a stronger foundation: A companion to science and engineering indicators-2006.* Retrieved from http://www.nsf.gov/statistics/nsb0602/nsb0602.pdf

Urban Libraries Council. (1996). *Partners for the future: Public libraries and local governments creating sustainable communities.* Retrieved from http://urbanlibraries.org/associations/9851/files/0110ulc_sustainability_singlepages_rev.pdf

Section 1

Included are chapters that have collaborations or partnerships that tie the public library better to the community, or use of social service agencies in partnership, or use those community resources to better serve an at-risk population.

Chapter 1
Neighborhood Resource Center:
The Library Partnership

Sol M. Hirsch
Alachua County (Florida) Library District, USA

ABSTRACT

The Library Partnership is a jointly operated facility that offers area residents full public library services and access to approximately thirty (30) social service agencies. The collaboration provides a unique environment for clients to receive counseling and advice from social service agencies and the resources, assistance, and services to address their needs from the public library all in one location. Clients are often referred to the library for a variety of eGovernment and other services. The presence of a public library allows potential and scheduled clients to come to the facility without the stigma often attached to entering a social service assistance center.

INTRODUCTION

This case study will provide an overview of the project, how and why the project was conceived, how the agencies work together, the project's effectiveness, and how this project has been a catalyst for other projects that have secured a new appreciation for the place of a public library within a community.

For several years, the Alachua County Library District (ACLD) has been shifting its focus from providing residents with the very best library services to providing library services that make a better community. This is reflected in its mission statement, "Alachua County Library District: a key to building a better community by creating opportunities to participate, connect, and discover" and through our tag line "…thinking outside the book…"[1] ACLD continues to value the importance of delivering traditional library services. But, ACLD recognizes that by positioning its services to meet community needs, the public library becomes more relevant to its residents and the community groups with which ACLD partners. In turn, these community organizations have become library advocates. The Library Partnership project

DOI: 10.4018/978-1-61350-387-4.ch001

is a prime example of this form of community librarianship that is described as "…being tied to the creation of partnerships that involve local people, multiple local government agencies, and business and volunteer organizations. Community librarianship also links to a commitment to concentrate on helping the information poor and a willingness to step beyond conservative practices in public librarianship."[2]

Alachua County is located in north central Florida. The 2010 county population was estimated at 255,692 of which 65% is non-Hispanic White, 22% is non-Hispanic Black, 9% Hispanic origin, and 4% other.[3] Gainesville is the county seat and also the home to the University of Florida.

WHAT IS THE LIBRARY PARTNERSHIP?

The Library Partnership, a Neighborhood Resource Center is a collaboration of ACLD, the Partnership for Strong Families, Inc. (PSF), the Florida Department of Children and Families (DCF), and the Casey Family Programs. The initial project concept focused on the desire by PSF and DCF to redesign traditional approaches to foster care and, through preventative services and programs, reduce the number of children who enter foster care due to abuse or neglect. They were supported in their efforts by the Casey Family Programs through strategic consulting and grant support.

The operating expenses for this 7,100 square foot leased spaced are split 60/40 between ACLD and PSF. The renovation expense was also split by the same percentage. ACLD and PSF pay for their own staff who work at the joint facility.

The goal of The Library Partnership is to strengthen families in the service area by providing a comprehensive array of information, programs, and services so families can help themselves and get the resources they need. The focus is on the basic elements that often lead to child removal

and include economic self-sufficiency, family support, child welfare, health, and safety. On site PSF staff coordinate the activities and schedules of the more than thirty (30) social service agencies that rotate through The Library Partnership.

Shared offices and meeting rooms are available for social service agency counselors to meet with clients. PSF staff perform an intake analysis for new clients, match clients to agencies, and set up initial agency appointments. PSF and participating social service agencies also present a variety of programs open to the public that are co-sponsored by ACLD and appear in the Library's online and print program guides. Programs include spousal abuse and parenting support groups, computer training, assistance with government housing applications, interview skills, clothing and food drives/distribution, and nutrition advice,

ACLD supports the social service agencies and their clients by offering a wide range of eGovernment services and library materials/resources tailored to complement client needs. For example, this library collection has a higher percentage of parent resource, job skill, early learning, and literacy materials than our typical branch. Library and social service agency staffs meet quarterly to discuss and coordinate services, resources, and programs.

WHY THIS COMMUNITY NEEDS THE LIBRARY PARTNERSHIP

The goal of this project by the primary agencies involved, PSF, DCF, and the Casey Family Programs was to redesign the foster care model and prevent children from being removed from their homes and families. Nationally, the traditional foster care focus has been on the care of the child after removal and then developing means to reunify the child with his/her family. More and more communities are realizing, through the efforts of agencies like the Casey Family Programs, that serious emotional harm occurs when a child is removed from a family even for a short period. It is more cost effective long term to provide preventive services than foster care and child and family rehabilitative services. Public library services became an integral part of the redesign approach.

The plan to redesign the foster care system started by selecting an area where the new approach could be tested. The three primary agencies analyzed data by zip code and identified 32609 as the area with highest number of reported child maltreatment, 98.5 reported incidents per 1,000 children ages 0 – 17. The next highest rate was nearly 20% lower. (There was high incidence of other factors related to maltreatment and child removal in 32609 that this project could also address.) In Alachua County, the 32609 area has the highest percent of teen births, the 2nd highest number of Medicaid births, the 2nd highest percent of adult residents without a high school diploma, and the 3rd highest rate of single parent families.

THE AGENCIES INVOLVED

The benefits of blending social service agencies and a public library services were not at first apparent to all the agencies ultimately involved in this project. In fact, as described later in this chapter, the inclusion of a public library was never considered during the initial phases of the neighborhood resource center project development. Only social service agencies were involved.

As background to understanding how The Library Partnership evolved and continues to succeed, it is beneficial to know more about the primary partners.

ACLD is an independent special tax district that provides public library services to the more than 250,000 residents of Alachua County, Florida. ACLD has a headquarters library, ten (10) traditional branch libraries, a branch library that operates out of the county detention center, and two (2) bookmobiles. The Library District receives exceptional community financial and programmatic support from the Friends of the Library (FOL) and the ACLD Foundation. Each year, the FOL's Snuggle Up and Read initiative provides funding to give every child enrolled in Head Start their own book. ACLD places a strong emphasis on children's services, particularly school readiness.

PSF is a non-profit agency under contract with the Florida Department of Children and Families to provide comprehensive child welfare services in the thirteen (13) counties that make up Florida Judicial Circuits 3 and 8. In 1998, the Florida legislature mandated that all foster care services be privatized (Florida Statutes 409.1671). The 3-year transition began in 2000. The privatized approach to these child welfare services is called Community-Based Care because the legislative intent is to create a strong effective system through a community driven process that is locally organized and empowered.

In Alachua County, there was not one existing agency that could provide the vast array of services necessary to adequately address the complex issues associated with comprehensive child welfare. A group of local social service providers including Children's Home Society, Family Preservation Services, and Meridian Behavioral Healthcare pooled their resources to create what is now called the Partnership for Strong Families, Inc. Since 2003, PSF has provided comprehensive child welfare services to this region.

DCF is the state agency charged with protecting children, the elderly, and the disabled from abuse and neglect. DCF is responsible for the nearly 20,000 Florida children in foster care and for finding permanent homes for children who cannot safely be reunited with their families. DCF services also includes protective services for adults, child care oversight, inspections, licensing and training, statewide domestic violence programs, Medicaid, food stamps, coordination of homelessness services, management of the state public mental health program, and coordination of substance abuse and refugee services with the federal government programs. The trend has been to move some of these areas from direct services provided by state employees to management and oversight by state employees of privatized programs.

The Casey Family Programs, headquartered in Seattle, Washington and with $2.1 billion in assets as reported in its 2010 Annual Report, is the nation's largest operating foundation focused entirely on foster care and child welfare systems. Their mission is to provide, improve and ultimately prevent the need for foster care. They provide consulting services and grants to child welfare agencies on the state and local levels to implement effective child welfare practices. The Casey Family Programs also provides research and technical expertise to members of Congress and state legislators so they may develop laws and policies to better the lives of at-risk children, their families, and children in foster care. The foundation was established in 1966 by the founder of the United Parcel Service, Jim Casey, and is one of several Casey Family foundations committed to the welfare of children and families.

HOW THE LIBRARY PARTNERSHIP STARTED

In retrospect, it seems obvious that public libraries and social service agencies should be working together closely, despite distinctly different missions. Social service agencies work with clients to comprehensively diagnose areas of concern and provide a treatment plan. Public libraries have the resources and staff expertise to guide social service clients through their prescribed plan. The focus on the client is what binds our collective work.

For several years, ACLD had been searching for a site for an Eastside Branch Library, ideally to co-locate with another entity. ACLD had funds in a capital reserve account to construct and furnish a free standing 8,000 square foot library and funds for staff and operations.

ACLD staff had spoken to county, city, school board, the University of Florida, and Santa Fe College representatives about sharing one of their sites for a public library. These other agencies all have operating facilities in the Eastside. Nearly all also have plans to renovate or build new facilities in the area. The agencies were, for the most part, favorable to sharing a site and common area maintenance expenses with ACLD. However, the economic downturn starting in FY 2008 caused these agencies to delay their new or renovation projects.

During the FY 2008/09 budget and planning sessions held in May 2008, ACLD staff advised its Governing Board that in the near term the likelihood of identifying a partner for the Eastside project was not good. However, the opening of a full service branch library serving the Eastside would remain ACLD's highest priority. Alternatively, staff proposed seeking a temporary storefront leased site in the Eastside area to have a library presence. No funds in the FY 2008/09 budget were allocated for the development or staffing of a temporary storefront library project because staff believed it would take a year to identify a site, approve lease terms, develop facility plans, and order furnishings.

In late 2007, PSF and DCF began working with the Casey Family Programs to redesign the foster care system. Their approach was to find ways to reduce the number of children entering foster care by increasing protective factors in vulnerable communities within Alachua County. Extensive demographic research was done to identify by zip code the verified reported "hotspots" of child maltreatment and removal. The zip code, 32609, with the highest number of verified reports and sheltering, was chosen for the project. Eastside, the area where ACLD was searching for a library site and a partner, is in the 32609 zip code area.

PSF, DCF, and the Casey Family Programs developed a one-page overview of the proposed Foster Care Redesign plan and a concept paper for services using a neighborhood resource center

(NRC) model with a list of existing agencies which could provide support and services through the center. The NRC is a one-stop center for social services used in many communities throughout the United States. There was never any consideration of including a public library in the NRC project. In their extensive research, the Casey Family Programs consultants had never come across a combined NRC and public library.

In early to mid-2008, Shawn Salamida, CEO of PSF, and Ester Tibbs, DCF Circuit 3/8 Administrator held planning meetings with staff from the key social service agencies serving the child welfare system to discuss the NRC concept and gain their support. In June 2008, more than one hundred potential partners and stakeholders were invited to a conference to discuss the Foster Care Redesign plan and NRC concepts.

The potential partners were asked to complete a survey and describe how their agencies could provide services to support the project. ACLD was not invited to attend the conference and was unaware this effort to redesign the foster care system and create an NRC was taking place. ACLD and several of the social service and other participating agencies attending the meeting regularly worked together on joint programs and projects. Yet, no agency suggested the public library be invited or included.

For example, DCF and ACLD were working together to promote the DCF ACCESS program, an online system by which persons could apply for benefits such as food stamps. Many DCF offices were being closed statewide due to budget cuts and DCF asked public libraries across Florida to make their Internet computers available to and assist persons applying for benefits. DCF recognized that many of the persons eligible for benefits did not have Internet access or would need assistance completing the application. In that instance, they recognized the valuable role public libraries could play to their clients. Yet, the value of adding public library services to the NRC project was not recognized.

The NRC concept was embraced by the social service agencies. Three (3) committees made up of social service agency representatives were formed, Self Sufficiency, Family Support and Child Development, and Health and Safety. The committees were to determine the types of services that could be provided at the proposed NRC. By late summer 2008, more than 25 agencies agreed to provide services at the NRC for families in the area. The agencies agreed to rotate staff through the center to provide an accessible and convenient way to deliver services to clients and families. PSF would manage the facility and coordinate the scheduling of services.

Through this process, PSF and DCF felt that at least one of the agencies would be willing to co-locate to the NRC and share operating expenses. The timing of the project coincided with the start of state and local budget reductions caused by the recession and lower property values. None of the agencies had funds to open a new office or relocate. The NRC project reached a serious hurdle.

In October 2008, Ms. Tibbs made a presentation about the NRC project to the Alachua County Children's Alliance. The Children's Alliance is made up of federal, state and local agencies including law enforcement, the State Attorney, the public library, and the school board, the United Way of North Central Florida, other not-for-profit organizations, and private citizens all with the common goal of ensuring the children of the county have the resources and environment to reach their full potential.

After the presentation, the ACLD library director approached Ms. Tibbs about considering the public library as a partner for the NRC. The successful implementation of the local ACCESS project between ACLD and DCF gave us the confidence we could work together well. At the same time, a Library Services and Technology Act (LSTA) grant had recently been awarded to ACLD to develop training and print and online support materials to instruct staff from rural public libraries in the region on eGovernment services.

It became apparent ACLD staff eGovernment expertise and interest would blend well with and complement the work of the social service agencies on the NRC project.

Immediately, ACLD, DCF, and PSF staff compared their site selection criteria for the Eastside Branch and the NRC. To our surprise, the criteria were nearly identical. Ideally, the library and NRC would be located on a bus line, near schools, within walking distance for many users, have sufficient parking, be in a highly visible location, and have attractive lease terms. Together, a search began and soon a site was identified that met all the criteria. The project was expected to take at least 12 months before the doors would open.

The location is a 7,096 square foot space at the end of a strip shopping center. The center includes a Dollar General Store, a laundromat, beauty parlor, and beauty supply store. A very popular barbeque take-out stand operated on a vacant out parcel. Demographically, the community is racially and economically diverse. The site is located across a 2-lane side street from an elementary school and a middle school is adjacent to the property. There are a charter school and a parochial school within walking distance. DCF has an office within 100 yards of the chosen site. And, there are more than 20 churches located within a 2-mile radius of the site. Though the site is less than 2 miles from the ACLD Headquarters Library, a large number of existing and new library users preferred this neighborhood branch.

In November 2008, the library director informed the ACLD Governing Board of the proposed collaboration and presented the concept for a joint facility. A fiscal and operational plan was also presented that would reallocate existing funds and staff for the project. The Governing Board strongly endorsed the project and gave the library director permission to develop cost-sharing and operating agreements with PSF and to negotiate a lease with the property owner.

In December 2008, ACLD and PSF entered into discussions about the building program. We realized our needs greatly overlapped. For example, we both needed a children's area and a meeting room and these became common areas. The entry area, restrooms and a large kitchen area to hold food preparation and nutrition programs were also considered common areas. Operationally, we both wanted a strong focus on children of all ages. ACLD would provide a teen room. An important component of providing eGovernment support to the social service agencies clients was the availability of Internet computers with high-speed access. ACLD would provide approximately 20 Internet access computers and Wi-Fi available 24/7/365 that reached into the parking lot.

Eventually, the lease space cost allocation was set at 60% for ACLD and 40% for PSF. The leased space needed a complete demolition and build-out. ACLD and PSF also agreed to split the renovation cost 60/40 like the operating expenses. It was agreed that ACLD would lease the space and PSF would be a sub-lessee. The lease agreement with the landlord contained a fiscal non-funding early termination without penalty clause if ACLD or PSF, the sub-lessee, did not have operational funds approved by their respective governing bodies.

It was during this period that the question arose about what to call the joint library and NRC. ACLD and PSF both agreed we needed this facility to be presented to the community as one resource and not two separate entities operating under the same roof. We agreed that we would be neither a branch library nor a social service center, but much more. The name needed to convey a seamless approach to service to all. However, we also understood that persons in the community would, through our name, need to identify the services we offered. We decided to be The Library Partnership, a Neighborhood Resource Center, a combination of our organizational names and how we wanted the facility to be viewed.

In January 2009, the ACLD Governing Board approved the lease and the PSF sub-lease. ACLD would be responsible for contracting for architectural services and use its facilities staff, including a general contractor, to oversee the renovation. ACLD and PSF staff together worked with the architect to develop the final layout and plans. One critical item creatively addressed by the architect was a layout that would allow ACLD and PSF to individually and securely access the common areas when only one of our agencies was present. For example, PSF or agencies and their clients can use the meeting room while the library remains inaccessible.

By the end of February 2009, the final demolition and renovation plans were developed and approved by ACLD and PSF. The City of Gainesville took 4 weeks to issue a renovation permit. The time was used to get construction contractors scheduled and start demolition. ACLD began the process of selecting furnishings and equipment. Renovations began in late March 2009. Construction was estimated to take at least 90 days and furnishings, collection, and equipment installation would take another 30 days. The project completion date was changed to August 2009, or 10 months from the time ACLD and DCF agreed to partner on the project.

GOOD FORTUNE

As construction began, ACLD started to address the project in more detail, especially the opening day collection, staffing and funding. We were very fortunate in all these areas and took it as a sign this project was meant to be. In October 2008, ACLD started a renovation and expansion project at one of it branch libraries. The building would close for 18 months and a temporary library would operate in smaller, leased space nearby. We planned to use the staff not assigned to the temporary library to fill vacancies as they occurred that year in order to save salary expense. From this pool of staff, 3.5 FTE were identified to assist with planning services and work at The Library Partnership for the balance of FY 2009. Funds for the new positions would be added to the ACLD budget for the following year.

There would need to be at least 15,000 items for the opening day collection, which we estimated to be valued at about $300,000. Again, a decision made years earlier came into play. ACLD was in the process of switching to a "floating" collection meaning ownership of an item was not assigned to a specific branch location. Materials would remain at the library location to which they were returned and not be sent back to their "home" branch.

The Library's Technical Services Section was assigned to identify appropriate materials that could be "floated" to The Library Partnership without diminishing any existing branch collection. This greatly reduced the expense of stocking The Library Partnership. ACLD staff was allowed access to the Friends of the Library materials being readied for their upcoming semi-annual sale. The ACLD Friends book sale is the largest in the southeast United States and they typically have 400,000 items available at each sale. Nearly one-thousand additional items were selected for The Library Partnership.

As publicity about the project spread, the ACLD Foundation became interested in providing support. (The Foundation had committed to making contributions to enhance the quality of the ACLD Snuggle Up Centers in each of our locations as they were renovated.) Snuggle Up Centers are spaces within our libraries designed specifically to support pre-school children and their parents and caregivers. The Snuggle Up Centers are part of a Success by 6 community-wide campaign coordinated by the United Way of North Central Florida to ensure children are adequately prepared to enter school. The ACLD Foundation donated $15,000 for The Library Partnership's Snuggle Up Center.

Our good fortune continued. The State Library of Florida became aware of our project in late February 2009 and recognized its significance in terms of their statewide focus on eGovernment services. The State Library desired to support our innovative project because of its potential to be replicated by other public libraries and it complemented other statewide eGovernment projects the State Library was overseeing. In March 2009, ACLD was awarded an LSTA grant for $93,000, of which $63,000 was used to purchase new materials for The Library Partnership. (In FY 2010, the State Library awarded an additional $120,000 LSTA grant for the operating support of The Library Partnership.)

We also were extremely fortunate with the construction and furnishings/equipment delivery schedules. There were no unforeseen delays. In fact, the project was ahead of schedule. ACLD, PSF, DCF, and the Casey Family Programs planned for a grand opening on July 8, 2009. However, The Library Partnership was ready earlier and we opted for a "soft opening" on June 15, 2009. The project was nearly 4 months ahead of the original schedule and opened to the public only 8 months from the time ACLD became aware of the NRC project. The entire project from inception to opening took only 240 days.

HOW THE LIBRARY PARTNERSHIP WORKS

The Library Partnership was designed from the onset to be a community center seamlessly offering a full range of services to assist residents. Together, PSF and ACLD staff can respond to nearly any user's question or need from referrals to intervention to information. The goal is, in one place and as conveniently as possible, to provide the user with services to address their need.

A person entering the facility is greeted in the lobby by a volunteer or PSF staff. First time visitors in particular appreciate a description of the services offered at The Library Partnership. When appropriate, the receptionist will refer the user to either library or PSF staff for assistance. Persons referred to the PSF staff often have questions about social service assistance. The PSF staff complete an in-take analysis to determine the type of and level of assistance. For simple needs, PSF staff can refer the user directly to library staff for help. In more complex situations, PSF staff will assist the user by making follow-up appointments with the appropriate social service agencies at this same facility. These agencies typically provide one-on-one or family counseling for services that include mental health, abuse, or food, housing, or job assistance. The Library Partnership provides office and conference room spaces scheduled by PSF staff and shared by the agencies rotating through the facility for individual, group, or family meetings.

At the meetings with social service providers, more thorough analysis of needs occur and a treatment plan may be developed. The public library is often the source for the plan components, especially in areas like job skill development, literacy tutoring, resume writing, interviewing, computer skill assistance, GED preparation, or parenting skills. ACLD staff are especially well trained and experienced in eGovernment services and can assist users with online benefit or job applications. In some cases, users only need access to free, broadband Internet services and may not have realized these are available at the public library.

Conversely, library staff can refer users to the PSF staff for in-take analysis. Library users asking for eGovernment help may volunteer more information about other service needs. In these instances, library staff can advise the user about the social service and legal assistance available in the same facility.

Some user needs can be easily addressed by The Library Partnership services. However, the impact of having access to relatively standard services should not be underestimated. For many persons in need, The Library Partnership is the first convenient and non-threatening service center they have used. Because of the public library presence, The Library Partnership removes any stigma attached to entering a social service center. In fact, one domestic violence center uses The Library Partnership as a secure, neutral meeting place for counselors and abused women because the victims can truthfully say they are going to the library.

Having easy access to services, resources, and advice can lead to a better job or home situation that can prevent more serious situations, like child maltreatment, domestic violence or dropping out of high school. A grandmother told library staff that a grandson who lived with her was going to repeat 8th grade because he failed math. She feared if left back, he would eventually drop out of school. However, if he could complete and pass an online math course over the summer, he could be promoted and attend high school. The grandmother did not have a computer at home or car to drive her grandson to the next closest library. The Library Partnership is within walking distance to her home and had computers, additional homework help tutors, practice tests, and online help databases. Her grandson passed the online class and went on to high school.

The Library Partnership hours of operation are determined jointly by the onsite ACLD and PSF managers. Work schedules are also coordinated to ensure the full range of library and social services can be provided during all hours of operation. Special events, like clothes drives and food drives, are also developed by both managers. The public programs are planned together and many are presented by the social service agencies. All programs presented at The Library Partnership are considered to be co-sponsored by ACLD in order to fully publicize the events through the library's website and marketing department. PSF also publicizes all public programs through their marketing department to ensure we get the widest

publicity. There is no distinction made between a PSF or ACLD program. From the user's perspective, everything is a Library Partnership program or event. ACLD and PSF even share volunteers.

WHY THE LIBRARY PARTNERSHIP IS EFFECTIVE

Some of the advantages of this collaborative project have been discussed, such as cost sharing and complementary services. There are two overriding factors from which all other successes emanate.

The first factor is that from the start ACLD and PSF decided this facility and its purpose could only succeed if it was a true partnership and collaboration. All significant program and operational decisions had to be made as equal partners. What was good for one organization had to be good for both. The second factor is related to the first. The ACLD and PSF site managers work together as equals and as though they both work for the same organization. The teamwork and passion they display for their community and work is remarkable. In addition to their work duties, they volunteer their own time within the community. As much as anything else, their collaboration has been a key to success.

There are more reasons why this project has been successful. However, this specific type of collaborative endeavor will not work in every community. The need for social services may not be high or the agencies that provide certain services may not be available in some communities. But the project does provide insight on how public libraries can work with social services and other agencies in the delivery of highly effective client-based services that are cost efficient. The project can be a model for creative approaches to 21st century library services that make public libraries more clearly relevant in the eyes of the community and in areas other than social services.

The same approach can be applied with local businesses to provide employee job-skill enhancement training or on-site research.

Libraries have experienced an explosion of eGovernment and other online services requests. In most situations, public libraries have designed their eGovernment services based on their client demand experiences. Library staff hear what users are asking and provide services and resources to address those requests. This is the traditional approach to library service, reactive in nature, and on the surface demand driven.

But what are social service agencies telling their clients they need? Does the library user request match what the social service provider has recommended or what is available? The Library Partnership relationships address this link by getting input from library users and the agency providers who recommend the services.

In the early stages of the project development, ACLD engaged in discussions of the purpose of a public library in this project. Frankly, most social service agencies thought the library presence was purely a way to reduce operating costs for the project. In fact, some local agency heads questioned the value of a public library to the project and that it might overshadow the social service and foster care redesign elements. It was surprising to ACLD staff to learn that agency staff with whom we had worked with closely for years had a very limited understanding of the full range of services public libraries provide.

Meaningful dialogues began between ACLD and the participating agencies to educate each other about the services we provide and how we could more effectively work together so that ultimately our users benefit. For the first time, many agency staff learned that libraries provide literacy programs, computer classes, job skill development resources, parenting materials, Internet access, and one-on-one assistance to persons with limited knowledge of how to access information.

Library staff, for the first time, sat with agency staff to learn what they were telling clients about addressing identified needs. This allowed library staff to focus their eGovernment training on specific areas and to develop or procure resources that serve social service agency clients. The Library Partnership materials collection is customized to address the types of services the agency staff tell their clients they need to have. For example, the collection contains a high proportion of high-interest, low vocabulary materials to assist literacy efforts. There are also a large number of GED and job testing materials to aid the unemployed and underemployed. The knowledge gained from social service providers about eGovernment through The Library Partnership has been shared through the Library District and with other public libraries in Florida.

ACLD has also experienced some indirect benefits as a result of this project. Through our collaborations, ACLD has added the social service agencies as new and strong advocates for library services. At the annual ACLD and state legislative delegation meeting, the speakers who addressed the legislators were primarily social service agency heads. The meeting was held at The Library Partnership where state legislators could see firsthand a cost effective and creative approach to addressing social service needs, and the important role public libraries could play in this area.

The Library Partnership provides an opportunity for ACLD to offer its services to many new users. This was especially true for the elementary and middle school students who now have a place to go after school and who never had access to a public library before. Many persons who come to the shopping center to shop and use the laundromat now use The Library Partnership, have library cards, use library resources, and make use of the social service agencies.

The Library Partnership is very involved in the community it serves. A clear goal identified at project inception was to strengthen families. The best way that can be done is to encourage families to participate in planning the services being offered. The Library Partnership has a Community Advisory Council that meets monthly to identify services that should be provided through the facility. The citizens who participate include local families, ACLD staff, PSF staff, other agency staff, and a pastor from a nearby church. The Community Impact Council is also an excellent way to promote Library Partnership activities throughout the community.

As previously mentioned, this project enhanced the place of the public library in the community. Rather than missing out on governmental or not-for-profit agency meetings, ACLD started to be invited to meetings. ACLD found itself being considered a critical element in community discussions about community redevelopment projects, job stimulus, and children's welfare.

OUTCOME MEASURES

Results are the only true way to measure the effectiveness of a project and participation in programs and use of the services are good measurement tools. As a collaborative venture, both ACLD and PSF consider The Library Partnership to be extremely effective and meeting or exceeding all the goals we set. The following information is the basis for that conclusion.

The project started with a goal to reduce the number of children residing in this zip code from entering the foster care system. It is nearly impossible to measure how many children would have entered the foster care system if not for The Library Partnership. In fact, PSF feel that it will take at least five years to collect sufficient data to determine the role of The Library Partnership in measuring the success of their Foster Care Redesign project.

However, the statistics reported by PSF for the calendar year 2010 could lead one to assume progress is being made. Throughout their service area, PSF has made significant progress related to child welfare. For the recent 12-month period, 92% of children reunified with their families are still in

their homes, the adoption goal was exceeded by 10% to 173 children, and the number of children entering foster care is declining.

The Library Partnership NRC-Related Use Measures

The measures we have for The Library Partnership are also better than expected and suggest a high level of satisfaction of the services. PSF staff collected three sets of information. The first set of data identifies the category of services requested by clients/users in 2010. The next two sets of data are satisfaction surveys. One survey polled clients/users. The other survey polled the agencies that see clients at The Library Partnership.

In calendar year 2010, PSF recorded 10,880 visits to the NRC component of The Library Partnership. This is separate from visitors to the library, though some visitors may have also used the library. There were 4,448 requests for social service assistance in 2010, including 1,130 requests by children.

Of those requests, 51% were in the category Self Sufficiency (Food, Job Assistance, Housing, etc.), 18% for Family Support and Child Development (Parenting Skills, Tutoring, mentoring, etc.), 17% in Misc. categories such as utilities, GED, furniture, and holiday assistance, and 14% in Health and Safety (Counseling, Medicaid, etc.). This data is used by PSF and social service agency staff to plan services and allocate resources.

PSF Client Survey Results

There were 241 completed client/user surveys. For the questions, "How pleased were you with services you or your family received?" 94% reported very pleased, 5% reported somewhat pleased, and 1% reported not very pleased.

For the question, "Would you return for additional services?" 94% reported most likely, 6% reported somewhat likely and 0% reported not very likely.

For the question, "Would you recommend others to The Library Partnership?" 92% reported highly recommend, 8% reported would recommend, and 0% reported not likely to recommend.

PSF Agency Survey Results

There were 35 social service agencies surveyed about The Library Partnership. The agencies did not respond to every question and reported the following:

For the question, "How satisfied have you been with the accessibility of Library Partnership staff when making inquiries regarding services, programs, room scheduling, etc?" 33 of 34 agencies said they were satisfied or very satisfied. One agency reported neither satisfied nor dissatisfied.

For the question, "How satisfied have you been with The Library Partnership's ability to resolve problems quickly and efficiently?" 29 of 32 agencies reported satisfied or very satisfied. Three agencies reported neither satisfied nor dissatisfied.

For the question, "How satisfied have you been with The Library Partnership's overall performance?" 29 of 34 agencies reported satisfied or very satisfied, 4 reported neither satisfied nor dissatisfied, and 1 agency reported dissatisfied.

For the question, "Typically, how satisfied are your clients with The Library Partnership's services, programs, interactions, etc?" 25 of 29 agencies reported satisfied or very satisfied and 4 agencies reported neither satisfied nor dissatisfied.

ACLD Use Measures

The branch library operating out of The Library Partnership facility had the following use during the 2009/2010 Fiscal Year.

The library was open on average 43 hours per week. During the year, 58,111 persons visited the library and 36,813 items circulated. There were approximately 150 library specific programs that were not co-sponsored by other agencies. Special co-sponsored programs included the spring and fall clothes drives where, at each on average, more than 4,000 articles of clothing were distributed to 640 persons, the Children's Book Give-Away where 500 books were distributed to nearly 100 persons, the Juneteenth Celebration with several hundred in attendance and featuring The Library Partnership Idol contest, and a special project where jackets were given to homeless adults and children through an collaborative effort with the Gainesville/Alachua County Office on Homelessness.

Other positive indicators include the issuance of approximately 750 new library cards despite being located 2 miles from the ACLD Headquarters Library, 43 children in formal tutoring programs, The Library Partnership hosting a Girl Scout Troop, and the use of the facility as the regular monthly meeting space for the Child Abuse Prevention Task Force.

THE LIBRARY PARTNERSHIP AS CATALYST FOR OTHER PROJECTS

The Library Partnership project has drawn attention within this county and throughout Florida. The combination of public library and social service agencies in one facility, sharing costs, and providing convenient, efficient services for citizens has been of particular interest during this period of budget reductions. The project has also drawn national attention after being recognized as a "Bright Idea" by the Harvard University John F. Kennedy School of Government Ash Center for Democratic Governance and Innovation and as a primary component of the process that resulted in Alachua County being named as of the 100 Best Communities for Young People by the America's Promise Alliance.

Locally, two significant projects were greatly influenced by The Library Partnership project, the University of Florida (UF) Mobile Health Clinic and the Southwest Advocacy Group (SWAG) Partnership project.

The UF Mobile Health Clinic (http://outreach.med.ufl.edu/) is a bus that has been customized to include two (2) examination rooms. Medical services are provided by an attending physician (often a volunteer) who may also direct medical students or a nurse practitioner. The bus stops in locations with a high number of persons on Medicaid and where there is limited medical service. Patients receive medical screenings and there is no charge or insurance requirement for services. Medications are prescribed or dispensed as needed.

As the UF Mobile Health Clinic concept was being developed, ACLD was approached by Dr. Nancy Hardt, Director of Health Disparities and Service Learning Programs, UF College of Medicine about using library locations as stops. Dr. Hardt was aware of The Library Partnership and believed ACLD services could provide a more comprehensive approach to health care than either the mobile clinic or the library alone. Here again, this new view of library services and relevance to other community services led to a unique partnership.

The first branch library site was selected to test the concept. Immediately, Dr. Hardt expanded the project by including a legal aid attorney on site during mobile clinic visits. The library meeting room is used for patient intake by UF College of Medicine and College of Nursing students. The library offers separate and private meeting space for the attorney. ACLD staff assist with eGovernment services as needed. The Mobile Health Clinic started operation in January 2010. Word spread quickly about the Mobile Health Clinic and it now stops at three (3) libraries and six (6) other locations.

SWAG is a grassroots effort to provide basic and essential services to residents of an area that has the highest crime rate in Alachua County. The Alachua County Sheriff's Office is actively involved in SWAG as a means of crime prevention. Both the Sheriff and SWAG members became aware of The Library Partnership, visited the site,

and became convinced the same approach would be effective in their community. In this case, ACLD operated a large branch library about 1 mile from the SWAG prime service area, too close to open another branch.

SWAG managed to procure funding from the county to buy two houses in the service area. One would be renovated for the SWAG Partnership and the other as a satellite clinic for the County Health Department. PSF met with most of the same social service providers that rotate through The Library Partnership. Nearly all agreed to participate in the SWAG Partnership. PSF will manage the SWAG Partnership. ACLD will provide library services such as children, teen and adult programs, literacy support, computer training, eGovernment assistance, and a deposit library collection at the facility. Library staff will be available to the SWAG Partnership though housed at the nearby branch library.

THE LIBRARY PARTNERSHIP: CONCLUSION

In summary, The Library Partnership project

1. Enhanced the place and value of ACLD in the community
2. Created opportunities to reach residents who never before used library services
3. Displayed the significance library services can have in meeting essential user needs
4. Enriched ACLD's ability to develop and deliver eGovernment and other library services
   a. Created dialogue between ACLD and social service agencies
   b. Allowed ACLD to design services based on client and service provider input
   c. Strengthened ACLD's ability to more thoroughly meet user needs
5. Created a new group of library advocates
6. Provided more opportunities for the ACLD to be included in community discussions

7. Provided opportunities for more cost effective collaborations
8. Provided a model for other public libraries

The Library Partnership project was significant to ACLD and to the way public library services can be integral to a community. Again, this project is not suitable for all public libraries for the reasons previously stated. The collaborations that were formed with agencies outside of the traditional scope of library services gave ACLD the confidence that our services did have impact beyond our walls and would be viewed in high regard. In general, the project showed public library services can provide greater value to the work of other organizations and vice versa.

By changing our mission statement from a focus on library services to reflect community librarianship and taking a broader, 21st century view to public library service delivery, ACLD is positioned to be a relevant contributor to Alachua County.

ENDNOTES

[1] Alachua County Library District Long Range Facilities and Service Plan Fiscal Years 2011-2016 (2011, February 24)

[2] Soy, Susan K.. "Understanding Community Librarianship: The Public Library in Post-Modern Britain. (Book Reviews)." Libraries & Culture. 2000. Retrieved February 07, 2011 from accessmylibrary: http://www.accessmylibrary.com/article-1G1-90042543/understanding-community-librarianship-public.html

[3] Population Estimate April 1, 2010, Bureau of Economic and Business Research, College of Business Administration, University of Florida

Chapter 2
Waking Up the Neighborhood:
Partnerships with Local Businesses and Art Communities

Catherine Hakala-Ausperk
Northeast Ohio Regional Library System, USA

ABSTRACT

With competition for customers, funding, and success at a premium these days, libraries must find ways to throw in their lot with neighboring organizations and businesses in order to best serve their shared constituencies. This chapter examines success stories born from collaborations showing that all libraries can share in this type of success—no matter how big or little their community may be—and partner with local companies, businesses, social, and non-profits groups in ways that are not only cost-effective, but can also result in innovative revenue streams for all parties involved.

INTRODUCTION

Success stories, at least at Ohio's Cleveland Heights–University Heights Library (CHUHL), always involve community partners and library staff members working together to bring innovative service to its customers. Consider these three examples: burgers were only $5 at the local Whole Foods store one summer day in 2010, when proceeds from their summer "Giving Grill" event all went to support the Friends of the Library foundation; baby showers, sometimes held simultaneously with wedding showers, are frequent Saturday afternoon activities in the library's meeting rooms. And "Hot Nosh," the name of a vending machine that offers such delicacies as pizza and knishes, available next to history texts and biographies, with our vendor sharing a portion of the profit with us. Throughout our building, food and drink can be enjoyed in any spot our users select. CHUHL has become *the* place where its residents meet and make good use of their community's central meeting space—the library.

As this chapter will show, CHUHL has engaged in numerous other community partnerships and celebrations that have helped support its technol-

DOI: 10.4018/978-1-61350-387-4.ch002

ogy and programming. It will outline successful, joint ventures from social events and parties to gallery showing and food sales, all of which contributed to improved services for library patrons and, often, financial and marketing benefits for local businesses and organizations. The objective of this chapter is twofold: to provide an overview of CHUHL's community focused that have helped ensure the library's financial well-being and to provide recommendations to other libraries around the country looking to find similar success. With little money, fewer staff and more competition of the customers' time and support, all libraries need to engage in such activities to ensure their own livelihood.

LOCAL BUSINESSES

All businesses want the same thing—a stable financial future. Small, local businesses like retail and grocery stores often wait on the same customers many of us see every day within the walls of our libraries. In fact, our visitor counts sometimes far outpace what might be recorded in a nearby grocery store. This begs the questions: Why would libraries not want to help that business neighbor by offering low-cost, targeted advertising of their services to its patrons? Why not form a partnership that helps both sides attract more traffic and revenue. Profit is no longer a four-letter word in library circles. Failure is. That's why CHUHL has openly courted, negotiated and profited alongside its business neighbors over the past few years and, in the end, our shared customers have benefitted as well. What follows are some examples of how CHUH reached out to its community to the benefit of all parties involved.

Grocery Stores

Grocery stores see many of the same people we see in libraries and usually almost as often. Because of that shared familiarity, a Branch Manager and

her staff decided in 2010 to ask one large, local store if they'd be willing to enhance our Morning Seniors' program by providing coffee and sweet rolls. We would in turn post a "thank you" note for all to see. The management of the grocery store agreed, asking if we could help them out by sending a librarian over to occupy children with stories while their parents attended an in-store cooking class. We also agreed, and a wonderful partnership was born that continues still and promises to grow! As University Heights Branch Manager Aurora Martinez explains, "Whole Foods is a different kind of business; their mission is not only to make a profit but also to be an agent for change and for improvement of the well-being of their customers and their community. Apart from the profit-seeking, their mission has a lot in common with that of the public library, and this has made for a successful relationship with many opportunities to collaborate. From babies to seniors, the library has teamed up with Whole Foods to present a wide variety of programs at their store, and in turn, we've welcomed the store staff to use our library meeting rooms free of charge for training and meetings. It's such an advantage for both organizations when customers see us working together for their benefit, and certainly our common hope is to win the continued support of our community. And it's always exciting to dream up new ways we can join forces to share our resources and services as trends come and go and community needs change."

Since then, we haven't run out of great ideas for enhancing each other's business. Another partnership we're planning to implement with the same grocery store we hope will involve canvas book/grocery recyclable bags—something both businesses need and use extensively. The library plans to ask them to help pay for a bulk purchase of bags with our logo on one side and theirs on the other. We would have them available for customers to use when visiting our respective places of bussines and, as our shared customers carry these bags around the city, both businesses would get low-cost advertising. While this has not happened yet, it's one of the expansions of this great partnership that we hope to introduce in the future.

CHUHL's Friends of Libraries group has made money at this grocery store, too, when it was selected to benefit from one of their summer "Giving Grill" events. While the store's staff cooked out burgers out in their parking lot and sold simple summer dinners, the Friends group set up a portable used- book sale. When all is said and done, we shared in the evening's profit!

Caterers

Workshops, library skills' training programs and even parties held at our library often feature food. We're learning that the benefit we can offer to local caterers, by connecting them to these events, can also benefit the library in terms of goods. It can even bring profit. Our Art Gallery Opening Nights is a good example of this. The local artists, who are selected to "show" their works in the library's gallery, we provided with a list of local caterers who have agreed to donate 10 percent of their profit with the Friends group. Since we exhibit local, amateur artists, many of whom have never hosted an opening before in the space of our library, they usually oblige and appreciate the help

CHUHL also frequently hosts library training workshops, on topics ranging from Readers' Advisory to Database Searching, Management and beyond in its branches all across Cuyahoga County. So, those same caterers used for gallery openings get another opportunity for more business while giving us the needed discounts. In addition, as discussed later in this chapter, the library's patrons use our meeting rooms for all kinds of social events, from family reunions to showers and birthday parties, which further contributes to the success of our caterer-library Return on Investment.

Camera Stores

A locally owned camera store in our community has helped the library provide technology expertise to our customers of all ages. For our YA patrons, the photo store in the past few years has sponsored a Teen Tech Week, by providing classes and sharing new, cutting-edge equipment we could introduce to them and by donating prizes. The camera store got some good publicity out of the event, with dozens of those teen's parents being able to see our "Thanks to _____ for Supporting This Program" signs posted prominently in the program area where it would be seen by attending parents and other residents.

After the successful partnership with the locally owned camera store, CHUHL forming a partnership with another camera store to introduce an Annual Digital Photography Contest, which is now in its third year. As was the case with the previous endeavor, the store donated free Digital Photography Classes at the library (which are usually offered for a fee at their store) and then helped with judging and by donating prizes, such as free attendance at photography classes. The judging panel included library staff and community leaders and finalists were displayed at each of our four locations, allowing our library customers to be part of the voting process. Again, with each display there was also a prominent sign thanking the store for its support. Publicity like that, for them, was certainly worth the value of the classes, the prizes given and the time invested. For the camera store, having both of these different opportunities to support the library helped them to reach a larger audience. While mostly teens, and some parents, were involved in Teen Tech Week, the Digital Photography Competition helped expose their business to local photo buffs of all ages.

Toy Stores

One of our business neighborhoods has the reputation for being a bit quirky and, in the middle of it sits a unique, historical toy store. We've had a lot of fun working with them to bring games and programs to our library at no cost by trading on the "advertising" their library support provides. One example of how we partnered with them was our Jeopardy-like trivia contest, one of the first inter-generational events our partnership created, which turned out to include contestants from middle school age to local seniors! Next came a Crossword Puzzle competition, which has also become a popular, annual event. Embedded in both events was our win-win philosophy of providing something for the store (publicity and goodwill amongst our thousands of local visitors) and prizes and monetary support for outstanding programming for library users. And we seemed to really hit the inter-generational goldmine with a co-sponsored "Historical Video Gram" display. It was wonderful to hear some first-time library visitors, who came to share techno-memories with their grandkids, compare the challenges of Pong with the newest online role-playing extravaganza. Library teens enjoyed hearing about how early video games worked and also loved demonstrating the newer games to the more senior attendees. Everyone in attendance learned something they hadn't known before.

Restaurants

Like our grocery store connection, our local restaurants have also found reaching the million-plus annual visitors to the library can benefit their own bottom line since, again, we all serve the same community. We've had a local coffee house offer everything from a travelling "barista" cart on programming days to teaching programs itself, including demonstrations of "coffee cupping" as part of our food series. We've also talked about the possibility of them selling pre-to packaged beans with special "literary" labels such as "French Fiction" or "Mocha Mystery." These products would actually be purchased at a cut-rate by our Friends group, and then re-sold in the vending/café area of the library.

Our local restaurants are also well used to library staff asking for support of our popular, summer reading programs. Almost always, with a promise of an acknowledgment of thanks in our community-wide newsletter, they contribute to our big, End of Sumer Party, helping to keep our programming costs way down. Often refreshments ranging from ice cream to Kosher popsicles are donated to the library for use in enticing and rewarding local kids' participation in summer programming.

Vending Machine Companies

Perhaps one of our most profitable business partnerships of the past few years has been the one we began with a local vending machine company that outfits all of our buildings with snack and drink machines and splits their profits with us. Originally, in exchange for new, fully-stocked machines at absolutely no outlay of cash from us, we agreed to take only five percent of the profit each quarter. Later, in response to the company's request to move the machines to a more highly-trafficked area and include a few more non-healthy snacks to boost profits, we hiked our portion up to ten percent. While still assuring that at least one half of each machine's offerings meet national health standard, we've added thousands of dollars to our programming budget as a result of this lucrative arrangement. And our hungry customers are happy to have the breadth of options available, and the option to choose for themselves what to eat. We even offer "Hot Nosh" kosher items heated in a convection oven inside the machine.

When we asked our vendor to provide an Office Supply vending machine as well, they complied (in an ongoing effort to keep us and our patrons happy) and provided a machine "loan" at no cost, which our Friends keep filled with paper, pens, travel drives, and more. One hundred percent of that profit comes right back to us. One more lesson from working with this vendor can be found for libraries—and that is that we can recommend them to one another. After seeing what a cash cow our branches would be, we had another "value" to barter in our recommendation of this company to other libraries. Due, in part, to a significant amount of business we directed their way, our partnership has been healthy and highly profitable on both ends.

THE ART COMMUNITY

In our communities, one can see art on almost every corner. Murals on the sides of buildings, artfully carved sidewalk benches and graceful archways reflect a strong, local focus on and appreciation of art in all forms. For our libraries, this provides yet another natural partnership. What better way to reach residents who might be otherwise considered "non traditional library users" than to partner with these arts groups and bring their music, sculpture, theater and dance inside the walls of our library? What follows is a rundown of a few of our more "artistic" partnership success stories.

Theater

A portion of our main library used to be a YMCA swimming pool. A local theater wanted to use that space as their permanent home, for rehearsals and presentations, and was willing to pay to build it out. At the theatre's expense, the entire "Black Box" theatre was built, lighting and sound were added and now, the "tenants" host plays, offer drama, lighting and dance classes and performances and partner with the library in everything. By combining their need for inexpensive, local space and the library's desire to expand into drama-type programs, with which our staff is unfamiliar, we increased our value to the public

and added an additional revenue stream as well, at a practically cost-neutral arrangement. Since the theatre has agreed to pay a monthly rent to the library, expenses for activites such as landscaping, security and cleaning are well balanced and end up not increasing library costs.. Plus, we practically doubled our marketing efforts in that arena as well, since we advertise for one another at all events and in all promotional materials. Just seeing our logos together can help demonstrate to our shared constituents that we are working productively together. .

Pottery

Similar to the theater arrangement, we rent space in the lower level of another of our branches to a local, non-profit ceramics group. Our goal is to keep our lease arrangements with both groups (and any in the future) similar in nature so we offer low-cost rent in exchange for free programming and events for library customers. We also often feature pottery "shows" in our display cases to help spread the word about this unique service to all of our visitors. Plus, of course, we try to supplement their work and classes with parts of our collection whenever we can. For example, if classes are focusing on a type of pottery from a particular age, the library collection may have supporting art history books to provide extra background information.

The "Computer Gallery"

A similar arrangement we had in 2006 with a local, non-profit visual arts group was unfortunately cut short, due to their inability to maintain a steady supply of volunteers to run it. Because we built out a full art gallery to support them, we were left with that treasure (what library wouldn't want its own art gallery right in the middle of their branch?) and a decision about how best to use it. Our "Computer Gallery" was the result.

When our art tenants were forced to move out, we were left with two problems. First, our current computer lab space was disappointingly small and, second, our gallery was empty, leaving our customers' desire for art shows unfulfilled. It didn't take long for us to open our "Computer Gallery" to solve both problems. Now, local artists of all types (and all levels of expertise) can apply to "show" their work and our computer users are surrounded by everything from watercolors to charcoals and oils.

Another positive side effect of this program was the implementation of "Opening Receptions" mentioned previously. Working together with local caterers, our "artists" are enjoying being able to invite their friends, families and neighbors to their show, allowing the library to attract more and more of those elusive "non-traditional library users," many of whom comment that the occasion marks their first ever visit to CHUHL.

Art in Landscaping

In a hugely popular move that appealed to our neighbors' aesthetic *and* environmental sides, our library has moved from traditional bushes and perennials to "sustainable landscape gardening" and our successes in that venture have had many dimensions. With beautifully selected and designed beds of colorful herbs and vegetables surrounding our buildings, we demonstrated to our users that we not only cared about saving them money but about "creating community" as well.

First, we shared our harvests with everyone who came into our buildings by setting up "Take Some, Leave Some" tables, complete with brown lunch bags for carryout. Library customers brought in their extra tomatoes and left them for others, while filling a bag of oregano for themselves. Gardening, cooking and nutrition books and articles also filled the table, helping to create a place where friendships grew as well as food. Next we shared our extra produce with the local Emergency Food Center, which doled it out to their usual customers—also our neighbors and friends—who needed additional support to keep their families fed. And, finally, we benefitted from the talents of a Library School Practicum student, who designed a wonderful "growing" window display (with associated bibliography), demonstrating to the youngest patrons the wonders of nature and harvest. Like the rest of this initiative, the experience was moving and defining of the library's place in the community.

The Written Word

Next to playing video games and spending time with friends and family, kids like to write and share their creations. A collaboration we've established with a local literary non-profit has provided us opportunities to help them do both. Our Writers' Clubs bring kids together after school to write, edit and "publish" their own stories, poems and even cartoons. How can we afford the tutors and facilitators who work with these young authors? The answer: we forge another partnership, or two. First, we have local foundations whose interests we're aware of because of strong relationships we've built with them through past programming. They are often willing to support literary programs that can also help children do better in school. Our "Writers' Clubs" combine our teen and "tween" collections and library services with real experience putting pen to paper (or fingers to keyboard, as it were) and then celebrating the creativity that results

According to Programming Coordinator Tonya Davis, "Working with the art community was an amazing way to demonstrate that our library knew what our community was about. Our local artists were so receptive to the space we had for them and so enthusiastic and creative about the way they approached using it. By working together, we built ongoing creative relationships that impacted everything from customers to programming!"

COMMUNITY EVENTS

Library advocacy training programs, such as PLA's "Turning the Page 2.0," teach that in order to have a presence in your community you need to *be* present in them. At CHUHL, we make it our priority to go out and find our customers in their neighborhoods whenever we can. From festivals to blocks parties, our patrons see their librarians everywhere and, in our support of local activities, we further strengthen our value in the community. What does not help the library, especially in these times of competition for public funding, is to be thought of a stagnant, myopic service where one can "go get a book." What can turn our funding, our support and our future around is the more accurate picture of today's public library as an integral, relevant and active part of our changing communities. We must keep up with how our customers are living their lives, not hang in the background, unwilling to change.

Meeting Rooms

Probably the single most successful community outreach initiative our library has introduced in recent years has to do with balloons and cake. We let our patrons have their own parties in our meeting rooms for a modest fee. When preparing to open our remodeled main library in 2006, we modified our traditional, stringent Meeting Room Guidelines so that our community members—the taxpayers who actually helped build the rooms—could better enjoy these new spaces. No longer restricted to quiet meetings by non-profit organizations only, these meeting rooms were opened for social, community or even celebratory purposes.

Since then, everyone has profited. The library has enjoyed a brand new revenue source that has provided several thousand dollars of additional income a year, much of it used for improvement of the rooms, the amenities provided, or for programming held there. But we've made much more than just money, we've made countless "friends" for the library. While many of these users might

have been formerly referred to as "non-traditional library users," we can now, hopefully, call them levy supporters, since we've found a way to make their neighborhood library more relevant in their lives.

Challenges connected to this increased, heavily used service were expected, met and resolved. Facility management issues, cleaning needs, food storage improvements and even noise containment were all manageable consequences of this new policy. So far, most would agree that solving all of these problems was well worth it. A favorite meeting room story involves a Saturday that saw attendees at a baby shower sharing the kitchen with attendees from a bridal shower, which was taking place in the meeting room next door.

According to Davis, "It was exciting to see all of the ways the community used our meeting room spaces: from baby showers to family reunions and from "home" offices to even wedding ceremonies, there was always something going on. By embracing the community, they embraced us and we were able to bring in entirely new customers to our library."

Block Parties

Block parties are big in our communities, owing in part to the fact that our residents want to create spaces that feel safe, cared for and shared. When one such part was heard about recently, an enterprising library staffer asked a resident if they'd like a door prize to give away from the library. Filling an always popular canvas library bags with prize books, for example, can lead to more appreciation for the library for a cost that's negligible at best. Think about adding another "gift" in the bag, too, to keep the connection growing strong after the party's over—and that would be a pre-paid, one-year membership to your Friends group. One must keep in mind here that block party planners have no budget. You can imagine the positive reaction you can get and the political capital you can bank when you offer something free to them.

Literacy Organizations

Some projects are expansive, involve a lot of staff and impact a large numbers of people at a time but others, like a program we've undertaken to grow readers, are more modest and touch customers individually. Still, both can have a life-changing impact. While reviewing our stated values several years ago, we paused to reflect on what we really meant by "our library supports literacy." We noted that we provided meeting rooms for tutors to use but, then, we provided meeting rooms to jugglers, too. We bought books written for adult new readers but, what good would they do those who continued to wait for someone to help show them how to read them? The outcome of this discussion was the creation of yet another partnership within our community, this time with a nearby adult literacy group, which allowed some of our librarians to become tutors.

In order to get behind this new partnership, our library not only pays for the day-long tutor training but also for the staff member's time for learning, as well as for the tutoring time they spend with the students each week. Any preparation time is put in on their own, as their personal contribution to this worthy program. After activating about eight new tutors in as many months, our library was proud to be awarded this groups' annual "Friend of Literacy" award. By helping our customers learn to read, we are helping to create another successful program and a lasting collaboration.

Parenting Groups

In addition to helping adults learn to read, our library is also dedicated, as many public libraries are, to helping students prepare to learn to read by the time they reach school age. In a joint effort with a neighboring parenting organization, we received a grant several years ago to open a literacy playroom, complete with toys, learning areas like a store, laundry and library and activities everywhere that build on and strengthen early reading and pre-literacy skills. We've also received a second grant to expand this playroom into another one of our branches and to expand its open hours to all the hours the library is available to the public. This P.L.A.Y. (Pre-Literacy and You) room will support and encourage parents and caregivers to learn skills that will help them better prepare children for the many years of schooling ahead.

While traditional funding may be shrinking, grants are ever-present for public and social entities that are working together to solve society's key problems. Libraries need to sharpen staff skills (and, perhaps, to utilize community volunteers' skills as well) to locate those funders, tell their "needs" story effectively and propose creative solutions – and the grants will come!

Hunger Networks

In 2010 our library experienced arguably the best and most impactful partnership in our cities' history when we joined with the local hunger center to help provide free summer lunches to our families. By the hundreds, children, parents, grandparents and caregivers filled our meeting rooms each weekday afternoon to share in a free, nutritious lunch. Along with a wonderful group of volunteers, our managers gave of their time to take part in this middle-of-the-day activity, and made sure the tables were covered with books, puzzles and games. Additionally, our staff came in daily to encourage "diners" to sign up for our Summer Reading program right after dessert and our participation numbers in that already popular program beat all previous records.

Besides all the statistics and cartons of milk and cookies, the single most important ingredient in this activity was community. Our residents, many of whom had never set foot in the library, got to see first-hand how much we strive to make the local library part of their everyday lives. We got to know new mothers, who brought their babies in strollers and chatted with each other over bologna. We were introduced to a group of grandparents who watch their offspring and who had no idea about the puzzle kits or puppet boxes we could loan them to lighten their load. And we strengthened yet *another* partnership with the Cleveland Foodbank and now, as a result of that summer success, we're beginning to work on ideas for after school snacks to share with our kids throughout the year.

Community Fairs and Festivals

Summer in Cleveland finds celebrations of everything from food and national origin to antique cars and balloon-twisting clowns on any street corner on any given weekend—and the library can be found there too. By scheduling staff to work alongside Friends and volunteers, we mobilize book sales, story times, take away crafts and more so that we can take advantage of meeting our existing and, hopefully, our future customers at these hometown events. An extra bonus is that taking part in these festivals and actually hosting some parts of them also give us the opportunity to work alongside local merchants and homeowners whose basic purpose is the same as ours, to make our communities the best places in which to live.

GROWING THE LIBRARY'S SUCCESS

In the CHUHL area, the arts play a huge role in local entertainment, study, small business and even in our schools. Our collaboration with artists and art support groups has been a natural avenue for successful partnerships. To maximize the benefit of partnerships within their communities, librarians need to pay attention to the needs and interests of their residents. For example, if their community is focused on local history, they could find a wealth of opportunity in creating partnerships along that interest that would capitalize on an already strong community focus. Same goes for education. If their town is home to a university or technical school, there are myriad partnership opportunities librarians could find around programming or supporting a speakers' bureau. In order to blend a community's interest with success in their library, librarians need only enforce and enhance the interests that are already there. They could start by involving their own staff, for example, taking a poll and creating a list of local clubs, organizations and projects in which members of the library staff are already involved. If they begin with such a list and build upon it, before long their successes in community partnering will become well-known and ongoing support from their community will be ensured.

Alone, we are a library. We focus on collections and programs and services that we all know are critical to both a democratic society and to the values of our towns and cities. But, together with partners and collaborators behind and around us, we are a larger and more impressive force of good, of change, and of effect.

Chapter 3

El Dorado County Libraries in Collaboration with First 5 of El Dorado Children and Families Commission and Partnering Agencies

Carolyn Brooks
El Dorado Hills Branch Library, USA

ABSTRACT

The partnerships of the El Dorado County Library system (EDC Libraries) with the First 5 El Dorado Children and Families Commission (First 5 El Dorado) and other public and private organizations have created a unique web of collaborations to enhance the pre-literacy competency and confidence of young children, newborn to five years old, and their families and caregivers in their communities. In recent years, the EDC Libraries have exponentially increased the number of library-based educational services for these young people and their families. In 2010, 43,000 young children, their parents, and caregivers participated successfully in the pre-literacy-based programs with EDC Libraries and their collaborative partners.

INTRODUCTION

EDC Libraries serve a diverse population from those who live in rural areas that have one-room libraries to those who live in suburban areas with state-of-the art libraries. Serving the unique needs of these young children and their families in their communities is a continuing challenge that has been dramatically addressed over the past four years by the six county libraries. The EDC Library system in California faces the funding and staffing challenges that other libraries are experiencing around the country. Yet in a significant contrast to this downward spiral of lost funds and services, the EDC Library programs have expanded to meet the pre-literacy needs of young children, newborn

DOI: 10.4018/978-1-61350-387-4.ch003

to five years old. This astounding phenomenon has occurred through collaborations and partnerships with external institutions and agencies. The term, *partnership*, in the context of this chapter, demonstrates how separate and autonomous organizations with different strengths can work together to achieve a common goal.

Together with First 5 El Dorado, the EDC Library system's goal is to improve early literacy education for children, newborn to five years old, with an emphasis on parent education. The coming together of this network of collaborations began with the serendipitous recognition of mutual goals by First 5 El Dorado and EDC Library staff. Initially, First 5 El Dorado provided seed funding for a pre-literacy children's program, and the EDC Library staff disseminated and expanded the program throughout their six library branches. The first year begin with $1200 and one children's program. In succeeding years, the EDC Library's network of collaborations with other First 5 El Dorado programs and additional other public and private institutions exploded into a myriad of interwoven partners to meet the mutual goals of pre-literacy intervention for young children and their caregivers.

The EDC libraries serve as the "go to" place for families with young children and additionally serve a diverse cross section reflection of the local communities. First 5 El Dorado supplies significant funding and support to the EDC Libraries for early literacy programs, and the branch libraries constitute the nexus of the expertise, audience, and physical sites. Although the library seemed a natural vehicle to both partners, to the surprise and delight of all those involved, this partnership of two uniquely different organizations took on a life of its own that has expanded into a network of collaborations with the other programs funded by First 5 El Dorado. Even more surprising to the uninitiated, the collaborations have not stopped there, but the partnerships continue to flow outward and inward to connections with additional county agencies and community organizations.

This chapter describes the role and activities of the EDC Library system in achieving the goal of pre-literacy readiness of young children, newborn to five years old, and EDC's multi-faceted collaboration with First 5 El Dorado and with other agencies and institutions. These organizations are listed in the next section and include other First 5 El Dorado Initiatives and programs, preschools, child care centers, non-profit organizations, federal, state, county agencies, and local educational institutions such as elementary schools and high schools and the El Dorado County Department of Education and the El Dorado County Department of Health. As a result of the interweaving of these collaborative partners into the fabric of the EDC Libraries' early literacy programs, each program is supported by many partners. Therefore, in this chapter, discussion focuses on individual programs and the collaborative partners that participate in each program.

BACKGROUND: EL DORADO COUNTY LIBRARIES AND PARTNERING AGENCIES

First 5 El Dorado Children and Families Commission

The statewide voter approval of California Proposition 10 funded the First 5 Children and Families Commission through a 50-cent tax on tobacco products. Throughout the state, local commissions, such as the First 5 El Dorado Children and Families Commission have been established to meet local needs and objectives. The primary mandate of First 5 El Dorado is that young children will enter kindergarten ready for school, academically, socially and physically. Since research shows that young children's need for literacy-based education crosses economic and social lines, all young children, newborn to five years old, are eligible and encouraged to participate regardless of income. Research has clearly delineated four factors that contribute to success in school: dental and medical care, parent/child reading together, quality child care and parent education. First 5 El Dorado has established initiatives to address these factors. Out of a specific initiative such as the Children's Health Initiative, one or more programs may be implemented. These programs often leverage relationships with established institutions throughout the community such as the partnership with EDC Libraries to provide early literacy education.

EDC Libraries in Partnership with First 5 El Dorado Initiatives

The *Together We Grow Initiative* was created in conjunction with the El Dorado County Office of Education in order to provide Early Childhood Education Specialists (ECE) and their services. ECE administer free developmental screenings and offer support for adult caregivers in every day parenting issues. Early intervention is offered when young children's developmental milestones are not met. Developmental screening occurs at the EDC Libraries.

The Children's Health Initiative's objective is to provide the opportunity for children, newborn to five years old, to receive health and dental care, as well as prenatal care for expecting mothers. The El Dorado County Department of Health Services receives First 5 El Dorado funding for ACCEL, a children's health program that works with parents and caregivers to find affordable medical and dental care for their young children. First 5 El Dorado has purchased and funds a mobile van with dental stations that visits sites throughout the county to provide free and low cost dental care for families that are without resources. EDC Libraries are an excellent site to maximize the dissemination of these services and for the mobile van to visit.

Best Beginnings Initiative: Local hospitals are provided funding so that a registered nurse

may visit every newborn and his/her family at their home within the first month of life. The nurses check the babies and provide the parents with information about available services such as *Together We Grow* developmental screenings and *Ready to Read @ the Library* programs (both First 5 El Dorado initiatives).

High 5 for Quality is also a First 5 El Dorado program that provides support and assistance to home and center-based childcare centers. The goal is to assist centers to successfully create outstanding developmentally appropriate programs to meet the needs of children and their families. *High 5 for Quality* also provides parent education so that parents will recognize quality early childhood education programs. A crucial component of *High 5 for Quality* is professional education and certification to teachers, aides and caregivers at preschools, home and center-based child care facilities to establish a high standard of excellence for educating young children. EDC Library staff is involved in providing this training and certification.

The Early Literacy Initiative's program, *Ready to Read @ Your Library* is a collaborative effort of the EDC Libraries, First 5 El Dorado and its other Initiatives, the El Dorado County Office of Education and many local community agencies. Programs, outreach and education for children, adult caregivers and educators are offered through the EDC Libraries at the library sites and at other community sites.

EDC Libraries in Partnership with El Dorado County Agencies and Local Community Groups

The El Dorado County Offices of Education, Child Support Services and Health Services are county agencies that provide services to teachers, families, and caregivers. First 5 El Dorado funds several positions at the Office of Education and Health

Services that enables them to present training, education and direct services to families in need and for children with special needs.

Lilliput Kinship Services is a unique organization that provides support for those caregivers raising a young child who are a family member but not a parent. They provide assistance with case management, advocacy, respite and support groups. Further information and referral is handled through this group, as well as recreation activities and tutoring for youth.

Cameron Park Medical Offices is a local collective of doctors that serve El Dorado Hills and Cameron Park who offer regular medical services, such as well-baby checks, routine medical appointments and follow-up for emergency services, as well as sick child appointments. They volunteer their expertise in presentations at the EDC Libraries.

Local Businesses

Target is a local retail store that is actively involved in supporting their local communities through providing grants in early literacy and the arts. EDC Libraries have collaborated with their local Target to provide programs and events for young children and their families.

EDC Libraries in Partnership with Other Participating State and Non-Profit Organizations

The El Dorado Hills Friends of the Library is a non-profit organization that conducts fund raising activities to raise money to support EDC Library programs. Their advocacy of the EDC Libraries garners support and creates visibility within the community.

The Rancho Cucamonga Library System in southern California is a leader in Early Childhood Education in the state and has presented at

several state conferences. They also provide Play and Learn Islands (PAL) to libraries all over the state through a grant from the California State Library. The PAL Island is a large table filled with sand and furnished with interactive tools used for manipulating sand. Putting the solid tabletop on the sand island creates a play surface with manipulative building toys such as blocks, towers, pegs, and interlocking units. These interactive manipulatives engage young children in imaginative play, developing fine muscle coordination and promoting parent/child interactions. The success of the PAL islands has been evident in the joyous interaction of parent and child with the island at EDC Libraries.

Sacramento Historical Maritime Education Organization is dedicated to the preservation and education of maritime history of the 16th and 17th centuries. They endeavor to bring history alive through live historical reenactment on a land-transportable stage that closely emulates a 16th century privateer ship that is 80' in length with a 40' high crow's nest. Dressed as pirates, each member shares the life story of their pirate character using improvisational acting that captures the imagination of children and adults. This education, regarding the daily life, duties, skills, terminology, and even the politics of the maritime life, is delivered in an unforgettable manner.

EDC LIBRARY EARLY LITERACY-BASED PROGRAM ELEMENTS

Literacy-based programs for newborns to five year olds at the EDC Libraries empower parents and their children to model best practice literacy activities that can be continued at home. Literacy is a continuous process of communication that includes oral language, listening, reading, and writing skills. EDC Libraries focus on the six emergent literacy skills that prepare children for reading readiness. Phonological awareness, print awareness and letter knowledge are the first three vital skills, which are considered decoding elements. These are coupled with vocabulary and world knowledge and narrative skills, important components of reading comprehension. Print motivation, which is the love of reading, is the guiding force. Good readers are excellent listeners, have strong language skills and have a love for books. A basic premise of the literacy-based programs is an association with reading that involves a joyful, playful atmosphere and attitude.

Individual literacy reading readiness programs at the EDC Libraries have been developed for specific age groups and for unique populations with emphasis on culture and language through literature-based reading readiness strategies. Because most of the literacy reading readiness programs focus on specific age groups, the pre-literacy activities are designed to be appropriate for the child's developmental phase. Reinforcement frequently occurs when specific objectives within age group programs overlap. All programs encompass pre-literacy building blocks such as fine and gross motor skills development, incorporating educational strategies such as visual representation of literature, musical oral alliteration, and oral storytelling.

Parents and caregivers participate with their children in each program, and they are encouraged to engage in toddler-directed talk such as expressive and receptive vocabulary, repetition, categorizing. Modeling correct language but not pointing out language errors in their child's speech is subtly modeled by the library staff. Our goal, in collaboration with our partners, is to promote pre-literacy competency and confidence of young children and their families and caregivers.

ON-GOING EARLY LITERACY-BASED PROGRAMS AT THE EDC LIBRARIES IN COLLABORATION WITH PARTNERING AGENCIES

Mother Goose on the Loose

A Nine-Week Pre-Literacy Program for Young Children, Newborn to two Years old

This program seeks to dispel the myth that reading with children is only for those children who have mastered spoken language. During the first year and half of a young child's life, exposure to language development can play a major role in pre-literacy development. During these early 18 months, the association of language and sounds with an external world is occurring within the brain. In a *Mother Goose on the Loose* session, parent and infants, sitting in a circle, engage in singing, finger plays, drumming, reading rhymes, rhythm and repetition, marching, interactive games, touching and talking games, naming games, and physical interactions with books. Young infants as young as four months reach out to tap the drum as it comes their way and gleefully wave their hands in time to the music. They play peek-a-boo with scarves, bells and rhythm instruments, and march with voice command interaction. Through this engagement with their children at *Mother Goose on the Loose*, parents learn strategies in which they can interact with their young infants in a positive and fun way at home.

The popularity of the program is demonstrated with the stories that the parents and caregivers share with each other and with the staff librarians and collaborative partners.

"When Sarah was four months, we came to her first *Mother Goose on the Loose*. When the singing and finger play begin, Sarah sat on my lap mesmerized, only moving her head to follow Carolyn moving from child to child tapping out a song. By our third program, she was waving her hands in concert with the other infants---okay I helped a little--and we were both having a great time. Sarah is four now, and she is insistent that we never miss a children's program at the library."

"I was sharing Stephen's baby scrapbook with my sister who is visiting us from the mid-West, and she commented in surprise that 'Stephen's book is filled with Stephen at the Library."

Collaborative Partners and Their Roles

Mother Goose on the Loose has been funded by Target, First 5 El Dorado, California State Library LSTA grant funding, and *Together We Grow*, a First 5 El Dorado Initiative.

At *Mother Goose on the Loose*, families are given the opportunity for infant and toddler developmental screening by *Together We Grow*. This developmental screening is completed by parents and caregivers at home and returned to the library. The Early Childhood Education Specialists from *Together We Grow* then score the screening worksheet and provide detailed individual reports and suggested activities that are mailed to the parents. Because of families' existing relationships with the library, they more easily participate in the developmental screening with confidence. Resources for parenting strategies are also provided. Parents frequently seek and receive advice on a number of issues, including sleep and eating habits. Families may also request and receive home visits and observations with our ECE Specialists for one-on-one assistance with every day parenting issues such as toilet training, poor sleep habits or temper tantrums. Parents and caregivers may also receive information and guidance about advanced services if their child has special needs.

Program Problem: The success of *Mother Goose on the Loose* eventually meant that there were too many children and caregivers in every session, which reduced the quality of the experience for all participants. The program also struggled with disruptions caused by newcomers, who joined several weeks after the program began. The infants, toddlers and their parents or caregivers usually need about three sessions to become acclimated to behavioral expectations in a group setting.

Program Solution: Additional sessions were added to provide room for more families to attend, which reduced the number of participants in any given session and improved the quality of the experience. The second session starts shortly after the first session, preventing attendance at more than one session by the same families, which allows more families to participate. Instituting a pre-registration for the nine-week sessions also allows an infant or toddler and their parent to begin the program at the same time with the other families, which has resolved the issue of latecomer disruptions.

Play to Grow

A Four-Week Developmental Play Session for Young Children, Newborn to Three Years Old

Learning does not take place in a vacuum so literacy education activities and programs have been set within a context of the basic needs for a learning safe environment. Dependable, loving relationships with adults, social interactions, active participation, positive emotional support, and good nutrition are key to children's success. The *Play to Grow* sessions connect a parent or caregiver to a local professional from the medical and education field at a time and place when the parent or caregiver's attention is focused on their child's pre-literacy development. For example, immediately after the opening circle of songs, a medical or educational professional makes a five-minute presentation. Although the rest of the session involves the participation in pre-literacy activities of the young children with their parents and caregivers, the professional remains available to answer individual questions from the parents and caregivers.

Colorful and inviting developmental play stations are distributed throughout the room. Individually parents and caregivers share with their young children in the exploration of the play stations. The parents and caregivers are encouraged to engage in toddler-directed talk such as expressive and receptive vocabulary, repetition, categorizing. Modeling correct language but not pointing out language errors in their child's speech is subtly modeled by the library staff. Pre-literacy building blocks are the focus of these play stations, such as the station that provides for pairing new words with new knowledge such as planting seeds after reading a book about plants. Other play stations are the drama play station, the story time kits with props, the memorizing and reciting poetry and rhymes play station, the drama play centers, the PAL Island and, of course, a display of books is always within reach of each child. Each *Play to Grow* session begins and ends with the participants in a circle sharing in a song together.

The success of *Play to Grow* was observed recently by a staff librarian who recounts this story. "A father and son were interacting at the PAL Island. The librarian observed that the father was tensely directing the child in the placement of the materials. In frustration, the father turned to the librarian and asked 'Why aren't there charts and diagrams so that we know how to put these together?' The librarian gently explained that exploration of the process is the most important part--not the product. 'There is no correct outcome." An 'aha' moment occurred in the father's eyes,

and later the librarian was delighted to observe a very different interaction between the father and the child as they happily explored the materials together.

Collaborative Partners and Their Roles

Play to Grow is funded by First 5 El Dorado. Rancho Cucamonga Library System provides the PAL Island.

Our great treasure are the professionals who volunteer their time and expertise, for example the psychologists, kindergarten teachers, speech pathologists, pediatricians, dentists, occupational therapists, yoga instructors, infant massage therapists, and elementary school principals. Many times, the sources for these professional contacts come from the recommendations of the collaborative partners.

At some time during the four-week session of *Play to Grow*, the County Department of Health Services helps parents locate low cost or free dental, medical and mental health services and insurances. Their puppet presentations to the children about how to care for their teeth are a highlight at *Play to Grow*.

Developmental screening by *Together We Grow*, a collaborative First 5 El Dorado Initiative, also takes place at *Play to Grow*. Families are given the opportunity for infant and toddler developmental screening. After the developmental screening is completed by the parent or caregivers at home and returned to the library, the Early Childhood Education Specialists of *Together We Grow* then score the screening worksheet and provide detailed individual reports and suggested development activities strategies to the parents at the next session. The ECE Specialists are available at the *Play to Grow* sessions to interact with the parents in a 'safe' library environment and answer any questions the parents might have and further explore any new topics that may have arisen.

The *ACCEL* staff, a Children's Health Initiative of First 5 El Dorado, in collaboration with the EDC Library staff works with parents and caregivers to find affordable medical and dental care for their young children. At times, a mobile van equipped with dental stations, funded by First 5 El Dorado, visits to provide free and low-cost dental health care for children.

The *Lilliput Kinship Services* staff present support material and information for those caregivers raising a young child who are a family member but not a parent. The *Play to Grow* Session provides a unique venue for EDC Library Staff and Lilliput Kinship staff to meet unique needs of young children and their families.

Musical Toddler Early Literacy Story Hour, Jazz Babies

A Musical and Movement Program for Young Children two to Three Years old

Francie Dillon, Sacramento State Professor and Musical Entertainment Professional, with her guitar, leads children through songs, dance, and chants at Jazz Babies. Parental interaction with children is the foundation of this musical early literacy program. The children and their parents manipulate instruments such as bells, shakers, maracas, and tambourines. To the toddlers' delight, Francie uses puppets to mimic animals, such as frogs jumping and cows mooing. Parenting strategies are modeled and discussed. This program is the EDC Libraries' most popular program with upwards of 130 people at each session.

Collaborative Partners and Their Roles

First 5 of El Dorado, Target, Friends of the Library, and patron donations have funded the program, *Jazz Babies.*

Ongoing developmental screening occurs as the young children mature since families are again given the opportunity for infant and toddler developmental screening by *Together We Grow.* Upon return of the scored developmental screens, new suggested activities are mailed with the developmental screening results to the parents. Parents are delighted with their ongoing awareness of their children's developmental growth. Many four and five year olds have been with the EDC Library System pre-literacy programs since they were infants.

Program Problem: The success of the program ultimately led to far too many children and caregivers in a session.

Program Solution: Another session was added to provide room for more families to attend. The second session takes place immediately after the first session to avoid repeat attendance by the families from the first session.

Let's Read Together

An Early Literacy Storytime for Families of all Ages

This pre-literacy family program is based on the early literacy program that includes both storytelling and craft making developed by University of California at Davis. The acquisition of early literacy skills and parent education is the intense focus of this storytelling and craft program. Modeling storytelling, finger plays, puppet use, flannel board stories, singing, music, and oral storytelling all contribute to the reading readiness activities. Interaction with stories rather than just reading and listening is particularly stressed. To reinforce the parenting education and activities at home, parent and child care providers are given take-home packets containing written brain research data, parenting strategies, developmentally appropriate math, science, and language activities, field trip suggestions, songs, finger plays and a free children's book.

Collaborative Partners and Their Roles

Let's Read Together is funded by First 5 El Dorado. The staff of ACCEL, a First 5 El Dorado Health Initiative program, does brief presentations relating to health issues such as how to obtain health insurance, dental care.

Families are also given the opportunity for infant and toddler developmental screening by *Together We Grow*, a collaborative First 5 El Dorado Initiative. This developmental screening is completed by parents and caregivers at home and returned to the library. ECE Specialists with *Together We Grow* then score the screening worksheet and provide detailed individual reports and suggested activities that are mailed to the parents. During and after the craft activity, the ECE Specialists mingle with the parents informally so that parents will feel comfortable discussing any every day parenting concerns that may have arisen since their last visit to the library.

Program Problem: The program is offered once month and did not meet the demand.

Program Solution: The *Early Literacy Story Time* for four and five year olds was created and is now offered each week in addition to the *Let's Read Together* program.

Early Literacy Story Time

An Early Literacy Storytime for Preschoolers

Although this program is similar to *Let's Read Together* and was created in response to the need to present *Let's Read Together* more frequently, it is specifically tailored to four and five year olds. In addition, the storytellers in this program include physically handicapped high school students in partnership with the Workability Program at the local high school. In the near future, sign language and a new version for Autism Spectrum Disorder will be incorporated into some of these *Early Literacy Story Times*.

Collaborative Partners and Their Role

Early Literacy Storytime is funded by First 5 El Dorado.

The High School Workability Agency partners with EDC Libraries in providing storytellers.

Because it is imperative that every child has an opportunity for development screening, evaluation, and support strategies, families are given the opportunity for infant and toddler developmental screening by *Together We Grow*, a collaborative First 5 El Dorado Initiative. This developmental screening is completed by parents and caregivers at home and returned to the library. After the ECE Specialists score the screening worksheets, they provide detailed individual reports and suggested strategies that are mailed to the parents. The weekly program allows for a more natural flow of conversation with parents and caregivers on a regular basis.

Spanish Storytime

A Bilingual Storytime for Young Children, Newborns to Five Year Olds and Their Families

This literacy reading readiness program has been developed for Spanish/English bilingual children with emphasis on culture and language through literature-based reading readiness strategies. Two formats at different times; one storytime is bilingual, using both English and Spanish, and the other program is Spanish language only. The majority of the audience of bilingual story time is English speaking parents and children who wish to be exposed to the Spanish language. The Spanish only story time has been very successful with the Spanish community. Because this story time brings Spanish families into the library, it has been a useful strategy in increasing participation by the Hispanic community in the pre-literacy programs and has encouraged regular use of adult and children library services.

Collaborative Partners and Their Role

The *Spanish Storytime* is funded by First 5 of El Dorado.

The developmental screening of infants and toddlers by Together We Grow, a First 5 El Dorado Initiative, has been especially important to the families attending this program. The developmental screening is completed by parents and caregivers at home and returned to the library. The ECE Specialists then score the screening worksheet and provide detailed individual reports and suggested activities and strategies that are mailed to the parents. Because of their existing relationship with the library, families more easily participate in the developmental screening with confidence. Since many of these families lack the resources to avail themselves of the county programs open to them, this allows our ECE Specialists to assist and guide them in procuring services, especially health care.

Program Problem: Getting the Hispanic community engaged in Library services is an ongoing outreach program, as not all of the EDC Libraries have a Hispanic Outreach Specialist.

Program Solution: We are searching for additional Hispanic community members to serve as our Outreach Specialists to involve the Hispanic community in the EDC Libraries.

DATA COLLECTION FOR EDC LIBRARY PROGRAMS

Informational data about the pre-literacy programs and their attendees is shared with partners and collaborators for their research. First 5 El Dorado requires that this data to be accurate and not duplicated (each child registered only once) so they can compile accurate reports for state reports. As we planned and hoped, the young children and their parents came frequently and repeatedly to the programs. However, distinguishing new children from regulars was a challenge, but one that

we needed to overcome to gather a true count of children served. The solution is a storytime punch card that is traded for a new book at the end of ten visits. EDC Library staff is now able to identify a child as a repeating attendee. Parents of newcomers to the EDC Libraries complete the brief data questionnaire when their children receive their complimentary book bags. This information is captured in a database, and quarterly reports are made to First 5 El Dorado. In the near future, these reports will also be made available to every collaborating agency and partner through the use of interactive media, such as tablets.

UNEXPECTED OUTCOMES

An unexpected outcome of our programs unfurled when we realized they provided an opportunity for caregivers and parents to meet on a frequent basis. As a consequence, a vibrant parenting network within the pre-literacy programs and outside the boundaries of the EDC Libraries has been built. Recently a grandfather and his young granddaughter attended the *Let's Read Together* pre-literacy program for the first time. Gradually, the other fathers sidled up to the newcomer grandfather, and a staff member overheard the other fathers ask, "Which one is yours?" The bonding that occurs through the shared joy of engaging with their children in the pre-literacy activities has been heart-warming.

DEVELOPMENT OF EARLY LITERACY MATERIALS FOR YOUNG CHILDREN AND PARENTS

Storytime Kits

Eighty (80) story time boxed kits have been developed by the library staff. These immensely popular kits are solidly grounded on the six emergent literacy skills discussed earlier in this chapter. During the pre-literacy program activities, these story time kits are a big hit. As parents and caregivers explore the contents of the story time boxed kits with their children, they become aware that reading books and reading readiness activities with their children builds letter print awareness and motivation, vocabulary and world knowledge. Parents comment on how they notice that their child's narrative skills are developed as they create a story on the flannel boards. These storytime kits are checked out by teachers, parents, caregivers and child care providers for home and classroom use.

Each colorful reading readiness box includes books, materials, and activities focused on a specific theme, for example, reptiles, ballerinas, trees, special needs, Caldecott winners, or firefighters. Each kit includes:

- Seven quality literature books about the chosen theme.
- How-to-book on developmentally appropriate art activities
- Finger plays and rhymes book
- Flannel board story: flannel board figures, script, flannel board
- Hand puppet

Collaborative Partner and Role: First 5 El Dorado, The Friends of the Library and Barton Hospital grants fund this project.

Problem: Storage space on EDC Library shelves for 45 boxed kits.

Solution: The popularity of these story time boxed kits solved the problem since only a few kits are available on the shelves at any one time, eliminating the need for a large storage area.

Children's Book Bag

Every child new to EDC Library programs receives a new children's book and book bag imprinted with the logos of the EDC Library and First 5 El Dorado. These colorful book bags are proudly carried by children and are seen at local grocery stores, parks and family picnics throughout the

county. These bags give children a safe place to keep their library books at home and has reduced the hunt for library books in the house when it is time to return them to the library. A brief parent informational data survey is completed by the parent or caregiver at the time the book bag is given.

Inside the brightly colored book bags are:

- New children's book
- Toothbrush with dental floss aka the "library string"

Information about the services of collaborating organizations serving children and their families such as First Five of El Dorado Initiatives and programs, El Dorado County agencies such as child support services, dental health, family health insurance for families

Story time punch card (ten visits equal new children's book and a new card)

COMMUNITY OUTREACH WITH COLLABORATIVE PARTNERS

Outreach to Medical Facilities

EDC Library staff members collaborate with medical professionals to create reading readiness opportunities for young children. At local medical facilities including the hospital, private doctors' offices and the County Health Care Center, the library provides collections of children's books and information about the reading readiness programs at the EDC Libraries.

Community Gateway for Caregivers and Parents

Through the EDC Library's pre-literacy program, the Library staff has found that they also function as an information gateway for families with young preschool children. Using the vehicle of storytime is only one way that the library is able to connect families with community agencies that provide essential services. Because of their experience in working with the collaborative partners, the EDC Library staff is a wealth of information. The EDC Library branches serve as a unique central source for the information of all our service agency partners, working together to serve young children and their caregivers.

Community Outreach Events

The dedicated members of the Sacramento Historical Maritime Education Organization

tour the community in their 80' pirate ship and its 40' high crow's nest, sharing their love of maritime history with children throughout the community. Annually for the past four years, the pirates have set up their village encampment and ship on the grounds of the El Dorado Hills Branch Library. This event draws over 1,500 families from the local community; many of who dress in pirate costume. The children and their families learn about the everyday life of a pirate. The program attracts new library patrons, who sign up for library cards. Partnering agencies such as the El Dorado County of Health, First 5 El Dorado Initiatives, sponsoring businesses and community agencies share information with the public at this popular event.

OUTREACH NETWORK OF COLLABORATIONS AND PARTNERSHIPS AT EDUCATIONAL INSTITUTIONS AND CHILD CARE ORGANIZATION

The partnership of the EDC Libraries with the First 5 El Dorado is deeply committed to reaching outside of the library sites to other sites within the local communities. The web of collaborative and external educational institutions and agencies that are equally committed to serving the literacy needs of young children (newborn to five year olds) and their families facilitate this process.

Outreach Training for Child Care Staff in Collaboration with Partners

The EDC Library staff is in a unique position to create a bridge across which *High 5 for Quality,* an El Dorado First 5 Initiative, and the personnel at preschools and day care centers can meet due to the Library's extensive outreach program to these facilities. *High 5 for Quality* staff assists child care centers to successfully create outstanding developmentally appropriate programs. As a further extension of this collaborative effort with *High 5 for Quality*, early literacy classes are taught by EDC Library staff, and these classes are certified for professional development credit by *High 5 for Quality*. This certification is highly regarded by parents and the child care centers, as the requirements for this certification are very stringent. Child care provider participants in these early literacy classes also receive printed educational material that they can use to share in an informal in-service training with others at their schools or child care centers.

Outreach at Public Elementary School Sites

Through the formation of partnerships based on the mutual goal of reading readiness programs for young children to age five, EDC library staff members regularly go out to the local preschools, Head Start programs and elementary schools to work with teachers and parents. Students and their parents are encouraged to attend the EDC Libraries' early literacy programs. Many of the kindergarten classrooms take a field trip to the EDC Libraries during the school year where they experience a tour of the library, participate in a storytime and craft making activities. After this tour, the children are eager to check out a book, and for many of them, this is their opportunity to receive their first library card. Prior to the library field trip, library card applications are sent home by the classroom teacher, and parents return the completed applications to the school. Two weeks before the trip, the teachers provide the library with the completed applications. Special Field Trip library cards that limit the students to a single book are then issued. Once the children have been to the library, they are eager to return to check out a book. Information about the library programs are sent home with the children. Later when the parents come to the library and show their photo identification, the children are assigned a regular library card.

Kindergarten Transition Programs

Each spring, local elementary schools invite parents of the fall incoming class of kindergarten students to the Kindergarten Roundup Evening and then on another evening, invite both parents and their preschool children. Staff members from the EDC Libraries and *Together We Grow* participate in both events at the local elementary schools. On the parent-only night, EDC Library staff members present best practice literacy activities for parents to use at home. At this time, written materials for activities and free children's books are also distributed to the parents. The EDC Libraries' staff extends invitations to the Library's early literacy programs such as Let's Read Together to the parents. To encourage parents to bring their children to the library, coupons for a free children's book that is redeemable at the library are handed out to all parents. At the Early Literacy evening that that is held separately from the Kindergarten Round Up Evening, preschool children do attend with their parents. In small groups, parents and their preschool children participate in early literacy activities they can replicate at home.

Outreach at Preschools, Head Start, State Preschools: Home-Based and Center-based Child Care

Each month Outreach Early Literacy Specialists from the EDC Libraries conduct on-site training

story times at over 150 preschools, Head Start classrooms, State preschools, home-based child care and center-based child care sites. The Outreach Specialists model storytelling, demonstrate puppetry, and disseminate information from collaborating partners. Developmentally appropriate books and story time kits are selected by the Outreach Specialists and checked out to each of the childcare sites they visit. When teachers and staff at a particular site are focusing on a particular theme such as fire safety, the Outreach Specialists select books from the library's resources and provide them to the site. A monthly newsletter is emailed each month to the sites to keep teachers and staff current about ongoing research as well as the activities of the EDC Libraries and partnering agencies. Developmentally appropriate activities for use with young children are a major focus of the newsletter.

Preschool Parties at the Library are also coordinated by the Outreach Specialists from the EDC Libraries. The parents, young children, and teachers participate together in this educational trip. At the library, they engage in pre-planned specific activities such as a tour of the children's library, a storytime and craft time. Parents and the young children are encouraged to obtain a library card and to check out books. At the conclusion of the field trip, the teachers/providers receive three free children's hardback books to add to their own permanent collection.

First 5 El Dorado funds this outreach program.

Parallel Outreach Collaborative Opportunities at Public Schools

Collaborations with teaching staff of grades K-5 spontaneously occur when EDC Library staff members are at the public elementary schools providing early literacy information and materials. Through the teachers and through the physical presence of the EDC Library staff, the accessibility of EDC Library staff and resources are conveyed to parents and instructors of other grade levels. As a consequence, teachers frequently initiate contact with the EDC Library staff. This collaboration to provide curriculum specific books and materials goes beyond providing library materials at the school to ensuring that curriculum specific books and materials are readily available at the EDC Libraries to support the children in the classroom and at home.

Local high school students engaged in Early Childhood Education programs and classes at their school receive training classes from the EDC Youth Services Librarians and often make field trips to the early literacy programs at the library to experience storytimes in preparation for doing their own storytime at local child care centers.

State Outreach and Training at Sacramento University and the El Dorado County Office of Education

At the invitation of the El Dorado County Office of Education, Youth Services Librarians at the EDC Libraries conduct pre-literacy workshops about early literacy development and education for young children, newborn to five year olds at the El Dorado County Office of Education. In addition, the El Dorado County Office of Education has videotaped the pre-literacy classes taught by the Youth Services Librarian at the El Dorado Hills Branch Library and has posted the videos on the El Dorado County Library website.

Sacramento State University

The Youth Services Librarian at the El Dorado Hills Branch Library are invited to make presentations to college students, majoring in teacher education, regarding early development in the brains of young children and early literacy strategies for young children.

FUTURE PLANS AND COLLABORATIONS

Future plans and directions are moving targets since the innate flexibility of the web of partnerships and collaborations encourages innovation and new partners. A few examples are listed below but by no means encompass all that may be currently happening.

Plans are underway for a monthly meeting at the EDC Library so that First 5 El Dorado program representatives can meet together to welcome new families in the community. First 5 El Dorado programs at this time include *ACCEL, Together We Grow, High 5 for Quality, Best Beginnings, Ready to Read @ Your Library*.

Collaborations and partnerships with additional First 5 El Dorado programs are planned, for example, *Best Beginnings*. In this program, babies born at Marshall Hospital in El Dorado County, receive home visit from nurse within the first few weeks. In addition, this program provides training and information for mothers on caring for their babies and provides library program information as well. *Best* Beginnings will deliver an invitation to all of these families to come to the library for a "birth day" party. All babies and their adult caregivers will be welcomed at the first *Mother Goose on the Loose* baby storytime of the month (no registration required), where they will receive a free hand-knitted baby hat (donated by our local knitting groups), a free book and we will sing 'Happy Birthday' to them.

In addition, plans are currently underway to also tell stories with sign language at the EDC Libraries.

The data collection conducted by EDC Libraries is currently sent quarterly to First 5 El Dorado only. Plans are underway to store this information in the 'cloud', of course without any identifying markers so that complete confidentiality is maintained. Soon, all collaborating partners and agencies will also have access to this information utilizing interactive media.

CONCLUSION

The EDC Libraries' collaboration with First 5 El Dorado has initiated and created a web of other collaborative agencies working in partnership to enhance the literacy capabilities of young children and to empower parents and caregivers. Each year the collaboration with other agencies takes on a life of its own as new partnerships of services and populations naturally leads to another in each participating group's drive to address the early literacy needs of young children. This successful collaboration works like the unique web of a spider with each fiber reaching out the next fiber, each made stronger by the other, and all leading back to the center to create a whole that encompasses the environment in which young children can succeed in reading readiness by age five.

Chapter 4
In Quest of Academic Achievement:
A Public Library's Partnerships in Onitsha, Anambra State, South East Nigeria

Nkem Ekene Osuigwe
Anambra State Library Board, Nigeria

ABSTRACT

This chapter describes various readership promotion activities undertaken by a Nigerian State Public Library in partnership with schools, churches, and the state owned television house. Massive failures in O' level national and regional examinations and the entrance examinations into the tertiary institutions have brought up the fact that the education sector in Nigeria is facing monumental challenges. This combined with a noticeable decline in user statistics, especially amongst school age children in Onitsha Public Library in South East Nigeria. This decline has long been associated with the school-boy drop-out syndrome. The State Public Library Board collaborated with agencies in its community to introduce intervention strategies to halt the trend. These were expected to increase usage of the public and school libraries, make reading attractive to children of school age, support school curriculum, and help students make better grades in examinations.

INTRODUCTION

Public libraries have always played a significant role in the education sector of its local community. They are crucial in inculcating reading habits into children and in improving and sustaining literacy skills throughout a lifetime. Celano and Neuman (2001) see the public library as one institution that plays a vital part in the reading achievement of children who do not have access to books and other reading materials in their everyday lives. Amongst the listed missions of the public library according to the Unesco Public Library Manifesto (2000) include the formation and strengthening of reading habits from an early age and aiding formal and informal education at all levels. For Koontz and Gubbin (2010), the public library is a dynamic institution working with other establishments and with individuals to provide a wide variety of library and information services to satisfy the ever

DOI: 10.4018/978-1-61350-387-4.ch004

changing needs of its community. Public libraries are therefore expected to meet the information and educational challenges of the local community even as the needs mutate.

The Anambra State Library Board (ANSLB) was established under CAP 82 Law of Anambra State Nigeria 2669 of 1979. The Board is a quasi-independent body under the Anambra State Ministry of Information, Culture and Tourism. It receives a monthly subvention for the payment of salaries and the provision of library services in the State. The Board has the sole responsibility for collecting, organizing, maintaining and making information resources available to the citizens of the State. The Board members are to be persons who appear to the Government to have wide knowledge, interest and experience in education, research, creative arts, the book industry and other allied fields (Ogbonna, 2010). The State Governor invariably ends up appointing politicians of various hues to the Board.

The Board takes policy decisions while the Director executes them. For any activity outside of normal library services to be undertaken, for example readership promotion campaigns or fund raising drive, the permission of the Board is sought by the Director. The Board is statutorily mandated to meet not less than four times in the year. The Director is also a member of the Board. The appointment of a Director is at the recommendation of the Board to the Governor who normally ratifies their decision. The Director is the chief executive of the Board and is solely responsible for the proper coordination of the Board's daily activities such as general supervision and control of staff and the management of the Board's financial affairs. The Director is also the Chairman of the Management committee which consists of the librarians in charge of the divisional libraries and heads of departments. The post of the Director is not tenured.

The Library which has three divisional libraries at Onitsha, Nnewi and Abagana and seven branch libraries at Atani, Ajalli, Amichi, Ihembosi, Ozubulu, Nkpologwu. Adazi Nnukwu is run centrally

from the State Central Library temporarily located at Ifitedunu while a new structure is being put up at Awka, the State capital. Books and other information resources are acquired and processed centrally at the headquarters. Sometimes though communities where the libraries are located in donate books with the firm proviso that the books remain in those libraries. Each of these divisional and branch libraries are manned by librarians who are directly responsible to the Director. The heads of these libraries receive funds for the running of the libraries but the salaries of all the staff are paid centrally. The Onitsha Public Library has the most functional and biggest children's section out of all the libraries in the system. An average of 621 users make up of 530 adults and 91 school age children use the Onitsha Public Library daily. The library is located in the government reserved area of the town. The Children's Section of the library runs a Saturday story hour program that incorporates other activities like debates, craftwork, quizzes and dancing competitions.

Onitsha is the hometown of Dr. Nnamdi Azikiwe, the first President of Nigeria. It has a rich crop of intellectuals yet 'money is the king' there because of the booming Main Market and other prospering and continually enlarging markets in and around the town. These markets supply all the other markets in the country and in some parts of West Africa with food items, wears, plastic wares, automobile parts, chemicals, cosmetics and other articles of trade. The presence of these markets impact negatively on the education sector in the town. Young people would rather go into apprenticeship with traders than complete their studies. They point out the fact that those who finished their education hardly get good paying jobs while trading enables the school dropouts to be independent and wealthy even before their classmates finish school. Mass failures in national and regional exams which are fast becoming a trademark in the country's education sector have not done anything to encourage children of school age to take their studies seriously within the community.

In fulfilment of the public library's role in meeting the educational and information challenges of its community, the Onitsha Public Library reached out to schools and churches in the town with the aid of state owned television outfit – Anambra Broadcasting Service. Reading competitions were held amongst primary and secondary schools, the bookmobile service was reintroduced to the schools and a Spelling Competition which ran for 13 weeks was held amongst children that use the library. Visits were made by the library staff to women's church meetings in the town. This was done primarily to appeal to them to allow their children and wards to participate in the readership promotion campaign. The visits also helped in creating a fresh awareness about the public library and its activities. All these were aired on the State TV at a reduced cost and this helped greatly in promoting reading activities amongst school age children in the town.

BACKGROUND

Onitsha is the commercial nerve center of Anambra State, South East Nigeria. Its Main Market with more than 65,000 stalls is reputed to be the largest of its kind in West Africa. Each stall owner who is the 'master' as a matter of exigency has at least two young boys that help him to market his wares and they are the 'apprentices'. This practice has encouraged the boy-child school drop-out syndrome in the town in particular and in the State in general. According to Akpunonu (2010), statistics from ETF (Education Trust Fund) reveal that over 71 percent of boys (male children aged between 6 and 18 years) drop out of school yearly in Anambra State. He went on further to state that Onitsha Main Market and other markets are some of the spots indicated where these male dropouts end up as apprentices to traders. Poverty, child labour, lack of sponsorship and the irrelevance of the educational experience to economic survival have all been touted as causes of the boy-child school dropout syndrome.

Meanwhile Nigeria as a country in recent times have been witnessing massive failures in the O' level examinations. These examinations are taken by children who have completed their secondary school education and who are averagely aged between 16-20 years. In 2009, 89.32 percent of the 1.2 million candidates that registered for the O' level exams were not able to pass the core subjects of English and Mathematics. Otti, (2011) reports that in 2010 only 20.4 percent obtained credit in English and Mathematics, 2005 saw 27.53 percent getting credit in the two core subjects, 15.56 percent passed in 2006, 25.54 percent in 2007 and only 13.67 percent obtained credit in the two core subjects in 2007. Between the years of 2007-2009 2,993,197 candidates sat for JAMB (Joint Matriculation Exam Board) examinations for into the nation's tertiary institutions, only 427, 77 of them secured admission. These higher institutions are universities and polytechnics which award degrees that are the basic requirement for getting white collar jobs. Parents and guardians blame the teachers, the teachers blame the government and the students blame everybody except themselves! In 2009 the Federal Government set up School Based Management Committees. According to Akpovwa (2010) this was to stem the tide of mass failures and curb the boy-child school menace in South East Nigeria.

Libraries were not a part of this intervention measure and it's not surprising that it failed because according to the Chartered Institute of Library and Information's (Cilip) report (2002):

All government initiatives aimed at developing literacy and learning opportunities or other services for children and young people, should involve library services, acknowledging the contribution which they have already made and enabling them to contribute fully in the future. p. 72

People come across various libraries throughout their lives, from private collections in homes to academic libraries in tertiary institutions. Public libraries however are in existence in communities for all irrespective of age, creed, background and educational status. They serve their communities by providing access to information resources for educational, recreational and personal needs. Nevertheless, due to the continuously developing technological environment in which libraries presently operate in, budgets constraints due to global recession, rapid increase in available information and the changing and diverse needs of clients, it has become obvious that no one library has the information resources to meet the information needs of a given community and that no one institution is self sufficient in its role as information provider Zobec (1990). Partnerships and collaborations are therefore needed between libraries not just to save costs but also for libraries to be able to meet the plethora of ever mutating information needs of their users and maintain their relevancy within the communities they serve.

Due to the obvious overlap between public and school libraries' goals, objectives, clientele and the type of information services provided, partnerships between the two types of libraries is most feasible and expedient, Shannon (1991), Williams and Grange (1989), are of the view that cooperation between the public and school libraries are often prompted by the public libraries trying to fulfil its traditional role of making information available to all in its community. Common goals create the passion and willingness to work together and solve problems collectively (Murray, 2004). It has been pointed out that the;

educational focus is a shared role and goal of schools and public libraries and is one of the most critical factors in rationalizing the need for cooperation and collaboration between the two. In today's information-rich society, both types of libraries can provide resources to complement students' curriculum and literacy needs. (Fitzgibbons, 2000, p.11)

Fenwick (1966) and Fitzgibbons (1983) had earlier asserted that cooperation between the two types of libraries may be the only viable option to providing sufficiently for the library needs of school age children. Czopek (1995) sees collaborations between public and school libraries as very workable because both share a number of related missions which include ensuring that students are information users by providing a wide range of current resources and motivating children and young adults to use library materials for educational and recreational needs. Public libraries have much to offer school libraries as larger and more established organizations with more professional staff and resources. However on the other hand, school libraries offer the public libraries a wider catchment of young clientele.

Collaborations between school and public libraries in Nigeria is most expedient considering the fact that according to Olanlokun (1996) and Aguolu (1975), there are a few schools with anything called libraries and even where one sees a 'school library', it is often a collection of books locked up in the principal's office This has been attributed to lack of space in schools (Ayorinde, 2005), meagre or non-existent funding (Fakoya, 2002) and low number of teacher librarians (Adeyemi, 2001). Okoye (2000), in reaffirming this observation went on further to note that;

40-60 percent of the secondary schools in Anambra State have no school libraries, while 70-80 percent of primary schools have neither a room or a building set aside as the school library. Books which the government donated are stored in the office of the head of the school and are never displayed for reading. (p.122)

The Federal Government had though, in the National policy of Education (1998) stated that schools should have functional libraries and provide for the training of librarians to work there.

However Mathews, Flum and Witney (1990), opine that collaborations between the public and school libraries will be challenging to both parties because of low staffing, funding and educational level of staff. LaMaster (2005) pointed out that territorialism or 'this is mine and that is yours' is an issue that must be dealt with in the partnership between public and school libraries. According to her, creation of joint mission statements and shared goals of achieving better grades for students through improved reading skills will help the collaboration between the two types of libraries move forward smoothly. Williams and Grange (1989) surmise that funding, time, attitude of the operators of the partnership and access are obvious impediments to collaborations between the public and school libraries. These challenges notwithstanding Busayo (2010), holds strongly that the library has a significant role to play and can help address the alarming failure rates of candidates in qualifying examinations in Nigeria.

Can the public library partnering with the school libraries make a difference in student achievement? Smith (2004) affirms that the school - public library combinations are particularly well suited for partnerships because the library can help students read better and if they read better, they will do better in schools. For the reading skills of students to improve so that they can study and improve their grades, they need to read and to have access to books that may or may not be on their reading list and the library is the only place they can have such an access. Small (2008) and Lance (2001) in their different studies agree that libraries contribute to the academic achievement of school age children more than other factors which may include experience of teacher, class size, number of computers available and the location of the given school. Cullinan (2000) believes that libraries do make vital contributions to student learning, however partnerships between public libraries, schools and other stakeholders are necessary if school library programs are to be effective in encouraging reading and academic achievement amongst students.

Reaching out for Collaborations within the Community

At the public library at Onitsha decreasing user statistics were noticed for three years running. Attendance to the story hour program at the Children's Section continued to decline, books were hardly being borrowed and the number of schools who were visiting the library with their pupils and students kept on dwindling. The library acquired new books, shelves and seats were rearranged to give the library a new look, attractive displays were put up, new activities were introduced in the Section but there were no noticeable changes in library attendance by school age children. A public library is only as vital as its host community perceives it to be. Non-usage of its facilities implies that the community did not understand what they stand to gain by making use of the information resources in the Library, The Library leadership decided not just to focus on collections and circulation but to reach out to create relationships that will enable the Library to form collaborations within its community so as to be able to fulfil its functions especially amongst children of school age. The partnerships would aid in providing more opportunities for the community to understand what the Library is doing presently and what it could do in the future.

Schools

Where are the kids? The Library had to go to where they are! Library staff visited primary and secondary schools in Onitsha. It was discovered that;

- Teachers were mainly apathetic about the non-usage of the public library facilities by their students.
- Extra lessons were being organized by different teachers for students after school hours for extra fees thus the children did not have time for visits to the library.

- Most of the schools did not have functional school libraries.
- Teacher - librarians were assigned subjects to teach thus their functions as librarians for the school libraries were seriously curtailed. The school libraries were not functional thus children did not have a proper concept of libraries whether school or public libraries.
- Students and pupils were excited at the idea of having access to books in the public library.
- School heads were open to the idea of a partnership with the public library so far as any activities undertaken would not disturb their academic lessons or stress the teachers and students unduly.
- No funds were allocated for acquiring information resources for the school libraries. Books in the libraries were dilapidated thus were of no interest to the children.

Women's Groups in Churches

Parents play a crucial role in the education of their children especially mothers who spend more time with them. If mothers are therefore made to understand the importance of inculcating the reading habit in children it will go a long way towards assisting the latter as they pass through different educational stages (Chew, 2005, Canlas, 2009 and Maduekwe & Oyenike, 2010). The Church is also a known agent for social change. The library staff therefore saw the need to visit women's church meetings in the mainstream denominations in the town. These include women groups in the Catholic (Catholic Women Organization) and Anglican (Mothers Union) Churches. The meetings are attended only by the married women of the community. These women meetings had become powerful in South East Nigeria since the end of the Nigerian Civil War (1967-1970). Women used these meetings to galvanize whole communities into undertaking development efforts in the war ravaged communities in the region. With the pas-

sage of time the meetings gave the women a strong voice in their different communities and became an avenue of moving the communities forward. They initiate and sometimes complete projects like construction of post offices, primary and secondary schools and civic centers. The women meetings also play crucial roles in settlement of quarrels in the communities. Letters were written to the Anglican and Catholic churches in Onitsha that we aimed to visit.

Our interactions with the women at the meetings were very interesting. The Library staff shared the statistics of dwindling usage of the Onitsha Public Library especially among the children and the dismal failures at external examinations. The women were also informed that use of the Onitsha Public Library would help the children learn to study independently and to read widely. The women were amazed at the failure rate and wanted to know why the public library in the town had waited so very long before reaching out to children to make use of library resources. However, the idea of allowing their children and wards to partake in the library's Saturday program met with resistance. According to them Saturdays are usually the busiest days in the Main Market and they need their children to keep tab of the dubious practices of their apprentices who make sales and pocket the money received or who hike prices unnecessarily so that they can pocket a part of the monies made in the day's transactions. They also felt that the extra lessons being organized by teachers was enough to make their children perform better academically.

The women were made to understand that the public library provides academic support and a good alternative to the traditional classroom environment. The advantages of forming good reading habits were outlined to the women groups. They were however most thrilled by the idea that reading provides great opportunities to unlock potentials in children and create pathways to greatness. They promised to allow their children and wards to use the Onitsha Public Library and to spread the word about the relevance of the library.

Anambra Broadcasting Service

The television and radio with its wide reach exert a great influence on children of school age. In order to reach a greater number of children, tell our story and to create a relationship with the Anambra Broadcasting Service towards the achievement of our goals, the Onitsha Public Library presented a proposal to the Anambra Broadcasting Service (ABS) to air our programs with the children. The TV/Radio house restructured our proposals. They broke down a proposed spelling bee to run for 13weeks on the TV while only the final of the Reading competition was to be aired. Fees for the broadcasts were reduced by as much as 50 percent. The broadcasting house was also excited that the Onitsha Public Library was taking such a step.

COLLABORATIVE INTERVENTION STRATEGIES

Re- Introduction of Bookmobile Services to Schools in the Community

One of the discoveries made when the library staff visited schools was that a few schools did not have libraries while most of the school libraries just had a scanty collection of text books, maps and a few dusty and torn story books usually donated by former students and the PTA (Parents Teachers Association) of the schools. This, according to Doust (1998),

is a very dangerous situation since children who meet badly stocked libraries with out of date books not only fail to find usable reading materials but are also led to believe that libraries in general are boring places and they are thus permanently discouraged from reading. (p.1)

Formerly through grants from UNESCO the bookmobile services were introduced in Nigeria by the regional governments in the 1960's and 70's. In 1991 when Anambra State was created, the service had become moribund. The scrapping of the mobile library services in Anambra State was a big blow to the efforts to get the general populace reading. The Onitsha Public Library reintroduced the service to make more books available to school children.

Three copies of one hundred titles suitable for secondary school reading were acquired by the State Library Board. The books included reference materials like general and subject dictionaries, novels, puzzles, English comprehension and objective questions and answers in different subject areas. A batch of hundred titles were each given to 3 secondary schools in the community to keep in their libraries for a one-month period at the end of which the library took back the books and gave to another batch of three secondary schools. The schools were instructed to allow the children have access to the libraries and the books. Teacher librarians were given a brief training on how to look after the books and still allow children to browse through the collection. Children were encouraged to make use of the books and they were given tips on how to take care of them. The same bookmobile system was used to move books around in the primary schools in the town.

Library staff visits to the schools to monitor the use of the books revealed that:

- More children now had a firm idea that good, interesting and relevant books can be found in the school libraries.
- More teachers and children use the school libraries because the presence of new books attracted them and they all wanted to benefit from the gesture.
- The books which children took home to do their home work were not always returned or when they were returned some pages

had been torn off or smeared with dust and grime!

- All the schools wanted the books to remain with them permanently.
- Teachers reported a gradual but noticeable improvement in the reading skills of the students and the ability to grasp new concepts as new topics are introduced in the classes.
- The public library staff acquired new skills in providing library services to children as they learned to serve in a new environment.

Young students do become encouraged to read when books are more easily accessible to them. The possibility increases that the more they have books around them, the more they see books as necessary tools for existence and survival. Teachers reported that even reluctant readers were excited by the presence of new books.

It was challenging getting the bookmobile program off its feet. There was difficulty in acquiring the right books to run the service. Promises of assistance from possible sponsors or donors were made but were not kept. Individuals and corporate bodies pleaded for more time but the great need to start the bookmobile services up again necessitated speed. Again there was a general apathy about issues concerning books and reading. Many would-be donors were hesitant, wanting the project to take off so that they would see how viable it was before becoming involved. However, the library believed that it would get more books as the program continued. All the books being used for the program were acquired by the Library Board. All the schools had to do was take custody of the materials and allow children have access to them.

Problems encountered in the implementation of this program mostly stem from the dilemma of whether to extend the bookmobile services to schools that neither had school libraries or teacher librarians. One issue was storage—where would bookmobile books be kept during the one month period. Another concern was how the children

would be able access the books. Also, there was a question of priority: the safety of the books so that the service would not be derailed or the obvious needs of the students and teachers to access the materials in such schools. The Onitsha Public Library decided to include a school without a library in the each trio of schools that receive the bookmobile services. The Library staff undertook to take the books to such schools without library twice weekly but to return with them after each visit. The excitement amongst the students was heart-warming but the visits seemed to disrupt the classes. We agreed with the Heads of such schools to allocate a period to be designated as library hour during the month that it's their turn to have the books so that they will benefit from the program.

Reading Competitions among Schools

Along with the 100 titles being rotated amongst secondary and primary schools in Onitsha, ten titles suitable for reading for different grades were also given to schools separately. These books were specifically chosen to get the children reading and to arouse their thinking. The books were not to be returned but were instead intended for a reading competition amongst the schools. Each school was to present their best four students who must have read the books enough to answer any questions that will be asked on the contents. These finalists from each school will compete against finalists from other schools then the first four winners will compete against each other for the final prize. The questions were set by a committee made up of the public library staff and a teacher from all the schools involved. It is hoped that the competition will help the children strive to surpass each other and in the process improve their mental capacity and eventually academic achievement. The program is still ongoing.

Despite their enthusiasm about the program and its advantages, school teachers were however of the opinion that they be allowed to make major input on which books were to be used for the contest next year. They wanted the books chosen for the competition to be those used in the class. This is not exactly what the Onitsha Public Library envisioned. The purpose of the competition is to get the students reading beyond their classroom texts so that they can learn to study independently, fall in love with books and have a better understanding of concepts whether they have been taught in the classrooms or not. The Onitsha Public Library would have to adequately share its vision for the reading competition with School Heads so that they can make their contributions. This would enable the two parties to agree on this issue so that the success of the program can be ensured.

The spelling contest was open to all school age children who used Onitsha Public Library. Awareness about the program was provided through publicity by the Anambra Broadcasting Service. Schools were told about the program as the bookmobile made service stops and the women in the community had been informed earlier about the contest when the library staff visited them during their church meetings. The contest was meant to encourage the children to learn words that might be considered difficult. It was also a way of getting them to get closer to books and to improve vocabulary, reading comprehension, and to make reading fun.

Each class, from primary one to senior secondary school six, had a day for their own contest. This was done so that bigger children would not take undue advantage of the younger ones. Each class was instructed to learn words that start with certain letters of the alphabet. This was meant to guide them and make them less terrified of the contest.

The contest was conducted in rounds. The first round was for all the children who were present and who wanted to participate in the competition. Words to be spelled were comparatively easy. Elimination at this stage took place after four

failed attempts to spell words correctly. Children are very creative. Once they understood that elimination was the end of the road for a participant, they started coming up with inventive spellings instead of not spelling at all. During the second round, the words to be spelled got a little tougher. The elimination took place after failure to spell three words correctly. The third stage was quite competitive; two wrong spellings sent a contestant packing. The final round was very challenging. A wrong answer was all that was needed to eliminate a participant. Word formations were also introduced at this stage. Children in senior classes were told to get 4 eight or nine letter words from 'Mediterranean Sea' - 'determine', 'sediment', 'terrains', 'mediates'. It made the children think, it made them realize that a lot can be achieved through reading and it inspired their competitive spirit to read more so that they would know more.

The competition was held only on Saturdays. It ran for twelve weeks and on the thirteenth week there was an awards ceremony to give prizes to all the contest winners. Government officials, parents and teachers were invited for the presentation of the prizes to the winners. The Anambra Broadcasting Service aired the thirteen weeks of the contest.

The program has been re-run twice fully by ABS. According to the Director of Programs in the media house, the Spelling Competition attracted wide attention from the general populace and that is why it had to be shown again, then again! This reiterates the view of Mordern (2003) that libraries, when partnering with media outlets, should recognize that the needs of the latter and that they are into the business of publicity. Obviously ABS needed the competition to shore up their ratings. However a non-governmental organization (Nkemefuna ICT Foundation), upon watching the broadcasted Spelling Competition, offered sufficient funds to the Library Board to organize the 2011 Spelling Competition with a proviso that all the public libraries in the State participate.

Advantages of Public Library and Community Collaborations

In order to be relevant and survive in these changing times, public libraries need to create a culture of collaboration and reach out for formal and informal partnerships in their communities for the attainment of common goals. Public libraries are generally known to provide services for the common good and have a strong focus on community development with no hidden political agenda attached. This makes it easy for the institution to partner with groups, individuals or corporate bodies in the community (Hovius, 2005). Ray (2001) posits that the public libraries need to have flexible and open boundaries so that they can partner with other agencies within the community. This viewpoint was re-echoed by Davis (2008), that public libraries are best placed to play a vital role in making connections within a community. Numerous advantages accrue from this. Jackson (1999) affirms that through partnerships the public library gains positive community exposure, heightened awareness of its programs, increased circulation and the registration of new patrons "(p101).

The Onitsha Public Library witnessed an upsurge in readership. Parents who brought their children to the Saturday program stayed back to use the library's facilities. Library staff has gained an additional set of skills, they now realize that teacher librarians have a lot to teach public librarians and vice versa. More children now come to the library and they have been asking when next they will be shown on TV! There has been an increased recognition of the importance of the library in the community. Schools are asking for more help with their libraries. The perception of the community about the library is changing. The opinions of Librarians are sought about issues even those totally unrelated to books and reading. It's as if the library has been 'born again'!

The Way Forward

The failure to adequately plan for these collaborations with other agencies in the community dovetailed into other problems. First, there was lack of understanding of what the public library was trying to do. Proper planning would have laid a better foundation whereby each agency would know what to give and what to gain in the partnerships. Planning would also have ensured that each partner knows boundaries so that no one would usurp any partner's position or function. Clay (2009), included lack of commitment, adequate staff, shared vision and common goals as impediments to successful collaborations of public libraries within their communities. This planning process would have entailed the formation of committees composed of the Onitsha Public Library staff, administrators of primary and secondary schools, teacher librarians and officials of the State Ministry of Education. This certainly would have ensured a firmer understanding and less awkwardness in the relationships that were formed.

Funding was a problem to the Onitsha Public Library as it entered into these partnerships with other agencies in the community. The availability of matching funds from the other agencies would have made a lot of difference. Again, the establishment of a coordinating agency to run such collaborations would give the move a big boost. The Onitsha Public Library is under the Anambra State Library Board which is controlled by the Ministry of Information, Culture and Tourism in the State. There were unnecessary administrative bottlenecks in dealing with the schools which are under the Ministry of Education.

Future collaborations will be undertaken after proper planning. Communications will need to be entered into and maintained at all levels with prospective collaborators so that the feeling of presenting them with a *fait accompli* will not arise and ego problems will be avoided on all sides.

Also the facilities of the library came under much pressure. There were many cases of book mutilation in the Children's Section, especially during the Spelling Competition. The library also discovered to its chagrin that it did not make adequate preparations to cater for new and returning clientele. Study carrels were not enough, newspapers were in high demand, dictionaries could not go round to all the children that were bent on learning new words for the Spelling Competition, the children took over the auditorium yet some children had to be sent away because of lack of space. Adequate planning by the Onitsha Public Library could have taken into consideration that reaching out to create relationships with other bodies would bring increased readership and usage of the library.

CONCLUSION

The public library despite its challenges has a fundamental role to play in ensuring that opportunities for lifelong learning are created within and outside the walls of the library for its community. Library services centered on the circulation desk are no longer enough. Present day financial realities make it impossible for the public library to do it all alone. Collaborations are therefore needed in order to reach a wider audience, increase usage of its resources, garner local support and justify its existence. Partnerships take time to mature as partners understand themselves. Despite problems and challenges encountered, collaborations with groups, agencies and schools in the community are necessary for the public library.

REFERENCES

Adeyemi, T. O. (2001). The school library and students learning outcomes in secondary schools in Ekiti State, Nigeria. *Asian Journal of Business Management, 2*(1), 1–8. Retrieved February 26, 2011

Aguolu, C. C. (1975). The school library as an instrument of education in Nigeria. *Integrated Library Review*, 46-50.

Akpovwa, D. (2010). FG step-up action to curb boy-child drop out in South East. *The Abuja Inquirer.* Retrieved February 10, 2011, from www.abujainquireronline.com/fetcher.php?fid=2812.

Akpunonu, C. (2010). 60% Imo boys drop out of school yearly. *Oriental Life News.* Retrieved February 10, 2011, from www.orientallifenewsonline.com/news/general/269.html

Ayorinde, S. (2009, March 22). Libraries not antiquity please. *Lagos: The Punch*, p. 3.

Busayo Oluwadare, I. (2010). The role of libraries in the unified Tertiary Matriculation examination. *PNLA Quarterly.* Retrieved February 24, 2011, from unllib.unl.edu/LPP/PNLA%20Quarterly/busayo74-4htm

Canlas, H. L. (2009). *Study tips for parents: How to motivate your children to read.* Retrieved November 11, 2010, from www.associatedcontent.com

Celano, D., & Neuman, S. B. (2001). *The role of public libraries in children's literacy development: An evaluation report.* Pennsylvania Dept of education, Office of Commonwealth Libraries. Retrieved February 10, 2011, from www.childcareresearch.org/location/ccrca5613

Chartered Institute of Library and Information Professionals (CILIP). (2002). *Start with the child: A report of the CILIP working group on library provision for children and young people.* Retrieved January 13, 2011, from www.cilip.org.uk/get-involved/.../children/start/...full

Chew, I. (2005). *Parents' role in nurturing the child's reading habit.* Retrieved September 13, 2010, from ramblinglibrarian.blogspot.com

Clay, S. E. (2009). The partnership between public libraries and public education. *Virginia Libraries, 55*(2). Retrieved February 26, 2011, from http://scholar.lib.vt.edu/ejournals/VAlib/v55_n2

Cullinan, B. E. (2000). Independent reading and school achievement. *School Library Reading Research, 3*. Retrieved January 12, 2011, from http://www.alia.org.au/groups/aliaschool/lamarca.ppt.

Czopek, V. (1995). Extending public resources into the classroom. *Emergency Librarian, 5*(22), 23–27.

Davis, C. (2008, June). Librarianship in the 21st century – Crisis or transformation? *Public Library Quarterly, 27*(1), 53–83. doi:10.1080/01616840802122401

Doust, R. W. (1998). *Provision of school library services by means of mobile libraries- The Zimbabwe experience.* Paper presented at the 64th IFLA General Conference, Amsterdam. Retrieved February 2, 2011, from http://archive.ifla.org

Fakoya, A. (2002, October 18). Bastardization of English language. *Lagos: The Punch*, p. 39.

Federal Republic of Nigeria. (1998). *National policy on education (Revised)*. Lagos, Nigeria: NERDC Press.

Fenwick, S. (1966). *School and children's libraries in Australia: A report to the Children's Libraries section of the Library Association of Australia Cheshire, Melbourne.* Retrieved February 24, 2011, from alianet.alia.org.au/publishing/alj/5.1/full text

Fitzgibbons, S. A. (1983). Reference and Information services for children and young adults: Definitions, services and issues. In Katz, W. A., & Forley, R. A. (Eds.), *Reference services for children and young adults* (pp. 1–30). New York, NY: Hawthorn Press.

Fitzgibbons, S. A. (2000). *School and public library relationships: Essential ingredients in implementing educational reforms and improving student learning.* Retrieved February 5, 2011, from www.ala.org/aasl/

Hovius, B. (2005). *Public libraries which add value to the community. The Hamilton Public Library experience.* Retrieved January 17, 2011, from archive.ifla.org/iv/ifla 71/papers/041 e-Hovius.pdf

(2010). IFLA public library guidelines. In Koontz, C., & Gubbin, B. (Eds.), *The Management of public libraries* (pp. 95–108). New York, NY: Grutyer Saur.

Jackson, M. D. (1999, Fall). Forging partnerships: Schools, school libraries and communities. *Teacher Education Quarterly*, 99–122.

LaMaster, J. (2005). Collaboration of Indiana Public and school media center services: A survey of current practices. *Indiana Libraries, 24*(1), 38–41.

Lance, K. C. (2001). *Proof of power: Quality library media programs affect academic achievement.* Retrieved January 21, 2011, from www.infotoday.com/MMSchools/sep01/lance.htm

Maduekwe, A. N., & Oyenike, A. (2010). *Parental involvement in children's literacy development in Nigeria: Empirical findings and improvement strategies.* Retrieved December 21, 2010, from http://www.linguist.org

Mathews, V., Flum, J., & Whitney, K. (1990). Kids need libraries! Schools and public libraries preparing the youth today for the world of tomorrow. *Youth Services in Libraries, 30*, 197–207.

Mordern, S. (2003). *Cooperation between public libraries and schools in Canada.* CELPLO report. Retrieved January 15, 2011, from www.sols.org/.../CELPLO.pdf

Murray, S. (2004). *Library collaboration, what makes it work?* Retrieved January 15, 2011, from http://www.iatul.org/doclibrary/public/conf_Proceedings/2004/Murray 20 Shepherd.pdf

Ogbonna, I. M. (2010). *Compendium of public library laws in Nigeria.* Enugu, Nigeria: His Glory Publishers.

Okoye Obi, C. (2000). The role of the library in the promotion of book readership: A Nigerian view. In Chukwuemeka, I. (Ed.), *Creating and sustaining a reading culture* (pp. 121–131). Awka, Nigeria: Nigerian Book Foundation.

Olalokun, S. O. (1996). Education and libraries in Nigerian schools. *International Library Review*, 476–481.

Otti, S. (2011). Mass failures worries stakeholders. *NBF News*. Retrieved February 23, 2011 from www.nigerianbestforum.com/blog/?p=78374

Ray, K. (2001, March). *The postmodern library in an age of assessment: Crossing the divide.* Paper presented at the National Conference of the College and Research libraries. Retrieved February 23rd, 2011, from http://www.ala.org/ala/acri/acrievents/kray.pdf

Shannon, D. M. (1991). Cooperation between school and public libraries: A study of one North Carolina county. *North Carolina Libraries, 49*, 67–70.

Small, R. V., Synder, J., & Parker, K. (2008). *New York State's school media and library media specialists: An impact study. Preliminary report.* Syracuse NY: Center for Digital Literacy, Syracuse University. Retrieved January 8, 2011, from fromwww.ciplc.net/attachments/179_Do%20School%20Libraris%20

Smith, M. (2004, January-February). California DREAMin'. A model for school-public library cooperation to improve student achievement. *Public Libraries, 43*, 47–51.

UNESCO. (2000). *UNESCO public library guidelines.* Retrieved January 12, 2010, from www.unesco.org/.../ev.php-URL_ID=4638&url-do=do-topic&url_section=201.html-

William, S., & LaGrange, J. (1989, Spring, Fall). Resource sharing between schools and public libraries in Texas. *Current Studies in Librarianship,* 28-34.

Zobec, H. (1990). Cooperation between schools and public libraries. *Australian Public Libraries and information Services, 3*(4), 245.

Section 2

Partnerships in this section are very specific to a particular purpose, such as a unique program, focus on a specific population or need, such computer skills for re-employment, financial education, responsible living, science education and film festivals.

Chapter 5
Lights, Camera, Library:
Building Community through World Class Film

Barbara Brattin
Wilkinson Public Library, USA

ABSTRACT

Providing public library services to a resort community whose members range from service industry workers to Hollywood moguls positions Wilkinson Public Library in Telluride, CO, as an institution bridging economic disparities. Community partnerships form the foundation for free library-based film series hosted by international festivals, including the acclaimed Telluride Film Festival and eclectic Mountainfilm. Both festivals enjoy a long history in this remote western ski town, and as a result of their national success, risk being disconnected from the average local. Through year-long partnerships with the public library, both festivals are strengthening ties with their home base. In turn, the library is fulfilling its role as the great equalizer and enhancing its facility through the benevolence of the festival organizations.

INTRODUCTION

Community partnerships serve a multitude of objectives. At the heart of the partnership is the affirmation that each institution matters, both to each other and to their shared community, a recognition that forges visible goodwill and lasting commitment to shared goals. At the small town level, these partnerships can become very personal, sustaining partnering organizations though hard times and raising the visibility of important services. For libraries with limited budgets, shared sponsorship of programs, services, or facilities is essential to innovation, but even libraries with strong financial support can dream bigger if they are willing to tap into the power of combined checkbooks, shared staff time and varied expertise.

As libraries strive to re-imagine their role in society, they are embracing new formats of the human story, whether it is in the form of dance, music, theater, lecture, film, or the written word. Just as in the past, when their roles expand they

DOI: 10.4018/978-1-61350-387-4.ch005

must seek outside experts to inform their success. Nowhere is that more evident than in the arena of public programming. In the traditional library, the youth or adult services librarian creates program content; the new library model positions the librarian as facilitator of community expression. Local musicians, amateur filmmakers and community activists often find their home in our spaces, redefining the library as a vibrant community center. Isolated by the individual nature of Internet searches and telecommuter jobs, our public yearns to gather together to discuss important issues, solve common problems and renew relationships. Library programming fills this need and positions the public library as a venue for building common ground through shared experiences.

This pressure for increased library programming is met in various ways. Typical partnerships occur between like-minded organizations such as universities, K-12 schools, and bookstores. The library's role is viewed as literacy and literacy is defined by the written word. A stretch of the imagination might yield electronic books and podcasts of author visits, but literacy is still boxed into a narrow set of formats. Looking outside the organization to partner with organizations that tell the human story in other formats is met with suspicion.

The resort library experience changes all that. Our users bring uncommon tastes and high expectations to isolated locations, expecting the public library, as the largest facility in town, to fill the role of children's museums, historical societies, performance halls, or other venues filled in large cities by other organizations. Partnering with world-class organizations is common and if done well elevates the image of the public library to noteworthy, driving a different clientele to library events—the elusive affluent demographic essential for library support. While these users would typically support the library as a "greater good" in their home towns, their engagement in civic affairs is considerably reduced in places where they own a second home. Libraries that

prove their worth to this demographic not only win lasting financial support; they also leverage high-quality library service for all members of the community.

Statistics show resort libraries typically fall in the upper-range of per capita funding. In Colorado, the public libraries in the ski resorts of Aspen, Vail, and Telluride rank as the top three earners per capita (Colorado State Library). What is not considered in the statistics are the unique challenges that resort libraries face in serving both an established population struggling to survive on service industry wages and affluent property owners with fleeting interest in community services. Mixed in with residents is the seasonal pressure of demanding tourists who use library services without contributing tax income. The impact of the tourist population can be quite dramatic, increasing the number of user accounts in Telluride to more than 196 percent of the service population and placing pressure on space, technology infrastructure, children's and ready-reference services. Each group of users has its own idea of what the library should bring to them, and each must be courted to participate in an institution that can be uncomfortably inclusive.

Typically serving small service populations, the resort library is naturally intimately connected to the lives of its year-round residents and easily disconnected from tourists and second home owners. Struggling local residents and guest workers seek a sense of community aside from the tourist ebbs and flows, looking to their public library for free services that keep them afloat on service industry wages. They often spend a large part of their free time in the library to access the Internet, borrow DVDs and other entertainment, or just stay warm. The concept of the public library as the community center is familiar and natural to them. Children's services are especially valued when access to children's museums or other educational opportunities outside of school is limited or nonexistent.

In contrast, affluent second home owners are often disinterested in supporting social services where they spend only a few weeks a year and may never enter the local public library facilities that their taxes support. They may feel like outsiders in a tightly knit community. Some assume that a remote library is unsophisticated and cannot match the experiences so readily available to them in major cities. But even in the most cosmopolitan urban areas served by major research libraries, the affluent do not see the value in the public library borrowing model in an age when books are easily purchased online or downloaded to mobile devices from anywhere in the world. While they may seek children's services on a rainy day or quickly scan the *Wall Street Journal*, they are unlikely to participate on a larger scale.

The challenge to the resort public library in a place like Telluride is to prove its relevance to all taxpayers and create a "third place" where every demographic comes together to create and sustain a broader community. To do this, it must reach beyond the expected and become a place of discovery where every visitor is met with an uncommon experience and invited to embrace the full manifestation of that experience—a lofty goal best served through partnerships with organizations that hold a reputation for excellence. That excellence must be matched by public library services in order to recruit a high caliber organization into a partnership and forge lasting trust with the partnership organization and the community.

Often the small public library is shy to approach another organization deemed too powerful or successful to associate itself with the underfunded, understaffed social service agency called the library, as if the relationship is altruistic and benefits only one party. Through its focus on Wilkinson Public Library's partnerships with Mountainfilm and the Telluride Film Festival, this chapter demonstrates the shared value of partnerships at all levels and encourages libraries to invite the most successful local organizations into their buildings and into the lives of their community.

BACKGROUND

Wilkinson Public Library (WPL) is a district library in rural southwest Colorado, serving 5,867 residents and 11,500 cardholders over a 50 square-mile radius in the San Juan Mountains and surrounding mesas of San Miguel County. The primary regional employer is Telluride Ski and Golf and the primary industry is tourism. The area is one of contrasts, not only in the landscape but in terms of demographics. Area property values are high. The 2009 median value of a house or condominium was $895,592, yet 14.4 percent of residents fell below the poverty line that year. (City-Data, 2009) Educational levels are also high, with 62 percent of residents having some college background in 2009 (USA Citylink, 2000), but diversity is low (94 percent white). (City-Data, 2009) Half the housing units available are classified as vacant by the U.S. Census Bureau, reflecting the prevalence of vacation homes. In 2010 the median age was 32.7 (City-Data, 2009) with men outnumbering women who are typically overeducated and underemployed. Under the umbrella of a forgiving and relaxed social structure, a small percentage of ski bums morph into entrepreneurs, managers and real estate moguls. The taste for quality runs high and residents from all walks of life expect outstanding performance and facilities from tax-supported institutions. Residents are well traveled, technologically savvy, read more nonfiction than fiction, and borrow as many books as DVDs. This kind of eclectic atmosphere attracts extraordinary talent. In 2007 alone, Telluride was awarded Colorado School Superintendent of the Year, Colorado Athletic Director of the Year, Colorado Teacher of the Year, and Colorado Librarian of the Year.

WPL maintains one 20,000 square-foot facility which opened in 2000 in Telluride, the county seat, and one library vending machine in neighboring Mountain Village. High property values translate to a full-time resident per capita budget of over $400 or a $200 per capita annual budget per cardholder. Stable funding supports a staff of 33, including a full-time program coordinator, part-time graphic artist, full time marketer and part-time program assistant. The library district administration confidently encourages experimentation and "getting to yes" with community partners. Social problems on the local, regional, national and international levels are of great concern to the local community and the library prides itself on educating the public as well as contributing to local solutions. In 2009, the library wrote a three-year service plan which earmarked creativity, comfort and curiosity as three service priorities. In 2010, WPL enhanced its plan through a community visioning event, broadening its role to coordinate local youth activities, build community capacity to make informed choices, and support community nonprofits. The final plan is entitled "Building Common Ground."

Awarded 5 Stars by *Library Journal* three times in a row, WPL places great emphasis on the experience of storytelling in various formats, whether through the visual arts, film, theater, poetry, dance, music, spoken or written word. Often the storytelling consists of activism through social issues film series or lectures by locals with expertise in the subject area. Nurtured by a liberal public living in the "bluest" county in America, the library enjoys the freedom of presenting controversial issues in a tolerant and thoughtful environment and prides itself on introducing intellectual opportunities such as streaming Bioneers, ITVS, and PBS film series premieres to an educated audience. Children enjoy Zumba classes, ballet, Yoga Storytelling, Brain Gym, Kindermusik, and Imagination Vacations in a setting compared to a children's museum enhanced by partnerships with local arts and science organizations to provide hands-on activities. The annual Children's Literature Celebration attracts children's authors like Todd Parr and Brian Selznik from every part of the country.

Discussion of local issues magnifies the polarity between environmentalists and developers, ranchers and ski bums, yet the library eagerly presents controversial ideas in all forms of media, keenly aware that the conversation must continue for the community to thrive. Stable real estate values ensure solid library funding and famous part-time residents combined with the lush beauty of the region position the library to easily attract performers with name recognition. Partnerships enhance the user experience and the library readily takes advantage of more than 60 local affiliations including theater groups, arts organizations, science institutes and history museums to broaden program offerings. In any given week, a local can participate in a creative writing workshop with Craig Childs, attend the screening of an independent film, design jewelry with a New York designer or watch Jane Goodall address the Bioneers conference live from California.

While building its creative programs, WPL has focused in particular on bringing a segment of every local festival into the library. Chamber Music Festival, Telluride Jazz Celebration, Blues and Brews, Bluegrass, Mushroom, Wine and Yoga Festivals all schedule at least one performance or lecture in the library on an annual basis. As the success of the library grows, more and more community groups seek partnerships with the library. By "getting to yes," Wilkinson Public Library has built and sustained partnerships that serve in fulfilling its long-term goals of inclusivity. It has gained the confidence of international film festival organizations to forge unprecedented year-long partnerships that both satisfy the tastes of the rich and include the common man in the experience of uncommon film. It has grabbed the attention of the affluent as a first-class organization and created a community center filled with discovery for its local residents, and guest workers.

The first Telluride Film Festival (TFF) was organized by Tom Luddy and began on August 30, 1974 with the intent of bringing filmmakers and theater owners together to celebrate new film and honor forgotten film. More than thirty years later, TFF remains uniquely eclectic and internationally recognized for selecting and premiering Academy

Award winning films. Indeed, perusing the list of 2011 nominations, 32 went to films premiered at TFF in 2010. Shunning the red carpet of Cannes and Sundance, the small venue allows Hollywood celebrities, independent filmmakers and screenwriters to mingle with participants on the sidewalks, making it a favorite with film aficionados worldwide. "Sundance has swag, Cannes has yachts... Telluride has class," says John Horn of the *Los Angeles Times* (Telluride Film Festival, 2011). "At this smallest of the world's major film festivals," Roger Ebert wrote, "there is always a controversy, and always a discovery, and always a moment when you stumble dazed out of a midnight screening into the clear mountain moonlight, convinced that cinema is worth saving after all."

Every Labor Day weekend for the past 30 years, the Telluride Film Festival has transformed a small mountain town of 2400 into an international venue for 5000 film aficionados, industry moguls, screenwriters, Hollywood stars and their adoring fans. Converting unlikely local spaces such as the elementary school cafeteria, hardware store loft and the historic Sheridan Opera House into world class theaters for four days of magic seems an impossible task, yet entering these spaces once transformed, ticket holders can well believe they are in a professional theater. Theater managers from all over the country vie for volunteer management positions and locals line up to volunteer and get an inside view of the production and a close-up of the stars while avoiding the high price of a festival pass. Attracting an average of 5000 participants annually, TFF strives to make the festival an experience everyone can enjoy. Admission to the Backlot Theater located in the library is free, as are open air showings of four premieres.

In addition to TFF, Telluride hosts another locally-based film festival, Mountainfilm. Currently in its 33rd year, Mountainfilm in Telluride is a four-day celebration of art, adventure, culture and the environment—a perfect fit for a town where every other resident is an athlete, activist,

filmmaker or artist. Filmmakers, photographers, conservationists, mountaineers and explorers from around the world come to this small mountain community to immerse themselves in independent documentary films and discussion on annual themes ranging from food to activism to endangered species. According to Jeff Hauser of the Raynier Institute, Mountainfilm "challenges, educates and inspires us to be the kind of caring and committed global citizens we should be." Guests are treated to such great minds as Nicholas Kristof, Greg Mortenson, Ken Burns, Maya Lin, and Joel Sartore in a typical festival celebration which includes a day-long symposium, art exhibits, book signings and student workshops. David Holbrooke, son of the late Ambassador Richard Holbrooke, is the current festival director, and continues to attract celebrity journalists and the politically powerful to the festival lineup.

In 2000, Mountainfilm in Telluride embarked on a new journey—Mountainfilm on Tour. Each year, festival staff takes a selection of films from the Telluride venue on the road to reach audiences who otherwise wouldn't have a chance to experience the festival. Those films display themes of adventure, mountaineering, remarkable personalities and important environmental and social messages. "Making Movies that Matter," a program offshoot of Mountainfilm, "introduces students to films and people who are deeply concerned and involved with the ways human beings interact with each other, with other species, and with the environment—and encourages them to get involved." Through a partnership with the Telluride Academy, a local nonprofit youth organization, students receive discounted tickets to the festival and vote for a Student Choice Award.

Telluride is proud to host both of these festivals, yet sometimes feels forgotten when the festivals leave town. TFF struggles to dispel the impression of elitism brought on by its affiliation with Hollywood superstars by sponsoring free Sunday films at the Palm Theater throughout the year and providing sustaining support to the Nugget

Theater, a small local historic movie theater. With a smaller staff and tighter budget, Mountainfilm has chosen to take its show to venues across the country and keep its presence in Telluride seasonal.

FORMATION OF A THREE-WAY PARTNERSHIP

In 2006 TFF approached WPL to create a Backlot Theater dedicated to the celebration of the history of film in the library's largest program room, a space measuring 870 square feet. The theater concept was new to the festival, an experiment intended as a bonus experience to satisfy the cinephiles that flood the festival each year. Although the festival had utilized the elementary school gym and the large high school auditorium for many years, this was the first time TFF had approached the library for theater space. In order to transform the room acoustically and visually, the festival proposed to permanently install hardware to hang heavy velvet draperies, add a temporary projection screen, remove existing hanging light fixtures and replace the library's video projector with a model specific to the scheduled films. The festival would pay for all components and labor, including risers and comfortable seating. All TFF equipment would be removed at the conclusion of the festival except the audio system, which the library would keep on permanent loan. The room would be returned to the library undamaged.

The offer to partner with an organization the caliber of TFF was exciting. Exposure to the affluent community the festival attracted was an elusive goal this partnership would fulfill. The majority of large donations to the library typically came from Los Angeles and San Antonio visitors who expressed delight with library services. Adding another 500 potential donors to the list of library visitors would hypothetically reap big benefits. But there were considerations specific to a tax-supported institution that had to be addressed before any agreement with the festival could be

reached. First, the library's meeting room policy required that no organization charge for admission nor make money in library meeting rooms, a rule fundamental to the library's values. In the interest of fair access, the policy also limited any organization's reservation to a much shorter time period than the seven full days requested by TFF. Meeting room policy required a fee of $50 per hour for reservations outside of normal library business hours, a fee the nonprofit festival wished to avoid. With no security staff on hand, the library expressed concern over the fate of memorabilia proposed for exhibits in the public hallway leading into the theater and with a long line of spectators sure to form outside the building, agreement had to be reached that the entrance would be carefully monitored so as not to block the free flow of library patron traffic. The impact on shared spaces such as public restrooms and the entry hall also needed consideration.

Luckily, there was a long standing partnership with the local community radio station that served as precedence for meeting room exceptions. The annual KOTO Community Radio Ski Swap is a favorite local event and a major fundraiser for the beloved station. Every year since the library building was completed in 2000, KOTO has held exclusive rights to the library's garage for its annual three day event in November, free from extended use fees, time limits, or from a restriction on income generating activities. This exception is not only expected by the general population of ski enthusiasts, but is a major factor in the library's popularity in the community, despite the inconvenience of temporary loss of access to coveted parking. Library administration entered into the TFF agreement, bolstered by the knowledge that if the locals recognized the same public good resulting from this new partnership as in the partnership with KOTO, they might accept temporary loss of access to the library's program room for other functions. While it was easy to see why locals would bend the rules for a radio co-op in which many were involved as volunteer DJ's, it remained to be seen if the locals were willing to be inconvenienced by an organization many considered elitist. TFF readily agreed to allow free admission to the Backlot Theater in its first year, both for pass holders and the general public. Based on precedence, and in consideration of the fact that room setup would take several days before the opening of the festival and takedown several days more, library administration made an exception on length of use and waived the after-hours fees for TFF. A festival volunteer was assigned to watch over the displayed memorabilia and the festival agreed to hold the library harmless for any theft or damage. The same attention to access for library users was promised. Responsibility for keys distributed to the theater manager was negotiated and the festival agreed to hire an outside contractor to clean the public restrooms, pick up the trash, and vacuum the hallway adjacent to the theater several times a day during the four days of the festival. All provisions of the agreement were outlined in a letter that was signed by both library administration and festival management.

In the tradition of TFF, a manager recruited from a small theater in San Francisco was assigned to supervise the crew of volunteers tasked with creating the Backlot Theater. He immediately met with Barb Brattin, the Library Director, and Dan Wilson, the library's Maintenance Supervisor, who would serve as the liaison between the library and the festival for the duration of the project. The crew began to transform the plain meeting room into a world class theater. Obsessed with perfection, they measured walls for authentic Rose Brand acoustical curtains, rented a full scale high tech screen, and ordered the latest evolution of projector flown in for the four-day event, courtesy of Panasonic. Risers bearing comfortable chairs were constructed, library lighting was replaced and new speakers were installed to maximize the theater experience. The Theater was finished just in time for the festival and received rave reviews from festival participants and no complaints from locals about policy exceptions. A grateful festival

delivered a handful of coveted tickets to library staff to show their appreciation.

For the next two years, the library and TFF gladly partnered to create the successful Backlot Theater and things ran smoothly. Then in 2008, another successful local film festival, Mountainfilm, approached the library for a similar partnership. Mountainfilm proposed a different model, however, in that the room would be treated like all other theater venues in town, showing the same films as other participating venues in alternating sequence and hosting follow-up discussions and celebrity breakfasts. Like TFF, Mountainfilm would bring in curtains, seating, screen, and projector. Unlike TFF, only pass holders would be admitted to the theater.

Library administration stood firm on the issue of open attendance and Mountainfilm eventually agreed to allow anyone into the theater on a first-come, first-served basis as a first-year experiment. All other provisions of the agreement mirrored those held with TFF, including exemption from limits on length of reservation, permission to make money in the library's meeting space, waiving of extended use fees. The theater was transformed as expected and a grateful community publically thanked the library for the comfortable space. Festival management, however, received complaints from pass holders about the difficulty of securing a seat at the library venue and questioned why those who did not pay to attend the festival were granted admission. In addition, several library staff members without passes were turned away by volunteers uninformed of the agreement. The library and Mountainfilm had reached an impasse that would only be solved by dissolving the partnership or amending the library's meeting room policy. In 2009, the library Board of Trustees changed its meeting room policy at the request of the Director, allowing nonprofit organizations to make money in its meeting rooms and allowing Mountainfilm to restrict access to its library theater to pass holders only. Mountainfilm returned to the library for a second successful year.

As these film partnerships progressed, the library began to ask for advice from festival managers on how it might permanently improve the acoustical and visual elements of the room for its own programming purposes. Recognizing the savings in equipment rental costs and time needed to set up their respective theaters, both TFF and Mountainfilm staff agreed to provide professional advice free of charge. Brandt Garber, an architect on staff with TFF, offered to sketch out drawings for a permanent screen. He calculated dimensions for drapes, identified associated hardware and suggested alternate lighting. Brandt also contacted vendors with ties to TFF to negotiate pricing. Mountainfilm Festival Producer Stash Wislocki proposed a monetary contribution of $3400 from Mountainfilm, which was one third of the projected cost of improvements.

Working with a combined budget of $10,000 for room improvements, work began in January 2010 to install a permanent wall-size screen made from high-tech materials. Black velvet curtains were purchased and hung to cover three walls of the room, completely blocking light from the north wall of windows and providing much needed sound abatement. The library contracted with a local carpenter to remove the existing equipment cabinet to a recessed corner of the room and paid for new carpet to be installed. The library's book drop, located in an adjacent closet, was acoustically treated to eliminate the noise of returned materials through a common wall. Lighting was strategically realigned to prevent interference with film projection. The library retained the borrowed sound speakers from TFF and its own projector.

In return for a few thousand dollars and shared expertise, the film festivals saved the time and expense of hanging acoustical curtains before each festival. They no longer needed to rent a high-tech screen and the screen in place fit the needs of the festival for size and placement. The community was pleased with the blooming three-way partnership and credited the festivals for the visible improvements in the library facility. Festival par-ticipants were granted a new, comfortable venue. Library program participants benefited all year from the acoustical and lighting improvements. Both festivals became convinced that the library was a reliable and friendly partner and the library quickly identified potential for partnership expansion. Soon the library's new Program Coordinator, Scott Doser, and WPL Director Brattin were drafting a proposal and calling TFF for a meeting.

For the past several years, the library had been developing a successful book club program. As the program grew, an idea came to Brattin for a parallel film discussion program led by local experts. In 2009, the library approached TFF for a partnership to bring regular classic films series and discussion led by experts to the library all year. The result is the Telluride Film Festival Cinematique, a monthly film series selected by TFF festival co-director Gary Meyer on such topics as French New Wave Films, Scorsese Films, Films of the Great Depression, and Food in Film. The library pays TFF $500 for each series of three film events for which it receives the list of films, background notes and discussion points, and a local moderator to introduce the films and lead the discussions. Past moderators include David Oyster, a filmmaker and former UCLA film school professor, Howie Movshovitz, a Colorado NPR film critic, and Gary Meyer himself. The $500 fee provides an additional revenue stream for the nonprofit festival and gains three events for the library's ambitious programs schedule. The library provides themed food for each film series, such as a mock "soup kitchen" for the Great Depression series and Italian cuisine for the Scorsese series. Marketing responsibilities are shared and multiplied between the combined organizational contacts. While the library first sought to associate with TFF because of its international reputation, TFF thanks the library for lending its good name to the festival at every event. "We would have never partnered with you," says Brandt Garber, "if you hadn't already proven yourself as a first-class organization."

During initial discussions with TFF concerning the Cinematique events, Brattin stressed the desire of the library to fulfill its role as the "great equalizer" and bring award-winning film and film discussion to every demographic. With festival passes priced from $390 to $3900, the average local works as a festival volunteer in order to participate and those whose work obligations prevent a week-long commitment are left surrounded by the festival activities, yet unable to participate. As a consequence, TFF risked developing a reputation with locals as an elitist organization pandering to the rich and famous, a far diversion from its original intention of an inclusive venue for the celebration of great film. Although Garber did not concede to the view offered by Brattin, he recognized the Cinematique partnership as one that could only strengthen ties with the festival's hometown. "The library is one of the few organizations in town of the caliber we seek for partnerships," said Garber. "We've reached the level of excellence where we have a reputation to uphold."

Bolstered by the huge success of TFF Cinematique, the library turned to Mountainfilm for a similar year-long monthly partnership in 2010. In January 2011, a series of favorite film shorts debuted as the first "Mountainfilm in the Library" to a crowd of 85 fans. Moderated by Seth Berg, 2007 Colorado Teacher of the Year, the film lineup was culled from past festivals for repeat performances. The structure of the Mountainfilm series has continued to follow this format--films with strong significance from past Mountainfilm Festivals are moderated by Mountainfilm volunteers. Mountainfilm staff selects and hosts the films at no cost to the library and the library provides the venue, marketing and refreshments. In February 2011, the library expanded its partnership beyond Mountainfilm, inviting the San Miguel Resource Center, a local domestic abuse advocacy group, and One Telluride, a community immigration integration group, to co-host "Presumed Guilty," a social issues film in Spanish shown at a recent Mountainfilm festival. The library paid for Mexican food prepared by locals to be served at the program. This partnership satisfied WPL's long-term goal to mingle the Hispanic demographic with its steadfast Mountainfilm participants and greatly enrich the conversation.

SOLUTIONS AND RECOMMENDATIONS

Despite our enthusiasm for creating enduring partnerships with local film festival organizations, concessions had to be made in relation to meeting room policies. Unlike TFF, whose Backlot Theatre hosted a unique agenda, Mountainfilm could not defend showing films in our facility for free while charging for the same films at another venue. The library had to weigh its options and decided that the partnership with Mountainfilm would in the end provide more free access to films over the course of the relationship than a few free seats over a four-day period could offer. Standing firm on free admission would have prevented the partnership from ever forming and our community would not be enjoying Mountainfilm in the Library. According to the meeting room policy in place at the time, the library had the right to charge each festival $50 per hour for every hour they used the facility outside of our regular open hours. The value of the year-long festival programs and the exposure to the appreciative film festival participants has yielded far more value than a few hundred dollars in room fees ever would have.

Over the past six years as Library Director, Brattin has found that policies must be continually evaluated in the face of changing circumstances. Local nonprofit organizations, even in Telluride, are struggling for survival. Allowing them to sell a T-shirt or bumper sticker in the library's meeting rooms makes sense for the organization and for the community and builds tremendous good will. Since its partnerships with the festivals, WPL has also experimented with removing limits to the number of consecutive reservations per organization, preferring to handle blatant abuses on a case-by-case basis. Brattin encourages every administrator to periodically review library policies with the staff members who are required to enforce them and ask such simple questions as "Does this work? Why not? How can this policy be amended?" or, the ultimate question: "Is this policy necessary at all?"

This re-examination of long standing policies has strengthened WPL in its quest to be more community-centric. As the library looks for ways to nurture community creativity, breaking down barriers imposed by traditional policies has proven essential. While Board policies had been written with the goal of equal access, close examination found that they were instead exclusionary and in the case of KOTO Community Radio, inconsistent. As more and more organizations perceived the library's commitment to community, they began to step forward, each with different needs and a desire to partner to accomplish shared community goals. The New Community Coalition, an organization charged with sustainability education, proposed a bicycle check out system using the expertise of local bicycle mechanics and the circulation system of the library. Now WPL checks out pink "Telluride Townies" and supports the program through collection of overdue fines.

Telluride Television, the local public access channel, followed suit, providing the community with film cameras and related training. The cameras are housed at the library and circulate like a book. The television station provides equipment, training and repairs and airs the films created by local residents as part of their regular programming. The partnership with Telluride Television has broad implications for the future of film partnerships at the library. The Director's Club, a program housed at the Telluride High School, has since moved to the library. Young students are paired with mentors to learn the craft of filmmaking. The library provides space, staff, and a "Creation Station" loaded with film editing and animation software. Telluride Television provides cameras. Participation in the program has broadened to the young adults who frequent the library but previously felt excluded from "the club."

For adults interested in film, the library has morphed into a training ground through a partnership with University Centers of the San Miguel, a degree granting institution dedicated to bringing accredited college classes to the remote San Miguel region. A recent series of classes, "Non-fiction Filmmaking" was hosted by the library and participants are provided with an additional "Creation Station" to hone their skills.

Recognizing the library as an established film venue, a small number of local residents stepped forward to form the "Jazz Lovers Film Club." The group meets at the library periodically to show a film and meet with like-minded people. The library willingly provides marketing materials and refreshments to support this community-inspired concept.

Not long after TFF was granted broader rights to the library's meeting room space, the Nordic Ski Association demanded the right to hold its own ski swap on library property and was granted that right based on precedence. Authors began to sell their self-published books in our meeting rooms. Soon the library received requests from independent filmmakers to screen their films and collect donations for their causes. The walls were coming down and surprisingly, the community feedback was nothing but positive. The domino effect of opening our meeting rooms to nonprofit fundraising has been heartwarming. Collections at one presentation by a local activist built a shower at a Tibetan girls' school. Local artists hoping for a public venue hang their work on the library walls through partnerships with local arts organizations. The same organizations now contact us to collaborate on combined programs at no charge to participants, elevating the quality of library programming by including the expertise of professional artists, dancers and writers and offering that expertise to community members with income limitations.

Recognizing the power of film to bring people together in the WPL eclectic community, the library has begun a series of films in Mountain Village, a tourist enclave located a short 20 minute gondola ride above the town of Telluride. Viewed as an underserved location within the library district, WPL began targeted service to Mountain Village a year ago by installing a library vending machine in the vestibule of the grocery store. Met with overwhelming praise, WPL then expanded its services to the village through programming targeted to an older audience. Partnerships with the Telluride Medical Center offered programs to retirees on ways to cope with high altitude at an advanced age and the biomechanics of skiing. Partnering with the Telluride Conference Center, WPL's Lawn Chair Classics film series brings family films to an outside venue in the summer months. The Conference Center serves refreshments and arranges for discounts at local restaurants, supporting local business and turning the films into events. Films from the library collection are projected onto a blow-up screen purchased by the Conference Center on the plaza outside the center's main building. Logistics are easy- all equipment is housed inside the Conference Center and refreshments are the responsibility of the Center. Alcohol sales permits are owned by the Center, bartenders come from Center staff, and all proceeds from food and beverage sales are captured by the Center, which is owned by the Town of Mountain Village. The library receives the good will of the people, local government officials, and through its film series reminds Mountain Village residents that they are valued members of the WPL district. Tourists enjoy a family activity after dark and respond by using other library services at the Telluride location during their stay.

Lawn Chair Classics is a simple partnership easily replicable by libraries of all sizes. Libraries should be prepared to overcome typical barriers to such partnerships by relinquishing control over profit making activities and concentrating instead on their mission to build community through inclusive programming.

Serving an inquisitive educated population has enabled WPL to take risks with programming that many libraries across the country remain intimidated to consider. Even in Telluride, library administration expected some backlash to relaxation of meeting room policies and partnerships with organizations that restricted access for short periods of time to ticket holders. Instead, the library has gained new relationships that broaden the impact of film festivals in the community and extend a year-long invitation to everyone in the community to experience the best film available. It has inspired local residents to begin their own film clubs and to bring those clubs to the library. It has positioned the library as a center for content creation through the use of camera equipment, computer software and college level film classes. Local nonprofits consider partnering with the library at every opportunity. The community looks to the library as both a community center and a strong foundation for nonprofit support.

FUTURE DIRECTIONS

While the Telluride Film Festival Cinematique continues to draw an audience of 60 or more at each event, we fail to see the variation in the socio-economic demographics of the audience we were seeking. The series has formed a following, but they are typically the same group that purchases a full festival pass each September. This could be due to the hosts, who are among the town's elite, or it could be due to the academic nature of the film discussion. The films selected by Meyer are classic and serve to educate the audience on the history of film from the Great Depression era to the 1960s, appealing to an older crowd who remember or relate to the time periods. While the library is pleased to have attracted elusive affluent community members to its program room, the question remains whether the Cinematique has become an exclusive social club or whether the selection of films drives the audience. While WPL studies this pattern of attendance, it will also watch to see if the TFF followers expand their attendance to other library programs.

Mountainfilm in the Library made its debut as a monthly series in January 2011. After two events, each attracting over 80 patrons, the demographic seems to be more inclusive, perhaps because an interest in outdoor adventure and political activism spans all socio-economic strata. Focusing on the Spanish-speaking demographic for the second film in the series by providing Mexican food and showing a Spanish-language political film has attracted many of the area service workers. Purchasing homemade food from this demographic also signaled the library's positive relationship with its small Hispanic community. It will be interesting to watch if that film series takes its own road toward exclusivity or whether it will continue to attract patrons from all segments of the population.

By embracing the Director's Club into the library's slate of services, there is potential to expand film programs by screening the work of participants. An expanded partnership with Telluride TV may lend itself to locally produced film screening events. There is talk of creating a film institute in Telluride, led by a Hollywood producer who recently moved to Telluride full time and the library is closely watching this project with an eye to partnership.

CONCLUSION

Developing lasting partnerships with important community groups requires an open mind, flexibility, and a willingness to change perspective on policy. The vision of a year-long film series free of charge required that the library first re-evaluate a meeting room policy that was unfairly administered and stood in the way of local non-

profit viability and enhanced library service. A cooperative attitude and consistent follow-though built a lasting trust that formed the foundation for expanded partnerships. While the library's main intention has been to connect all demographics with transformational film experiences, the main demographic attending the Telluride Film Festival Cinematique continues to be homogeneously affluent. It is the library's hope and mission that as the film selection evolves, the disenfranchised will begin to attend this series, mimicking the mixed audiences of Mountainfilm and fulfilling the public library's role as the great equalizer.

WPL's partnerships with local film organizations have unexpectedly evolved into a new community role for the library: a hub for content creation. Telluride Television now films interviews in the acoustically friendly and appropriately lighted program room that was upgraded through the film festival partnerships. KOTO Community Radio records interviews in the same space and local musicians may reserve it to record their music at no cost. Through the library's affiliation with the Director's Club and UCSM's nonfiction filmmaking classes, the library is the new space for budding filmmakers to explore their own creative impulses and unveil their creativity to the world. Who knows? Maybe the next Scorsese lives among us and will discover his passion within the library's walls.

REFERENCES

City-Data. (2009). *81435 zip code detailed profile* Retrieved from http://www.city-data.com/zips/81435.html.

Citylink, U. S. A. (2000). *Telluride demographics* Retrieved from http://tellurideco.usl.myareaguide.com/demographics.html.

Colorado State Library. (2010). *Public library annual statistics.* Retrieved from http://www.lrs.org.

De, R. C., Johnson, J., & OCLC. (2008). *From awareness to funding: A study of library support in America: A report to the OCLC membership.* Dublin, OH: OCLC Press.

Telluride Film Festival. (2011). *Purchase passes.* Retrieved from http://telluridefilmfestival.org/passes.html.

ADDITIONAL READING

Community Radio, K. O. T. O. (2010). *Home page.* Retrieved from http://www.koto.org.

Mountainfilm. (2010). *Mountainfilm in Telluride.* Retrieved from http://www.mountainfilm.org/.

Telluride Television. (2010). *Home page.* Retrieved from http://telluridetv.org.

University Centers of the San Miguel. (2010). *Home page.* Retrieved from http://ucsanmiguel.org.

Wilkinson Public Library. (2010). *Home page.* Retrieved from http://www.telluridelibrary.org/.

Chapter 6
A New Evolution in Science Collaboration

Erica Segraves
Mamie Doud Eisenhower Public Library, USA

ABSTRACT

The Mamie Doud Eisenhower Public Library is a single site, medium sized, municipal library in Broomfield, CO. After receiving an initial matched grant of $50,000 from the Sandoz US Foundation ten years ago to build the Sandoz Science and Education Center located on the first floor of the library, the continued partnership with Sandoz Pharmaceuticals, Inc. has evolved into the development of a Science Task Force composed of scientists in the community willing to volunteer their time to bring science programming to the library. This chapter details the initial development and subsequent growth of these partnerships as well as how the evolution of this collaboration has impacted the Young Adult Department science programming and education services. The chapter also focuses on developing collaborations with local companies as well as finding volunteers in the community. Procedural information regarding the recruiting and retaining of volunteers as well as key points in program planning, executing, and evaluating are also shared.

INTRODUCTION

The Mamie Doud Eisenhower Public Library is a single site, medium-sized, municipal library in Broomfield, CO, a northern suburb in the Denver-Boulder metro area with a population of about 55,000. Given its amazing view of the mountains and a strong support system for the library's Young Adult department, I was immediately drawn to working there and accepted a position as a new graduate holding a Master's of Librarian and Information Science (with a certification in information management). Prior to becoming a librarian at Mamie Doud, I had worked as a project manager for a technology in education non-profit organization and was therefore used to managing and communicating with a team of 12 people in an organization that had 60 employees. When assigned the task of devoting part of my 28-hour work week to being the library liaison to our Science Task Force, I felt thrilled about the opportunity to possibly expand the program.

DOI: 10.4018/978-1-61350-387-4.ch006

What has now become one of our most popular programming series has gone through quite an evolution that began with one 400 square feet of space and ended with nine monthly programs that are not only full but often have waitlist of more than ten participants.

After the initial grant award and the creation of the Sandoz Science and Education Center, a Science Task Force was established to help the library staff solidify the role of science programming in the library. The Mamie Doud Eisenhower Public Library Science Task Force is a community-based group of citizens formed to share information and combine resources to promote science and technology knowledge and literacy. This includes activities and events aimed at expanding knowledge, investigating technology, practicing modern science, and informating community members of the well of technology and resource in Colorado. The group accomplishes these goals through development, presentation, and sponsorship of programs and events for young people ages 9-14 years of age and for general audiences in the communities of the Denver-Boulder corridor of Colorado. The Science Task Force continues to reach out to the surrounding communities and businesses and find partnership opportunities that help us achieve our goals of providing free, quality science programming to our community's youth. We currently have three types of collaboration: programming in collaboration with Sandoz, programming in collaboration with the Mamie Doud Eisenhower Science Task Force, and programming in collaboration with community expert volunteers.

EVOLUTION OF COLLABORATION

History of Sandoz Partnership

In 2000, the Broomfield Library Friends sent a grant application to the Sandoz US Foundation to request funding for a Sandoz Science and Education Center to be built inside the new library building. The Library Friends stated that the Mamie Doud Eisenhower Public Library must address the needs of the children and youth in the community to have life science education materials, basic education resources, access to databases, software, and online information to support scientific education and development of competency in basic skills to become productive adults. Print materials, hands-on educational games and toys, scientific equipment and audiovisual learning materials were also needed to provide the resources for youth to develop marketable skills in a safe environment during non-school hours. At that time the Library Friends also asked Sandoz to provide support for additional evening and weekend storyhours to address the needs of working parents unable to attend during the work week and in addition to provide storyhours for daycare centers and homeschool children at off-site locations.

There were four objectives and tactics of the grant.

- First, to increase educational skills and knowledge of science in children and youth from 18 months to 18 years by purchasing and making available scientific and educational materials to the public.
- Second, to increase reading skills in children and youth by purchasing and providing computers with software and circulating print materials specifically designed to increase reading proficiency.
- Third, to help youth develop marketable skills in a structured learning environment by purchasing materials and software to assist in preparing for a high school diploma or taking the GED test as well as preparing for college entrance or employment examinations.
- Fourth, provide storyhours one evening a week and Saturdays as well as special storyhours for daycare and homeschool children by hiring a qualified person to prepare for and conduct these special storyhours.

This grant included all of the various library departments by ensuring the Children's Librarian, Young Adult Librarian, and Reference Librarian, along with the Director and Assistant Director, would be directly involved in the collection development for the Sandoz Science and Education Center. The public service librarians would also provide assistance to the public so that users of the science center would be able to maximize usage of all materials and technologies. They would train and supervise all assistant librarians who work in the public sector so that staff would be knowledgeable of the content and comfortable with the technologies. The cataloger would handle all the cataloging of the items and supervise all assistant librarians who complete the data entry and volunteers who process all materials. The Library Director and Assistant Director would assume the responsibility for supervising all aspects of setting up the Sandoz Science and Education Center and its daily operations.

This was a matching grant and the $50,000 awarded from the Sandoz US Foundation went towards the collection development of the scientific and educational materials. The matched library portion went towards creating an approximately 400 square foot room in the library that would house the Sandoz Science and Education Center and provide a dedicated space for scientific enrichment. There were no other centers such as this in any of the libraries in the surrounding areas. The diversity of material types, the depth of knowledge included in the collection, and the focus on children from toddler to teen created a unique center in Broomfield.

The Sandoz Science and Education Center is located on the first floor and is one of the first areas that patrons view as they enter the library. The grant also enabled the creation of the new Sandoz collection which includes books, videos, games, databases, models, posters, hands-on kits and scientific equipment aimed at enhancing learning from a variety of subjects for children age 18 months to 18 years. The interactive and exploratory nature of the collection makes this a unique center for scientific learning.

With a back wall of glass windows looking west across Community Park and out towards the mountains, this room offers a causal learning environment where experiments take shape and learning is encouraged. The other two side walls are lined with books from the Sandoz collection with the purpose of assisting students perform scientific research for school projects or personal interests. There are low counters with ample workspace on top and neatly organized models and kits in bins in the shelving below the countertop. There is also a high bar in the center of the room that contains more storage shelving for kits and posters as well as a computer area for patrons to access the science databases and computer games. Two glass-front cabinets are in both of the front corners of the room and these house models, artifacts, and scientific equipment like compound microscopes. There is also a video viewing area with a TV, VCR/DVD, and headphones.

Creation of the Science Task Force

With a new emphasis on science due to the dedicated Sandoz Science and Education Center on the first floor, the library staff recognized an opportunity to focus more heavily on science programming. However, in order to do science-centered programs, scientific minds were needed. Therefore, a volunteer position was posted calling for scientists in the community to create a Science Task Force. Several community members responded. The initial goal was to have the Science Task Force volunteers staff the science center and help patrons in need of guidance. They would also be in charge of cleaning up and maintaining the area after patrons used the educational kits or scientific equipment. This goal was never fully reached, because the Science Task Force changed its focus from being collection centered to becoming program centered and leading science based hands-on programs for the children and youth of the community became the priority.

The Sandoz Science and Education Center collection was highlighted in these first few years of science programming, because the one to three programs held each year utilized the posters, kits, media, and print materials in the newly acquired Sandoz collection. The earliest Science Task Force programs were called Foundations and Frontiers events. They were designed to build inquiry and reasoning skills and to investigate the frontiers of science discovery, research, and technology. For example, the first program was called Life Matters. Science Task Force facilitators used a Sandoz kit of seven hominid skulls. The program focused on cloning, organ transplants, animal super senses, and genetics as well as genetic engineering. There were demonstrations and hands-on activities with microscopes, chemistry, and measurement. This program and others were offered to children and teens ages 9-14 and had a healthy average attendance rate of 12 participants.

Then in 2005, the library was awarded a $2,500 NOVA's "Einstien's Big Idea" grant. These series of programs were entitled Einstein in October. One of the programs included in the series was called Walking Lightly – A Portrait of Einstein, which was a stage performance of Einstein's life. Other programs presented included a Trivia Night at the Science Kaffeehaus for grades 6-12, a Tapping Your Inner Einstein: Hands-On Science for ages 9-14 years, and an Einstein's Big Idea PBS/ NOVA film showing for general audiences. The positive community turnout to the Einstein in October science series brought a new awareness to the library staff that not only was scientifically centered programming successful, but that it would also bring larger numbers of people to the library's events. The number of programs increased from one to three programs held in 2005 to a total of six scheduled in 2006, with the average attendance rising to 25 people at each program.

During this time the Libray's organization and staff time commitment was also growing. In 2007, the library's Young Adult Department created a new professional position with time specifically dedicated to the subsequent growth of the partnership with Sandoz and the nurturing of the Science Task Force as well as the further evolution of the yearly science programming series. I have now held that position for four years and have been able to coordinate and participate in this process of expanding our science programming.

Dedicated Science Task Force Led to Increased Programming

By 2007, the Science Task Force and library staff solidified the role of science programming in the library by writing a mission statement to unify our goals. The mission statement is as follows:

The Mamie Doud Eisenhower Public Library Science Task Force is a community-based group of citizens formed to share information and combine resources to promote science and technology knowledge and literacy. This includes activities and events aimed at:

- Expanding knowledge of scientific discoveries
- Investigating technology and current areas of scientific research
- Reinforcing and practicing the methods of modern science
- Informing community members of science and technology resources in Colorado.

The group accomplishes these goals through development, presentation, and sponsorship of programs and events for young people ages 9-14 years of age and for general audiences in the communities of the Denver-Boulder corridor of Colorado. This volunteer-based group is motivated by curiosity and interest in sharing their professional knowledge with the community.

The call for members of the Science Task Force is always open and is advertised on the Teen Zone webpages of the library website. The City and County of Broomfield website also has a page that lists contacts for volunteer opportunities. The library receives several emails a week from people interested in volunteering at the library. Those with scientific backgrounds are automatically routed to the Young Adult Department to see if they would be a good match for our Science Task Force. Though we do get quite a few adults wanting more information about the science program and wondering what volunteering for the Science Task Force entails, we do not have a lot of new members joining. This is in part due to the immense time commitment it requires. We do not mislead prospective volunteers or skim over the requirements; they need to know upfront what is expected from them being on the Science Task Force. Members are expected to be at each of the programs planned for the upcoming year, which usually means nine Saturdays out of the year. We usually do not have programs around the major holidays or during the summer months. Each program also includes at least one planning meeting beforehand to discuss who is leading the hands-on learning stations and what activity each station will contain. These stations are designed based on personal interests related to the topic of the program by the member who is manning the station. That means the Science Task Force members must also dedicate personal time to create and test whatever scientific experiments and theories they will be highlighting at their station. We also have one long planning meeting for the upcoming year each October. If prospective volunteers wish to continue with the process of volunteering after acknowledging and accepting these time commitments, they must fill out a City and County of Broomfield volunteer application and disclosure. We also request a copy of his or her résumé to determine the areas of scientific expertise held by the applicant. A background check is then performed for the applicants and

once the background check passes an approval process by the City of Broomfield, the Young Adult Department conducts an informal interview to ascertain whether the applicants will work well with tweens and teens. Once this whole process is completed, the new member is introduced to the rest of the Science Task Force.

We currently have four members on our Science Task Force. This is a diverse group of volunteers that are from different cultural and scientific backgrounds. A mix of men and women on the Science Task Force helps in promoting scientific interest and learning to all genders. One of the members is a founding father to the original Science Task Force and has a background in computer science. The first female member actually began volunteering for the Young Adult Department to help with a Lord of the Rings program in 2002. Staff learned about her structural engineering background and she happily joined the Science Task Force. The other female member began volunteering in 2004 and has a background in botany. The last volunteer to join the Science Task Force came to the group through the biannual Chemistry programs. He was an Sandoz employee and decided he wanted to volunteer more than twice a year. He joined the Science Task Force in 2007 and has even started a weekly Boost Your Brain tutoring night from students in grades 6-12 needing help with math or science homework. We have had one other person complete the process and join the Science Task Force only to find that it was not what she was looking for afterall. Other parties have been interested, the time commitment usually prevents people from being able to join, especially since most of the meetings and programs take place on weekends.

The personal reasons behind each members' desire to volunteer on the Science Task Force are similar. Several members expressed that they find it rewarding to share their knowledge and excitement about science with the students. One member noted that the questions and curiosity expressed in the program by the tweens and teens in attendance takes him back to when he was younger, and makes him re-evaluate what he knows about science while trying to explain it. Knowing that he is making a difference in our youths' education and perspective on life makes the large time commitment worthwhile. Another member stated that seeing happy kids and grateful parents was what made her thankful for volunteering. Many members recalled volunteers who helped educate them as they were growing up, and the members feel that this is their way of returning the favor and passing along what they have learned. Because it can be hard for students to understand and connect theory to practical applications, they hope to bring excitement and wonder to science, so that students can find their passion and are driven to learn for themselves.

The goals of the Science Task Force are to offer hands-on scientific and educational programs geared towards the 9-14 year old population. There are also occasional programs that the whole family can attend. This enables joint participation between the Children and Young Adult departments. Currently, the Young Adult Department staffs six of the nine yearly programs. The Children's department staffs the other three.

Input from participants in the science programs give the Task Force ideas about the type of science to focus on each month. At the end of each program, the participants fill out a very short, half-page survey and write down any suggestions or requests that they may have for future programs. Each October the Task Force and I sort through the evaluations and make a list of selected topics. We then choose the most popular requests to highlight in the coming year. By planning so far in advance, we are afforded the time to create new partnerships. It allows us to quickly form a big picture of the year and then narrow in our focus to each individual program and devote our attention to the particulars for each event.

The overarching goal for program content is for hands-on, experiential activities that maximize mental and physical engagement of the participants. Each program allows between 30-50 participants. However, we usually have a full registration list over a month in advance and routinely have waitlists of 10-20 interested tweens and teens.

Strong Programming Led to Community Experts

The popularity of our programs has directly led to one outcome that we were not expecting. Almost on a monthly basis, a scientist in the community will call, email, or stop by the library to offer his or her services or ask to be involved with one of our already planned programs. This is an immensely helpful predicament to be in especially for a medium sized library with a small programming budget. Many times the expert isn't expecting our programs to be in place for the coming year, so often times the Science Task Force finds room to welcome him or her into an upcoming program or we ask if their information can be saved for the coming year. What is particularly important to note is these community experts are mainly donating their time and just wishing to be a part of something that they feel is benefiting their community in a positive way. Many times the experts are actually parents of tweens or teens who participated in one of our previous programs.

Fortunately, the Science Task Force has a strong line of communication that is always open through email. Any interested parties are often introduced to the Science Task Force via email and then we continue the conversation to see how the community expert would like to donate his or her time and in what type of capacity. We also have a Science Task Force binder that is kept at the library. In it, there are business cards, emails, and contact information for those experts who have aided us in past programs and those who are waiting to volunteer for future programs.

Current Types of Programming Collaboration

There are three main types of programming resulting from this evolving collaboration. The first is programming offered by the original partnership with Sandoz Pharmaceuticals, Inc. The second is programming created and developed or sponsored by the Mamie Doud Eisenhower Science Task Force. The third is programming presented by community expert volunteers who are not otherwise part of the Science Task Force. Several of these collaborations produced programming that repeats on an annual basis.

Programming in Collaboration with Sandoz

Our first type of collaborative program is headed by Sandoz Pharmaceuticals, Inc. Fortunately for the library and the patrons in our community, after awarding us the matched grant Sandoz continued their collaborative efforts. They formed a unique partnership with the library and adopted us as their community outreach headquarters. The scientists at Sandoz began holding an annual chemistry program during National Chemistry Week in October. It quickly became one of the most highly attended science programs each year. In 2008, Sandoz agreed to conduct two annual programs, one in spring and one in October.

Sandoz brings in a team of 12 chemists to lead this intensely interactive program. The 50 participants are divided by age range into four groups. Usually, there are two groups of age 9-11 and two groups of ages 12-14. This allows the two chemists leading each station to speak appropriately to the elementary versus middle school groupings. Each of these biannual programs contains different activity stations and four main group demonstrations, including a culminating event that takes place outside due to its messy chemical reactions. During the Chemistry Creations event this past March, the four activity stations

included distinguishing between endothermic and exothermic reactions, fabricating bouncy balls, experimenting with long-chain molecules by creating stained glass glue, and studying the properties of polymers by making slime. Before rotating to the next new station, two other chemists performed large group demonstrations while the activity stations were being cleaned and readied for the next group rotation. These large group demonstrations included creating a vacuum to crush a water cooler jug, formulating oxygen-filled foam called elephant toothpaste, and making ice cream with cream, sugar, and liquid nitrogen that all the participants could then eat. After all four groups visited each station, Sandoz handed out goodie bags and all the participants along with their parents who returned to pick up their child were welcomed to meet outside for the grand finale of the group demonstrations. The crowd favorite has been the chemical reaction between Mentos candy and Diet Coke experiment that sends sticky fountains of sugary liquid into the air.

Programming in Collaboration with Mamie Doud Eisenhower Science Task Force

Our second type of collaborative programming is headed by the Mamie Doud Eisenhower Science Task Force. They conduct two types of programming: either homegrown or outsourced. The programming budget for the science programs is obtained through a Broomfield Library Friends grant which awards us about $400 a year to buy outsourced programs as well as supplies and refreshments for all other programs.

For the homegrown programs, the Science Task Force creates, prepares, and leads the programs. They start from scratch to produce a program that has been sparked by the past participants comments on the evaluations. Such programs have included *Who Are You?: Hands-On Genetics, Battle of the Brain Trivia Contests, Structures: Build 'Em and Break 'Em, Bountiful Botany,* and *Artists' Lab,*

We find that most of our programs with live animals are very popular. The city's K-9 police unit agreed to send Officer Jason Collins and his dog Nik. Together with another officer acting as the perpetrator, Officer Collins and Nik demonstrated the powerful bond between a highly trained dog and his commanding officer. After this exciting demonstration, another one-time volunteer from the Longmont Human Society spoke about training therapy dogs and related it back to the mentality of a pack of wolves. Afterwards, the 30 participants were divided into four groups to attend the five hands-on activity stations. These stations included visiting Officer Collins and Nik, discerning the correlation between height and hand measurements and discussing the skeletal system, discussing selective breeding and the hearing and smelling senses of dogs, visiting the therapy dogs, and getting ideas on how to train your own dogs at home.

The most far-reaching and unifying program led by community experts was the EcoTracks program. For EcoTracks, the Science Task Force obtained free assistance from local experts in the community, from the local 4-H organization, the Colorado State University Extension, the Birds of Prey organization, and the Environmental Systems Research Institute (ESRI), which is a local geographic information systems (GIS) mapping software firm, as well as other City and County of Broomfield employees from the GIS Department and the Public Works Department. The purpose of the program was to develop and deliver a family GPS scavenger hunt that focused on sustainability in the community. With the help of a local company, ESRI, (specializes in global information systems), we were able to set up a scavenger hunt with geocaches at four points within a half-mile radius of the library campus. The GPS units were pre-programmed by the ESRI worker to point the four teams in a varying circuit of the set locations in order to ensure that more than one team did not go to the same location at the same time. The ESRI employee and our own employee from the GIS department in the City

and County of Broomfield opened the program with a short lecture on GIS technologies and the importance of sustainability in our community. Then the 40 participants were divided into four teams and went outdoors to complete the scavenger hunt. Each of the four stations was staffed by members of the Science Task Force or local experts who had willingly volunteered three hours of their Saturday afternoon to lead this program. The local wildlife station was led by a City Trails and Open Space volunteer. The local farming station was led by a Science Task Force member who is an expert in botany. The Xeric garden station was led by two Colorado State University Extension Master Gardeners and another city employee. The water station was led by another member of the Science Task Force.

Whether the program is led by the original partnership with Sandoz, created by the Mamie Doud Eisenhower Science Task Force, or presented by community experts, the resulting impact on the community is positive. Many parents relay the excitement that their tweens and teens express for attending these science events. Often the teen has an interest in pursuing a certain career in science, and this is a wonderful way for him or her to experience one-on-one time with a scientist working in that specific field. After our Wildlife Science 101 program led by the Denver Zoo, a grandmother reported that her granddaughter wants to be a zoologist and it meant so much to her that she could speak to one in person and see the small live animals up close that the zoologist brought with him. Teens and tweens that have an interest in science but aren't necessarily pursuing it as a career say they love that the programs are interactive and they enjoy experimenting to learn new things.

Solutions and Recommendations

Though the beginning of our relationship with Sandoz was established in 2001, it has taken years of dedication and patience to develop this science collaboration into the series of programming it is today. It has also taken a dedicated library staff person and devoted Science Task Force to allocate the needed time and energy that goes into planning the yearly programs. Concluding recommendations focus on acquiring the right type of volunteers, having a dedicated library staff liaison, marketing throughout the community, approaching local companies and organizations for help, and, finally, applying for funding to help support a programming budget.

The initial goals of the Science Task Force were not unified between the members of the founding Science Task Force due to different learning styles and different expectations of the scope and scale of programming. It is essential to find volunteers who work together as a cohesive unit with a common interest of educating and enhancing the local community youths' experience involving scientific exploration. I had to refine the process of obtaining volunteers by explaining the amount of paper work, background checks, and time commitment involved. This is not meant to be a deterrent or to dissuade people from applying to be members of the Science Task Force, but rather to make sure they are fully aware of the dedication and responsibility involved. Being part of the Science Task Force does not mean that they volunteer just a few hours nine months out of the year. They work on the presentations during their personal time at home, meet for planning meetings here at the library, respond to email communications on a weekly basis, and then arrive early and stay late after each program. It is a very large time commitment and it is exceedingly important to the library staff and patrons that our volunteers are prepared to contribute this much time to our science programming. The library is incredibly fortunate to have such dedicated volunteers and that is one of the key factors in having such a strong collaboration.

The other key ingredient is having a dedicated library staff person. In the beginning, multiple staff members were managing different aspects of the original approved grant. There were several ports of communication and no staff member had

designated time to nurture the Science Task Force or manage the collection in the Sandoz Science and Education Center. When my position was created in 2007, the managing members of the library knew that one of the key roles I would play would be to work hand-in-hand with the Science Task Force and give them the attention they deserved as such stalwart volunteers. I do not have a background in science and though I gather feedback and help decide the overall plan every year, the Science Task Force members are the ones that do all the scientific legwork while I act as a support person and help them with any material and organizational needs they might have. I rely on the Science Task Force to do develop and lead the programs. My role during the actual programs is to welcome the attendees and answers any questions from the parents, monitor the room dynamics during the program, provide refreshments during break, hand out and collect program evaluations, and thank the participants for attending. Though the yearly planning of the science programs requires extensive work from October to January, usually the rest of the time I allot towards planning and preparation of each program is relatively low. Many of the Science Task Force planning meetings that take place before each meeting happen at a table right next to the Teen Zone desk. The Science Task Force usually plans these meetings on the one Sunday each month that I work so that I can take part in them, but if that date does not work, we communicate through email as to what supplies and support they need from me at the upcoming program. Of the 28 hours I work each week, approximately one hour is spent on Science Task Force business. Then I usually work one Saturday afternoon for six of the nine programs and a Children's Assistant Librarian works the other three programs. The program sharing was designed to aid me in not always working two weekends a month.

In order to have success and recognition in the community for the Science programming, it is our experience that the Library staff needs to reach out to the local schools and businesses to market the programs. Apart from advertising the programs in the library, we also have a list of 10 schools in the surrounding area to which we mail flyers and newsletters. We also send these dissemination materials to our local Borders® Bookstore, the Paul Derda Recreation Center, the city Health and Human Services Department, and make them available at the Community Assistance Center at the City and County building. The upcoming programs are also announced on the library Teen Zone webpages and in the local newspaper. This saturation of program flyers is one of the reasons why each of our programs fills up a month in advance and why we sometimes find ourselves in the unfortunate position of turning participants away due to not having the facilities or facilitators to handle such a large amount of interest.

Marketing to the homeschool community is also important. Homeschoolers make up 18% of those individuals attending our past events. Often we find that this population is using our Sandoz Science and Education Center on the first floor so we have included science program flyers there as well. Many homeschool parents say that they attend our programs as added enrichment to their science curriculum.

It is also highly recommended that libraries interested in starting their own science collaboration, or growing the partnerships they currently have, not be timid in contacting local businesses and organizations. We have found that many of these institutions are actually extremely welcome to the idea of sponsoring or donating their time to lead a program. Many of these institutions also have company or organization goals that focus on outreach in the community, but are lacking the outlets to do such a thing. As the old adage says, it never hurts to ask.

For libraries with already small programming budgets, it is essential that you find other outlets for funding. Though many of the collaborations already discussed were provided to the library free of charge, securing additional funding helps relieve some of the stress from the Science Task

Force by providing a few of the purchased outreach programs each year. Good places to look for additional funding and grants are your local library Friends groups, your city, and even national entities like NASA and NOVA. In 2010, we applied for and received a grant of $1500 from the city's Art, Cultural, and Science Grants to help us with our 2011 programming.

A final recommendation is to be prepared to handle the popularity of the programs. The science programs are advertised quarterly to allow ample time for families to sign up. Many families will sign up their tween or teen for one or two of the upcoming programs at one time. Therefore, the registration lists do tend to fill up quickly. When all available spaces for the program are filled, a waitlist of 10 to 20 people is allowed. A few days before the program, library staff contacts registrants to confirm attendance.. If anyone cancels at this time, the next person on the waitlist is notified that there is now an available space in the program. We also encourage the first four people on the waitlist to plan on attending, since we normally have four to six people who do not show on the day of the program even when they confirmed their seat. There are typically several calls the week of or even the day of the program from parents wishing to register their child for the program. Almost every science program is full by the week of the event, but parents are invited to sign up their children for any other upcoming science programs. We also let them know to check our website and newsletter for upcoming science programs and to call as early as they can so their child can be guaranteed a spot. Most parents are grateful for the opportunities the science programs give their child and are more than understanding when the programs are full. If we have an overwhelming interest in the program with a very large waitlist, we will do our best to run the program in two back-to-back sessions to accommodate more people. Recently, we did this for our Mr. Roboto robotics program. Having concurrent sessions of a program is really more realistic to do when the program is outsourced or lead by a community expert. Unfortunately, it is a rare occasion that we are able to negotiate resources, instructors, and time in order to offer a second session, but we are keeping this in mind when planning future programs. For example, during the upcoming You Are Here: 2011 Teen Summer Reading Program, we have purchased the From Tombs to Treasures program from the Denver Museum of Nature and Science and have scheduled two concurrent sessions to accommodate the high volumes of participants we anticipate having during the summer.

CONCLUSION

While programming is an ongoing and evolving aspect of library offerings, the Mamie Doud Eisenhower Public Library has experienced a unique, yet replicable, relationship with local science-based businesses as well as other local experts. These collaborations took many years to develop and blossom into the popular science series they are today. However, continued efforts have helped us reach our science programming goals and brought our ideas to fruition for the benefit of community youth.

Chapter 7
Cross – Generational Learning Case Study:
A Working Partnership between Malahide Library and Malahide (Post-Primary) Community School

Susan Lovatt
Fingal County Libraries, Ireland

ABSTRACT

"The public library, the local gateway to knowledge, provides a basic condition for lifelong learning, independent decision – making and cultural development of the individual and social groups." (IFLA/ UNESCO Public Library Manifesto, 1994)

No public library, however large and well funded, can meet all the needs of its customers on its own (2010, IFLA, p. 28). With fewer staff resources, collaborations and partnerships have become even more important in today's economic environment to help deliver a quality service to library customers. The working partnership established between Malahide Library and the local post-primary school delivers mutual benefits to both. It has enabled the library to meet its customers' needs through sources of volunteers who assist in the delivery of technology-based classes within the library. The cross-generational approach of the partnership has enabled the students to fulfill their school requirements of engaging in social responsibility and developing life skills. The partnership has assisted in enhancing the role of the library within the community and fostering good relationships with its future customers.

INTRODUCTION

The working partnership between Malahide Library an Community School (MCS) has developed over the last three years, proving beneficial to the library, the students involved and the wider community. The students participating in the partnership are part of the Transition Year (TY) Programme run in the school.

DOI: 10.4018/978-1-61350-387-4.ch007

Transition year is a one year "stand alone" pro-gramme designed by individual schools within the framework of national guidelines. It occurs after the compulsory three year cycle (age 12-15) and Junior Certificate state examination, and before students embark on a Leaving Certificate pro-gramme for the final two years of their schooling. Transition year programmes build on the idea that mid-adolescence is very much a time of change and there is a strong focus on facilitating transi-tion from the dependence of childhood towards the relative independence of adulthood (Jeffers, 2004, p. 54).

29,000 students drawn from 550 schools throughout Ireland currently participate in a Tran-sition Year program. The Transition Year program calls for the students involved to participate in social responsibility and self – directed learning and to develop life skills. In this chapter, I will outline the background to the partnership, its delivery, benefits and progression over the last three years. Examples will be given of how it is meeting the individual needs of all participating in the partnership and how, through its cross-generational learning approach, it is contributing to breaking down some of the barriers that exist in our digital society. Cross-generational learning not only supports bridging the digital divide; it also can be seen as bridging the gap between formal and informal education. The partnership with the local school has given the library the opportunity to be seen as an educational partner, highlight-ing the influence it can have on the students' lives. This is demonstrated through the school's openness to move the partnership into different directions. Foremost outlined within the chapter will be how the partnership with MCS supports Malahide Library in delivering an efficient and quality service to meet the various needs of its customers.

BACKGROUND

Malahide Library is part of Fingal County Coun-cil which administers the County of Fingal in North County, Dublin. Fingal covers an area of 450km² and is Ireland's fastest growing county, with a 22% population increase between 2002 and 2006. A network of nine public libraries and a mobile library service are uniquely placed to reach all citizens of the county to deliver a quality service. In addition, a housebound service and an archival and local studies service are available to all residents. Four of the libraries are open fifty-six hours a week; two are open fifty hours, while the remainder are part-time (30 hours per week). At present, there are 140,337 registered users of Fingal Libraries out of a total population of 273,051(Census 2011).

Malahide Library is located in the coastal village of Malahide; the library is a Carnegie building dating back to 1909. It serves Malahide Village and surrounding area and the adjoining suburbs of Kinsealy and Portmarnock. In 2007 the library reopened after a major refurbish-ment and expansion. The refurbishment allowed the library to increase the stock and facilitate a larger range of activities and events. The floor space has increased to 1,200 square meters, the opening hours have been extended to 56 hours a week, and the number of public access computers has increased from two to sixteen. The library, in retaining its position as a focal point in the village and surrounding area, strives to meet the needs of all in the community. In ascertaining these needs, Malahide Library continually asks its customers for suggestions on activities and events that they would like facilitated within the library. There are many requests for children's activities. However, the main request is for computer classes to be organised and run in the library. The main responsibility and focus of librarians in Malahide library is organising activities and events. This focus has led to collaborations and partnerships with the MCS .

The Irish School System is set up as follows:

1. Primary School (ages 4-12) - Children from the age of 4 upwards enter primary school into Junior Infants class. They progress from there into 1st class through 6th class.
2. Secondary School (post-primary, ages 12-18) – The secondary education system is divided into two examination cycles with Transition Year taking place in the middle.
3. The first cycle is from first year to third year, leading to a state examination at the end of third year called the Junior Certificate Examination
4. Transitition Year (Fouth Year) – non examination year introduced to allow students develop and mature as individuals.
5. The Second cycle includes fifth through sixth year leading to final state examination at the end of sixth year called the Leaving Certificate Examination. Eligibility for undergraduate courses is determined through a points system on the results of the Leaving Certificate Examination.

MCS (a state-funded School), originally called Pobal Scoil Iosa, is a co-educational, inclusive post-primary school that welcomes pupils of all religious denominations. MCS is the only post-primary school within the Malahide area, and caters to 1,200 pupils. It is run in the belief that "the benefits of a well ordered and structured school environment facilitates and encourages learning". As a community school, it has a "special responsibility to facilitate continuing education and leisure activities for the local community" (https://sites.google.com/a/malahidecs.ie/malahide-community-school/). The Transition Year Programme within the school has called for the students to partake in social responsibility, thus opening the school to suggestions of collaboration and partnership.

PARTNERSHIP

The establishment of the partnership with the local community school has allowed Malahide Library meet its customers needs. Beth Hovius (2005) notes that the "starting point of a partnership is the tendency to talk about what can be done for each partner, as opposed to what can be done together. It is only as both sides communicate their issues, and share a common language that the areas of mutual benefit and concern can be identified (p.8)". In establishing a working partnership with the local community school, the needs of the library to provide computer classes and children's activities and the needs of the students to engage in social responsibility coincided.

Initial collaboration with the local school occurred in May 2008 during the celebration of Bealtaine (an Irish festival celebrating the older person). Transition Year (TY) students participated in and ran a class in the library called "Learn How to Text for the Over 55s". The success of this collaboration laid the foundations for the library- school partnership, and a pilot project for this initiative began in September 2008. The first set of classes ran over a ten week period.

Cross-Generational Learning

Cross-generation learning is a major aspect of the partnership between the school and the library. Smith (2010) comments about the mutually beneficial, two-exchange that takes place between those engaged in this kind of learning. Both teacher and student:

...share their expertise and experience with each other across generations, they can capture and share their hard won expertise of retiring boomers, blend it with the energy, skills and the knowledge of a new generation of young teachers and together create teaching and learning beyond what any generation could do alone (p.10).

The generations that are affected directly and indirectly by the partnership in the library can be described as:

- Silent Generation (individuals born between 1925-1942)
- Baby Boomer Generation (individuals born between 1943-1960)
- Generation X (individuals born between 1961-1981)
- Generation Y (individuals born between 1982-2000)
- Generation Z (individuals born between 2001-2010)

By engaging in the partnership students are actively communicating with and learning from the different generations they encounter. The partnership allows the students to develop an understanding of others, foster healthy growth and adjustment and develop effective interpersonal communications and relationships. This cross-generational learning experience enables Malahide library meet its customers needs and build a good relationship with the "next generation of library customers and supporters, ensuring the future of the library". (Cross, 2005, p. 217)

Student Teachers

The TY students that volunteered to take part in the computer classes in the library were part of a Transition Year module entitled *Third Age Anthology*. In preparing the student teachers for the classes, we initially followed a manual provided to us by Age Action Ireland, a charity- run organisation which promotes positive ageing and better policies and services for older people. They have provided volunteers on occasions to teach basic computer classes within the library. The modules in the manual were guides for the student teachers. The classes they gave were on a one-to-one basis, allowing the student teacher to cater for the needs expressed by their particular student. From the first session with their student, the student teachers prepared a class plan for the next meeting. The main areas the student teachers have covered are basic Microsoft Word applications and how to use the internet for setting up e-mail accounts, booking golf sessions, paying car tax online, booking flights, and many other tasks.

To complete the Transition Year, students must engage in "education for maturity with the emphasis on personal development including social awareness and increased social competence" (Department of Education, 1993). Social responsibility, broad educational experience and self-directed learning are some of the key features also expressed in the Transition Year Guidelines for students to develop. These objectives are achievable through partnership with the library. Students address the area of social responsibility in running the classes; the student teachers are imparting their knowledge to allow their students gain new skills to become part of the digital social network. Their level of social awareness and social competence is engaged in their interaction through informal cross-generational learning. Self-directed learning and broad educational experience routinely become part of the one-to-one classes. The student teachers, through conversation with students, are automatically involved in self-directed learning. They have been set the challenge of preparing and developing class plans for subsequent weeks, giving them ownership of how the classes are approached.

Library Arrangements

Library staff provides customer education and training in online resources, especially those to which the library subscribes. Due to a public service recruitment embargo, "the existing staffing level would not have permitted the library staff to commit to giving basic computer classes on an ongoing basis" (Lovatt, 2010, p.23). Without advertising, the library has a list of about one hundred to one hundred and fifty people who are interested in basic computer classes in the library. Those on the list are mainly older persons and women who have been out of the workforce and education for a long period of time. They have found themselves lacking in basic IT skills that are relevant in aiding their grandchildren in their homework and contributing in today's digital society. The cultivation of the partnership with the local community school has allowed us to satisfy these customers' needs.

Library personnel manage the booking of the computer system and maintain the waiting list for classes. When people register their interest, library staff note their level of experience and give them a choice of class with volunteers provided by Age Action Ireland or one-to-one tutoring with TY students. In a majority of cases, the one-to-one tutoring format is preferred. The library has twelve public computers that are used for computer classes. When the school provides their dates for the classes, library personnel match a learner to a student teacher, thus allowing twelve people to be removed from the wait list each time. The added advantage of the partnership with the student teachers is that there is no age criteria for the people taught. Age Action Ireland and other organisations that have given classes in the library have an age limitation: the person they teach must be over 55 years of age. The partnership with the school facilitates an activity that is open to all local citizens.

Review and Evaluation

The first sets of classes run in the library were carried out as a pilot project. With the success of the project, the library decided to move forward with another series of classes. Before proceeding, librarians reviewed and evaluated of the first set of classes and came up with solutions to any issues that were highlighted. The areas that needed to be addressed are outlined below:

1. The classes were run over a ten week period, though there were only six weeks of classes in all. In the middle of the ten weeks, the student teachers engaged in two weeks of work experience (a compulsory part of the Transition Year Curriculum) in various companies organised by their school. There was also a two week mid-term break in the middle of the classes. This proved disruptive to their students, who found that after the breaks, they had forgotten a lot of what they had learnt. To solve this problem, the library now runs classes in six week blocks with no interruptions.

2. The first day of the first set of classes was a little manic: the students had not visited the library before the classes and were unsure which computers they were to use or how to log on to the library computers. Due to certain technical requirements by the IT Department regarding security and virus protection, the set up of the computers is slightly different from that with which the student teachers were familiar. As a solution, a new element was added to the program: before any new classes are run, the student teachers are brought down to the library to familiarise themselves with the computers, dissipating any confusion on the first day. The sessions before the classes have proven beneficial from an educational and library perspective. At these sessions librarians introduce the student to the online databases, how to use the library catalogue and renew and reserve books online, since not all are necessarily familiar with these facilities. Students are encouraged, if they get the opportunity, to pass on this information to their students, enabling them to use their library in all formats, and thus, bridging any digital divide.

3. Absenteeism among the student teachers meant that on one or two occasions, one of the learners did not have a tutor. To rectify

this, the next time classes were run, other student teachers were placed on standby in case of absenteeism. These substitutes communicated with various student teachers, to get an idea of the learner's level and experience. Since this backup system has been put in place, no learner has been left without a tutor.

4. From the school's perspective, the first set of classes was run as part of a single period class. This caused disruption to the next class the students were attending, as they returned late back to the school from the library. Subsequent classes were organised when the students had a double period of the module *Third Age Anthology*. This allowed the student teachers to take more time with their students and not rush the end of the lesson. In addition, the students did not interrupt any other class back at the school.

5. When people sign up for the library classes, library staff gauge their level of competence. However, "one or two people taking the class were not complete beginners and the students found that they were ill equipped to meet their demands". (Lovatt, 2010 p. 24) Library personal double-check the level of competence of each person signing up to participate in the classes before they assign a person to a TY student. These incidents have not occurred since the first set of classes.

There is a constant review and evaluation after each set of classes between myself and the teacher supervising the classes. Each time we meet, we find further ways of developing the programme between the library and the school.

Music and Story-Time

In all there are between twenty to twenty five students signed up to the module *Third Age Anthology*. It is not possible for all these students to teach computer classes in the library at one time due to the number of computers available. In point of fact,

not all of the students participating in the module are interested in teaching computer skills. Through conversations with their teacher, the library noted there was an interest from the public in children's activities to be facilitated within the library. The students with no interest in the computer classes were asked if they would like to facilitate a music and story-time session for parents and toddlers. The level of interest from the students was extremely high. On the mornings the computer classes are run, other TY students set up and run parallel music and story – time sessions for parents and toddlers. In preparation for these classes, they have organised a musical instrument session, a puppet show, craft sessions and they have acted out various children's stories and nursery rhymes. When Jeffers (2007) is looking at innovation in the transition year programme, he comments that "student's interests can be stimulated by imaginative and appropriate activities, inside and outside the classroom" (p.113). The level of motivation and imagination in the preparation of the music and story-times sessions is impressive; the level of independent learning and responsibility shown by the students has been noted by their teacher.

ASSESSMENT

One of the purposes of Transition Year is to move the student away from the pressures of examinations. In doing this each school can devise different ways to asses their students' work. Jeffers states:

Some schools have responded to this opportunity by developing systems of portfolio assessment, often shifting from a traditional reliance on terminal, written examination towards a greater emphasis on presentations of work, practically and orally. Project work, by individuals and by groups, student journals and log books, as well as reports from work experience and community service placements, also feature in some schools' assessment procedure. (2004, p.57)

In developing the programme between the school and the library, the teacher's assessment of student work has evolved over time. Initially, the students did an essay on their experience of teaching in the library. Now they fill out a learning log after each session, developing skills of reflection on their work. The teacher and I have also developed a feedback sheet to be completed by the student, the student learner and parents in the music session after the set of classes are finished. Finally, a student's overall mark will be given for a report they produce of the whole experience.

Benefits and Feedback

According to the International Federation of Library Associations and Institution (IFLA) Public Library Service Guidelines, one of the most important institutional relationships for a public library is that with the local school and the educational system in the service area (2010, p.53). Ihanamäki (2010) observes that "partnerships involve concrete activity based on mutual needs and objectives. The goals of this activity are deemed so important that the various participants are solidly committed to achieving them". (p.18) In the partnership between the school and the library, there were clear objectives, and needs from both sides that were laid out and met. Individual and mutual benefits resulted from the partnership. The importance of these relationships can be demonstrated through the benefits acknowledged from each of the players connected to the partnership.

I. Benefits for the Transition Year Students and the School

Underpinning the rationale of Transition Year is the need for the students to learn by experience through the curriculum set by the school. The curriculum devised by the local school and its openness to enter into a partnership with the library have established a "bridge to help pupils make the transition from a highly – structured

environment to one where they will take greater responsibility for their own learning and decision making" (Department of Education, 1993 p.4). The benefits for the students participating in the partnership and its cross-generational approach has contributed to their development of skills in communication, teaching, and project/time management (of the content of their sessions and how they are delivered), along with a mutual respect and understanding for the people they are teaching. Each of the skills they have learnt has given them a foundation and experience of adult working life, which they can bring forward. Along with the educational aspects of the partnership, students indicated that they really enjoyed giving the classes and "having a chat" with the people they where teaching.

Another benefit noted came from one of the students who participated and ran the music and story-time sessions: she commented that the experience had confirmed her career aspirations of becoming a primary school teacher. From participating in the partnership she was able to make the decision on what subjects to take in her final two years of school. These benefits show that learning can occur quite effectively outside the classroom.

This partnership has given the school the benefit of 'projecting the school's image as innovative and progressive to the local community' (Jeffers, 2004, p.61). When the students run the classes, they wear their school uniform, marketing the school in a positive and responsible light.

II. Benefits for the Library

The overall aim of this partnership was to meet our customers' needs in bridging the digital divide. The partnership enabled us to give people an opportunity to become computer literate and more confident in using computers. By catering to the needs of those on our waiting list for computer classes, the library is fulfilling its mandate to be proactive in helping people become more independent and capable on the internet, thus allowing them to become more active in their citizenship. "It is important that libraries as impartial centers of learning should assist all members of the public in acquiring ICT-skills, thus contributing to the basic principles of inclusion, participation and democracy". (Rødevand, 2009, p.13)

III. Marketing Benefits

Similar to that of the school, an added benefit of the partnership regards marketing. We find a drop in the active use of the library by young adults between the ages of 14-17 years. The participating TY students fall into this age group. Some of the students had become lapsed users while the library was in temporary premise during extensive refurbishment, and they were pleasantly surprised and impressed with the new library and the added stock we had to offer. In the pre-session to the classes, we have started to give the students a tour of the library, bringing to their attention the range of stock we have to offer. One student was so impressed that he posted a comment to that effect on our Facebook page.

Another positive element of the marketing for the library is the spread of the classes through word of mouth. We have not advertised the classes, yet everyday someone new is signing up on the waiting list. The partnership has helped increase our rate of new users.

After the learners have set up and used their new e-mail address, they have asked to receive the library's monthly e-mail bulletin, informing them of the activities and events organised for the next month. The e-mailing list has grown by 25% from 393 to 523 in the year 2009-2010, an increase reflected in improved attendance of events. Figures for event attendance for 2009 stood at 6,382. In 2010 this figure had increased to 7,112. To date figures for 2011 continue this upward trend already standing at close to 6,000.

IV. Benefits for the Customers

The main benefit for the customer is that the library is providing a service that they require. Some of our customers were reluctant to participate in the group classes we organised, so when the one to one classes were offered, they were delighted. The nature of the one to one classes allowed them to learn at a speed with which they were comfortable. The area of Malahide according to the 2006 Census has a high level of home computer ownership. A majority of our customers were given presents of laptops from their family so they could keep in touch. However, they did not come with instructions! As part of the classes, these students brought in their laptops so they could learn how to use them. In one instance, a student had an Apple computer, and we were able to pair her with a student teacher who had Apple experience. During past classes the library did not have WI-FI so they were unable to access the internet on their laptops. Since February 2011 WI-FI has been installed in Malahide library.

Another advantage for the customers is they are able to come to the library and practice what they are learning. This practice has been observed by staff on several occasions; for example, one of the learners was worried about not finishing the homework the student teacher had set her! Our customers have reported that they feel like a "whole new world has opened to them"; they no longer need to wait on family to help them with online transactions. There has only been positive feedback from our customers, regarding the classes; they have loved the "bit of learning" and "chatting to the young folk".

Lifelong Learning

The final report of the IFLA project on 'The Role of Libraries in Lifelong Learning' (2004) defines lifelong learning as an "all purposeful learning activity undertaken on an ongoing basis with the aim of improving knowledge skills and competence" (p2). That lifelong learning can contain various forms of education and training formally and informally. The report reflects that lifelong learning can be based on a more "holistic view on education and recognises learning in and from many different environments" (Häggström, 2004, p1). A key feature of Transition Year is the wide range of teaching and learning methodologies used to move the student beyond the traditional (formal) way of learning. The different learning approaches in Transition Year augment and promote the student's skill for future activities in lifelong learning. An affiliation with a school involved in Transition Year points to the present and future role public libraries can play in students' lives through their lifelong learning experiences.

The Curriculum of Transition Year under the direction of the guidelines points out that the "pupils will participate in learning strategies which are active and experiential and which help them to develop a range of transferable critical thinking and creative problem solving skills", which can be used for their future learning (Department of Education, 1993). MCS individual criteria and guidelines to achieve in their Transition Year Programme include:

- To challenge students in all areas of development
- To develop life skills
- To encourage variety in teaching and learning
- To encourage students to become independent self-directed, learners.

The library is responsive to all the criteria above through the delivery of the computer classes and the story-telling sessions. These activities call for the student to take centre stage in the learning process. Because different generation participate, these sessions not only facilitate the development of life skills in the digital age, they contribute to the growth of skills that each participant can bring to their interaction and continuing life learning experience.

Log On, Learn

During the summer 2008, as Malahide library and the school planned the pilot stage of the project, a similar collaborative initiative was being discussed elsewhere. An Post (Ireland's Postal Company), Microsoft and Intel, as part of their corporate social responsibility, launched their project 'Log On, Learn' in October 2008 by Minister Máire Hoctor. Log On, Learn started in September 2008 in twenty schools as a pilot programme. This programme, similar to the library and school programme, involved Transition Year students teaching computers to older people. The classes in this programme are taught in the school computer room.

On hearing of this programme, there was a moment of apprehension that the school would prefer this option rather than continue its collaboration with the library. However, this was not the case: the school did sign up and register for the *Log On, Learn* pack but decided to keep the classes in the library as well. By registering to be a part of the *Log On, Learn* programme, the school received certificates from the organisers for each learner that completes their course with a student teacher. A ceremony was held at the end of each course, giving a sense of pride to those who completed the course and a sense of accomplishment and respect to the student teachers for their patience and skill in imparting their knowledge to bring their student into the digital age.

The school considered several aspects of the library partnership before deciding to keep running the classes in the library. From the school's viewpoint, the first consideration was holding the classes in the library; using the library as a space for classes meant that the school computer room could be used for other purposes. Secondly, a component of Transition Year is learning social responsibility, which can occur outside the school and the classroom. Having the classes in the library allowed the students take part in social responsibility activities and to experience self-learning through a customised learning activity in a neutral environment. Thirdly, for the teacher of the class, having the classes in the library gave an opportunity to all her/his students to take part in an activity that suited their interests, i.e. music and story-time sessions in addition to computer classes. Fourthly, having the library organise the matching of a person to the student teachers saved the school the responsibility of advertising and starting a new list of prospective students.

Part of the decision to continue with the classes in the library came from consideration and feed-back of people who had been participating in the classes. A few concerns they expressed were firstly, the location of the school compared to the library. The library is situated in the centre of Malahide village, whereas the school is located slightly outside- and uphill- making it more difficult reach. Secondly, those participating in the classes found the library an ideal place to learn with which they are comfortable. In addition, those who did not have a personal computer at home were able to practice what they learnt in the library anytime they wished.

The press release for the Log On, Learn initiative reported, "research shows computer training classes offered/delivered (evening classes) through the usual channels are not successful in reaching (2008)" older persons; rather, "experience shows that training which is delivered in a local setting, on a one-one basis, at a pace which is suited to each individual, proves more successful (2008)". This is proving relevant in both the Log On, Learn programme and the library partnership with the school. Both are fulfilling their mandate to teach and bring those excluded by computer illiteracy into a socially inclusive world. As John Davies (2008), Intel General Manager, World Ahead Programme comments, "To survive and thrive in this growing knowledge-based economy, our older citizens must be equipped with 21st century skills to stay in touch." The management of and participation in the classes allows this to transpire.

Evolving Technologies

Evolving technologies are continually changing the way libraries work and deliver services to the public. The IFLA Public Library Guidelines comment that "public libraries must, whenever possible, make use of the new technologies to improve services and provide new ones" (2010, p.56). Over the last year, Fingal libraries have adopted new technologies to enhance our service delivery; these include the introduction of WI-FI, Self-Service System (RFID), a self- service management system for the public to manage their own booking and printing of computers, and the option to download audio/E-books. Along with online databases, online catalogue and the ability to renew and reserve books online, evolving technologies enable library users to take a certain amount of ownership of their transactions with the library, making the library available seven days a week, twenty four hours a day. The integration of new technologies allows the Malahide Library to deliver a quality and efficient service, which falls into line with the core objectives and values laid out for the organisation of Fingal County Council. These objectives and values include:

- A good value, efficiently run service provided to our citizens
- A structure that releases the potential for staff to contribute creatively and positively to the council
- The enhancement of local democracy.

Cox notes that "excellent customer service is something which libraries have always emphasised, and its value is even higher in a climate which combines recession, higher student numbers, greater complexity in information provision and increased pressure on time (2010, pp 12-13)". Providing these services is only one step in delivering an efficiently run service; showing our users how to make the best use of the services is the next step. The collaboration and partnership with the Transition Years is proving vital in this task. As part of the computer classes, the student teachers will teach their students how to log on to the computers, print from the computers and connect to WI-FI. They will also briefly show them how to use the library catalogue and navigate to the online databases and downloadable books. The combined efforts of the student teachers and staff in relating our service to our customers has increased their level of usage, releasing staff for other projects and bringing our customers into a digital and democratic society.

Libraries as Digital Arenas

The IFLA Public Library Guidelines state that "public libraries are instruments of equal opportunity and must provide a safety-net against alienation and social exclusion from technological advance by becoming the electronic doorway to information in the digital age" (2010, p. 54). Since 1999, when public internet computers were introduced to Irish public libraries, Fingal Libraries have been proactive in "breaching the digital divide by providing supporting steps to computer literacy" (Lovatt, 2010 p. 22). The refurbishment of Malahide Library and the increase in computers galvanised our efforts to bridge the digital gap that exists within our community. The physical expansion of the library allowed for more light and space, opening the library environment as an area that is warm, safe and neutral, an ideal venue for learning and promoting projects to encourage digital knowledge and skills. In an era were ICT is counted as an elementary skill along with reading, writing and math, the role of libraries as digital arenas, providing computer and internet access along with the opportunity for people to learn skills in these areas, has never been more important. The significance of the partnership entered into with the school has been a key element in breaking down barriers that exist for those in our community who are computer illiterate, missing out on both social and democratic inclusion.

This view of libraries as digital arenas is universal: Gundersen (2009) reports, "in Norway, A Norwegian Government Report No.17 (2006-2007) - An Information Society for All - pays particular attention to libraries as arenas where the general public can develop digital skills" (p.7). The results of this report led The Archive, Library and Museum Authority in Norway to select four public libraries as arenas of learning for digital competence. The libraries selected were guided by a development master model that was intended to be implemented nationally throughout all public libraries in Norway. Outlined below are some of the criteria of the master model that were used as a starting point for the project in classifying libraries as digital arenas.

- The development of the library as a learning arena must be an intrinsic part of local or regional planning. The service must also have the positive backing and acceptance of the library staff involved.
- The service must be based either on individual instruction or on theme structured mini-courses with only a few participants per instructor. Teaching should include an introduction to Internet-based services offering the greatest everyday benefits, such as e-mail, searching for information, electronic trading, banking and social technologies.
- The library must have computers capable of meeting requirements with regard to number, quality, Internet-access and other features suitable for learning purposes.
- The service must be part of the library's normal activities and the staff must be directly engaged in its shaping and execution
- There should be regular and systematic contact between the library and other relevant participants in this field (Gundersen, 2009 p. 8).

Measured against the standards mentioned above, I feel confident in describing the Malahide Library as a digital arena. To improve and maintain our status as a library for digital learning, it is vital to maintain the ongoing partnership between the library and the school and to look at other libraries' projects which can be described as "best practices" for a digital learning experience. The Norwegian model describes a framework in which we can judge ourselves as a library for digital learning. However, there are other initiatives and projects throughout the world which may not firmly fit into this model but must be considered when assessing ourselves as an arena of digital learning.

The Role of Libraries in the TY Program

The Transition Year Guidelines (1993) state that "curriculum content is a matter for selection and adaptation by the individual school" and that "the school should also take into consideration the possibilities offered by employers and other work-providing agencies and the wider interests of the local community" (p.5). This message is also stated in the guidelines, goals and objectives that the school uses in deciding its curriculum. Principles should involve "the wider community as educational partners in all aspects of the programme and ensure efficient and effective delivery of the programme" (Department of Education, 1993, p.5). The working partnership currently operating between the school and students engaged in the module *Third Age Anthology* has opened up the door for other collaborations within the school and the integration of the library into the curriculum content of Transition Year.

Jeffers (2007), in his research on the attitudes towards Transition Year, finds that a main area of concern for parents whose children are undertaking Transition Year is they might loose academic focus in their work. He argues that striking a balance between the values of Transition Year, such as social development and self-directed learning and

the "pragmatic reality that students will proceed to a Leaving Certification course immediately after TY, is especially challenging" (2007, p. xxi). Miller and Kelly have noted in their research that

While it cannot be concluded that participation in TY is the cause of this gain in Central Applications Office (CAO) points, the data do point to a strong relation between enhanced academic performance and TY (Millar and Kelly, 1999, p. xxvi).

Taking into consideration these attitudes and knowing the rationale behind Transition Year and the differing modules within the school, the library has approached other teachers of Transition Year, proposing various projects that have the potential to promote and engage students in combined academic focus and self-directed learning projects.

During Malahide Library's centenary in 2009, a successful project was the publication of the '*Carnegie Library Malahide: Centenary Celebration 1909-2009*'. This collaboration transpired between Transition Year students engaged in a local history module. As part of the project, I approached the teacher of the local history module, with the idea that the students would research and develop a booklet on the history of Malahide Library. To aid the students in this endeavour, various members of staff with skills and knowledge in research and resources gave lectures to the students on how to carry out the project. We organized guest lectures from our archival section and from the local historical society. The students engaged in this module were planning to take history in the Leaving Certificate examinations. Students taking history are examined in part by the production of a research paper called a "special topic", which accounts for 20% of the overall mark. Through this project, these students learnt the skills to aid them in their research project for the Leaving Certification. As an additional benefit, the booklet was sold to the public, raising 3000 euro for the school. This collaboration is still progressing; new students of the module are given a topic to research and as part of their research development, they attend lectures within the library on various resources.

There is huge potential in developing the role of libraries in Transition Year. I believe Transition Year is a real opportunity for any library to engage with their local school and develop initiatives and projects that can be mutually beneficial. While writing this chapter, I have been approached by three other post- primary schools within the Fingal area, regarding the teaching of computer classes in the library and the development of a library module as part of their Transition Year programme. I have directed the Principals of these schools to libraries in the catchment area of their schools that can facilitate their requests. The partnership between the local school and Malahide Library that started as a pilot project has evolved into a more sustainable program and has been replicated By September 2011, three Fingal libraries (including Malahide) will be engaged in similar partnerships, enabling them to meet the growing needs of their customer base.

Community of Practice

The working operations of public libraries are best illustrated by Wenger in his works on communities of practice. Wenger (2006) defines

...communities of practice as groups of people who share a concern or a passion for something they do and learn how to do it better as they interact regularly... Members of a community of practice are practitioners. They develop a shared repertoire of resources: experiences, stories, tools, ways of addressing recurring problems—in short a shared practice (www.ewenger.com).

Working in a community of shared information brings many initiatives and ideals to the forefront that can be modified and adapted to suit individual libraries. One of the main challenges facing Irish public libraries currently is detailed in a recent report by the Organization for Eco-

nomic Co-operation and Development (OECD). In its latest Programme for International Student Assessment, it reported that the reading ability of Ireland's 15-year-olds was ranked 17th out of the 39 countries that were studied. According to the report, ten years ago the figures placed Ireland as the fifth nation for literacy skills among this age group, indicating a decline in reading levels. It must be noted that over the last ten years, the number of non-nationals has risen quite dramatically, and this may have a bearing on the report. However, the drop in literacy levels is a concern, and libraries are in a position through various collaborations and partnerships to halt the drop in literacy levels.

Valerie Cross (2005) describes a partnership called "A+ Partners in Education," which formalized the public library as a full partner in education with Howard County Public School System in Columbia, Maryland. This partnership highlights the importance of libraries and library professionals as educators. We adapted some of the key components from the A+ partnership; for example, we contacted the local community school about initiating a programme to ensure that every student entering the school is signed up with a library card. This programme has expanded to connect new incoming students to the library. Upon entering the school, a new student is paired with a TY student, and as part of the buddy system, the TY students will bring the first year student to the library explaining the way it works.

In her study of cross-generational learning, Smith (2010) argues the case of bringing retirees back into the classroom for particular topics to aid in the education of students. In adopting this concept and in looking at initiatives in other libraries, Malahide librarians can help to bridge the gap in literacy levels and adopt new ideas of how to expand and enhance their role as educators with the local school. The partnership with the local school is one example of a successful working partnership between a public library and the local post -primary school.

Another library's project, the "Human Library Experience," organized evening events where people from different backgrounds presented themselves to the library to answer any questions the public might have about them, giving the human experience of their lives and culture. In looking and learning from these experiences and initiatives, along with the knowledge of the key components of Transition Year, we hope to develop a "Human Library Experience" of our own for Transition Years to aid them in their decisions of what subject to study for the leaving. Currently, we are contacting persons in different careers to volunteer their time to this project; we hope the experience will be beneficial to all taking part. Libraries and library professionals are fortunate to be in a profession that is run as a community of practice. The shared repertoire of resources, experiences, stories, tools, and ways of addressing recurring problems enables librarians to champion themselves as educators and show relevance within the community.

FUTURE CONSIDERATIONS

In times of economic uncertainty, staff shortages and budget cuts, libraries are increasingly under pressure to show relevance, value for money and efficiencies in the delivery of their services. Instead of seeing the economic difficulties as being detrimental to the service, there is optimism and opportunity in developing alliances and partnerships that can enhance and promote libraries, proving relevance to their organization and the community. The partnership with the local community school has opened the possibilities of future projects and a long-term systematic cooperation between the library and the school into the future. The introduction of Transition Year with its extensive range of subjects into the Irish Education System, has given libraries the opportunity to integrate themselves through various partnerships in the school that will have mutual benefits to all. At present

the Malahide Library is in talks with the media and art teachers of Transition Year in developing future projects. Projects under discussion include the design and production of a poster that they feel will attract kids of their age group, (apparently the library's posters are boring!) and the design and production of a viral video on the library and what it has to offer. Fingal Libraries, including Malahide library, are constantly developing and looking for alliances and partnerships to promote and aid us in delivering a quality service to our customers. The partnership with the school has exceeded expectations from its conception and will likely continue to do so into the future.

CONCLUSION

Within the current economic climate, for libraries to provide a quality service that satisfies our customer's needs, the development and cultivation of partnerships are vital in complementing and adding to our service delivery. The partnership entered into by the school and library has shown how one initial contact and collaboration has grown into a long-term working partnership that is meeting the needs of each partner along with the local community. There have been clear benefits for all involved, directly and indirectly in this partnership. The cross-generational learning approach of the partnership has allowed the students involved to meet their social responsibility requirements to mature and develop life skills that will stand them in good stead for learning formally and informally in the future.

For the library this partnership is proving extremely advantageous in numerous ways. It helps the library meet customers' needs through the facilitation of computer and story-time sessions. Likewise, the partnership bridges the digital divide that exits within the community by making the library become a place of digital learning for all. Most importantly, the partnership with the school has developed the educational support role the library can play with the present and future students within the school. In turn, it will help to foster good relations to connect with the 'next generation of library customers and supporters, ensuring the future of the library' (Cross, 2010, p.217).

REFERENCES

Age Action Ireland. (n.d.). *Home page*. Retrieved February 26, 2011, from http://www.ageaction.ie/

Census2006. (2006). *Beyond 2020*. Retrieved February 26, 2011, from http://beyond2020. cso.ie/Census/TableViewer/tableView. aspx?ReportId=76524

Census2011. (2011). *CDP01: Population and actual and percentage change 2006 and 2011 by sex, province county or city, year and statistic*. Retrieved September 7th, 2011, from http://www. cso.ie/px/pxeirestat/Statire/SelectVarVal/Define. asp?maintable=CDP01&PLanguage=0

Cox, J. (2010). Academic libraries in challenging times. *An Leabharlann: The Irish Library*, *19*(2), 7–13.

Davies, J. (December, 2008). *Intel, Microsoft and a post join forces to Promote "Log On' Learn"*. Retrieved February 26, 2011, from http://www. logonlearn.ie/News.aspx

Department of Education. (1993). *Transition Year programmes guidelines for schools*. Dublin, Ireland: The Stationery Office. Retrieved February 26, 2011, from http://www.education. ie/servlet/blobservlet/pp_transition_year_guidelines_school.doc

Dublin, Ireland. Retrieved February 26, 2011, from http://www.fingalcoco.ie/Publications/Council/Corporate%20Plan%202010-2014.pdf: Fingal County Council. (n.d.). *Website*. Retrieved February 26, 2011, from www.fingalcoco.ie

Festival, B. (2011). *An Irish festival celebrating the older person*. Retrieved from http://bealtaine.com/

Fingal County Council. (2010). *Fingal County council corporate plan 2010 –2014*.

Fingal Libraries Department. (n.d.). *Website*. Retrieved February 26, 2011, from www.fingalcoco. ie/libaries

Gundersen, B. (2009). The DIGIKOMBI project library initiative for a national model to improve digital competence. *Scandinavian Public Library Quarterly, 42*(3), 8-9. Retrieved February 26, 2011, from http://splq.info/issues/vol42_3/04.htm

Hovius, B. (2005, August). *Public library partnerships which add value to the community: The Hamilton Public Library Experience* (041-E). Paper presented at the World Library and Information Congress: 71th IFLA General Conference and Council, Oslo, Norway.

Ihanamäki, S. (2010). Partnerships in the North Calotte area. *Scandinavian Public Library Quarterly, 43*(3), 18-19. Retrieved February 26, 2011, from http://splq.info/issues/vol43_3/09.htm

Jeffers, G. (2004). Implementing the Transition Year Programme in the Republic of Ireland. In A. Burke (Ed.), *Teacher education in the Republic of Ireland: Retrospect and prospect* (pp.54-61). Armagh, Northern Ireland: The Centre for Cross Border Studies.

Jeffers, G. (2007). *Attitudes to Transition Year: A report to the Department of Education and Science*. Maynooth, Ireland: Education Department, National University of Ireland. Retrieved February 26, 2011, from http://eprints.nuim.ie/1228/

Jeffers, G. (2008). *Innovation and resistance in Irish schooling: The case of Transition Year*. Unpublished doctoral dissertation, University of Limerick, Co. Limerick, Ireland

Koontz, C., & Gubbin, B. (Eds.). (2010). *IFLA public library service guidelines*. New York, NY: Saur, IFLA.

Lovatt, S. (2010). Making connections: The library and the community. *An Leabharlann: The Irish Library, 19*(1), 22–27.

Malahide Community School. (2010). *Website*. Retrieved February 26, 2011, from https://sites. google.com/a/malahidecs.ie/malahide-community-school/

Malahide Library. (n.d.). *Website*. Retrieved 7th September 2011, from http://www.librarybuildings.ie/library.aspx?ID=72

Millar, D., & Kelly, D. (1999). *From junior to leaving certificate: A longitudinal study of 1994 junior certificate candidates who took the leaving certificate examination in 1997 (Final Report)*. Dublin, Ireland: Educational Research Centre & National Council for Curriculum and Assessment.

OECD. (2009). *PISA 2009 assessment framework - Key competencies in reading, mathematics and science*. Paris, France: OECD. Retrieved February 26, 2011, from http://www.oecd.org/dataoecd/11/40/44455820.pdf

On, L. Learn. (2008). *Press release*. Retrieved from http://www.dohc.ie/press/releases/2008/20081001b.html

Rødevand, A. M. (2009). Learn computer technology in your library. *Scandinavian Public Library Quarterly, 42*(3), 13. Retrieved February 26, 2011, from http://splq.info/issues/vol42_3/08.htm

Smith, K. (2010), Multi-faceted, cross-generational learning teams for the 21st century. *MASCD Perspectives,* Spring, 10-12. Retrieved February 26, 2011, from www.nctaf.org/.../KarenSmith-Multi-facetedCross-genLTsfor21C-MASCDPerspectives-Spring2010.pdf

Transition Year Support Service. (n.d.). *Website*. Retrieved 8 September, 2011, from http://ty.slss. ie/ UNESCO/IFLA. (2011). *Public libraries manifesto*. Retrieved 26 February, 2011, from http:// www.unesco.org/webworld/libraries/manifestos/index_manifestos.html

Wenger, E. (June, 2006). *Communities of practice: A brief introduction*. Retrieved 26 February 2011, from http://www.ewenger.com/theory/index.htm

Chapter 8
Smart Investing:
Partnering to Promote Financial Literacy – The Orange County Library System Experience

Paolo Melillo
Orange County Library System, USA

J. Clay Singleton
Rollins College, USA

Robert K. Prescott
Rollins College, USA

Susan Bach
Rollins College, USA

ABSTRACT

This chapter describes the Orange County Library System's financial literacy workshops and highlights the partnerships that made them a success. While the library system received a grant that helped get the project started, its partners brought expertise and a connection with the target audience that the library alone could not have provided. This project illustrates how community partnerships are a mutually beneficial way for public libraries to establish themselves as a resource for unbiased and reliable information. In addition to the describing the partnerships, this chapter will also focus on the ingredients believed to be the keys to success. The authors hope the experience can serve as a motivator and template for public libraries everywhere wanting to further establish themselves as information resources with community partnership assistance.

INTRODUCTION

In 2008, with the help of a grant opportunity, the Orange County Library System (OCLS) in Florida partnered with a local business school and began offering a successful series of financial literacy workshops in Spanish. Survey results show that the series helped reinforce the perception of the Library as a community resource for unbiased and reliable financial literacy information and programs. The series exceeded everyone's expectations and more workshops were developed

DOI: 10.4018/978-1-61350-387-4.ch008

and offered in English to target the area's African American community. Plans are currently underway to repeat the process and offer similar series for other target markets in the near future.

Five key factors were instrumental to the project's success. We:

- identified a target market,
- researched the needs of the target market before planning the workshops,
- obtained a funding source,
- developed a marketing plan,
- used surveys to obtain feedback and adapt future programs to what was learned.

Last but not least, we were able to establish effective partnerships with community agencies to help us in planning, promoting, and even facilitating the workshops. Most of the partnerships were for outreach and promotional assistance.

Our main partner, however, was the Rollins College Crummer Graduate School of Business, a well known and nationally ranked business school in the area. This partnership was the crux of the project which allowed us to profit from the partner's credibility in the community. The School's faculty also provided finance expertise and MBA students served as program instructors.

This chapter will focus on the above cited ingredients for success and the partnerships which made the financial literacy workshops an achievement we are proud to promote. We hope our experience can serve as a motivator and template for public libraries everywhere wanting to further establish themselves as recognized places for unbiased and reliable information via informational programs developed and offered with community partnerships.

BACKGROUND

The Orange County Library System serves nearly one million residents in the Orlando area of Central Florida. This area is known as having a one

of the fastest growing Hispanic populations in the United States (Fishkind & Associates, 2007). According to the U.S. Census Bureau's American Community Survey, the population of Hispanics in Orange County was 25.6 percent in 2009. This survey also reported that close to 33.7 percent of this community claimed to speak English less than "well" (U.S. Census Bureau, 2009).

Staff working directly with the community noted an interest in financial literacy from Spanish-speaking users but a lack of appropriate information. Several staff stated that the Spanish-speaking patrons they worked with knew that budgeting, saving and investing were important to their lives but they were unsure where to turn and whom to trust. Many of the books and media materials on the topic were in English and many in the community believed the topic was intimidating.

In 2007, the Library received an invitation to apply for a Smart Investing @ your library® grant. Smart Investing @ your library is co-sponsored by the American Library Association (ALA) and the Financial Industry Regulatory Authority (FINRA) Investor Education Foundation. The program addresses the "growing need for unbiased financial and investor education at the grassroots level" (American Library Association [ALA]). This opportunity could not have come at a better time. Based on staff observations, we knew there was an interest and need in the growing Hispanic community for a program on financial literacy.

Understanding the Target Market

Our background research helped us better understand the relationship between our target market and basic financial services. The Federal Deposit Insurance Corporation [FDIC] describes the unbanked as people without a checking or savings account. The under-banked are in turn described as "those that have a checking or savings account but rely on alternative financial services" such as a check cashing services, payday loans, pawn shops and rent-to-own agreements (Federal Deposit Insurance Corporation, [FDIC], 2009, p.

3). A 2003 Chicago Federal Reserve article on changing Hispanic demographics reported that 23 percent of U.S. Hispanics did not have a checking or savings account, compared to 2 percent of the general population (Toussaint-Comeau, 2003).

Furthermore, the FDIC's *National Survey of Unbanked and Underbanked Households* cited Hispanic households as accounting for 24 percent of the nations "underbanked" population (FDIC, 2009, p.4) A total of 43.3 percent of Hispanic households were said to be either unbanked or under-banked (FDIC, 2009, p. 4). A FINRA survey also observed that up to 43 percent of Hispanic respondents may have difficulties making ends meet (FINRA, 2009, p. 5). We concluded that our target market was unlikely to be familiar with banking and investment services.

We also recognized that we had to design financial literacy workshops specifically for Hispanics. The studies and reports cited here as well as feedback from branch staff highlighted significant barriers that the Hispanic community faced. We agreed with experts who advised that "programs directed to minority audiences may need to be more specifically tailored to overcome barriers to participation in financial education efforts that are related to general barriers to minority participation in financial markets" (Gutter & Mountain, 2007, p. 3). The barriers most often cited by staff and the research included:

- **Familiarity**. Not being familiar with how the banking and investing systems worked. In a national Financial Capability survey, Hispanics and African American respondents scored the lowest among ethnic/racial groups when it came to correctly answering questions eliciting awareness of basic personal finance concepts (Applied Research, 2009, p. 41). A focus group report observed that "Many Hispanics pointed out that they knew so little in regard to financial information that they would not know if they were receiving bad informa-

tion or advice in any situation.. ."(Gutter & Mountain, 2007, p.15).

- **Trust Factor**. Not knowing who to trust for financial advice. The Financial Capability Survey cited Hispanics as the ethnic/racial group least likely to ask for professional advice (Applied Research, 2009, p. 45). Another report stated, "The most important qualification for anyone giving financial information to the Hispanic subgroup is trust, which is a very big obstacle for them to overcome. They feel more comfortable talking to a friend or friend of a friend than to someone perceived as a salesman. Along the lines of trust, they [Hispanics] felt that a person who has their best interest in mind is not trying to sell them something" (Gutter & Mountain, 2007, p.15). In another survey, many Hispanic participants revealed that they had had a negative experience with at least one financial professional (Toussaint-Comeau, 2003, p. 3). Reading financial literature available in libraries and bookstores can be challenging to understand for the general population and even more daunting for Hispanics with less trust of financial institutions (Fredrick and Rodriguez, 2001).

- **Language**. Language was often cited as a barrier. "A barrier that prevents this subgroup from seeking information. ... is a lack of ability to speak or read English at a level necessary to acquire financial knowledge. Spanish translations would be preferred, however, it was pointed out that translations often have severe limitations (Gutter & Mountain, 2007, p. 12). "Translations may have little meaning when there is no exact equivalent concept or word in Spanish that Hispanics might have heard in their native country (p. 16).

- **Role models**. Hispanics "... want to hear financial success stories of people who are of the same ethnic group to make them aware that financial success is attainable." (Gutter & Mountain, 2007, p.20).

- **Child care issues**. Staff often cited adults wanting to attend library programs but faced the difficulty of finding convenient child care.

Planning the Workshops

Based on the information we analyzed to understand the needs of our target market, we concluded that the financial literacy workshops needed to be offered in Spanish to address the language barrier. We planned on having our Spanish speaking library staff develop the workshops and present them in an effort to help garner trust as well as serve as role models. We also prepared to offer simultaneous children's programs to address the childcare barriers.

The FINRA Foundation web site had ample information in English and Spanish which could be used to develop content for the workshops. We planned to have Spanish-speaking library staff go through the content and develop the workshops tailored to the needs of the target market. We anticipated a challenging project for busy time-strapped library staff who were not very familiar with teaching financial literacy to develop the curriculum and present it in Spanish.

DEVELOPING A PARTNERSHIP TO SUPPORT THE WORKSHOPS

As library staff began drafting an outline of the proposed workshop curriculum we approached Professor Clay Singleton at the Crummer Graduate School of Business at Rollins College. We proposed having the College's faculty and MBA students review the curriculum. They had the appropriate financial expertise to ensure that the content we put together was correct.

In addition, having the approval of such a prestigious institution was intended to give our workshops more respectability. The Crummer Graduate School of Business has been nationally ranked by Bloomberg Business Week as well as by Forbes.

Upon hearing of our proposed plan for the partnership, Dr. Singleton thought the partnership could be deepened with mutual benefits. He proposed that rather than have library staff focus on putting together content – which was not their subject expertise – he could get some of the School's faculty to develop the curriculum instead. The faculty was naturally very familiar with financial literacy concepts and could more readily cull the curriculum's broad content supplied by FINRA and adapt it to the needs of our targeted audiences.

Furthermore, six Hispanic MBA students would be selected by the faculty to assist with the project. These students came from different Hispanic countries and cultures and could better translate the curriculum prepared by the faculty into Spanish. Being Hispanic, from the community and students of finance, they were in the best position to translate the content using appropriate Spanish terminology that would be understood by the target market.

These same students would also be well-suited to present the workshops. Hispanics from the community could more easily relate to students with whom they shared a similar national and ethnic background and who they could more readily see as role models.

Benefits of the Partnership – The Library

Several beneficial advantages to both the Library and the Crummer School were outlined with this developing partnership

Some benefits for the library:

- More credibility in the community. By offering these financial literacy workshops in Spanish with the imprimatur of a respected academic institution, the workshops would help promote the role of the Library as a place for unbiased and reliable information for the community. Mentioning the School's participation would also attract some Hispanics who may not have been interested in previously visiting the library or attending an informational library program.
- Save staff time and effort with curriculum development. Having the School's faculty develop the curriculum rather than library staff who were not experts in the subject saved us a lot of time and effort.
- Save staff time and effort with translations. Having the Hispanic MBA students whose first language was Spanish translate the content and present it in Spanish saved library staff from being committed to doing something which was not their expertise.
- Save staff time and effort by not having to present the workshops. The Hispanic MBA students could more easily and effectively present the content which was in their field of study. This saved the library from having to schedule staff to prepare and present the workshops.
- Focus on supporting the workshops. Library staff developed displays in the host locations featuring library materials. Library staff also came in at the end of each workshop to give brief presentations on library resources which were available to assist with what attendees were learning.

Benefits of the Partnership – The Rollins College Crummer School of Business

Some benefits for the Rollins College Crummer School of Business:

- Develop presentation skills. By presenting these community workshops, the MBA students would hone their presentation skills.
- Improve expertise. By translating the curriculum into Spanish and preparing to present the workshops in Spanish, the MBA students would develop and improve their knowledge of finance and investments.
- Community service and awareness. By working with the community in presenting and answering questions, the MBA students would develop good awareness of community needs and community work. The MBA students could understand first-hand the value of their education in the community and the responsibility of the business sector in building a strong economy.
- Leadership development. As emerging leaders, the MBA students applied the leadership training they received as part of the curriculum and came to more fully understand the contributions they can make as leaders. Because the students were Hispanic, they will face challenges associated with striving for leadership positions in a corporate climate that is still opening the doors and removing ceilings for minorities (Thomas & Gabarro, 1999).
- Positive publicity for the school. The School would be seen as contributing to the community and supporting financial literacy needs. The School also competes in national programs, such as Beyond Grey Pinstripes, that recognize innovative full-time MBA programs that are integrating issues of social stewardship into their curriculum.

The Partnership Plan to Address Barriers

The partnership plan allowed the Library to directly address, in a more efficient manner, several of the barriers which were cited above as limiting

99

Hispanics' financial knowledge. The barriers and how they would be addressed with the partnership are listed below:

- **Familiarity**. Being from the community, the MBA students had first-hand knowledge of the target market's needs and interests. They identified with the community and could directly address their questions.
- **Trust Factor**. Students were seen as trustworthy by the community because not only did they have the knowledge but they were also not salespeople in the program to make a profit. They were more approachable than "experts" yet still knowledgeable.
- **Language**. The students came from different Hispanic countries and cultures: Columbia, Panama, Puerto Rico, and Mexico and they helped adjust the presentation to reflect a common terminology.
- **Role Models**. Being from the Hispanic community and studying for an MBA at one of the nation's top business schools, the students could serve as role models. They had a solid knowledge of finance and shared their personal success stories with budgeting and investing. Each workshop was facilitated by a male and female student, thereby also addressing the general need for gender role models.

Developing the Other Partnership – HBIF

The need for role models was further addressed by a partnership with the Hispanic Business Initiative Fund (HBIF). HBIF is the leading Hispanic economic development, non-profit organization in Florida that specializes in providing bilingual assistance to Hispanic entrepreneurs trying to establish or expand their business in Florida. We contacted the local director of the organization with our project. We wanted six of their Hispanic clients to record short motivational videos on how they have been successful with managing money. We proposed to post these videos on the Library's dedicated web site for Smart Investing: http://www.ocls.info/sudinero. In turn, the Library would mention that these individuals were clients of HBIF on the web site.

Six HBIF clients visited the library in July 2008 to record the footage. The videos highlighted successful Hispanic business people in the local community. The videos included testimonies from male and female financial advisors, an attorney, marketing director, business owners, as well as the Orlando Hispanic Chamber of Commerce President. The eight videos can still be viewed online at www.ocls.info/sudinero.

Implementing the Workshops

The series was given a Spanish-language title to make it more appealing to the target market. It was called, "Alcance más con su dinero" which can be translated as "Get More for Your Money."

The workshops' content consisted of four modules. Each module was repeated at different times at two branches serving the county's largest Hispanic populations.

The MBA students developed PowerPoint presentations for each session. These PowerPoint presentations were printed as booklets to allow attendees to follow the workshops as well as take notes and have something to take home and refer to in the future.

As mentioned, each session in the series ended with a library staff member from the host location giving a short presentation in Spanish on the library resources available– both in English and in Spanish – to support what was learned at the workshop. The host branches also displayed personal finance materials available in their collection. In addition to books, these displays showcased DVDs, CD Books and informative staff prepared bookmarks on the topic in question. Participants were informed that the library had the resources as well as knowledgeable bilingual staff who they could ask for assistance. In short, the library was positioned as a source for reliable and unbiased financial information as well as a welcoming place for Hispanics who may have otherwise felt it was an unknown and intimidating institution.

The workshops were offered weeknights and on Saturdays at two selected branches, rather than our larger Main Library downtown. This thereby placed the workshops directly in the Hispanic community and at convenient times for the target market.

Responding to the need for childcare, the library offered simultaneous children's programs. A local storyteller was hired with grant funds to provide craft and stories to children while the adults attended the workshops. The children's programs included decorating piggy banks and games with play money. The children could, therefore, do something similar to what their parents were learning in the adult program. A total of sixty-five children attended the programs over the course of the series.

At the end of the series, participants were entertained with a party with refreshments and raffled prizes. The gifts were popular Spanish language finance books. The participants were given certificates with the Library's and the Rollins Crummer Graduate School of Business' logos. The certificates were signed by the library's director as well as representatives from the School. At the party, several Rollins faculty and the student presenters congratulated the attendees and answered questions. Library representatives were also present to congratulate the attendees and thank the Rollins partners. In all, sixty-nine adults and nine children attended the closing events at both locations.

About 60 percent of the grant funds were earmarked for marketing the workshops. The library had not had much success in attracting adult Hispanic audiences for informational programs in the past. With the exception of ESL and computer classes, informational programs rarely attracted more than ten participants. Based on past experience, we knew that one of the biggest challenges

when offering information programs, especially in Spanish, was ensuring their proper promotion.

Marketing and Promoting the Workshops

Thanks to the grant funds, the library was able to earmark a substantial sum to the marketing of the series. The library used a local marketing firm, SayitLoud, for design assistance and to develop the visual identify for the Smart Investing workshops. The firm is owned and operated by a local successful Hispanic businessman. SayitLoud developed several proposals for a logo which would brand the series and make it easily recognizable. Select library staff arrived at a consensus for the final selection. The logo branded the series and was used in all ads, web site, and promotional materials.

As planned, the Library placed:

- Five ads in *El Sentinel*, Central Florida's full-color, Spanish language weekly newspaper.
- Five ads in *La Prensa*, a leading Spanish language newspaper in Central Florida.
- Tail pin (back of buses) ads were placed on city buses on routes through the city's heavy Hispanic areas served by the selected host branches.
- Online advertising via targeted email, online newspapers and a blog
- Ads were run in the Library's newsletter

The Crummer Graduate School of Business also promoted the workshops which generated additional interest. A write-up was placed in their school newsletter. They also issued a news release which garnered more attention in the local media. In addition, the MBA students took flyers and promotional materials to community organizations they knew as well as to family and friends.

Our partners at HBIF, being well connected with the Hispanic community, were able to spread the word across the county. They mentioned the series at their events and on their web site.

Figure 1. Spanish language logo for the financial literacy series targeting Hispanics

Based on survey results and user comments, we know that this joint marketing effort was effective. Most attendees cited the library newsletter and flyers together with newspaper and radio announcements as the sources from which they first heard of the series.

Before we knew it, quite a bit of interest was generated by the combined efforts of the Library's marketing outreach and that of our partners. Having heard of the event through the press release, local media contacted the library asking to feature the series:

- The local *La Prensa* newspaper ran two articles introducing and promoting the series to the community (Figueroa, 2009). One article was published in the city's other Spanish newspaper, *El Sentinel.*

- A local TV show on Telemundo discussed the series in a nighttime talk show called "A la medianoche."

Workshop Successes

The workshops were exceptionally successful. The library's typical informational programs usually averaged up to ten attendees and the attendance figures were typically lower for Spanish language versions. In contrast, the financial literacy workshops averaged 19.4 attendees. In all, 311 people attended the workshops and 65 children were at the simultaneous craft and story programs.

As we prepared to start the series, the economy started coming to a standstill and the Great Recession of 2008 began. This change in the economy served to heighten awareness of the importance of managing money and investing cautiously.

The attendees asked questions throughout the series. It was obvious that the community felt comfortable with the students from Rollins who were presenting.

The students were seen as approachable and from the community. This was obvious to us as we observed that most attendees were asking questions throughout the series. Many attendees stayed after the workshops ended to speak to the presenters about their experiences and interests in the program topics. Survey results were also very favorable and 98 percent of respondents stated that the workshops helped them feel confident enough to start budgeting and apply what they learned. We believe these results show that the attendees could relate to the presenters. We believe our goal of having the presenters serve as role models and guides was reached.

Circulation was also impacted by the workshops. Librarians from each host site gave a small introduction to the Library's resources on the topic at the end of each workshop. The Southeast branch location reported a circulation increase of 76 percent in financial economics materials during the series. The Spanish non-fiction collection saw a circulation increase of 44 percent. At the other host location, South Creek, the numbers were more modest. The difference may be attributed to the fact that the Southeast Branch had a large display of material on the topic outside the meeting room. At the South Creek location, a few items were brought into the meeting room as show and tell – there was no regular display set up.

Surveys were distributed to attendees at the end of each workshop. The surveys were developed by library staff and the Rollins students. Their purpose was to measure the effectiveness of the series against the goals we had established before embarking on the project. One hundred and forty nine surveys were filled out and returned. The survey results showed very high satisfaction rates.

The table in Appendix 2 shows the results of these surveys.

Sustaining the Partnership and the Project

When initially writing the grant application, we had agreed to repeat the series in English. The workshops proved to be very popular and we actually had several requests from the public for the workshops to be presented in English. From the beginning, Dr. Singleton and his faculty team liked the idea of continuing the partnership and repeating the workshops.

A new group of students was selected for the next round of workshops. The presentations were adapted for the needs of another group of the population with a large number of unbanked members – those living in the service area's lower income African-American communities.

Similar strategies were implemented this time around as with the previous series in Spanish. We offered the workshops in three branches serving large numbers of the targeted community in question. Rather than simply translating the workshops back into English, the selected Rollins students researched the population's demographics and financial needs and tailored the workshops specifically for them. We used both white and African-American male and female students to serve as approachable role models and strengthen the trust factor.

We also branded the English language series with a logo. Given the successful branding of the series in Spanish and the fact that the logo, we kept the artwork. The only difference with the new one was that the title was now in English, "Smart Investing @ your library."

In planning the new series, we also implemented things we learned could have been done differently. Feedback from the Spanish series showed that given time and scheduling issues, many attendees would have been preferred to have fewer workshops. The MBA students in turn condensed the material into two workshops. We scheduled the series and spread them across three branches.

Figure 2. English language logo for the financial literacy series

As planned, the grant funds were depleted with the Spanish language series. The English installment did not, therefore, have a budget to support a strong marketing campaign.

We partnered with the local chapter of the National Black MBA Association for marketing and promotional assistance to the African American communities. The chapter promoted the series on their web page, in their newsletter as well as in meetings. In turn, the library mentioned their support in our flyers and publicity.

We also used members of the Association in short motivational videos. In all, six members came to the Library to be videoed. The members were all African American and included male and female business owners, a manager, an investment professional and an MBA student. The videos served to offer role models and were placed on a dedicated web site created to promote the series: www.ocls.info/smartinvesting.

The English language workshops were popular as well. Although we did not see the high numbers as we did with the Spanish series, 62 people at-tended the workshops and 15 children participated in the simultaneous children's events. These lower numbers are attributed, in part, to the fact that we did not have a large marketing campaign.

Rather than full videos of the presentations, a copy of the PowerPoints used by presenting Rollins students was posted to a dedicated web site for the series. The PowerPoints are very helpful in conveying the information to the community even after the end of the series.

Solutions and Recommendations: Lessons Learned

Several of the lessons learned after the Spanish language series were implemented when we planned the English language version. We condensed the number of workshops in the series from four to two. We also did not repeat the videotaping of the workshops. When we viewed the videos loaded to the web site, it was believed that, because the workshops were designed to be interactive, the format did not lend itself well to video. When we repeated the series in English we posted the PowerPoint on the website. If we were to do this over again, we would choose a PowerPoint presentation with a voice over for increased effectiveness.

Flexibility and adaptability were key ingredients ensuring success. We originally went to our partners at Rollins to have them review the content prepared by library staff. Staff had already begun the workshop outlines and drafts. When our partners wanted to take this part of the project over, we changed our plans. Our staff was relieved of the duty to prepare the material and present. We drew on our partner's expertise with the material and in developing presentations entirely. The focus on library resources was maintained by having staff present a promotional segment at the end of every session.

Another major change had to do with the plan of the workshops. When we initially planned on the series, the national economy was still in good order. Our focus was going to be on investing. As the economy hit a recession, we switched gears and focus became getting out of debt, saving and then investing. While the recession heightened interest and probably motivated many of the participants to attend, we believe their satisfaction came from the content.

FUTURE DIRECTIONS

Given the successful results of the partnerships and the positive participant feedback regarding the Spanish and English language series, the library was asked to apply for another Smart Investing @ your library grant. The library used this opportunity to continue working with our partners at the Rollins College Crummer School of Business on another financial literacy project.

This time we chose to focus on the area's service workers. Orlando has a large tourism and service industry. According to the Metro Orlando Economic Development Commission (MOEDC),

the Leisure and Hospitality Industry comprises the largest segment of Orlando area employment. As of December 2010, 20 percent of the area's workforce is employed in this field. (Metro Orlando Economic Development Commission, 2011). Data from the MOEDC indicates the median hourly salary for a hotel desk clerk is $10.11 and for a waiter/waitress is $8.73. The current economic recession has hit the area hard and Orlando faces the third highest rate of home foreclosures in the country (Baribeau & McGrail, 2010). The city also ranks 10th nation-wide with an average consumer debt of $25,316 (Burnett, 2010).

Workers with financial stress are less productive. (Personal Finance Employee Education Foundation, 2000). Given the current economic and financial situation in our area, we are certain that financial literacy workshops geared to this targeted market will be welcome and needed.

We plan to partner again with the Rollins College Crummer School of Business to draw on their expertise and develop the workshop content tailored for the needs of the target market. Male and female MBA students will again be selected to teach the workshops and serve as knowledgeable, approachable, and trustworthy role models.

We also asked the President of the Central Florida Lodging Association to be our partner and help us market the programs. The President also serves on the Library's Board of Trustees and is enthusiastic about the program.

CONCLUSION

As can be seen, our partnerships made the financial literacy workshops a success. While the FINRA grant was critical in providing initial funding, the program would not have been as effective without our partners. The Library benefitted by positioning itself with the Hispanic community as a trusted source of unbiased financial information. The Crummer Graduate School of Business benefitted by providing an opportunity for their students to gain experience developing and presenting practical material relevant to their education and by giving back to the community. The other partners gained from being associated with a successful community program. We hope out experience can serve as a model for other public libraries that want to be seen as a source of unbiased and reliable information via informational programs developed and offered with community partners.

REFERENCES

American Library Association (ALA). *About Smart Investing @ your library*. Retrieved February 3, 2011, from http://smartinvesting.ala. org/about/

Applied Research & Consulting LLC. (2009, December 1). *Financial capability in the United States*: *Initial report of research findings from the 2009 national survey* (A component of the national financial capability study). Retrieved from http://www.finrafoundation.org/web/groups/ foundation/@foundation/documents/ foundation/ p120536.pdf

Baribeau, S., & McGrail, B. (2010, September 10). Florida issuers sell $442 million with debt cost at record high. *Bloomberg Businessweek*. Retrieved February 6, 2011, from http://www.businessweek. com/news/2010-09-10/florida-issuers-sell-442- million-with-debt-cost-at-record-high.html

Burnett, R. (2010, May 13). Orlando ranks 10th with average consumer debt of $25,316. *Orlando Sentinel*. Retrieved February 6, 2011, from http://articles.orlandosentinel.com/2010- 05-13/business/os-orlando-ranks-consumer- debt-20100513_1_credit-card-debt-personal- debt-consumer-debt-counselors

Fajt, M. (2009, September 21). A twist on reaching out to unbanked Hispanics. *American Banker*. Retrieved February 6, 2011, from http://www. progressfin.com/A_Twist_on_Reaching_Out_ to_Unbanked_Hispanics.pdf

Fajt, M. (2009, November). How to reach Hispanics: Give them credit. *US Banker, 119*(11), 28-29. Retrieved February 6, 2011, from http://www. americanbanker.com/usb_issues/119_11/how- to-reach-hispanics-give-them-credit-1003190-1. html

Federal Deposit Insurance Corporation (FDIC). (2009, December). *FDIC national survey of unbanked and underbanked households: Executive summary*. Retrieved February 6, 2011, from http:// www.fdic.gov/householdsurvey/executive_sum- mary.pdf

Federal Deposit Insurance Corporation (FDIC). (2010, September). *Addendum to the 2009 FDIC national survey of unbanked and underbanked households*: *Use of alternative financial services*. Retrieved February 6, 2011, from http://www. fdic.gov/householdsurvey/AFS_Addendum.pdf

Figueroa, C. (2009, January 8). Charlas en Español orientan a ahorrar. *La Prensa*, p 3.

Figueroa, C. (2009, February 4). Enseñan ahorro a estudiantes hispanos. *La Prensa*, p. 3.

Financial Industry Regulatory Authority (FINRA) Investor Education Foundation. (2009, December). *Financial capability in the United States: National Survey—Executive Summary*. Retrieved from http://www.finrafoundation.org/ web/groups/foundation/@foundation/documents/ foundation/p120535.pdf

Fishkind., & Associates. Inc. (2007). *Hispanic communities of Central Florida: Economic contributions to the region. Executive Summary*. Orlando, FL: Orlando Regional Chamber of Commerce.

Friedrich, A., & Rodriguez, E. (2001). *Financial insecurity amid growing wealth: Why healthier savings is essential to Latino prosperity*. National Council of La Raza, Issue Brief, No. 5, August.

Gutter, M. S., & Mountain, T. P. (2007). *Understanding minority preferences for investor education: Results from African-American and Hispanic focus groups*. Accepted for presentation at 2007 Academy of Financial Services.

Hispanic Business Initiative Fund (HBIF). (n.d.). *Website*. Retrieved from http://www.hbifflorida.org/

Metro Orlando Economic Development Commission. (2011, January 21). *Employment by industry: Metro Orlando*. Retrieved February 6, 2011, from http://www.orlandoedc.com/core/file.php?loc=/Solodev/clients/solodev/Enterprise%20Main/Documents/EDC%20Documents/Data%20Center/workforce/Workforce_EmpbyInd_1210.pdf

Packaged Facts. (2005, July 1). *Market trends: Opportunities in the "unbanked" consumer market*. Retrieved from http://www.packagedfacts.com/Trends-Opportunities-Unbanked-1079258/

Personal Finance Employee Education Foundation. (2000, May 5). *Workers with financial stress are less productive*. (Press Releases). Retrieved February 6, 2011, from http://pfeef.org/press/press-releases/Workers-with-Financial-Stress-Less-Productive.html

Thomas, D. A., & Gabarro, J. J. (1999). *Breaking through: The making of minority executives in corporate America*. Boston, MA: Harvard Business School Press.

Toussaint-Comeau, M. (2003, August) *Changing Hispanic demographics: Opportunities and constraints in the financial market*. Chicago, IL: Chicago Fed Letter. Retrieved February 12, 2011 from http://www.chicagofed.org/digital_assets/publications/chicago_fed_letter/2003/cflaug2003_192.pdf

U.S. Census Bureau. (2009). *S0201: Selected population profile in the United States, Hispanic or Latino (of any race)*. *Orange County, Florida*. American FactFinder: American community survey 1-year estimates. Retrieved from http://factfinder.census.gov

ADDITIONAL READING

Beyond Grey Pinstripes. Beyond Grey Pinstripes is an independent, biennial business school survey and ranking hosted by the Aspen Institute. Retrieved February 12, 2011 from: http://www.beyondgreypinstripes.org/index.cfm

Consumer Interests Annual. (2007, January). Articles retrieved month day year from The Free Library by Farlex http://www.thefreelibrary.com/Consumer+Interests+Annual/2007/January/1-p51773

Figueroa, C. (2009, January 8). Charlas en español orientan a ahorrar. *La Prensa*, p. 3.

Figueroa, C. (2009, February 4). Enseñan ahorro a estudiantes hispanos. *La Prensa*, p.4.

Greene, W., Rhine, S., & Toussaint-Comeau, M. (2003, August). *The importance of check-cashing businesses to the unbanked: Racial/ethnic differences* (Working Paper Series, WP 2003-10). Chicago, IL: Federal Reserve Bank of Chicago. Retrieved February 10, 2011, from http://www.chicagofed.org/digital_assets/publications/working_papers/2003/wp2003-10.pdf

Marks, D. (2008, Aug 13). The unbanked Hispanic market. *Spanish Hispanic Marketing Internet.* Retrieved May 28, 2009, from http://www.ahorre. com/dinero/hispanic/services/the_unbanked_hispanic_market/.

Miley, M. (2008, June). *Expanding financial skills in low-income communities: A framework for building an effective financial education program.* Newton, MA: Massachusetts Community & Banking Council [MCBC]. Retrieved February 10, 2011, from http://ctmoney.org/Resources/Documents/Miley_ExpandingFinSkillsLICom_2008. pdf

Stone, G. (2004, June). Financial Literacy. *LOMA.* Retrieved June 2, 2009, from http://www.loma. org/res-06-04-literacy.asp.

Sumo, V. (2007, Winter). Bringing in the unbanked: Banks are increasingly turning their attention to Hispanics without bank accounts. *Region Focus, 11* (1) 32-35. Retrieved February 6, 2011 from http://www.richmondfed.org/publications/research/region_focus/2007/winter/pdf/feature3.pdf Suro, R., Bendixen, S., Lowell, B.L., & Benavides, D.C. (2002). *Billions in Motion: Latino Immigrants, Remittances and Banking.* Los Angeles, CA: Pew Hispanic Center.

Wang, C., & Hanna, S. D. (2007, January 1). Racial/ethnic disparities in stock ownership: a decomposition analysis. *Consumer Interests Annual.* Retrieved from *The Free Library* http://www. thefreelibrary.com/Racial/ethnic disparities in stock ownership: a decomposition...-a0167842521

KEY TERMS AND DEFINITIONS

Alcance más con su dinero: The Spanish language name of the Orange County Library System's series of financial literacy workshops geared for the Hispanic community. The name translates as: "Get More for Your Money."

Financial Literacy: The understanding financial matters. The ability to make informed judgments and effective decisions regarding the use and management of money.

FINRA: Financial Industry Regulatory Authority (FINRA) is the largest independent regulator for all securities firms doing business in the U.S.

FINRA Investor Education Foundation: A FINRA Foundation which supports research and educational projects aimed at segments of the public who could benefit from additional finance resources. The Foundation's mission is to provide underserved Americans with the knowledge, skills and tools necessary for financial success.

More for Your Money: The English language name of the Orange County Library System's series of financial literacy workshops geared for the African American community.

Smart Investing @ Your Library®: A grant funded program developed by the American Library Association and the FINRA Investor Education Foundation. The program addresses the need for unbiased and financial and investor education at the grassroots level.

Unbanked Population: Persons without a checking or savings account.

Underbanked Population: Persons with a checking or savings account but rely on alternative financial services such as check cashing, payday loans, pawnshops and to rent to own organizations.

APPENDIX A

Module 1

Money Fundamentals – this module focused on the very basics of saving, budgeting and getting out of debt. It was repeated three times at each of the two selected branches.

Module 2

Investment Fundamentals – this module focused on the basics of investing. It was repeated three times at each of the two selected branches

Module 3

Practical Investments – this module offered a more detailed outline of investing. It was repeated once at each of the two selected branches.

Module 4

Retirement Options – this module was presented by Dr. Clay Singleton. It was offered in English with simultaneous Spanish translation as required. It focused on retirement plans. This module was given once at each location and ended the series. This session finished with a party.

APPENDIX B

Survey results from the Spanish-language workshops.

Goal # 1: Program participants will be knowledgeable about key investment concepts and information resources available

Based on the 189 collected survey results:

- 98 percent of survey respondents felt more confident when it came to creating a personal budget after attending the series. Our original goal was 70 percent.
- 100 percent of survey respondents felt they were more confident with basic money management techniques after attending the workshop. Our original goal was 70 percent.
- 95 percent of survey respondents stated they could identify at least 10 key financial concepts after the workshops. Our original goal was 70 percent.

Goal #2: The target audience of the Hispanic community will value the library as a place to get accurate, unbiased investment information.

Based on the 189 collected survey results:

- 97 percent of respondents reported that would recommend the library as a place to get accurate, unbiased investment information. The remaining 3 percent was not sure. Our original goal was for 90 percent to respond favorably.
- 97 percent stated they would often use the Library as a resource for investing information. Our original goal was 80 percent.
- 97 percent stated that they considered the Library to be a "very good" resource for investing information. 3 percent stated they considered it to be a good resource. Our original goal was 80 percent- 100 percent of respondents answered that the information they received during the program helped them feel more confident saving money. Our original goal was 80 percent.

Goal # 3: Library staff at participating locations will be knowledgeable about investing resources.

The staff at both host locations were trained on basic finance resources and were asked to identify three questions to ask a patron to guide him/her to correct sources. Staffs were also tested on the usage of key resources on investing.

- 100 percent of tested staff at both locations were able to identify three questions to ask a patron to guide him/her to correct sources and were able to identify key resources on investing.

Goal #4: Effective marketing and outreach result in awareness among the target audience.

Most of the 189 survey respondents stated they learned of the series though the Library's media publicity and outreach efforts.

- 8 percent through radio
- 29 percent through newspapers
- 13 percent through bus ads
- 3 percent through community events

Regarding the Library's in-house publicity efforts, the survey 3 respondents stated they learned of the series:

- 32 percent through the Library Web site
- 5 percent through the Library newsletter

Chapter 9
The Hampstead Carbon Challenge

Peggy Thrasher
Dover Public Library, USA

ABSTRACT

In 2008, the Hampstead Public Library partnered with the New Hampshire Carbon Challenge to encourage Hampstead residents to reduce their carbon emissions. The multi-faceted month-long initiative included programs, services, and resources designed to educate people and motivate them to take the Carbon Challenge and help the environment. The project provided activity and publicity, which helped the library position itself as an information resource in the community. The partnership provided fresh ideas and enthusiasm to both the library and the Carbon Challenge. The Hampstead Public Library pioneered some best practices for future Carbon Challenges in other locations, and leveraged the knowledgebase of the Carbon Challenge to provide a meaningful and memorable experience for its patrons. The Hampstead Carbon Challenge was a lot of fun for everyone.

INTRODUCTION

The Hampstead Public Library established a productive partnership with the New Hampshire Carbon Challenge in 2008. The New Hampshire Carbon Challenge later became the New England Carbon Challenge™ (http://necarbonchallenge. org/about.jsp). The partnership helped to move both organizations closer to their goals. For the Carbon Challenge, our library provided a successful platform for spreading the word about carbon emissions and educating people about simple things they could do to reduce their household carbon footprints. For the library, the Challenge brought the staff and community together and positioned the Hampstead Public Library as an information resource in the community.

The New Hampshire Carbon Challenge is structured around the simple premise that households can make easy reductions in their use of fossil fuel energy and that these changes, when coupled with the actions of other households, can have a significant impact in reducing greenhouse gas emissions and stabilizing the risk of climate change. Households that have *Taken the Challenge* have, on average, reduced their annual energy us-

DOI: 10.4018/978-1-61350-387-4.ch009

age by 16%, are saving more than $700 a year, and most actions can be implemented in less than an hour. Since many homes and families waste a lot of energy unknowingly and are unaware of how easily they can reduce their energy consumption, the Carbon Challenge also appeals to residents for whom frugality and energy independence are greater motivators than reducing one's environmental footprint.

The Hampstead Public Library's month-long Carbon Challenge initiative provided a way for the library to publicize that it is a place for people to get information that will help them make important decisions in their lives. It energized the staff and involved them in a meaningful project. The combination of programs with related services and resources positioned our town to vie for the honor of having more households from Hampstead take the Challenge than any other town. This project helped the library to be more visible, educated our patrons, and helped make a difference to the environment. Working with our community partner, the New Hampshire Carbon Challenge, enabled the Hampstead Public Library to expand its reach and influence.

BACKGROUND

The Hampstead Public Library

Hampstead is a town of almost 9,000 people situated in the southern tier of New Hampshire, near the Massachusetts border. It is primarily a bedroom community, with residents traveling to larger communities in New Hampshire and Massachusetts for work. There are three campgrounds and many seasonal residences with access to the lakes in town.

U.S. Census Bureau (2009) statistics show that Hampstead is an affluent, educated town with little diversity. As is common in New Hampshire, almost all Hampstead residents are white. Only 2% of Hampstead residents live below the poverty level. Ninety-three percent of residents over the age of 25 have high school diplomas, and 34% have Bachelors degrees.

The Hampstead Public Library was founded in 1888. The library is open six days a week including four evenings for a total of 54 hours. Its current home is in a building originally constructed as office condominiums (Figure 1). Ten thousand square feet are utilized on the first and second floor. The library holds 48,000 materials, including books, audiobooks, movies, magazines, and newspapers, with a total annual circulation of 70,000. Ten computers are available for public use, but since most people in town have computers and high speed internet access at home there are usually no waiting lines. Three meeting rooms, which accommodate 136, 62, and 10 people, provide space for library programs and for local non-profit groups. Two study rooms are also available for smaller groups. The basement houses a Thrift Shop which is run by the Friends of the Library, as well as storage space. Storybook Garden, behind the library, is maintained by the Hampstead Garden Club.

I joined the Hampstead Public Library (HPL) in March of 2008 as its Director. I earned my MLIS degree online from San Jose State University that same year. I had worked part time in another library in New Hampshire for 10 years. Before that, I had been a software engineer and engineering manager. The library staff, including two additional full time librarians (one with a MLS degree) and seven part time employees, worked a total of 243 hours each week (6.08 FTE). We also had two high school pages and two part time custodians.

In addition to the library's appropriation from the town ($396,000 in 2008), which comfortably met the library's needs, we received significant donations. In 2008, the Friends of the Library, civic groups, and individuals donated funds to purchase the library's 13 museum passes and added $5,000 to our $1,000 programming budget.

The library focuses on providing informational and recreational reading and programming. An active summer reading program draws 250 children, and storytimes are held both during the school year and in the summer. A home schooling group meets once a month. Two library book groups meet on a monthly basis. Meetings are held twice a month by a spinners and knitters group and a needlecraft socials group. Adult storytimes, which are targeted towards developmentally delayed patrons, are also held twice a month. The library's Wii™ gaming system is set up for adults to use on Tuesdays, and for the Senior Drop-In Center on Thursdays. The Friends of the Library sponsor ten programs each year in conjunction with their monthly meetings. The library provides an additional 35 programs each year, including lectures, performances, movies, events, and workshops.

The library's website (http://www.hampsteadlibrary.org) includes a library catalog, calendar of events, and access to downloadable audiobooks and e-Books. The site provides the traditional access to electronic databases as well as an online newsstand interface that encourages browsing through the online magazines. The library's Facebook feed is also displayed on the homepage.

The Library in 2008

In 2008, the Hampstead Public Library, like many small public libraries, was seen by the community more as a source of recreational reading than as a source for information. One of the biggest challenges for libraries is to let patrons know about all the wonderful resources that they have. We had more than 13,000 non-fiction books for adults, a small collection of non-fiction videos, 30 electronic databases provided by the State Library, and seven electronic databases funded through our budget. Our reference desk was staffed every hour that the library was open, primarily by our full-time MLS reference librarian. Yet, our strong resource collection was underutilized. Circulation of adult fiction titles was 3 times the circulation of adult non-fiction. I wanted to find

a way to publicize our non-fiction collection, and to engage patrons so they would begin to come to the library for information that would help them to solve real problems in their lives.

The library already had an effective publicity mechanism for programming. There are two weekly free newspapers in town (*Tri-Town Times* and *Carriage Towne News*) and one daily newspaper (*Eagle Tribune*). The library sends press releases to each of these papers weekly announcing special and ongoing programs. There is also a sign in front of the Town Hall, which can be read by people driving by, that displays most of the library's significant programs. We provide announcements to the local cable access channel, which displays them throughout the day.

I wanted to utilize these effective publicity channels to inform patrons, and other residents in town, of the information resources in the library. Programming can be used as a marketing tool for other services and resources. As a library publicizes its programs, it reminds the public of the types of information that are available at the library. I decided to promote a series of related programs that would help to introduce the concept that the library is not just a place to get the latest hot novel or book group choice, but is also a source of information.

The central topic for this project needed to be an issue that our patrons were interested in or concerned about. The best choice would be a subject that was familiar to most people, but that people typically did not have a firm grasp on because they had not invested sufficient time to understand it. Many people recognize that they should give more attention to broad topics such as managing finances, maintaining a healthy lifestyle, and taking care of the environment. Providing specific information on topics like these could help people make meaningful changes in their lives.

At a staff meeting in mid-2008 we discussed ways that the library could make a difference to the community. A couple of staff members expressed interest in helping the environment, and wondered if the library could get the town excited about saving the planet. The enthusiasm of the staff bode well for this to be an engaging topic for the community. One staff member drew up a long list of ways that the library could be "greener", such as recycling cellphones, ink cartridges and used batteries; reusing scrap paper; using recycled paper, napkins, plates and cups; using environmentally friendly cleaning products; improving air quality with plants; and installing programmable thermostats. Janet Arden, the Adult Programming Coordinator, began looking for speakers on "green" topics.

One of the outreach services that the University of New Hampshire (UNH) provides is a Speaker's Bureau (http://www.unh.edu/universityevents/speakersbureau). Over 500 different presentations are offered to New Hampshire non-profits, civic groups and schools. Each organization can request up to three programs each year. Janet asked the University of New Hampshire Speaker's Bureau if they had any "green" programs, and was connected with Denise Blaha from the New Hampshire Carbon Challenge.

The Carbon Challenge

The New Hampshire Carbon Challenge was an initiative started by Denise Blaha and Julia Dundorf through the University of New Hampshire in 2006 to increase awareness of residential carbon emissions and to encourage individuals in the community to reduce their carbon footprint and thereby, their contribution to greenhouse gasses in the Earth's atmosphere. The Carbon Challenge chose to focus on individuals rather than businesses because 40% of carbon emissions come from individuals' use of heat, electricity, and transportation (U.S. Environmental Protection Agency, 2008). The Carbon Challenge program's goal was to educate people about the planetary impacts of carbon emissions and how an individual's actions contribute to their carbon footprint. It also wanted to inspire people to make

small, manageable changes in their daily lives that would reduce carbon emissions.

The New Hampshire Carbon Challenge website promoted action as well as providing information and links on sources of carbon emissions such as heating and electricity use in the home, transportation, and recycling. Website visitors were asked to *Take the Carbon Challenge* for their household. Challenge takers filled out a short survey about their current energy use, and then pledged to make changes that would reduce their carbon emissions. Suggested changes included reducing the temperature in their house, switching to compact fluorescent light bulbs, retiring older appliances, purchasing a more fuel efficient car, etc. The Carbon Challenge's New England Carbon Estimator™ (their on-line carbon calculator) determined the quantitative effect of those changes on the household's carbon emissions and provided estimates of the dollars saved from implementing these changes.

The Carbon Challenge tried to encourage groups of people to take the Carbon Challenge, by setting up a competition between towns on their website. When someone took the Challenge (filled out the online energy survey and pledged to make changes), they identified their town or city. The Carbon Challenge website tracked the number of households taking the Challenge in each town and provided two rankings: the towns with the largest number of households who had taken the Challenge, and the towns with the largest number of households who had taken the Challenge in the past 30 days.

THE HAMPSTEAD CARBON CHALLENGE PROJECT

Denise Blaha could present a kick-off program for a Hampstead Carbon Challenge. This program would educate our patrons about carbon emissions and introduce them to the New Hampshire Carbon Challenge. This was a program that would draw a crowd and allow us to highlight paper and electronic resources in the library. Denise suggested that the library also do a time limited project that would encourage as many patrons as possible to take the Challenge. A month long Challenge sounded like fun to us. I decided to expand the project to include series of additional environmental programs that we would arrange. These programs would attract more participants to the Challenge and to HPL. Hampstead was the first library to organize a Challenge. Previous Challenges had been sponsored by environmental groups, towns, schools and businesses.

The Carbon Challenge was a good choice for our project because the underlying issue, the environment, impacts everyone. This meant that our series could be of interest to a majority of our patrons. Even those for whom environmental concerns are not a top priority could be receptive to energy reduction as it offers additional benefits such as cost savings, reduced reliance on imported fossil fuels, and less waste of our natural resources; core values that resonate with frugal, independent-minded New Hampshire residents. For these reasons, it seemed like a safe, broad based topic. The general topic also included a range of subtopics that would allow our programming to have diversity, while still fitting into a theme.

Planning

A month before the kick-off program, Denise Blaha came to a library staff meeting to explain the Carbon Challenge. This presentation had two purposes. The first was to educate the staff about the causes of carbon emissions and their effects on the planet. Some of the staff were already environmentalists, while others were hearing the message for the first time. The second purpose was to introduce the staff to the Carbon Challenge's online survey and carbon calculator so that the staff would be able to answer patrons' questions.

Denise encouraged our staff members to take the Challenge before the series started. We did,

and thereby became more comfortable with the online interface. This also gave us a better idea of the specific actions that the Challenge was suggesting. Our participation jumpstarted the statistics; also, it was also easier and more effective to encourage other people to take the Challenge when we had taken the Challenge ourselves.

While Janet Arden, the Adult Programming Coordinator, set up the programs, other staff members contributed in their own way before and during the month-long project. A page was added to the HPL website that contained links to online resources on "green" topics (http://www.hampsteadlibrary.org/greenwebsites.asp). We solicited donations of items from a variety of local and national suppliers. The local grocery stores and a few web merchants donated reusable shopping bags. A local hardware store donated compact florescent light bulbs and electrical socket insulation. Later in the month we received donations of books and some very attractive reusable bags. These items were used as incentives to the first people who arrived at the kick-off program, for the first people who completed the Challenge online, and for other raffles during the series. We contacted the schools, and some teachers offered extra credit to their students who attended our kick-off program.

Even by the day of our kick-off program, we had not identified all of the other programs in the series. In part this was because we were all learning during the series and the more we learned the more ideas we had for ways to engage our patrons. Part of the excitement originated from the way that the project evolved over time. Library staff remained flexible enough to incorporate new ideas as we better understood the topic and our patrons' interests. Managing the changes, however, was challenging. It was difficult to make sure that all of the staff knew what was going on as the plans changed. As we got closer to the end of the project, we had more good ideas than we had time to implement. In particular, the lead time required to properly publicize a program is three weeks.

Since the project was only a month long, just as we were becoming more knowledgeable and more inspired, we ran up against publicity time limits.

The program series ended up with five programs (http://www.hampsteadlibrary.org/carbonchallenge.asp). The kick-off program by the Carbon Challenge group was followed by programs that Janet organized on recycling and composting, energy audits, renewable energy, and energy efficient home construction. These programs were chosen because they touched on a variety of green topics without too much overlap. We investigated a number of other topics as well, but chose not to include them. In many cases, this was because we could not find an appropriate presenter for the topic.

To help maintain interest during the series, and to provide a highly visible symbol of our goal, we constructed a "thermometer" to display the number of Hampstead households who had taken the Challenge. The graphic was a dark footprint, which was filled in with increasing amounts of green paint as more families took the Challenge. This five foot plywood sign was placed in front of the library next to the library's main sign (Figure 2). I had no idea how many people in Hampstead might take the Challenge, so I chose a goal of 100, an ambitious number. While we never met my goal (we had 70 households take the Challenge), the sign showed the public that we were making progress while demonstrating that we still needed their participation (Figure 3). The Hampstead Carbon Challenge garnered significant interest in the local press, with the *Eagle Tribune* printing a front page article including a picture of me painting the footprint sign (http://www.eagletribune.com/newhampshire/x1876451833/Hampstead-library-accepts-carbon-challenge).

The Programs

The kick-off program was presented by Denise Blaha and Deb Cinamon Waylan, a volunteer with the New Hampshire Carbon Challenge, on October 22, 2008. They gave an educational talk that explained the issue of carbon emissions. They encouraged attendees to take the Challenge and reduce their individual carbon footprints by reducing their consumption of fuel and electricity, and by reducing waste. At the end of the talk they dumped 56 empty water bottles on the floor. They said that this was the number of water bottles discarded by a family of four in a week. Since only 10 percent of water bottles are typically recycled, most of the bottles would end up in a landfill. We had welcome packages of donated items for the first 25 people. This program attracted 65 residents, a huge turnout. Some members of the audience were already familiar with carbon emission issues, but it was a new topic for many. At the end of the presentation, we encouraged the audience to go home and take the Carbon Challenge. Within the next 24 hours, 12 Hampstead residents took the Challenge.

Our second program, attended by eight residents, was "Composting and Recycling 101". The local Solid Waste Committee chairman, Pat Bracken, came to talk about the town's recycling for paper, metal, glass and plastic, as well as how to recycle more unusual items. The audience was very active, asking many questions and sharing solutions of their own. Most of the attendees for this program were people who were already passionate about recycling. We raffled off a composter that was donated to us by the Town of Hampstead.

In preparation for the third program which was about energy audits Paul Button, from Energy Audits Unlimited, conducted an energy audit of our library building. The Friends of the Library paid for half of the audit. Its purpose was to identify ways that the library was being inefficient in its use of energy. The audit included a door blower and thermal imaging, as well as inspection of the heating system, electrical system, and insulation in the building. The audit report provided the library with a list of projects that could be completed to increase the energy efficiency of the building. We found that the windows, even though they were 20 years old, were reasonably energy efficient and the building had fairly tight construction. The insulation in the attic was acceptable, but could be improved. There was a significant problem found with the size of the air intake to the furnace rooms. Energy could also be saved by replacing the fluorescent exit signs with more efficient LED signs. The largest problem (termed by the auditor "the mother load"), was the fluorescent lights on the first floor, which had magnetic rather than electronic ballasts, and used T12 bulbs rather than the more efficient T8 bulbs. The library decided to invest $7,700 in retrofitting the lighting fixtures on the first floor. This work was eligible for a $2,800 rebate from the electric company and would pay for itself in two years. The staff also became more aware of our energy use and began to reduce the library's carbon footprint by making simple changes such as turning off the lights in meeting rooms when they are not in use.

The auditor's presentation, which was our third program, attracted ten attendees. Paul described the audit process and explained the areas in a home that are inspected. He then presented the results of the audit that he had completed on the library. We put a copy of the library's Energy Audit Report into our circulating collection.

Our fourth program, "The Sun, the Wind, and the Mighty Dollar" was presented by Gary Bergeron, from Planit Green Renewable Energy, to 20 people who learned about the advantages, disadvantages, and costs of solar and wind energy. A major part of his talk was about tax incentives available for families who implemented alternative energy projects.

Our final program, on energy efficient home construction attracted 35 people. Norman Mancusi (Mancusi Builders, LLC), the son-in-law of one of the library's staff members, was a contractor who had recently completed the first house in the area that had achieved the internationally recognized green building certification known as LEED. He described the energy efficient systems in the house,

and the challenges that he encountered during its construction.

To supplement our programming, we also instituted recycling of batteries, cell phones, ink cartridges, and CDs at the library (Figure 4). We collected the items and then sent them on to organizations that could recycle them. Our patrons appreciated the convenience of these services. To this day (2011), we continue to recycle cell phones, ink cartridges and CDs.

Our patrons loved that we recycled batteries, and we did so for the next year, but that project became problematic. Modern standard batteries do not require special handling. In the past, batteries could not be thrown in the trash because they contained mercury. Current batteries do not have this problem. However, many people remember the days when batteries did need special handling, and thus were happy to have a convenient location to drop them off. We found an organization that would take the batteries. The handling required to send them, however, was more than we could justify for the long term. The batteries needed to each be taped on both ends, and then no more than six batteries placed in a zip-lock bag before they could be mailed to the organization. We used volunteers to prepare the batteries, but we were receiving large quantities of batteries and even with the volunteers' help the task became overwhelming. When we finally announced that we would no longer accept batteries our patrons were quite disappointed, as was the staff.

We also purchased two Kill a Watt EZ Energy Usage Monitors that we circulated. These monitors are plugged in between an electrical outlet and something that uses electricity (such as a floor lamp, coffee pot, or computer). The monitor shows how much electricity is used over a period of time, allowing people to understand which items in the home are consuming the most electricity.

We provided information and handouts on carbon emission topics, including bookmarks encouraging patrons to take the Challenge and listing the programs in our series. We had a worksheet that they could take home to record the data they would need to enter in the calculator. We had catalogs from Public Service of New Hampshire, the local electricity provider, offering reduced cost energy efficient light bulbs and fixtures. We posted information that we found at various sources on a bulletin board to inform and inspire our patrons.

The Challenge

Our goal was to have as many Hampstead residents as possible take the Challenge. Each person who took the survey and chose energy saving actions would be likely to associate the library with environmental awareness, action and saving money. They would also be likely to spread the word to their neighbors and friends. If enough people took the Challenge, then Hampstead could have the highest number of households participating and would be the number one town in the Challenge rankings.

The process of taking the Challenge provided the taker with a number of benefits. First, the taker learned information about carbon emissions and actions they could take to reduce their carbon footprint. Second, they generated a plan of beneficial actions that they pledged to take. Third, they were provided with a quantifiable measure of the outcome of the plan, both in environmental terms (pounds of carbon dioxide (CO_2) saved) and in monetary terms (dollars saved). This last benefit was particularly important because it left the taker with the understanding "I saved X pounds of CO_2 (or Y Dollars) because I went to the library today". This is a much more concrete statement than "I learned something today at the library".

Taking the Challenge required collecting a small amount of data including electric bills, heat bills, car mileage and distances traveled. This information was entered into the survey, which then determined the current carbon footprint for that household. The second step involved deciding which changes the family was willing to make. The calculator determined the carbon emissions and dollar savings for each change that the family committed to.

Challenging Obstacles

There were many obstacles to getting residents to take the Challenge. First, we needed to make sure the public were aware of the Challenge. This was an ongoing task which included newspaper publicity, prominent notices on our website and library bulletin boards, bookmark handouts, and constant reminders as patrons came to the circulation desk.

Library staff was directed to ask each patron who checked out materials if they had taken the Challenge. Some members of the staff were more comfortable bringing up the Carbon Challenge at the circulation desk than others. There is a fine line between enthusiastically promoting library activities and pressuring patrons. We had a number of discussions among the staff about what level of promotion was appropriate. In the end, most of the staff learned to moderate their approach through this exercise. Those who tended to be pushier became a bit mellower, and those who were reluctant to bring the topic up at all saw that the patrons often appreciated the information we provided.

Initially we encouraged people to take the Challenge by stressing the environmental impact that was possible with simple changes. We did find, however, that a significant segment of the population was not motivated by environmental concerns. We changed tactics in the second week and explained how much money could be saved by making the changes, emphasizing that the typical household taking the Challenge was saving over $700 a year in reduced energy costs. Saving money was motivating to many people. In the third week, we played up the competitive aspects of the Challenge. It was clear that we had a real chance to become the number one town. We were competing against Rye, NH (a smaller town) and Williamstown, MA (a town the same size as Hampstead). Making Hampstead number one was motivating to some people. In the final week, we stressed that reducing our carbon footprint would lessen our nation's dependence on foreign oil. This topic cropped up in the news during the final week, and we took advantage of that fact to help diversify our encouragements.

Changing the focus of our banter at the circulation desk helped to keep the project fresh for both the staff and the patrons. An informal survey had recently shown that, of the unique patrons who came to the library in a two week period (and who chose to participate in the survey), almost half visited the library every week or more than once a week. This meant that after the first week of our project, most of the patrons had already heard our initial message. The staff also was losing enthusiasm because of the repetition. When we changed the focus each week, we were able to motivate a new segment of our patrons and relieve the boredom of the staff.

Another significant problem was that many of the environmentally motivated patrons felt that they had already made changes and that the Challenge was not going to give them any new ideas. It was difficult to get the idea across that we were looking for people to make changes, but we were also looking for participation. The Challenge ranked towns based on the number of households that had taken the Challenge, not on the amount of carbon emissions that people pledged to save. While the reduction of carbon emissions was the ultimate goal of the Carbon Challenge, both the Carbon Challenge organization and the library recognized that the act of participation by individuals was also important. An individual who was already consciously reducing their emissions would be reinforced in their efforts by taking the Challenge. In addition, they would be likely to speak to others about the fact that they had taken the Challenge, helping to spread the word. Finally, an individual who took the Challenge realized that the process was not difficult, and this would allow them to encourage others who might be less familiar with carbon emissions to also take the Challenge. These early adopters and opinion leaders have been shown to be effective ambassadors in spreading the adoption of environmen-

tally beneficial changes in a community (such as recycling, composting, and energy conservation) (McKenzie-Mohr, 1999).

Some of our patrons had difficulty taking the Challenge because it was a computer based survey. We publicized that they could use library computers, and that we would help them take the Challenge. All of the staff understood that helping a patron take the Challenge was a very high priority task. Still, some patrons were hesitant to ask for our help.

Getting the Data

In order to take the Challenge, an individual needed to collect data about his household's energy use for the past year. Four pieces of information were needed: amount of fuel used for heating, cooking, and hot water; amount of electricity used; number of miles driven for each vehicle; and the vehicle's fuel efficiency rating (miles per gallon). For some of our patrons, collecting the information was an eye-opening experience. They were amazed at the amount of fuel and electricity they used over the course of a year.

As the HPL staff took the Challenge and as we helped our patrons take the Challenge, it became clear that obtaining these numbers was difficult for many people. First, many people do not keep records of their utility bills. For those who do keep records, it was often easy for them to find out how much money they had spent, but much harder to figure out how many gallons of oil or kilowatts of electricity they had used. Each hurdle a patron faced increased the chances that the patron would give up and not take the Challenge.

To simplify data gathering, the Challenge calculator allowed people to omit information and use an average figure if the exact figure was not known. In fact, a patron could take the Challenge without entering in any of their actual energy use. They could still pledge to make changes, and the calculator would estimate what those changes would save the average household.

To assist participants with this aspect of the program, I added a page to our website with answers to Frequently Asked Questions (FAQ) about the Challenge (http://www.hampsteadlibrary.org/easychallenge.asp). Answers included suggestions such as calling an oil company to ask how many gallons of oil had been delivered in the past year, where on the electric bill the historical usage amounts were located, a method of estimating the number of miles driven each year, and a website that gave the fuel use numbers for most cars. The FAQ page also stressed that the staff at the library would be happy to help patrons find the needed numbers and take the Challenge.

One of the side benefits to the library of the Challenge was that it gave the staff a chance to publicize that we really were ready, willing, and able to provide individual assistance to our patrons. Since the Challenge was a very high priority in the library, staff felt that any time they spent on the Challenge would be supported by me.

Working with a Partner

Denise Blaha worked closely with us before and during the month long Challenge. The training she provided to library staff not only familiarized us with the logistics of the survey and calculator, but it also inspired us to start thinking about carbon reduction both on a personal level and as a library. As we became more familiar with the topic we were able to generate new ideas for programs and other ways that we could engage our patrons. Denise helped by sharing her contacts with us. In particular she helped us to find an energy auditor who could perform the audit on the library and present the results at our program. Periodically, Denise would send me statistics indicating the number of people who had taken the Challenge from Hampstead. In addition, the map on the Carbon Challenge website indicated the number of pounds of CO_2 that Hampstead Challenge takers had committed to save. This data allowed the library to track the progress of the Challenge.

Two days before the kick-off program, Denise sent me a spreadsheet of people who had taken the Challenge. This report did not show the details of each person's carbon footprint, nor of the changes that they had agreed to make. It simply showed the name, email address, town and date when the Challenge was completed. Based on this report, Denise told us that if we had one more patron take the Challenge that we would be listed as the #10 town. We achieved that goal the day before the kick-off program. As milestones like this occurred, I shared them enthusiastically with my staff through email.

The first group of Challenge takers from Hampstead encountered a problem that Denise had not seen before. One of the data items requested by the calculator was the amount of propane used. Propane is sometimes measured in gallons and sometimes in cubic feet. The calculator expected the quantity to be measured in gallons, however many Hampstead household deliveries were measured in cubic feet. When Denise saw the results of one Challenge taker who had entered cubic feet, she added some text to the Frequently Asked Questions page of her website that explained how to convert cubic feet into gallons. Throughout our partnership, she responded very quickly to any issues that came up.

During the kick-off program, Denise asked the audience to go home and take the Challenge. In the first two hours following the program, nine Hampstead patrons did take the Challenge. Denise was amazed and wrote in an email: "In all the talks that Julia and I have given, only ONE time did ONE person immediately go home and take the challenge. One time! And Hampstead had NINE!! Just phenomenal..." (personal communication, October 22, 2008).

We identified a second issue on the day of the kick-off, as well: Only whole numbers were accepted by the calculator. Denise quickly added an instruction to use only whole numbers. She would have preferred to have the calculator require only whole numbers, but they did not have the funding to pay a programmer to make the changes needed. She asked me if I could write a letter of recommendation which would help the Carbon Challenge organization to obtain additional funding that could be used to pay a programmer to enhance the calculator. At the end of the Hampstead Challenge, I did write a letter for them.

We tried a number of ways to show people how the Challenge was progressing. The first was the footprint thermometer. This plywood sign was on display inside the library for about a week before it was moved outside next to the main library sign. Denise suggested a graphic for our website that showed the commitments that Hampstead residents had made in terms of pounds of CO_2 reduced and the amount of money that would be saved. Displaying this information from a date before our Challenge program began as well as showing current information gave our patrons an idea of the progress that we were making (Figure 5). As the Challenge transitioned to focusing on the amount of money that people could save, I created a poster with an image of a piggy bank. We taped green dollar signs, that had the number of dollars saved by each individual, on the piggy bank, and invited our patrons who had taken the Challenge to come and record their savings on the poster (Figure 6). The poster had a number of purposes. First, it provided an action that people could take which would reinforce their commitment to make the changes. Second, it provided patrons who had not yet taken the Challenge with proof that others had already taken it. It also showed the amount of money that was typically saved. Over time, our patrons could see the number of dollar signs increase, which gave us another visual way to show people that their friends and neighbors were participating.

Newspaper coverage helped us to spread the word about the Challenge. *The Eagle Tribune* printed both a Letter to the Editor from me which described the Challenge and the article on the front page the morning after our kick-off program.

We also had a significant article in the *Tri-Town Times* in advance of our energy efficient home construction program. As a result of our weekly press releases, notices of our Challenge programs were included in the local weekly papers each week during our month long Challenge. *The Concord Monitor* publishes a "Green Living" supplement twice a year. In November of 2008, the Hampstead Challenge was featured in this publication.

Denise and I communicated frequently about a range of topics via email. She let us know that she was seeing significant referrals to the Carbon Challenge website both from the library's webpage and the town's webpage. She sent us updates on the number of Challenge takers, and the amount of CO_2 and money that they would save. She told me about a meeting that she attended where she was "bragging about" our footprint thermometer idea. She reported a time when one of the links on the library website was broken, which allowed me to correct the problem quickly. I let her know that a map on the Carbon Challenge website was malfunctioning at one point, and she investigated the problem which turned out to be an incompatibility between Microsoft and Google Maps.

The competition between towns was perhaps more motivating for the staff than for the patrons, but town pride is a strong incentive for many people. As the month drew to a close, Hampstead was just behind Rye and Williamstown in the number of households that had taken the Challenge. Denise provided me with updates on our count, and how many more we needed to overtake the other towns. She sent these updates every day and sometimes multiple times in a day. Her enthusiasm and encouragement helped motivate me to make sure that we succeeded in taking the number one spot. We finally made it to the number one spot on November 24, one month and two days after our kick-off program (Figure 7)! We posted signs around the library thanking our patrons for making Hampstead number one.

The Carbon Challenge Today

In May of 2009, the New Hampshire Carbon Challenge expanded to become the New England Carbon Challenge™ (http://necarbonchallenge. org/about.jsp), a joint initiative of the University of New Hampshire and Clean Air - Cool Planet. The Carbon Challenge's online calculator was retooled and enhanced and is now called the Personal Energy Planner™ (http://myenergyplan.net/estimator). Through New Hampshire's participation in the multi-state Regional Greenhouse Gas Initiative (RGGI), the NE Carbon Challenge debuted a new website, My Energy Plan™ (http://myenergyplan. net) in April 2010, expanding their online resources for households, including a searchable database of contractors and vendors who provide energy efficient solutions in New England, and the federal, state, and utility incentives to reduce the costs of these energy improvements.

As of March 2011, Challenge takers have committed to reduce their CO_2 emissions by 22,651,944 pounds through actions that will save residents $2.5 million dollars a year in reduced energy costs. Hampstead contributes 410,799 pounds towards that total. Hampstead ranks as the number eight town (out of 487 towns and cities of all sizes in six states), just behind Rye and ahead of Williamstown.

The Hampstead Public Library was listed as a Carbon Challenge Climate Hero in February of 2009 (http://necarbonchallenge.org/heroes. jsp). The Hampstead Challenge has also been featured prominently in the presentation given by the Challenge organizers to groups that are considering holding their own Challenge in the future, as an effective model of how to engage residents in household energy reduction.

RESULTS

Benefits to Library

The benefits to the Library of partnering with the Carbon Challenge were significant. While we chose and arranged for the programming on our own, the Challenge provided a structure for our series. Initial contacts with the Challenge organizers helped to ease the startup efforts for our new initiative. The organizers had a clear focus which we could adopt, making it so that we did not need to define the boundaries and, instead, could use that energy to flesh out our initiative within their boundaries. Since we were early participants in the Challenge, and the first library, we received a lot of attention and support. Denise was as interested in our success as we were, and helped to brainstorm ideas with us. When we came up with new ideas they were excited and encouraging, this helped to keep our interest high.

The month-long initiative generated a lot of buzz in town. Each new program provided an opportunity to re-publicize the Challenge, bringing the message to new people. At each program, we encouraged the attendees to come to the remaining programs in the series. While the kick-off program had the highest attendance, the attendance figures increased steadily for the second through fifth programs. We did find that we needed to continue to talk about the Challenge at the circulation desk for the entire month. Toward the end of the month it was common to hear people say "I've heard about the Challenge, but I don't really know what it is." Clearly, our message was getting out, but our experience underscored that people will often hear only the surface message without understanding the details. It was clear from our experience that a message needs to be articulated over and over again, and in as many ways and forms as possible.

For the library, participation at all levels was the goal. Each person who took the Challenge was a potential new ambassador for the library. Each program attendee could help to spread the word about the information that was available at the library.

The Challenge did help us to spread the word that the library was a place to get information as well as recreation. Unfortunately, this has not translated into increased circulation of our non-fiction titles. The density of programming (a program every week) kept the initiative in the forefront of our publicity and people's minds. The variety of programming attracted a range of attendees.

Benefits to Carbon Challenge

The Carbon Challenge was pleased to partner with us. Libraries can serve as effective partners because they have communication channels with the community. They also can provide space for groups of people to get together to share the message. Libraries also have good internet connectivity and helpful staff members, eager to assist patrons who are not as comfortable with technology or are in need of extra assistance. The Challenge's main goal was to educate people and motivate them to make positive change. The library was able to add its resources to those of the Challenge to make the message more accessible to the public. The sense of community found in the library helped to encourage people to not only learn about the issues but to take action.

For the Carbon Challenge, our initiative helped crystallize the essential elements and best practices of a successful challenge. Over two years later, the NE Carbon Challenge still utilizes the building blocks used in our initiative. These are: a solid organizing structure that "leads by example" by taking the Challenge themselves; effective communication strategies; incentives, reminders, public pledges and commitments; a definitive start and end date for the Challenge; and celebrating success after the Challenge concludes.

In fact, while all communities are encouraged to promote the Challenge, NE Carbon Challenge staff resources are focused and prioritized toward those communities that adopt the "Hampstead model" in hosting a Challenge, since it greatly increases the likelihood of success.

Benefits to Community

The Challenge increased connections within the town of Hampstead. The contacts established for the program on recycling and composting with the Solid Waste Committee helped the library be more supportive to the town when it later decided not to change to a pay-as-you-throw system. The Selectmen attended many of the programs, and helped us to publicize our events by announcing them at their regular meetings which are televised on the local cable channel. The Challenge made a significant difference in the Selectmen's impression of the library. They began to see the library as a relevant, active resource. Today, I promote a timely program or service at most of the Selectmen's meetings which helps to spread news of the library to my patrons but also to other residents who do not come to the library.

When our Carbon Challenge initiative began in October of 2008, one family had taken the Challenge, pledging to reduce their carbon emissions by 5,486 CO_2 pounds and saving \$878 per year. As of March, 2011, 75 households in Hampstead have committed to reduce their carbon emissions by 410,799 CO_2 pounds, a savings of \$49,786 in reduced energy costs.

Lessons Learned

Our Carbon Challenge experience taught us that a month long series provides an effective way to maximize publicity and "buzz" in town. We can easily get information to our regular patrons who visit the library at least once a week. They see the posters in the library, pick up the handouts describing upcoming programs, read the weekly email newsletter, as well as seeing our publicity in the press and on our website. While our newspaper, cable TV, and Town Hall sign publicity effectively get our message into most Hampstead households, convincing a non-patron to act on that information and come to the library for a program is quite a challenge. The program series provided us with a mechanism for repeating our message ("You can get information about environmental issues at the library") over the course of a month without sounding too monotonous.

We have since held two other month long series, the first on surviving the recession, the second on health and wellness. Both of these series were successful, but not as successful as the Challenge. The Challenge was different from the subsequent series as more of the staff was involved in the Challenge than in the other series. This required significant effort on a daily basis to keep the energy levels high and to keep the staff informed. The Challenge had the advantage of being our first series, so the process was novel. In addition, working with the Challenge organizers meant that when our interest and energy lagged, they could encourage me with new statistics or a new feature on their website. Having energy coming in from outside of the library was invaluable. In turn, each time we had a success, the enthusiasm from our library helped to invigorate the Challenge organizers.

It was helpful to be part of a larger cause. This allowed us to feel as if our small efforts could have a larger impact because they were combined with others' similar efforts. The competition between towns was also helpful in that it gave us both incentive and clear goals.

The staff needed to be engaged in the topic in order to effectively brainstorm ideas for the project. While we had talked about how the library could be involved in saving the planet, the staff really started coming up with ideas only after the staff training. Since there was only a month between the staff training and the kick-off program, there was not enough time for ideas to germinate and be executed. I would expect that there is also a danger to involving the staff too early, in that their enthusiasm could peak before the project begins.

CONCLUSION

The partnership between the Hampstead Library and the Carbon Challenge kindled creativity and enthusiasm. Combining our expertise and brainstorming solutions together produced innovative ideas. Being part of a larger cause helped to motivate us by showing that our small efforts could contribute in a meaningful way. It was fun to work with new people who were as committed to our success as we were.

Personally, I began this program as someone who was fairly indifferent to saving the environment. I am now much more aware and interested in the issues. As a result of taking the Challenge, I made a number of changes in my house, including reducing the thermostat, installing programmable thermostats, and using compact fluorescent light bulbs. Maybe this year I will replace my old dehumidifier. The library also continues to make changes. We have covered up the large air intake for the furnace rooms, now bringing in only the air that we need for combustion for the furnaces. We have also sealed cracks in the heating ducts. I hope to replace the exit signs this year.

The Carbon Challenge in Hampstead was beneficial to the library, the community, the Challenge, and individuals in Hampstead. Working with the Challenge organizers helped the Library stay focused and enthusiastic. While it was an exhausting month, the Carbon Challenge helped the Hampstead Public Library reach out to the community in a very meaningful way.

REFERENCES

Hampstead Public Library. (2011). *Easy to take the Carbon Challenge*. Retrieved from http://www.hampsteadlibrary.org/easychallenge.asp

Hampstead Public Library. (2011). *Green websites*. Retrieved from http://www.hampsteadlibrary.org/greenwebsites.asp

Hampstead Public Library. (2011). *Hampstead Carbon Challenge*. Retrieved from http://www.hampsteadlibrary.org/carbonchallenge.asp

Hampstead Public Library. (2011). *Hampstead Public Library*. Retrieved from http://www.HampsteadLibrary.org

McKenzie Mohr, D. (1999). *Fostering sustainable behavior: An introduction to community-based social marketing*. Gabriola Island, Canada: New Society Publishers.

New England Carbon Challenge. (2011). *Climate heroes*. Retrieved from http://necarbonchallenge.org/heroes.jsp

New England Carbon Challenge. (2011). *My energy plan*. Retrieved from http://myenergyplan.net

New England Carbon Challenge. (2011). *My energy plan: Estimator*. Retrieved from http://myenergyplan.net/estimator

New England Carbon Challenge. (2011). *New England Carbon Challenge*. Retrieved from http://necarbonchallenge.org/about.jsp

Sullivan, M. (2011). Hampstead library accepts carbon challenge. *Eagle Tribune*. Retrieved from http://www.eagletribune.com/newhampshire/x1876451833/Hampstead-library-accepts-carbon-challenge

University of New Hampshire. (2009). *UNH University events & programs: Notable events & programs: UNH speakers bureau*. Retrieved from http://www.unh.edu/universityevents/speakersbureau

U.S. Census Bureau. (2009). *2005-2009 American community survey*. Retrieved from http://factfinder.census.gov/servlet/ACSSAFFFacts?_event=Search&geo_id=&_geoContext=&_street=&_county=hampstead&_cityTown=hampstead&_state=04000US33&_zip=&_lang=en&_sse=on&pctxt=fph&pgsl=010

U.S. Environmental Protection Agency. (2008). *Inventory of U.S. greenhouse gas emissions and sinks: 1990-2006* (pp. ES-8). Retrieved from http://www.epa.gov/climatechange/emissions/downloads/08_CR.pdf

Section 3

Public libraries can extend services to incarcerated populations, complimenting or enhancing existing education initiatives in those institutions.

Chapter 10
A Second Chance

Kathleen Houlihan
Austin Public Library, USA

ABSTRACT

This chapter describes the history of the Second Chance Books Program, a partnership between the Austin Public Library and the Gardner Betts Juvenile Justice Center. It covers the initiation of the partnership in 2002, through the early days and challenges, the growth of the partnership in 2007, and the maturation of the program in 2010. The focus is on the challenges encountered by a maturing community partnership and the resolution of those challenges. Topics include coordination of administrative tasks, transitional leadership, maintaining partnerships through staffing changes, strengthening partner buy-in, and funding concerns for long-term partnerships. The goal of the chapter is to help librarians with established or budding long-term partnerships strategize ways to prepare for and resolve problems encountered along the way.

INTRODUCTION

Second Chance Books is a nearly decade-long collaboration between the Austin Public Library (APL) and the Gardner Betts Juvenile Justice Center (GBJJC) of Travis County. The library provides two satellite libraries at Gardner Betts, as well as programs targeting reluctant readers. This case study details several of the challenges the program faced while establishing and maintaining a long-term community partnership, and the efforts to improve and expand the program over time. While some difficulties outlined here may be unique to working in a correctional facility, the majority will be relevant to the establishment and maintenance of lasting partnerships.

Our specific challenges over the past eight years reflect the complexity of a partnership such as this. One of the program's earliest challenges was simply securing library administration support for what could be seen as an extraneous program, particularly in a time of budget cuts. The program also went through a transition of leadership, where the program's founder passed control to a program administrator, to ensure its longevity and continued growth. This required

DOI: 10.4018/978-1-61350-387-4.ch010

the transition of longstanding relationships with community partners, a process that was made more challenging by the departure of several key staff members at the partner agencies.

Additionally, due to a lack of models of public library service to incarcerated youth, and the learning curve in developing this partnership, many of the policies that might otherwise have been put in place at the outset of a new venture were not implemented until later when the program had already solidified. Reluctance of correctional center staff to work with the library in the process of developing new policies meant that some later attempts to improve the partnership through policy changes were thwarted. Following a period of intense challenges for our partner agency, the program suffered from a lack of staff support, making it more challenging for the librarians to work with the partner agency and straining the limited time that library staff had available for programming at the facility. These tensions in turn contributed to library staff burnout, leaving the programming team short-handed.

Other long-term challenges included coordinating programs for very overbooked teens, with partner staff who were understaffed and overworked themselves, causing frustration for librarians on the team who felt like their time was being wasted. The program struggled each time it lost team members to attrition— librarians who moved up or moved on—because recruiting new team members had not previously been a standardized or formalized process, and training new members took a significant investment of time. Today, many of these challenges have been resolved and the partnership is stronger as a result. We hope that the exploration of our efforts will be beneficial to others in earlier stages of their partnerships.

BACKGROUND

Second Chance Books has a vision of decreasing the recidivism of incarcerated youth in the Austin community through increased literacy skills and an engagement with reading for pleasure and personal betterment. The goals of the Second Chance Books Project are to improve the literacy levels and literary engagement of incarcerated youth in Austin and to increase incarcerated youths' awareness of the library and librarians as beneficial resources to their lifelong success once they re-enter society. We do this by intercepting at-risk youth at a critical juncture in their lives, introducing them to reading for pleasure through sustained relationships with librarians skilled at working with reluctant readers. We also provide special programs to enhance residents' engagement by hosting author visits, writing workshops, art and technology programs, and other special events.

The youth that we work with often have not read much outside of school and very rarely for their personal enjoyment. Their reading levels are low for teens— often on a fifth grade level— and their experiences with reading have been a dreary struggle, when they attempted to read at all. Incarceration cuts youth off from both the personal interactions with friends and family, as well as the hyper-connected outside world, where those with similar experiences are only a click or text away. Denied nearly all personal and virtual connections with people outside the facility, the solitary experience of incarceration becomes doubly isolating. For these youth, a character in a book with a similar history to their own can become a lifeline, and a friend.

When a librarian is able to connect a teen with a book that he or she needs, not only is the teen given a tool to cope with their own challenges, but a powerful bond of trust is formed. Librarians are not the only adults interacting with these teens— they are surrounded by correctional center staff, who form a family unit and provide a stability that many of them have never experienced. The staff can become surrogate parents to a teen, and if a staff member is a reader, the teen will take notice. Many of the program's biggest successes are those in which the correctional staff actively participate in book discussions and request and recommend books for the teens in their care.

I first became involved in the Second Chance Books program when I was hired as the Youth Program Librarian for the Austin Public Library in 2009. This position was created to serve as a point contact for the library's two large youth outreach programs, including the longstanding partnership between the Austin Public Library and the Gardner Betts Juvenile Justice Center, which is part of the Travis County Juvenile Board. Previously the program had been managed by a team from Youth Services, who served the facility on a rotating basis, and divided the administrative duties of the program amongst the team. As the library's Youth Program Librarian, I coordinate the administrative side of the Second Chance Books program, including recruitment and training of new team members, promotion and advocacy for the program, communication with partner agency staff, coordination of special presenters and programs, creation of policies and strategic plans, application and administration of grants, and selection of books and materials for the program. My background is in public libraries, collection development, strategy and marketing, outreach, community partnerships, and customer service, and my experiences in each of these areas have shaped my responses to the challenges of this partnership.

THE PARTNERS

Austin Public Library's Youth Services Department

APL has a long history of innovative programming for youth, and the Second Chance Books Project enabled the library to make those programs available to those who were unable to access them, and had been chronically underserved. Through the Second Chance Program, APL oversees the collections at both the Detention facility and the long-term Leadership Academy facility at Gardner Betts. The Second Chance Books Team is made up of five to seven Youth Services librarians and staff at any given time, each joining the team because of an interest in serving at-risk youth. Team members each sign up to serve one or two units at Leadership, and two team members provide bi-monthly visits to Detention.

While the rules at each facility differ slightly, for the most part, the library has tremendous freedom when selecting materials for inclusion in the two satellite libraries at Gardner Betts. Recently, the selection of which titles to include in the collection has been the biggest cause for disharmony between the librarians and correctional staff, with each having very different philosophies about appropriate content. The library has gradually increased support of the Second Chance Books Program over the years, including the creation of the Youth Program Librarian position, which coordinates Second Chance Books and other youth outreach programs for the library.

Gardner Betts Juvenile Justice Center

Comprising two parts—a short-term Detention facility and a long-term Leadership Academy— the Gardner Betts Facility serves youth from across Travis County. The short-term residential, pre-adjudication facility (Detention) houses youth who are detained before and during their trial. The Leadership Academy is a long-term residential sentencing alternative to the larger Texas Youth Commission (TYC) prison. Travis County believes that it is important to keep youth in their communities, even while incarcerated, so they have an opportunity to form relationships with support agencies and other organizations during their incarceration, and to ease the transition and improve the success of those returning to the community. Residents at the facility are ages ten-17, and their stays average seven to ten days at Detention, and three to 18 months at the Leadership Academy. The population at Gardner Betts is predominantly Hispanic and male. Male and female residents are kept separate at all times, attending classes and programs with their assigned units.

The teens at the facility often struggle with reading, with the average reading level being that of a fifth grade throughout the facility. The Leadership Academy operates on a therapy-based model, with residents participating in a variety of programs, which could include group therapy, cognitive behavioral therapy, and individual counseling for substance abuse. There is also a court-mandated expectation that parents and guardians will be significantly involved in the rehabilitation of the youth in the program. Following a 2007 investigation, where youth were found to have been abused and neglected in a larger TYC facility, the number of youth incarcerated at Gardner Betts increased dramatically, as the county attempted to retain as many Travis County youth as possible in the local facility, rather than sending them to the troubled state agency. As the population rose, so did the severity of the crimes of the youth being detained there. The facility struggled for several years to adapt to the state's need to house youth who would have gone to TYC in a facility that was not designed to address their specific needs. Due to other innovative developments in the state's Juvenile Corrections program, the population has steadily decreased over the past year, and the facility is reporting record low numbers in their short-term Detention facility.

Austin Independent School District

The Austin Independent School District (AISD) provides school year-round to the residents at both facilities in all the traditional subject areas, with classes being offered year-round, with half-days during the summer. At both facilities, classes are made up of discrete units, with each unit being grouped based on similar infractions and treatment needs. This means that a single class may have teens as old as 17 in the same room with 11 year olds— a very challenging learning model, and one that AISD handles with true skill. AISD is also offering a new program at Leadership, DELTA, which provides an accelerated education program for incarcerated teens to get them closer to graduation upon release. DELTA had its first high school graduation ceremony in December 2010, and has high hopes for helping incarcerated teens achieve success through increased academic achievement. AISD is a strong partner of the Second Chance Books program at Gardner Betts in both the long- and short-term facilities. Historically, AISD has not had the resources to fund a library collection at either the Detention or the Leadership Academy, but in 2010 and 2011, teachers at both facilities received grant funding to improve the library collection, which they did with the support and recommendations of APL.

Writers' League of Texas

The Writers' League has been a tremendous resource for the Second Chance Books Program for several years, providing access to a wealth of local authors who regularly visit with youth at the center. Two grant-funded programs, Project WISE and Project INK, have provided over a dozen author visits and author-led writing workshops with incarcerated teens at the Gardner Betts facility in

2009 and 2010. The authors themselves report that the workshops and visits are tremendously rewarding, with many of them returning each year to work with the teens at Gardner Betts.

MAIN FOCUS

Issues, Controversies, Problems

In 2002 the Gardner Betts Juvenile Justice Center had no library to speak of at either its short-term Detention facility, or its long-term Leadership Academy. Youth at the facilities spent their time in school, in therapy, in group, in gym, and writing in their journals—but spent very little time reading, unless they were fortunate enough to have parents who sent them reading materials. At Detention, the room designated as the library was simply a store room full of boxes of donated materials of little interest to reluctant readers, containing outdated information or topics irrelevant to teenagers. The Austin Independent School District was also unable to provide library services to the facility. When Austin Public Library staff member, Devo Carpenter, discovered that these teens had no access to leisure reading materials, she approached the library's Youth Services Division to see if there was any way the library could help. While the library had no monetary resources available for the partnership at the time, it had an abundance of books which had been weeded from the collection and were destined for the library book sale, and a dedicated staff who were passionate about engaging with at-risk readers. Initially, the Gardner Betts facility was reluctant to allow outsiders access to their facility, but Carpenter was determined, and APL was ultimately granted permission to provide library services to the short-term Detention facility, though they were not permitted to provide the same services to the long-term residential facility until 2007.

Beginnings

Although the Second Chance Books Project officially began in 2002, it started slowly, and took several years of fact-finding, research, development, partnership building, grantwriting, and advocacy, before it became a fully functioning program. Once Carpenter gained permission from the library to select books for Gardner Betts from the library's weeded materials, she recruited other youth services staff to help go through these materials and begin building a collection for Gardner Betts. The fledgling group sought out and received a small grant from the Tocker Foundation to launch the program in 2003. Carpenter also partnered with the AISD Reading Teacher at the facility to get the library into shape by removing the boxes from the library room and installing shelving for the library at Detention. In the early days, the Second Chance Books team was a small group of library staff members who visited the center twice a month during the Reading Teacher's Friday class period in the new library. Team members served the facility on a rotating basis to lessen the burden to their already packed schedules. For each visit, a team member brought more books for the library, promoted books and provided Reader's Advisory services, encouraged the residents to read, and talked to them about visiting the library upon release.

Over the next few years, the team enlarged the library at Detention through donations from publishers, collection development grants, and more weeded items from the library's collection. There were many challenges in the early years as the team worked to communicate the importance of reading and caring for the books in the library to the youth at Detention. There were several incidents where residents destroyed the covers of materials by tagging them or tearing them off, but on the whole, the information between the covers stayed intact, which gave the team hope that the residents valued the ideas inside the books, and were benefitting from the program. The team applied for more grants and awards to improve the collection and pay for special presenters to visit the facility, and from 2005 to 2007, they received several grants and awards, including statewide attention with the 2006 Texas Library Association Award for Project of the Year. The team's partnership with the AISD Reading Teacher remained strong, with the teacher advocating for library funding from AISD. While AISD had previously provided funding for classroom book sets and materials, the teacher was able to successfully lobby for a small book budget, which she used to purchase materials for the newly created library.

The team was still determined to provide services to the long-term facility, and through sustained advocacy for the program and success from their work at Detention under their belt, they were invited to provide library services for the residents at Leadership. The James Patterson Pageturner Award enabled the partnership to expand into a second satellite library at Leadership in 2007. In addition to this second library, the team began the Rolling Bookclub at Leadership, which rotated through each of the long-term residential units every few months. The administrator at the long-term facility was very impressed with the program, noting that the number of physical altercations among residents had decreased since the programs' inception, and gave the team a great deal of support and a free hand when developing the collection.

During this time, the team created a web site to promote the program, and began writing a strategic plan for the partnership. With the growth of the program, and the loss of several of the founding team members, keeping up with both the administrative duties of the partnership as well as providing programming was becoming problematic. The team firmly believed that the program needed a coordinator to take over the administrative tasks of the partnership, and serve as a liaison between all the partners, and consistently advocated for the creation of this position.

By applying for grants and awards, the team sought to increase the prominence of the program, and highlight the work being done through the partnership. A 2008 Library Journal Mover and Shaker Award for Carpenter's work with at-risk youth, along with a Texas Humanities Award, dramatically increased interest in the program, and that same year, APL began financially supporting the program through a $2000 yearly budget for books and materials. The library also began looking for a librarian to coordinate the youth outreach programs for the library. For the partnership, these were major milestones, providing much-needed legitimacy and support for the partnership between APL and GBJJC.

Evolution

With the 2009 hiring of the Youth Program Librarian to oversee the program, and a number of challenges faced by the Gardner Betts facility during that year, there were many changes in store for the Second Chance Books Program. The transition of administration of the program from the team to the new program coordinator was convoluted, as the program had grown very complex, yet lacked unity. Aside from the administrative tasks, a number of contact persons needed to be introduced to the new coordinator and those relationships needed to be strengthened.

By the summer of 2009, the coordinator had identified several problem areas with the existing service model, and a strategic planning session in summer 2009 fleshed out these challenges and offered solutions. One of the biggest problems was the logistics of scheduling unit visits at Leadership. When the program expanded to include Leadership in 2007, the team did what they had always done at Detention—divided the visits amongst themselves in a rotation. However, since they were not offering their programs during a teacher's class period, as they had in Detention, the complexity of scheduling at Leadership meant that there was never a single point of contact that the program could rely on for scheduling. Because so many staff persons were involved in the process, any break in the communication chain might cause a cancelled program, resulting in wasted staff time and weakened relations between library and correctional center staff, which hastened librarian burnout.

The lack of any formalized training for new team members also contributed to apprehension of newer team members, as they learned to navigate the correctional system environment. Although new librarians were mentored by existing team members, and most team members contributed to a private blog chronicling the program's history, there was no way for new team members to learn about how best to serve a particular unit, and no way to evaluate the service to any particular unit. There were also no guidelines on commonly encountered problems and solutions to help new team members prepare for and cope with the challenges of service.

The rotation schedule for service was also problematic. Since librarians were only at the center once every few months, they weren't there frequently enough to form positive relationships with either staff or residents, which made a challenging programming environment even more so. The ever-changing librarians also meant that none of the correctional center staff who worked with the residents got to know any of the librarians, and were therefore less apt to support the librarian visits with the residents. This played out through repeated book clubs, where staff hadn't encouraged the residents in their unit to read the book, so none of the residents had; visits where programs were abruptly cut short due to some previously unmentioned scheduling conflict; and even a few visits where isolated correctional staff were openly disruptive or dismissive of the program.

Statistic collection had also suffered from a lack of attention and regularity. The team wanted to begin collecting more statistics on circulation than they had previously, but had no mechanism in place to do so. Since residents most frequently used the library on the days when no library staff members were present, there had never been any checkout system in place at either facility. As a secure facility, a checkout had seemed unnecessary to prevent item theft, when an item could easily be tracked down by visiting each of the units and checking the bookshelves. This meant that the library had no accurate record of what books were in the library, and circulation counts were simple estimates of how many materials it was believed were read by residents each month.

At this same time, several of the long-term contacts and administrators at the center and AISD changed positions or left the facility altogether, necessitating the creation of new contacts, many of whom had a complete lack of awareness of the Second Chance partnership. Because so many administrators and staff members at the facility had changed, due to the high turnover among correctional facility staff, the program was in need of significant promotion within the partner agency, to help agency staff understand who the library was and what library programs were about.

Another problem with the new staffing changes was the adoption of partnership principles and policies, which had previously been verbal agreements. I began attempting to formalize the partnership and the policies about the library's role at the center, but ran into several obstacles in this process. The first misstep here was an attempt at formalizing the partnership between the library and the Gardner Betts facility. Several of the longstanding problems at the facility seemed to stem from correctional center staff not being trained in how to interact with the library, the librarians, or the library materials. Because new correctional center staff never received any training with regards to the library, it seemed plausible that such training would be beneficial to both librarians and correctional staff. It also seemed likely that such training would be useful in educating correctional staff about the library's collection development policy and reconsideration request procedures. These policies had been sent to the facility administrators as drafts, with explanations about the importance of such policies in a library setting, but with little of the negotiation necessary to craft policies for use in a correctional setting for juveniles.

In an effort to initiate some administrative changes with regards to staff training at the facility, I initiated contact with the upper administration of the facility. The Second Chance Program had had no previous contact with the upper administration of the facility, since the program had been supervised by the division heads of each of the two facilities. It quickly became apparent that neither the City Administration nor the Travis County Administration were willing to enter into a formalized agreement for the provision of services at the facility, as such an agreement could quickly become entangled in legal and financial hurdles that might jeopardize the success of the partnership.

In 2007, the Texas Youth Commission, the state juvenile corrections agency was embroiled in a series of scandals at several of its facilities, including accusations of sexual abuse, physical abuse, and squalid conditions, among other mistreatment of inmates (Ratcliffe, 2007). Due to these statewide crises in the juvenile correctional system, Travis County courts began sentencing more residents to Gardner Betts than it had in the past. Many of these residents were being detained for more serious legal infractions than had been traditionally accepted at Gardner Betts. The facility had not been designed to detain more violent offenders, but was being asked to house them with other juveniles with lesser offenses. This necessitated an increase in security at the facility, more restrictions during programs, and higher correctional staff turnover. This environment often left residents more sullen and less willing to participate in programs than ever before.

Funding was another concern for the partnership. Although the library had committed to a small budget each year for the program, it was not enough to provide new books for librarians to take

on every visit, or improve some of the neediest portions of the collections at both libraries—in particular nonfiction and Spanish-language materials. It was also not enough to expand the program in some desirable areas, such as technology and audiobooks for struggling readers. Funding was also critical to bringing special presenters to the facility.

SOLUTIONS AND RECOMMENDATIONS

Although the challenges facing the Second Chance Books Project were significant, each one represented an opportunity to strengthen the partnership, use resources and staff more efficiently, and improve the impact of programming on the residents at the facility. The diversity of the administrative roles involved in this partnership meant that the new program coordinator had to interview and train with each team member to gather all the reins of the program together. The program's founder took great pains to facilitate the transition of leadership to the new coordinator by introducing the coordinator to all the administrators and key staff repeatedly, and redirecting any queries to the new coordinator. She also did her best during this transition to keep a low profile administratively, while still providing programs at the facility. This facilitated the transition of contacts to the new coordinator, by reducing partner staff confusion about who was the primary point person for Second Chance. Once the administrative tasks were transitioned to the program coordinator, team members were freed from the responsibilities of grant writing, collection development, strategizing, marketing, giving them more time to do what they did best—encouraging at-risk youth to read.

A new service model did much to improve the communication challenges that team members were having with partner agency staff. In fall 2009, the team changed their model of service at the Leadership Academy from a rotation to a direct service model, with each team member signing up to serve one or two units at Leadership on a monthly basis. This model enabled each librarian to take responsibility for their unit, allowing them to form a bond with the staff of that unit, as well as the residents. This connection to the staff has significantly improved communication, with fewer cancelled programs, and increased staff support and engagement in library programs. This model actually increased the number of visits that each librarian was responsible for, up from four to 12 visits a year, but after being freed from the administrative responsibilities of the program, team members agreed that once-a-month visits were preferable. In the nearly two years since this model was adopted, we have experienced much greater team member satisfaction with the partnership, and reports of greater impact on the youth that we serve.

While we have had some team member attrition after transitioning to the new service model, the majority of the team has remained steady, with three new team members joining in 2011. These new team members are currently undergoing careful training and mentoring to ensure their success at the facility. They each received training from the program coordinator, and the Gardner Betts volunteer coordinator. This training gives them a clearer picture of our partner, and our mission, and how to achieve individual success with their programs. The program coordinator also encourages team members to contribute their experiences to the Second Chance Books wiki. The wiki facilitates the finding of information on particular units or past programs, and also contains many resources for new team members as they are learning their way around the program, such as discussion guides for book clubs, worksheets for unit visits, and tips on working with particular units.

Circulation statistics are still collected unconventionally at the center, but the addition of a formalized volunteer internship for the program has enabled us to collect circulation statistics from the returns shelf at Leadership with enough

granularity to provide assistance in collection development efforts. Creating internships for Master's students in Information Studies has been a great way to provide these students with experience, while giving them a tangible way to improve the program. At Detention, a new AISD Reading Teacher is instrumental in supplying us with circulation collection through reading logs collected each week.

Two years, and many meetings later, the program coordinator is now a well-known face at the facility by the administrators and teacher partners at Gardner Betts. In the first six months, the program coordinator added her photo to the signature block of her emails, to ensure that her face was familiar to the administrators and staff she was interacting with. This was a simple step, but proved very effective in transitioning the point person identity to the new coordinator, and helped greatly with face recognition at the facility. The program coordinator also met repeatedly with key administrators and teachers, to discuss the program, any difficulties in implementing our programs, and ways that the library might help Gardner Betts or AISD further their own mission and goals. These conversations proved invaluable in cementing the position of the library in the minds of these administrators as a true partner, focused on not just our own agenda, but those of our partner agency as well. As an indicator of the level of trust and respect the administration has for the library,, we have been regularly asked to provide recommendations for purchases that would aid in the continuing education of correctional center staff. The center administrators have also offered to support the library by purchasing and installing fixtures and furniture to support library programming.

Although a formal partnership agreement initially seemed beneficial to the longevity and legitimacy of the program, it was clear that formalization had consequences that the administrators of both partners were not prepared to entertain. The matter of an official partnership agreement has been laid aside, and there are no plans to pursue it further. For this partnership, at least, it was better to keep things on a casual and unofficial level, from a legal standpoint. Collection policies in juvenile correctional facilities can be a tricky negotiation between the land mines of external perceptions, staff discomfort with materials, and the needs and rights of residents. It is for this reason that they must be developed jointly between librarians and correctional facility staff, and must be sensitive to the unique rehabilitation needs of the residents. As of this writing, the development of a collection policy and reconsideration committee were nearly complete at the Leadership Academy. A committee has been formed with staff from Gardner Betts, counselors, AISD teachers, and Library staff to finalize a collection development policy to guide our purchases for the facility. This same committee has also formed the basis of a reconsideration committee, and discussions are ongoing to address challenges to materials in the collection and aid the library in the development of the collection.

Time has resolved many of the challenges that Gardner Betts faced in 2009 due to the TYC scandal. The numbers of residents at both facilities has decreased significantly as TYC moved into conservatorship and modified its practices. Currently, the population and types of offenses seen at the facility are more in line with the traditional Gardner Betts Leadership Academy philosophy of treatment, therapy, and community engagement. This decrease in security threats has meant less stress and turnover in the correctional staff, which has resulted in improved library program participation and support.

Securing sufficient funding will likely always be a challenge for the partnership, but the program is currently on stable financial footing. A portion of our APL collection budget was lost during the financial crisis of 2009, but some of this funding was returned in 2010, and the team continues to advocate for its reinstatement and ultimate increase. The program has benefitted from several library-wide grants where our collection projects

were small write-in additions, which has enabled us to significantly improve our nonfiction and Spanish-language collections, and our strong relationship with AISD and Gardner Betts has resulted in significant partner expenditures on additional library materials.

The program has also taken advantage of the vibrant author community in Austin, and local authors come out to the facility regularly to work with the residents as part of the Writers' League of Texas's two grant-funded programs: Project INK and Project WISE. These visits, which are grant-funded, are tremendously popular at the facility. The program coordinator also made several new community contacts in 2009 and 2010 that enabled us to recruit authors visiting the community for other programs—the Austin Teen Book Festival, and the Texas Book Festival. Partners at each of these festivals worked with Second Chance to get nationally-renowned authors to visit the facility at no charge. Our strong ties to the teachers at AISD provided a financial windfall for the program, when the teachers received substantial collection development funding from both the Federal and local government, and spent the funds to improve both collections at Gardner Betts with the library's assistance.

Present

As of the spring of 2011, the program has stabilized and services have become more frequent and regularized, with each Leadership Academy unit being assigned a Unit Librarian from the Second Chance team. Unit Librarians provide monthly Reader's Advisory visits to their assigned unit, bringing new books to highlight at every visit, and also offer book clubs three to five times each year. Librarians also visit the Detention facility twice a month, helping residents there find books that will engage them during their shorter stay at the facility. The team is expanding, and membership has been opened to other divisions within the library, as well as to librarians in the community who are interested in working with at-risk youth, including some from local area schools. Both satellite library collections look better than they ever have, with thousands of brand new, high-interest titles lining the shelves. Authors regularly visit both halves of Gardner Betts as a result of other community partnerships with the Austin Teen Book Festival, and the Texas Book Festival, and we have several more visits planned for the upcoming year. We have some new branding projects in the works, including a display in the library where we can highlight new books, upcoming programs, and library services and locations to strengthen the connection between the residents and the library. We are also working on one of our long-term advocacy and prominence goals—to create a program blueprint, in book and web site format, for others wanting to learn more about how to provide library services to incarcerated youth.

The administration at Gardner Betts has become much more aware of the benefits of having regular library services at the facility, and has been promoting the library's efforts and results through their own channels. Results of a recent survey show 100 percent correctional staff support and approval of the library's programming, although they still disagree with us on some of our title selections—a problem we hope to resolve through the reconsideration committee process and the inclusion of library-specific training at upcoming staff-training days. Due to the advocacy of the teachers we work with, the administrators at AISD have also provided glowing feedback about the library's programs, in particular the success of our summer reading programs at Gardner Betts.

Audience

In the past two years, APL has tripled the number of small-group programs offered at the facility, with each librarian developing strong relationships with the residents on their unit. While incarcera-

tion will continue to be an extremely difficult time for the youth we work with, it is the rare student who we are unable to connect with over time. The consistency that the unit librarian program provides is key to the success of the program. By the time of their release, residents who may have been resistant or hostile to our encouragement to read initially, will become our strongest readers, providing book talks to their peers, and asking us for numerous book recommendations every week. When they know they are about to be released, residents often ask which branch we work at so they can come visit us and get more book recommendations. These relationships were much rarer when we were not consistently working with the same kids every month.

We currently collect circulation statistics each week, along with summer reading program logs, and surveys. In the past year, our circulation numbers have increased significantly, with each resident at Detention reading an average of two books a week, and each resident at Leadership reading upwards of ten books every month. Much of this increase in reading is due to the sustained Reader's Advisory experience, combined with a wealth of new, high-interest titles—funded in large part by the efforts of our community partners and generous funding support from programs like the Loan Star Libraries Grant. Over 85 percent of residents who reported not reading at all prior to incarceration say they are reading five or more books every month, and plan to continue to read after they are released. Over 90 percent of our residents tell us they were introduced to their favorite book through the program, and that they plan to continue to read once they are released. We also recently heard from Elizabeth Polk, Director of Library Services for AISD, that the AISD librarian at our local alternative high school can always tell which residents have come to her from Gardner Betts, because they always head straight for the library.

WHAT WORKED AND WHAT DIDN'T

Every partnership will have peaks and valleys, and the Second Chance Books Program has had plenty of both. What follows are some of the key takeaways from the experience.

Strategic planning has been tremendously helpful for this partnership. Because Second Chance Books is such a large-scale operation, involving so much staff time and coordination, and because there are so many parties involved, it was essential for the team to figure out what our core mission and vision were, as well as what challenges we were facing and how to address them. Taking time out to talk strategy with regards to future plans, as well as funding, has been immensely beneficial to the program.

Having a program coordinator is a luxury that not every program will be able to afford, but for this type of partnership it is indispensable. Without a program coordinator, library staff must spend large portions of their limited time doing administrative tasks, as well as replicating the work of others if there is no system in place for sharing resources. By having a coordinator in place, you ensure that your skilled employees spend as much time as possible doing the things they are best at. The unification of leadership also gives the administrator a bird's-eye view of the program, enabling them to anticipate problems for the partnership, eliminate inefficiencies, evaluate services, and plan for growth. It should be noted, however, that our program didn't start out as big as it is today—the initial program could easily be handled by staff in their spare time. But successful programs have a way of growing, and if your program gets big enough, there will be a time when it can't flourish without someone to administer it full time. The program coordinator is also extremely beneficial when forging lasting relationships with the partner agency. Having a single point person puts partners at ease and gives them the security of knowing who to go to if they have a question or problem. A program with many contacts can seem fragmented and disjointed, and may raise fears of being too labor-intensive to maintain from the partner's perspective.

Although developing policies in tandem with your partner agency at the very outset is a best practice, it was one that was impossible for our partnership, due to the lack of other service models that we could use to guide us in our earliest steps. Without knowing what our partnership might look like, or what services we might offer or problems we might encounter, there was no way for us to develop policies, and no way to initiate a conversation with our partner about what policies might be beneficial. It was not until several years into the partnership that we were able to identify problematic areas, and not until recently that we have made any headway with the creation of a shared set of partnership policies and expectations.

FUTURE RESEARCH DIRECTIONS

The future of the Second Chance Books Partnership is bright. With strong partner buy-in and support, we are able to successfully accomplish our goals of increasing literacy rates among the at-risk youth in our community. Residents who are barely able to finish a few chapters a month when they first arrive are devouring multiple books per month upon their departure. We hope to have our collection development policy revised and approved by summer 2011, and look forward to the continuing discussions of our reconsideration committee. We are working on an information sheet about library services that can be included in the Gardner Betts staff training manual, educating partner staff about the importance of the program, and how they can support it. We also hope to expand our partnership outside the Gardner Betts facility to some of the halfway houses around Austin, which will necessitate additional funding and partner development. Our long-term goals include implementation of a program modeled on Changing Lives Through Literature, a probation program where libraries host book discussion groups with Probation Officers, Judges, and the juveniles under their guidance in attendance, and a focus on personal betterment through literature. This type of program will require a solid network of community partners from the juvenile justice community throughout Austin, but we hope that the work we have done at Gardner Betts will provide a strong foundation and compelling reasons to support such a broad community partnership.

CONCLUSION

The Second Chance Books Program has grown significantly from its earliest days as a used book depository program. Today, we make thousands of new books available to incarcerated teens, and offer hundreds of programs every year, with library staff forging lasting relationships with reluctant readers at a point of crisis. Through diversification of our programming and unification of the administrative tasks of managing such a partnership, we have improved our award-winning program to a level of service that is truly outstanding. None of this success would have been possible without the strong support of our partner agency, and the dedication of library staff to serve incarcerated teens. By inviting the library into their facility, Gardner Betts has made a significant contribution to the well-being and success of at-risk youth in Austin.

REFERENCE

Ratcliffe, R. G. (2007, April 29). *TYC abuse claims poured in amid debate*. Retrieved from http://www.chron.com/disp/story.mpl/metropolitan/4758560.html

Chapter 11
A Rite of Passage:
New York Public Library Passages Academy

Lindsy D. Serrano
New York Public Library, USA

ABSTRACT

In New York City, over five thousand young adults are taken in to custody by the city's department of juvenile justice. (Fenster-Sparber, 2008). While in detention, they do not have easy access to books, and literacy is not always a priority. Although attempts have been made to incorporate library sites throughout New York City's juvenile correctional facilities, students there have limited access to educational materials. Research shows that a higher literacy rate in such facilities can play a vital role in an incarcerated teen's rehabilitation process. The New York Public Library (NYPL) saw an opportunity to reach students who might otherwise not be able to get access to information and build a long-lasting outreach program with Passages Academy, a multi-site correctional school run by New York City's Department of Education and the Department of Juvenile Justice. This case study describes New York Public Library's mission at Passages Academy, which started shortly after Passages was established in 1998 and continues to be a strong community partner today. The author, who also participated in the project, interviewed NYPL librarians and Passages Academy librarians and educators to gain a better understanding of their challenges.

INTRODUCTION

Libraries have always been centers for local community involvement, often able to reach communities that would otherwise not have access to information and educational resources. This chapter examines how young adult (YA) librarians from New York Public Library (NYPL) embarked on a mission starting with a few librarians in

1998, to provide outreach to New York City's most overlooked citizens: the incarcerated youth.

NYPL already has a well-established relationship with Riker's Island, New York City's jail for adult offenders. However, there are many other juvenile detention sites throughout New York City's five boroughs that are often overlooked. One of them is Passages Academy. Since 1998, YA librarians from NYPL arranged outreach

DOI: 10.4018/978-1-61350-387-4.ch011

programs for many of Passages' sites by giving gently used books to teachers who work in the detention centers. Some sites gathered enough books to make their own small libraries. During their site visits, NYPL librarians often provided an introduction to the library and a chance for the students to receive their own library cards. They also prepared book talks that highlighted the books already on site or brought in donated books for the teens to choose from and keep.

The outreach project was spearheaded mainly by the passion of NYPL's librarians and librarians and educators of Passages Academy. It was sometimes difficult to make time for regular visits to detention centers, even if they were in the local area, and the effort itself at times seemed discouraging as librarians were not always sure if they were really connecting with the students. However, weeks later, when they read the evaluations and heard how much the students enjoyed their presentations and appreciated receiving books from them, some of which they could keep for their own private collection, the project became much more meaningful for everyone involved.

This case study first focuses on the how the educational system works in the department of Juvenile Justice. Passages Academy is not a single school building in New York City but a collection of sites throughout the Bronx and Brooklyn and serves a student body which changes almost daily. A brief history of NYPL's outreach services for the city's incarcerated patrons is also provided, as well as information on how the library first started working with New York City's juvenile offenders. The focus will then shift to the most recent collaboration between NYPL and Passages, with a special emphasis placed on class visits and the challenges librarians and educators confronted when faced with underserved young students. While outreach programs started at Passages Academy in 1998, the focus of this case study will be on the experiences of YA librarians from 2006 to the present day.

BACKGROUND

NYPL has a long-standing tradition of service for incarcerated patrons. Its Prison Library program started in the mid 1970s with the help of state funding. It was coordinated through the office of special services and became an integral part of the library's outreach program. Today, there is a department established solely for the support of New York's incarcerated adults. This outreach is three-fold. First, there are regular visits to Riker's Island where the Correctional Services volunteers deliver books that have been donated for the inmates and run four mobile libraries throughout the Island. Second is the reference work. Each week the Correctional Services Department receives about 60 letters from inmates who are usually looking for information that they will need after their release. The demand for this information is so great that NYPL started a publication called "Connections," an annual guide for recently released inmates that can be downloaded from NYPL's website for free. Most library branches also have a printed copy available at the reference desk. The third and final component are the various programs, one of which is the recently implemented "Daddy and Me" program at Riker's Island. There, fathers take literacy classes and then record themselves reading popular children's books. The recordings are then sent to their children.

Since the mid 1970s, outreach services between NYPL and Riker's Island flourished. Juvenile detention centers did not receive the same kind of attention. Although library outreach for these sites started around the same time as outreach for adult inmates at Riker's Island, it was conducted in a less official way. In the mid 1970s, Ma'lis Wendt, who was a YA Spanish specialist for NYPL, started paying visits to schools and community centers in the South Bronx. One of these visits was the Spofford Detention Center, which she visited several times, each time taking 16mm films and a projector to the center to show educational and recreational films from the NYPL collection.

Such initiatives were extremely popular and well received, but the efforts of one person could only go so far. Karlan Sick, NYPL's former director of YA services in the Bronx, was among the first to see the need for more outreach and took action immediately thereafter: "I began working in the Bronx in 1983 and realized that outreach to high schools was needed. Knowing the juvenile detention centers in the Bronx had high schools called Passages, I tried to set up visits but learned that the adult prison outreach staff also visited Passages. Several years later, I learned by accident that their staff had been cut and that they no longer reached the incarcerated teens. I was able to add the two sites to my schedule." This marked the beginning of a regular visiting schedule between NYPL and juvenile detention centers and the start of using book talks and library information as part of the outreach.

In January of 1998, New York City's Board of Education, in partnership with the Department of Juvenile Justice, began to operate Passages Academy, a full-time education program that would give credits to juvenile offenders and try to minimize the interruption to the students' education while they were incarcerated. Today there are four sites in different detention centers; where students go depends on whether they are in a secure or non-secure facility. Passages Academy tries to stay close to a high school curriculum but has a special education program as many of the students have low-level reading and math skills. In the beginning, libraries were not part of Passages' offerings. In her article "New York City's Most Troubled Youth: Getting Caught Reading at Passages Academy Libraries," (Fenster-Sparber 2008) Passages school librarian Jessica Fenster-Sparber notes, "When it opened in 1998, Passages Academy was lucky to have a visionary teacher in Rebecca Howlett. Hired to teach social studies, Howlett was shocked and saddened to find that no libraries were available to students who were locked inside a building for twenty-four hours a day, seven days a week…Each individual dorm

area had books, but they were, more often than not, one of three titles: GED Prep, The New Testament, or The Cross and the Switchblade. There were some other random books around like The Von Trapp Family Singers." Howlett worked hard to build the first library at the facility in 2003 and since then, five other libraries have formed in other sites to create a small network of libraries that "satiate the students' hunger for reading materials, and to support students' and the faculty's information needs." (Fenster-Sparber 2008)

Today, Passages has two certified school media specialists, two literacy teachers, a library coordinator, a library assistant, and an education professional. Its libraries work diligently to promote literacy and social responsibility to the students using their services. They also want to make sure that students have a great support system after detention. While some will have to go to a more secure facility for the remainder of their sentence, many are released and sent back to their old neighborhoods, friends, and sometimes their old habits. This was one of the main reasons why librarians at Passages reached out to the YA librarians at NYPL, asking them to talk to students about their options and to make them more aware that libraries are available to them on the outside just as they were on the inside. It was also important to convey the message that continuing their education after detention was easier than they thought.

CASE STUDY

Since the founding of Passages in 1998, many NYPL librarians have included its schools in their outreach programs. The program is very similar to what one would expect at mainstream high schools, but there are significant challenges that can make this kind of outreach difficult for both librarians and teachers. Each day, students from ten facilities, similar to group homes, attend Summit, the largest non-secure detention site at

Passages. Summit is also home to a freestanding library with a computer lab and one of Passages' only circulating collections. This is very helpful for the students who attend Summit because their literacy needs are significant. According to Anja Kennedy, school librarian at Summit, "Most of [the] students are reading below grade level. They need and want high-interest books and [require] access to them. Circulation is challenging because it requires a lot of communication, but it is worth the extra time." Low reading levels are a great challenge for librarians and teachers at Passages. Sydney Blair, Passages' founder and first principal, notes some staggering statistics: "90 percent of the students are two years or more behind in their school grade level; 95 percent are reading two or more years below grade level; and 45 percent are reading below the fourth-grade level."

In an environment like this, Kennedy's challenges extend past readers' advisory. She rarely knows which students will be in her library and cannot always predict what their day-to-day needs are. According to Kennedy, "The transitional nature of the school is one of the biggest challenges in promoting programs. Because we get new students every day, and students are always in and out of court, medical visits, parole officer interviews, etc., it is nearly impossible to prepare all of the students at the same time." Before getting involved, librarians at NYPL recognized that they could be a valuable support system to librarians like Kennedy, who were already accomplishing a great deal on their own. Therefore, the main goal for NYPL's outreach program with Passages was to supplement rather than replace the existing collection of books, assist with literacy programming at various sites, provide book discussions and other activities to further stimulate dialog, and promote NYPL's resources that the students could use after their release from the detention center.

During outreach visits, NYPL librarians gave books to the classroom libraries, or if allowed, to the students directly to take back to their group homes. Many of the students initially didn't want to take books or complained that there was nothing in the collection they would want to read. In the end, however, they would usually settle on something. The pool of books that they could choose from was very limited, and this remained a challenge for everyone involved. Sometimes they were donations from publishing companies or advanced readers copies; other times they were books that have been weeded out from the YA collections in NYPL's own branches. Many of the students would request books with subject matters like true crime that were not allowed at the facility. For example, books by publishers like Triple Crown, which produces extremely popular street novels often accused of glorifying criminal activities, were not permitted. NYPL librarians tried to find titles with more urban themes but would also bring books with a broad range of topics, including books about sports and magic, series like Harry Potter and Bluford High, and comic books. According to Jessica Fenster-Sparber, also a librarian at Passages, there was always "the issue of finding relevant, accessible, appropriate texts for the students...but [Passages] benefited tremendously from the partnership with NYPL."

As important as it was to select the right materials, it was equally important to get the students excited about reading. This is why book talks became an integral part of NYPL's outreach programs early on. Jenny Baum, one of the first librarians to take frequent trips to various Passages sites, said that the book-talking portions of her visits (usually once a month over the course of several years) were very similar to the ones she would normally do at mainstream schools throughout the city. There were, of course, some notable challenges: "The main difference was that library materials could only be photocopied by the resident librarian upon request, so we tried to bring discarded paperbacks that [students] could bring back to their rooms. Having multiple copies of a book was always helpful. The class size was much smaller than most school classrooms. The audience tended to be respectful and, like any audience, responded best to book talks that were delivered with enthusiasm and a good story." Sick, also included successful book talks in her own presentations, noting: "Students often looked skeptical when I first arrived, but as soon as I started book talking, they were interested. One group of boys immediately selected the books they wanted to read, sat down and began reading quietly. I assumed that this was the practice at the end of a lesson, but the teacher said silent individual reading was not tried before. It was wonderful to see the teens caught up in the books."

As NYPL librarians became more comfortable with their visits, the students at Passages became more open and engaging during the process. They were eager for more interaction and seemed to enjoy talking about the books that were brought in. Baum says, "Students responded best to the stories in the book talks. They wanted to have a conversation about the characters I was discussing and talk about similar books they'd read, or about totally different books they'd enjoyed. Some students would be hesitant to select a book; some would ask if they could have two; most would take one. Occasionally, students would complain that I didn't bring some other genre of book, but they usually found something that they were at least somewhat interested in." Chris Shoemaker adds to this: "I got the best response from book talks and giveaways, since the students were free to choose from many different books and explore the authors and the stories that they were most interested in."

Book talks and independent readings are great ways to get students interested in what the library has to offer, but could be challenging as well. NYPL librarians also wanted to give students a chance to learn how the library works and show them that their opinions mattered to the library staff. Chris Shoemaker, who had worked with Passages as a YA librarian and then as an NYPL administrator, went beyond the book talks and together with several other colleagues (including the author of this chapter) quickly realized

that traditional library instruction would not be as effective at Passages. Shoemaker says, "It was impossible to do traditional library instruction - the booktalk choices were limited, there was no internet for database instruction, and the students were unable to immediately attend any of the afterschool programs I could discuss." Shoemaker saw that one of the main hurdles he faced reaching the students is that they did not realize the extent of what the library had to offer. Shoemaker says, "While some students could identify the library branch that was nearest to their house, most indicated they were not checking out books or speaking to a librarian for help. They were unaware of the variety of books that could be found in the library's collections, and it was a positive experience to see how many of them would take a book and flip through it, even after stating they were not readers and not interested in books or libraries." After this discovery, many YA librarians started to bring a large amount of books for teens to flip through and discuss, showing a wide range of materials that the library has to offer. Shoemaker was on YALSA's Quick Picks committee, and was able to bring in that year's nominees for the students' inspection. This was a great way to let the students feel a sense of ownership in the library's collection and ordering procedures.

Librarians often grapple with challenges when facing even the regular classrooms. Students could be bored, unruly, or completely uninterested in what they are presenting. This author has been known to take her glasses off before a presentation, so she can't see anyone's face while nervous. Once a librarian starts to believe in his or her mission, the fear starts to fade and the enthusiasm spreads throughout the class. However, sometimes even having a strong belief in the work couldn't solve the challenges at Passages. Sick explains one of them: "The biggest challenge was dealing with the security system. The Department of Juvenile Justice and the Board of Education both ran Passages and did not always agree about the importance of a visit. Once I was kept waiting in an outer office because the head of the facility and the principal had had an argument about a completely unrelated matter...It was also difficult to carry enough books to offer three groups of students a choice of materials. Coming by subway with a short walk afterward was also not easy."

Another challenge was the simple act of getting into the facility. If librarians at Passages knew an NYPL librarian was paying them a visit, the guards in the facility were not always informed or ready for their arrival. This could cut into the time they had allowed for such a visit. In some detention centers, outside librarians needed to go through metal detectors and all of the materials they brought with them needed to be scanned. There were times when a delay in the program could not be helped, such as, for example, if there was a breach of security or a change in class schedules. NYPL librarians often came well in advance in case they needed to go through a checkpoint or security had to confirm their program with the teacher. Sometimes multiple forms of identification were required, both work and personal IDs. The best way to avoid unpleasant surprises was to ask a Passages teacher or librarian about security before even scheduling a visit.

Travel was also a challenge. Sometimes NYPL librarians would run out of giveaway books because they could only carry so much to the facility at a time. One way to handle this was to gather several boxes of donations and discarded books every couple of months and mail them directly to Passages. That way, outside librarians always had books waiting for them "on the inside," which then allowed them to make selections from the stored boxes each time they visited Passages. The constant changing of the student body was also a problem. Baum notes: "The students came from all parts of the city and were often changing locations (i.e. going to court, going upstate, going to a different facility, etc.) at a moment's notice. This made it difficult [for NYPL librarians] to focus [on their mission] and to ensure that the book they

selected would be able to go with [the students]." Because students at Passages are always waiting for their court dates, they may be sent home or upstate for the rest of their sentence. One never knows when a new group of students is arriving or if those currently there may be leaving the next day, which means there is no guarantee that the students will always be able to keep the books they've received.

The same is true for library cards, which can be even more of a challenge. As Shoemaker observes, "Library card sign ups are tricky, since the cards must be held by staff at the academy or by parents until the students are released." When the author of this article started giving out library cards, she would have the students fill out a form and then give them an actual card. When she got back to the branch each time, she would activate the cards and erase any fines they had on previous cards as part of NYPL's fine amnesty program. However, in many sites, students were not allowed to carry cards in their pockets in fear that they would be used as a weapon. So the cards often had to be given to the security guards who would be asked to deliver them the students, but this was not guaranteed. So in lieu of cards, Fresh Start Slips were used as an alternative. These were forms that students could bring into an NYPL branch after their release to receive a new library card and to get their fines erased. Most students would be able to take the paper with them after the outreach program. If not, the Fresh Start forms would be given to the teachers or librarians at Passages and they would distribute them closer to the students' release. This was one of many examples of how NYPL creatively overcame some of the obstacles that stood in the way of their mission.

The main goal of these visits was to expose the students to what the library had to offer, including its vast print collections, online resources, and various programs, and to make sure that the students understood that the library would be there for them in a number of ways later in life. Shoemaker says, "Working with young adults at

Passages was very interesting, since part of doing outreach is a sell to bring youth into the library. When students are physically unable to travel to the library, it requires you to bring materials that will make a lasting impression with readers and connect them with the long-range programming activities. There are also restrictions on the types of materials you can bring, the resources you have available, and the amounts of access students have to digital resources." To help promote the library's resources, NYPL librarians often brought in pamphlets with book suggestions, played games like Pictionary, and gave book talks to illustrate what readers' advisory looked like in the regular public library branches. The idea was to give the students a glimpse of what the libraries in their own neighborhoods looked like.

SOLUTIONS AND RECOMMENDATIONS

The partnership between NYPL and Passages Academy was a rewarding experience for everyone involved. At this time, the visitation program has stopped, mainly due to the lack of staff members able to make the visit to Passages. But there is hope to reboot the program and build an even stronger, long-term relationship. The outreach program at Passages was very popular, but it left much to be desired. It was completely up to the YA librarians of the NYPL to set it up from the start. If they hadn't been able to set aside time for the monthly visits and fully commit to engaging with the students while overcoming many obstacles, the program would never have taken place What is needed next is for a dedicated professional or a group of professionals to make such a program more official and to advocate for more funding that can help support its unfinished mission. Fenster-Sparber proposes that an expert NYPL librarian be trained to become a permanent and dedicated partner with Passages and other schools serving detained youth, much like NYPL already provides

services to incarcerated adults in New York. She adds, "Many students are unaware of the role the public library can play in their lives when they leave detention, and this is an untapped resource for a desperately underserved population."

A challenge that many of the YA librarians faced was working with both the department of juvenile justice (DJJ) and the Department of Education (DOE) at the same time. Both groups are very large institutions with a different mission when serving the students at Passages. Safety is a key issue when it comes to serving NYC's detained youth and there are many rules and regulations that librarians face when visiting Passages that they do not usually face when visiting community schools. If there was staff designated at NYPL solely for outreach to juvenile detention centers, it may be easier to navigate the politics between these two institutions. It could be possible that library staff could serve as a mediator between the DJJ and DOE and together they could develop a plan for making it easier to facilitate programs in detention centers. Until then, librarians could collaborate on a centralized checklist to be used to provide information on what to expect when visiting a detention center so that there would be no surprises once they arrive there. Librarians should also go through a training session before they start visiting the centers so that they know what security procedures they might face depending on the site that they visit. As always, forming a strong connection with the educators and the detention centers is crucial as they will be the librarians' most powerful ally in this partnership.

A lack of reading material has always been a major challenge for both the YA librarians and the Passages Staff. Recently, NYPL started an educator library card program as a way to help teachers bring more books into the classroom. Shoemaker suggests the following: "I would love to see Passages take advantage of the NYPL educator cards, where teachers are able to deliver a larger range of materials to their students, and where students have the opportunity to connect one-on-one or in smaller groups as they complete their time at the academy." These new library cards would allow the students to have more access to NYPL's collection while they are still in detention and it would also allow teachers at Passages to temporarily supplement their own classroom libraries.

Collaboration between public libraries and juvenile detention centers has been the focus of many recent articles and publications (YALS: Young Adult Library Services and VOYA is a good example) because more and more librarians are looking to juvenile detention centers as places for positive outreach services. These partnerships can go beyond traditional outreach models. Librarians could, for example, set up technology training and book clubs at detention centers or host author visits and read-ins. The possibilities are endless. In return, librarians get a valuable perspective from patrons that they might not get in the branches. After those visits to Passages, this librarian was much more knowledgeable about street lit and the needs of readers who live in the neighborhood that she served.

CONCLUSION

It is regrettable that juvenile detention centers are often forgotten when it comes to library outreach. Students in these sites greatly need the support from their community, and the library is an important part of the process. While it takes a great deal of commitment and effort to establish an effective relationship with juvenile detention centers, the outcome is overwhelmingly positive. It is often easy to forget—even for those who work in libraries—that many people do not know about the opportunities that the library offers. As this case study shows, the partnership with Passages gave NYPL librarians a chance to make an impact outside of the library by reaching out to students who otherwise would never have set foot inside a library. It was because of all their efforts that students were left knowing that there was a place for them to pursue their own interests and support their education after detention.

Section 4

Public libraries and schools are common partners, though a good relationship must first be established, and then a myriad of collaborations and partnerships are possible, from small and specific, to larger and ongoing.

Chapter 12
Bridging the Divide

Hillary Dodge
Clearview Library District, USA

Erica Rose
Clearview Library District, USA

ABSTRACT

The purpose of this chapter is to provide an example of a productive working relationship between a public library and a public school district. For years the Clearview Library District (CLD) struggled with an estranged relationship with the Weld Re-4 School District. Various contributing factors made it difficult for staff to proactively connect with educators and school administration. In 2008, CLD made a commitment to reassessing its role in the community and began exploring ways to better serve more members of the community. CLD selected schools as a priority because they presented a tremendous opportunity to touch a large percentage of the population. This new relationship became a major focus for the Youth Services and Outreach Departments of the Clearview Library District, who worked together to develop a plan to bridge the divide.

INTRODUCTION

As the role of public libraries continues to evolve, it has become increasingly important that libraries insert themselves into communities as necessary partners. To accomplish this goal, CLD opted to pursue a strong partnership with the Weld Re-4 School District. Both districts share the same boundaries and are centrally located within the town of Windsor, Colorado, a bedroom community of roughly twenty thousand citizens. CLD is a dual-branch library district consisting of a "brick and mortar" main branch and a new mobile branch. The Weld Re-4 School District is comprised of

five elementary schools, two middle schools, and one high school.

The library-school partnership was optimal because of the similarity between both entities. "The educational focus as a shared role/goal of school and public libraries is one of the most critical factors in rationalizing the need for cooperation and collaboration between the two" (Fitzgibbons, 2001, 4). When library service takes place only within library walls, it is only possible to reach those who come through the library doors. Taking library services into the schools allowed CLD to have direct access to every student, parent, and educator in the district, thus strengthening the

DOI: 10.4018/978-1-61350-387-4.ch012

community's educational network while simultaneously conducting a large-scale promotion of CLD services.

As CLD expanded its outreach services via a new bookmobile (the Clearview Library District Mobile Branch), it also sought other avenues of connection within its community. Building a relationship with the School District was a clear way of connecting with a large portion of the community and was therefore selected as a major focus of outreach. Several major players contributed to the fostering of this successful relationship: Karen Trusler, Weld Re-4 Superintendent; Jen Maley, Weld Re-4 Information Literacy Coordinator; Erica Rose, CLD Head of Outreach Services; Hillary Dodge, CLD Head of Youth Services; and the CLD and Weld Re-4 administrations. Forging strong relationships among these individuals resulted in a shared sense of purpose and responsibility across departments and organizations.

The following case study will outline the steps taken by the Clearview Library District in the creation of this partnership. It will discuss the history of collaboration between the Districts, the creative process of molding the relationship, and address the challenges and successes of making it beneficial for both parties.

BACKGROUND

A survey of the current literature revealed a number of different approaches to the school/public library relationship. Many articles were repetitious in that they described similar ventures and practices. A few incorporated new thoughts or were particularly well written. Interestingly enough, there appeared to be an equal distribution of articles geared towards educators as well as librarians. Below, a few of the stronger articles are listed as examples.

By far, articles on best practices and collaborative programming were most prolific. Margaux

DelGuidice's article, "Are you Overlooking a Valuable Resource?," is a good example of a piece aimed at educators. Her approach on best practices focuses on creating lines of reciprocal communication. Likewise, Sara Ryan, shares tried and true practices from the public library's perspective in her article, "Be Nice to the Secretary." Ryan addresses cross-promotion, bringing schools to the library, and using outreach as a tool to reach schools outside library walls. Two articles of note that address successful program collaborations are "School and Public Librarians Working Together" by Julie Scordato and "Hand in Hand" compiled by Jana Fine. Scordato's article, a column in Library Media Connection, describes a joint teaching venture involving the public librarian and online research classes. Fine's article, geared towards public librarians, is a compiled list of mini-stories – each one describing a fruitful project or program.

Articles concerning best practices and programming were followed closely by articles with a historic or theoretical perspective. Shirley Fitzgibbons explores the changing climate in education alongside movements within the professional library world. Her article, "School and Public Library Relationships," emphasizes the rationale behind bridging the divide between these two entities and provides an impetus for understanding and overcoming various barriers and challenges. Fitzgibbons also provides several key recommendations for moving forward. Another great article detailing from a historical perspective, the relationship between the school and public library, is Edwin Clay's "The Partnership Between Public Libraries and Public Education." Aimed at demonstrating the commonalities between the two institutions, Clay draws from primary sources to make connections between the past, the present, and the future.

Rarer was the piece that sought to educate teachers and librarians about the differences between public library and school cultures. Mostly, this sort of information was incorporated into the larger article about theory, history, programs, or practices. Also scarce throughout the literature were stories of the whole process – from point A to points B and beyond. Individual stories about specific projects were presented in abundance; however, complete case studies focusing on the evolution of a school and public library's relationship were not common.

Although this case study was written from the perspective of a public library, every attempt was made to speak to the cultural and organizational differences between the institutions and elaborate on how those differences affected the growing relationship. Every library's approach will, necessarily, be different. Resources, staff, and various networks will vary. What the Clearview Library District attempted in documenting their case, was to piece the whole process together – best practices, collaborative programs and projects, cultural discoveries and differences, and need-based design and evaluation.

THE CASE STUDY

The First Step: Creating a New Partnership

This inspiration for this project stems from several motivating factors. First, relatively new to their departments, both the Head of Outreach Services and the Head of Youth Services became keenly aware of a constant stream of negative dialogue flowing between CLD and the School District. They noted repeated observations and feedback from staff and educators regarding the adverse feelings existing between the two districts. This negativity seemed to exist predominantly at the educator/librarian level. As a result, the lack of educators utilizing CLD services was painfully evident. This was a great concern as both Department Heads understood that educators are one of the most powerful influences on a tremendous portion of the community-students and parents.

Further inspiration for the project revolved around the fact that CLD space and manpower was limited. In-house programming numbers were at a maximum. Staff and space was being utilized at full capacity despite the recent expansion. Therefore, it became necessary to begin thinking about ways that CLD could impact more patrons outside of library walls.

Relationships between schools and libraries are notoriously difficult to create and maintain. A variety of factors – staff, time, physical resources, and a willingness to think outside the box – contribute to the successful school/library relationship. The CLD had struggled for many years to build and sustain such a relationship with the Weld Re-4 School District. Until recently, the right factors were not in balance and attempt after attempt to connect still had not resulted in a sustainable program.

Partnerships between the districts have been sporadic at best over the past thirty years. The CLD, then still an entity of the town of Windsor, first partnered with the Weld Re-4 School District in 1981 when the district added a new school, Skyview Elementary. Upon opening, Skyview had yet to build its school library collection; CLD stepped-in and shared books with the fledgling school library. In 1988, the School District returned the favor by acting as a major supporter of the Library's campaign for special districthood, which was ultimately established using the same boundaries as the school district. The Districts also partnered on a few smaller-scale projects, such as *TV Turn Off Week*, off and on throughout the following years. Additional attempts were made to bring together the major players via monthly meetings between the public librarians and the school media specialists but such an arrangement was never maintained for more than a few months at a time.

Despite building a strong foundation of support for each other, the Districts were unable to maintain a consistent, viable relationship. While some previous collaborations had gone smoothly, others had not. Obtaining material from the public library was a challenge for educators who generally needed items longer than normal loan periods allowed. The administrations of the Districts were not communicating on a regular basis about wants and needs, resulting in a large amount of misinformation and misunderstandings. Educators would check out items that would get lost "in the system." Children thought library cards cost five or more dollars to obtain. Resource sharing and program collaboration were non-existent. All this changed when CLD made the decision to make the school/library relationship a priority. While the change certainly did not occur overnight, once the focus was narrowed, small steps created a momentum that led to major progress.

In 2008, a change in staffing and a massive expansion and renovation project at CLD provided the right leverage for a big change. Furthermore, Library administration began to focus on outreach as a way to expand library services. Paradigms of library service were changing; no longer was the library a repository of books and no longer was the librarian the gatekeeper. In keeping with the times, CLD opted to transform itself into an information utility for its community. To achieve this goal, it was important to assess the current environment, both within the library and without.

As previously stated, the boundaries of the Clearview Library District are identical to the boundaries of the School District and encompass not only the town of Windsor but also parts of several surrounding towns as well. It was decided that both the School District and CLD would greatly benefit from a strengthened relationship. Reaching out to the Schools would bring in more patrons while simultaneously helping CLD become a more vital resource within its community. By extending its resources and programming to the schools, CLD was able to help support and enhance the school's curriculum and the educational experience of the students.

Moving forward to create this new partnership meant letting go of the struggles of the past and starting with a clean slate. Two ideas were implemented immediately - bringing CLD to the Schools and bringing the Schools to the CLD. With limited time and staff being the major barrier to most school/public library collaborations, these two options seemed like relatively easy and viable ways to start creating connections.

First, CLD opted to create a presence at the schools by attending various events at the schools, including literacy nights, back to school nights, the annual Kidz Expo, parent-teacher conferences, and other special school events. These events were ideal for a library presence and allowed CLD to promote its services to the entirety of the School District population. The logistics were simple, requiring only the set-up of a table or booth of CLD information and giveaways. The tables were staffed by librarians and paraprofessionals for, at most, two hours at a time. As these school events were spread throughout the school year, there was no major time commitment required from library staff. Initially, CLD found out about these events via invites from teachers or school media specialists. Once these events were on CLD's radar, a few phone calls and a keen eye on the School District website during the year kept CLD staff on top of all special School events. Taking a more active role in event participation was much appreciated by the schools' various administrations.

Second, CLD offered its main facility to the Schools by sending invitations for public library field trips. This was certainly easier said than done for some schools – those that were located within walking distance to the main facility jumped at the opportunity to visit, while the schools father away took longer to express an interest in visiting. School field trips required a little preparation in advance, including ensuring that the circulation desk was well staffed to handle requests and checkouts and planning for activities that would work well for the various age groups visiting. Discovering the best way to handle school visits at CLD took a little trial and error but it was found that the best visits lasted roughly one hour and accommodated a group of no more than thirty children with at least two to four engaged teachers or chaperones. A typical school visit would consist of a story time (yes, even for elementary school children, though it requires careful book selection), a craft, and a tour.

These two efforts - taking the CLD to the Schools and bringing the Schools to the CLD - proved to be immensely successful. Not only did they allow for the children to learn about the library, but they also allowed for the CLD staff to meet the educators. Additionally, these efforts allowed CLD to promote its summer reading program, which keeps children reading all year long. Gaining the interest and respect of the educators - teachers, school media specialists, and administrators alike – helped further the CLD's goal of becoming an information utility within the community.

In early 2010, CLD tried a new way of getting into the Schools via a lunchtime book club at the Windsor High School. Connecting with the school media specialist, CLD advertised the potential group within its own facility and in the School via fliers and announcements. The first meeting was an unexpected success with sixteen teens attending. To make the club work within the structure of the school day, the school media specialist proposed that the club become an official school group, led by the students and advised by the specialist. The group decided to meet every other Friday during the lunch hour. They would begin with discussions about what they were reading and end with a social activity or game. CLD supplied the books via inter-library loan and prepared for the discussions and activities. In exchange for participating in the club, students' library fines were forgiven.

A major motivation for creating the book club within the High School was to create a program that complemented the structure and schedule of students and teachers. It also allowed CLD to get an insiders' view of the School District environment. This information was highly useful in creating a model of service that would appeal to the educators for the future of this partnership.

The Second Step: Molding the Partnership

Understanding the environment in which educators work is paramount when creating a plan for partnership between the public library and the school system. School faculty members maintain demanding schedules. In addition to rigorous time constraints, they are also under the constant pressure of adhering to strict protocol. All of this is a necessary part of the responsibility of supervising and educating large groups of children. However, it leaves little time for miscellaneous conversations with people outside of the organization. It is important for public librarians to find ways to integrate themselves into the culture of the school without creating additional work for the educators.

The work that was done in attending literacy nights, conducting school tours, and organizing in-school book clubs allowed CLD staff to gently introduce themselves into the schools. Beyond providing meaningful ways to promote literacy to the children and families in the community, these programs created regular opportunities for the CLD staff to communicate with school principals and media specialists. Not only were the public librarians becoming acquainted with many of the students, they were also building positive working relationships with the faculty.

As strong proponents for education and literacy, CLD feels it is important to examine ways that services might be manipulated in order to provide support to the schools and reinforce their efforts. With this in mind, staff began brainstorming about ways to expand the efforts in the school. In order to do this, it was crucial to gain administrative support from both organizations. Encouraged by the success of the initial efforts, data was gathered from these programs and used to demonstrate the value of the partnership. By the end of the second quarter of 2010, programming statistics had increased over 100 percent and the positive feedback from parents and educators was overwhelming. This information was compiled into monthly reports that were consistently presented to both the library director and the library board. With impressive statistics supporting the positive verbal feedback that was shared, both the library director and board enthusiastically agreed to support a commitment to fostering the partnership.

The presentation of this information was equally effective in gaining the support of the Weld Re-4 School District Superintendent, Karen Trusler. Mid-way through the school year, an email was sent to Ms. Trusler documenting CLD's efforts in the school district and expressing CLD'S appreciation of the School Districts' support of the partnership. This exchange led to a meeting during which both sides expressed a commitment to a long-term partnership. Meeting with the superintendent was an ideal opportunity for open conversation about ideas and expectations of both parties. Ms. Trusler reiterated the need for education and support beyond school grounds, which was exemplified in an interview conducted at the Severance Middle School during which Ms. Trusler articulated that "It [education] doesn't stop inside these walls." CLD staff expressed the hope for increasing public library usage and enhancing a positive perception of the CLD within the community. Understanding and appreciating each entity's priorities made it possible to make plans that would garner mutual administrative support.

After gaining top-level support on both sides, more aggressive planning began. Following the conversation with Ms. Trusler, CLD staff understood that she was looking for ways that CLD might help educators in acquiring resources for the classroom. This was a concern as financial prudence is a necessity for any tax-funded organization. A national economic downturn that trickled down and led to budgetary concerns at the state level provided even further impetus for finding ways to share resources for the benefit of both organizations. In turn, as a public library,

the goal was to expand the use and benefit of resources within the community. CLD began to formulate a plan that would help both entities achieve these goals.

Support from administration was an important first step. Fostering a consistently harmonious relationship with the District's educators was the next goal. Because of the common ground that both parties share, approaching the media specialists was a logical first step in this process. Meetings were set up with every media specialist in the School District. Topics covered during these meetings included the structure of the media centers in the school, informational challenges facing media specialists and educators, and brainstorming about ideas for partnership. The media specialists welcomed the opportunity for partnership and they continue to serve as liaisons and advocates between CLD and the School District's educators. Using the information that was gathered during conversations with media specialists, several services were designed and implemented intended both for the benefit of students and educators and to further the promotion of CLD within the schools. These services include Educator Cards, CLD library cards on school supply lists, sharing resources, and cross program promotion.

Educator Cards

Educator Cards were designed as a response to teachers' needs in supplementing their curriculum. The major benefits of the Educator Card include:

- Extended check-out periods (six weeks as opposed to two)
- Increased holds (ten holds as opposed to five)
- Increased Interlibrary Loans (five as opposed to three)

CLD received considerable feedback from educators indicating their desire to check out public library materials to supplement a teaching topic.

However, the two-week checkout policy presented a difficulty as teachers often spend four to six weeks teaching a particular unit. Increasing the check-out period to six weeks brings educators into the public library to look for supplemental books. In turn, it has increased the circulation of items of an academic nature that often sat untouched on the shelves.

Increasing the number of holds is also a successful way to aid educators who are looking for supplemental material. Planning ahead is crucial for educators; allowing them to place more items on hold aids them in organizing and planning for their units. Increasing the number of interlibrary loans benefits those who are seeking unique materials for their classroom, and expanding this service allows educators to plan and structure curriculum using materials that otherwise would not have been available to them through standard check-out with the local library. Educators who look to their public library to help meet their research needs will pass this perception on to their students.

Educator Cards were formally implemented at the start of the 2010-2011 school year. As of March 2011, 47 educators in the district have acquired Educator Cards.

Library Cards on School Supply Lists

Using the media specialists as liaisons, CLD staff approached the principals at District schools to request that they place CLD library cards on their school supply lists. Principals were presented with a set list of criteria as to why this would be a benefit to their students. Doing so gave them articulate documentation to present as justification for their decision in the event that questions might arise. This list of benefits included:

- Children who use the public library are more likely to develop expanded skills in research that will enhance their ability to

continue their education beyond the formal school setting.
- Children with public library cards have access to all of the free educational programs offered by the library.
- Children who read for pleasure are more likely to excel in all other areas of academics. Encouraging the use of the public library fosters the notion of reading for pleasure.
- CLD makes an effort to acquire databases that are beneficial for student research. Students with a public library card have access to these technological resources. Students with a CLD card have the ability to check out books from the CLD Mobile Branch (Bookmobile) during its regular visit to the schools.

As of early 2011, five of the nine schools in the district required CLD library cards on their school supply lists. CLD's goal is to add two more schools to this list in the next year. To date, 4,895 students in the district have library cards; this represents a large portion of the 34.66% increase in library cardholders since 2009.

Sharing Resources

The idea of sharing resources with the schools was approached with care. As a public library, CLD staff had to be cautious not to set a precedent in which the schools counted on the Public Library to purchase resources specifically for their use. Yet one of CLD's priorities was to create a collection that would help supplement education within the community and support the work of educators. The solution was to work with the media specialists to determine a list of resources that the public library might acquire for their mutual use. This is a discussion that is continued throughout the school year. CLD looks for every opportunity to converse with educators about their collection needs and then incorporates as many of the suggestions as possible into collection development. The requirement is that these resources must be equally beneficial for both the schools and for the general population of Public Library patrons. This discussion involved all types of information resources including books, audio-visual materials, and databases.

Databases were of particular interest for both parties. CLD had just begun a large campaign designed to encourage increased database usage. The schools presented an opportunity in which to heavily promote these resources. Media specialists often work with a limited budget and the prospect of eliminating a portion of the cost of databases was very appealing to them.

CLD committed to acquiring a database each year that would be highly useful for educators and students in research. To date, the databases that are heavily used by the students and educators include EBSCO, Transparent Language, Global Issues in Context, and Books and Authors. The selection of these databases was and will continue to be based on feedback gathered from educators, media specialists, and students throughout the school year.

Beyond databases, educator suggestions for print materials are also considered. If it is determined that the request will be a meaningful addition to the collection for both educators and general patrons, CLD purchases it. This benefits both parties as it provides supplemental resources to educators and it broadens the scope of criteria that CLD uses when reviewing potential resources.

Cross Program Promotion

CLD benefits greatly from the network of communication that is now in place with the Schools. This network is used as a key tool for marketing library programs to specific age groups. Depending on the target demographics for each program, school contacts are emailed accordingly and asked to disseminate the program information to the appropriate groups. For instance, by informing the high school English teachers about poetry programs, these teachers are often willing to give students extra credit to attend these types of programs at the public library. Alternatively, high school English teachers send their students to CLD to complete assignments in collaboration with CLD staff.

Mass flyer mailings are conducted by asking school secretaries to place a program flyer in every student's mailbox at the schools. In order to do this, the flyer must be approved through a formal process at the district level. Following approval, the flyers are printed and delivered to school secretaries for distribution. CLD finds this method particularly effective for advertising the Summer Reading Program, author visits, and other high profile events.

The Final Step: Evaluating the Partnership

While some of the challenges to creating a successful school/library relationship are clear – time, staff, and physical resources – some are less so and require a little more work to not only identify, but also to conquer. Further, encountering new challenges is a constant reality and does not go away once the relationship is established. This is true of the CLD/Weld Re-4 relationship. As the partnership continues to be shaped by both Districts, unforeseen difficulties continue to surface. Being flexible and ready to adapt is crucial to the sustainability and future enhancement of the partnership.

The initial challenges faced were logistical – staff, time, and making the right connections. Educators are notoriously busy. Finding ways to connect was no easy task. Making the first contact can be especially daunting. At the time the partnership was formed, the school district did not have a Media Specialist Coordinator for CLD to use as an initial contact. This would have been the first point of entry if that had been an option.

Instead, CLD worked individually with school principals and media specialists. While this got the job done, so to speak, it required infinitely more work as relationships had to be fostered within each school rather than on a district-wide basis.

Maintaining open lines of communication between the Districts proved to be yet another challenge. Effective communication is key to the sustainability of the partnership. In the past, CLD had participated in several successful projects with the School District; however, the relationship wasn't viable long-term because consistent communication did not occur. While both Districts attempted to hold joint meetings, CLD discovered that extra meetings were never the answer. However, having a presence at regular staff meetings allowed CLD to present its resources to the educators while, at the same time, educators received an opportunity to have their voices heard about their wants and needs. Gaining visibility with the Schools and constantly reminding the educators of CLD's presence and willingness to help provided the necessary glue to hold the relationship together.

Once the divide had been bridged and regular communication was in place, both Districts faced the challenge of give and take. Remaining within the parameters of the Public Library's mission while striving to provide specially catered services for the School District was a distinct challenge. The Library needed to exercise balance, specifically with regard to resources and collection development. As an example, CLD would be unable to purchase twenty copies of a particular title for a specific school project because policy dictates that multiple copies are purchased based on current library collection needs and public demand. In a library where multiple copies typically mean no more than six copies, twenty copies would be outside the bounds of reason. However, CLD could certainly purchase a few more copies of the required title within the stipulations of policy to assist the schools with this need.

Another hurdle that presents itself when considering is the logistics of the collaboration is the issue of limited time on the part of the educators. Public educators are often overworked and understaffed, leaving little time for additional projects. It is important to respect that the Schools' administration may be protective of staff time. For this reason, CLD attempts to think creatively about collaborative opportunities that require little to no time commitment from schools and educators. The programs that are implemented are streamlined – simple but meaningful. Additionally, CLD makes an effort to seek out educators who are hungry for collaboration. Time commitments and motivation differ among individuals and once the right connections are made, more intensive program planning can take place. Finding these individuals is a matter of constantly fostering relationships and networking with educators in the district. Continuing to gently probe for information and names of individuals who might support the effort eventually leads to the right people.

Finally, there is the challenge of convincing individuals to approach things differently and try something new. The services in this discussion are regarded as non-traditional library work. Both professions, public libraries and schools, are steeped in tradition and are often bound by policies and procedures that have been in place for years, and may sometimes be antiquated. Educators and librarians alike are sometimes handicapped by the need to follow the rules and maintain precedent. But the dynamics of the educational environment continue to shift dramatically and new problems require a different approach if there is to be hope for successful solutions. Jen Maley, Information Literacy Coordinator says it best; "People [need to be]…willing to step outside their comfort zone." Therefore, CLD used delicate persistence when approaching all the parties involved. Staff gave careful thought as to how ideas could be presented in such a way as to generate enthusiasm. Every concern that surfaced was taken seriously and addressed immediately. The focus of the presentation for each potential program revolved around the benefit to the students.

Despite these and other more banal challenges, the benefits to both Districts and the community at large far outweigh any of the difficulties encountered. In fact, careful consideration of the challenges often leads to better service solutions. The benefits of a strong partnership between public library and the school district are many and varied. The benefits for both districts include additional resources and expertise, cross-promotion for events, extra help for special programs and projects, collection development assistance, improved public relations and more opportunities to advocate for the library. The benefit to the public library and the young residents of the community is worth expending the majority of the effort in nurturing the partnership.

Moving Forward

CLD credits much of the success of this partnership to the unwavering support of the School District Superintendent, Karen Trusler, and the Information Literacy Coordinator, Jen Maley. Their willingness to promote CLD to teachers and students gave the project a level of credibility it otherwise wouldn't have had. CLD benefited greatly from these individuals' accessibility and enthusiasm.

While many important relationships have been formed and wonderful services have been implemented, there are still many unchartered opportunities to enhance the school/public library partnership. "When the staff in the public library know, and regard as colleagues (and even better as friends), the staff in the schools whose children they serve, the potential for effective collaboration is tremendously expanded" (Del Vecchio, 1993). In the future, CLD staff hopes to create more connections with individual educators and students. These connections will generate more opportunities for programming in the schools and will provide additional feedback towards enhancing the collection. The greater the number of teachers who consider the public library as an

indispensable resource and support for education, the greater the number of students that they will infuse with an attitude of goodwill toward the Public Library.

In order to foster connections with more teachers, CLD will host a District-wide staff meeting at the beginning of each school year, which will take place at the public library. Because this meeting is intended to be a "welcome back celebration", CLD will provide food and raffle prizes. During this meeting, key library staff will have an opportunity to introduce themselves, give a general presentation about the resources offered to educators, and provide verbal affirmation of their support for teachers and community education. CLD staff will also request invitations to individual school staff meetings in order to provide more detailed and comprehensive presentations about databases, resources, programs, and services. these initial meetings, CLD staff will maintain regular contact with educators by sending out a quarterly e-newsletter. The content of this newsletter will contain brief articles about upcoming programs, lists of new books and resources beneficial to educators, and other miscellaneous information about CLD's activity in the School District.

Expanding Book Clubs

CLD established its school book club prototype within the Windsor High School. Facilitating a book club at the school during school hours was the key to success. Often children are unable to even make it to the public library because of the logistical issues of transportation and time constraints. The school book club attracted a larger and more diverse number of participants than in-house library book clubs as it eliminated some of those logistical hurdles. Conducting book clubs during lunchtime created a safe and enticing atmosphere as students gathered to talk and laugh over food. This book club formula was particularly appealing to the media specialists as it provided an opportunity to promote their collection and their spaces in a fresh and dynamic way. Building on this proven success, CLD plans to expand these in-school book clubs to the School District's two middle schools. Cognizant of the larger developmental differences that exist between the grade levels in middle schools, CLD will offer a book club specific to each grade level. In order to do this successfully, more staff time will have to be dedicated to the organization of the school book clubs. This includes preparatory work of reading the book, researching discussion questions, designing interactive activities, and gathering supplies. Actually facilitating the book clubs will require a time commitment of several hours on multiple days each week. After the implementation process is complete, CLD will be offering seven in-school book clubs throughout the School District. Preparing for this significant expansion includes acquiring a budget to create book club book kits. The kits, which will include books, questions, and activities, will be used throughout the clubs in the District and shared among other public libraries across the state.

Mobile Service

Examining ways to connect with more students is another essential piece of the future success of the partnership. CLD hopes to utilize its Mobile Branch (Bookmobile) service as a powerful means of connecting with many District students on an individual level. Bookmobile service was implemented in accordance with the CLD's vision for expanding library services through outreach into the community. A mobile unit gives CLD extended flexibility for providing services during unique hours and at a variety of locations. This flexibility has great potential for the partnership work with the school district.

New to CLD in 2010, the Bookmobile completed a trial semester of service to the schools in spring 2011. Having experimented with informal lunchtime and after-school stops as well as more formal stops during classroom time, CLD has found that each stop requires something different. Having gathered valuable information about how to maximize each unique school stop, CLD hopes to implement Bookmobile stops at a majority of the schools in the district in the next two years. The major goals of Bookmobile service are to supplement the resources available to students in their school media centers and reinforce the idea of reading for pleasure.

Many public school media centers operate with unsatisfactory levels of administrative support and extremely limited funding. The media centers within the Weld Re-4 School District are fortunate to have strong administrative and parental support, yet they still face funding challenges. According to the American Association of School Librarians, "On average, schools annually spend about $15.00 per student, less than the cost of one hardcover book, on print and non-print library resources" (AASL, 2010). Regular visits from the CLD Bookmobile extend each school's media center resources by approximately 2500 titles.

School media centers are organized in such a way that learning and research is the primary focus. Promoting recreational reading is an important secondary focus, but schools often have little time and limited resources to dedicate towards this endeavor. The Bookmobile can substantially supplement a school's effort in promoting recreational reading and its benefits. A giant bus filled with books is something of a phenomenon in and of itself. These aesthetics coupled with the enthusiasm of savvy librarians make it appealing even to the most cynical students. Students can come on the bus to find a book for no other reason than pure enjoyment. Often they walk off with several books, a piece of candy in their pocket, and a smile on their face. The unique experience of the Bookmobile creates a positive perception of books, reading, and the library. CLD looks forward to providing Bookmobile service to an increasing number of students throughout the District.

Measuring Success

CLD gathers both qualitative and quantitative data in order to evaluate the successes and pitfalls of the project.

It is imperative to gather numbers that can provide tangible evidence that the cost/benefit ratio of the library's efforts is favorable. Though it is sometimes a difficult concept for librarians to swallow, hard data is the most powerful motivational tool when communicating with administration. This is one of the very positive pieces regarding programming in the schools. Though there is the occasional instance of having to report low statistics, overall CLD has found that the numbers gathered from the partnership programming efforts have been very positive.

CLD tracks programming statistics using the theory that every interaction counts. When attending a back-to-school event or literacy program every individual who takes a flyer, signs up for a library card, engages in conversation with staff, or gives library feedback is counted as a participant. Often this will generate statistics in the hundreds. Though this may seem extreme to some, CLD feels these numbers are completely justified. All of these interactions have a positive impact on the library. People who take flyers often decide to attend library programs for the first time. The feedback received is used to evaluate CLD services and often leads to an improvement in procedures and policies. Children who take a piece of candy stamped with the CLD logo associate the library with a positive experience.

All of the program statistics are carefully documented in a spreadsheet organized by date/program type/number of attendees. A special section of the statistics spreadsheet is dedicated to "School Programs" in order to make it easy to track the success of school programs. These statistics are reported monthly in the Outreach Department report. Following the implementation of the School partnership program, CLD programming statistics rose 90 percent. The facilitation

of the weekly high school book club along with attending one special school event per month generates a minimum of 260 additional program participants per month.

In addition to tracking programming statistics, CLD utilizes the reports feature of its Integrated Library System (TLC –The Library Corporation) on a regular basis. Every six months, staff generates a report gathering data pertaining to the number of CLD card-holders between the ages of 5-18 years. This number rose 30 percent between 2010 and 2011. Additionally, the Youth Services Department runs regular collection reports and has seen a ten percent increase in Juvenile Non-Fiction circulation and a five percent increase in Young Adult Fiction circulation.

In addition to gathering a surplus of data, CLD also listens to the voice of patrons. As is often the case in library work, the nature of the school/library partnership is not always conducive to gathering quantitative data. Who can put a quantitative value on the work of helping one child learn to love reading? Qualitative feedback is highly significant as it is an extremely effective way to understand the positive and negative aspects of a service from the patron's perspective. Positive feedback is good for staff morale as well as for generating goodwill with administration. Gathering and then sharing success stories motivates staff to continue to pursue excellence and helps staff and administration comprehend the impact of library efforts in the schools on a personal level. These stories create a positive emotional perception of this work.

Qualitative feedback is obtained verbally and electronically via email, although verbal feedback tends to be the most valuable as well as the easiest to gather. In order to gather this data, CLD makes it a priority to have regular conversations with the contacts in the schools, which, as mentioned earlier, is crucial for sustainability. In addition to speaking with educators, conversations with parents, students, and other community leaders allow CLD staff to obtain a realistic understanding of the community's reaction to its efforts in the schools. Staff documents the conversations and these interactions are passed onto higher levels via email and in verbal reports.

Careful documentation of statistics for programs, collection circulation numbers, dissemination of Educator Cards, and Bookmobile circulation allows Department heads to justify the value of the partnership with solid numerical data. This data, coupled with the many wonderful stories gathered from our patrons is communicated to the Library Director and Library Board on a monthly basis. Besides generating the solid support of administration, this data helps us all celebrate yesterday's successes, evaluate today's service, and plan for tomorrow's challenges.

CONCLUSION

This project is based on the formulation and maintenance of relationships. Quality, lasting relations take time and effort. CLD staff offers these key pieces of advice to other public libraries that are considering building these relationships and extending services into the schools:

Persistence is Key

While one must be careful not to become an annoyance, it does not hurt to leave more than one message, send email reminders, and occasionally present a face in the school office. Busy educators may be difficult to pinpoint and initiating contact often requires several attempts. This isn't an insult –it's a symptom of a hectic schedule. Understanding and empathizing with this will help alleviate stress and/or bitterness when it comes to creating school contacts. Be persistent in programming and service efforts as well. Do not conclude failure if statistics are disappointing after the first attempt. Examine programming plans carefully, adapt them, and try again two or three times before discontinuing a program or service.

Throw out the Model

Every public library district and school district is a unique creature. What works in one district may not be practical in a different district. Understanding the targeted district and the tools available to the public library will help in ascertaining what works in that district. Do not be afraid to tweak or radically modify ideas from other districts in order to succeed. Candid conversations with the educators and administration are crucial in discovering the mechanics of a particular school district.

Serve Dynamically

No matter what the specifics of a particular school/ public library relationship look like, it is important to go the extra mile whenever possible, no matter what. An extra phone call or a gentle reminder often makes a great difference. It is necessary to keep the service to students as the top priority. If the relationship between the public library and schools goes sour, it is the thousands of students who lose. Always remember that reaching into the schools is a powerful way to positively impact many young lives and create a host of life-long public library supporters. Any challenges that one faces are worth overcoming for the sake of those students.

Building the school/ library partnership is a cyclical project and is ongoing. As student demographics and administrative staffing changes, so too will the service cycle. Assessing the need, recommending the solution, and evaluating the outcome will inevitably lead to further assessment, recommendation, and evaluation. Maintaining the assessment cycle will allow the public library to continue enhancing the lives and futures of the school district's youth. "School and public libraries cannot solve all the problems youth have, but they can and do make a significant difference" (Matthews, 1991, 201). In this way, the Clearview Library District will continue its work as an information utility within the community.

It takes a village to raise a child. CLD board members and staff take their role as villagers seriously. Our efforts in the school district are investment in young people and an investment in the future of our community. -Bill Karr, CLD Board member

It is very exciting to see the school district and the library leveraging our resources to promote our common goals of literacy and learning in our community.- Scott Wildman, CLD Board member

REFERENCES

American Association of School Librarians (AASL). (2011). *The school library center: Quotable facts.* AASL website. Retrieved April 2, 2011, from http://www.ala.org/ala/mgrps/divs/aasl/aaslissues/toolkits/schoollibraryfacts.cfm

Clay, E. (2009). The partnership between public libraries and public education. *Virginia Libraries, 55*(2), 11–14.

Del Vecchio, S. (1993). Connecting libraries and schools with CLASP. *Wilson Library Bulletin, 68,* 38–40.

DelGuidice, M. (2009). Are you overlooking a valuable resource? A practical guide to collaborating with your greatest ally: The public library. *Library Media Connection, 27*(6), 38–39.

Fitzgibbons, S. (2001). School and public library relationships: Déjà vu or new beginnings? *Journal of Youth Services in Libraries, 14*(3), 3–7.

Matthews, V. (1991). Kids need libraries: School and public libraries preparing the youth of today for the world of tomorrow. *School Library Media Annual, 9,* 201.

Scordato, J. (2004). School and public librarians working together. *Library Media Connection, 22*(7), 32–33.

ADDITIONAL READING

American Association of School Librarians. AASL. (2007). *Standards for the 21st Century Learner.* Chicago, IL: American Library Association.

Bush, G. (2006). Walking the Road between Libraries: Best practices in school and public library cooperative activities. *School Library Media Activities Monthly, 22*(6), 25–28.

Fine, J. (2001). Hand in Hand: Public and school library collaborative projects. *Journal of Youth Services in Libraries, 14*(3), 18–22.

Jackson, E. (2005). Formal and Informal Opportunities for Public Libraries to Partner with Schools. *Bookmobile and Outreach Services, 8*(2), 45–67.

Ryan, S. (2001). "Be Nice to the Secretary" And Other Ways to Work Successfully with Schools. *Journal of Youth Services in Libraries, 14*(3), 18–22.

Wepking, M. (2009). From Communication to Cooperation to Collaboration: School and public librarians as partners for student success. *Library Media Connection, 28*(3), 24–26.

Chapter 13
A Furry Partnership

Mary L. Hall
Bedford Public Library, USA

ABSTRACT

This case study describes the partnership between the Bedford Public Library and an elementary school. This partnership consists of a program designed to assist grade school children with literacy skills. Third grade students read aloud to a Pet Partners team made up of a therapy dog and a handler who is a professional public librarian. The team visits the school weekly with books selected from the public library's collection to provide animal assisted therapy. School staff and teachers collect and provide assessment data on students to create goals and track progress for the students. The librarian, teachers, and school staff work together to create new methods of assessing progress attributed to reading to the dog. During the summer months, the Pet Partners team visits a local Summer Meals site to help address the problem of summer reading loss. Children of all ages are invited to read aloud to the team to participate in animal assisted activities.

INTRODUCTION

"Bridget! Today is our school day. We're going to read with the kids!" I tell the Golden Retriever, who jumps to her feet and heads for the door. When we leave the Library building, she leaps eagerly into the car, and as we approach the elementary school, she stands up on the car's seat in antici-

pation. We head into the school building to read with the third grade students who are waiting.

Bridget and I are a therapy dog team focused on helping children love reading. We are part of a unique partnership between our public library and our local school system, designed to help improve literacy in our community.

Since 1999, therapy dogs have been used to help children with reading. Reading aloud can be a very stressful experience for children, but research has found that just the presence of a

DOI: 10.4018/978-1-61350-387-4.ch013

friendly dog can reduce children's stress levels. When children read to a trained therapy dog and handler, not only are they more relaxed, but over time, their reading fluency improves. Therapy dogs also provide comfort, reinforce learning, motivate speech, stimulate the senses, encourage positive social behaviors, foster feelings of safety and acceptance enhance self-esteem, decrease loneliness, provide the opportunity for touch and for nurturing, inspire people to smile, laugh and have fun, and offer unconditional love and acceptance (R.E.A.D., 2010). When children read to dogs they start coming to school more consistently, volunteering to read aloud in class, being late less often, turning in more homework assignments, and forming trusting relationships (R.E.A.D., 2010). Although this is a new idea, it is growing rapidly with the number of trained therapy dog teams and programs increasing nationwide.

The Bedford Public Library has endeavored to create its own such program, but in a unique way. Most 'Reading Dog' programs take place either in schools or public libraries. In most library programs, volunteers bring their therapy dogs to the library for informal reading sessions. In schools the programs are more structured, but also generally use volunteers. However, in this program, I am working both as a professional librarian and therapy dog teammate to bring the program to the school. There, we partner with school teachers and staff to work with each student and to document and assess each student's progress.

This program is made possible because of a long-term partnership between our library and the local school system. The Library's administration has long considered partnerships to be important. However, recent economic events in our area have made partnerships even more vital. Lawrence County, Indiana, has been hit hard for the last several years by a wave of job losses, which has dramatically changed the lives of many residents. This has added to the number of adults and children whose lives are increasingly confusing and

stressful. This situation has made learning more problematic for many children.

We've all heard how higher education and literacy skills are increasingly important for future American workers. This contrasts with the sobering statistics we frequently see about U.S. students' poor test scores. Meanwhile, many American children live in poverty and in family situations that make learning and high achievement even more difficult. Our community is no exception. In response, the Bedford Public Library has implemented a variety of programs to address the community's needs. Many of our programs involve partnerships with other local organizations.

Our program began its first full school year in the fall of 2010, and so the program is very much in development. It has two components, which make it a year-round endeavor. During the academic year, we provide animal-assisted therapy at one elementary school. During the summer, we provide animal-assisted activities at a Middle school.

This chapter will describe how the program was created and how it functions. Background information will be included about the increasing use of dogs to help children. I will discuss future plans and recommendations and suggest that programs like this have a role in addressing children's literacy, an important issue facing communities, schools, and public libraries today.

Definition of Terms

Accelerated Reader (AR) is a software program designed to interest students in reading books outside of class (http://www.renlearn.com/ar/). Students select a book to read, and then take a test that assesses their comprehension of the book. Points are awarded based on the book's reading level and correct answers. Schools use this software to create enthusiasm for reading by rewarding students for points accumulated throughout the semester.

Animal Assisted Activities (AAA)

Animal Assisted Activities provide opportunities for motivational, recreational, and/or therapeutic benefits to enhance quality of life. *AAA* are delivered in a variety of environments by specially trained professionals, paraprofessionals, and/or volunteers, in association with animals that meet specific criteria (Delta Society, 2010). Progress is not usually monitored or documented (Intermountain Therapy Animals, 2010).

Animal Assisted Interventions (AAI)

A broad term that includes animal-assisted therapy and animal-assisted activities (Fine, 2010).

Animal Assisted Therapy (AAT)

AAT is a goal-directed intervention in which an animal that meets specific criteria is an integral part of the treatment process. AAT is directed and/or delivered by a health/human service professional with specialized expertise, and within the scope of his/her profession. *AAT* is designed to promote improvement in human physical, social, emotional, and/or cognitive functioning. AAT is provided in a variety of settings and may be group or individual in nature. This process is documented and evaluated (Delta Society, 2010).

Delta Society is a national non-profit organization that facilitates the use of therapy, service, and companion animals. Their *Pet Partners* program screens people and their pets for visiting animal programs in hospitals, nursing homes, rehabilitation centers, schools, and other facilities. *Pet Partners* is the only national registry that requires volunteer training and screening of animal-handler teams (Delta Society, 2010).

Intermountain Therapy Animals (ITA): Pets Helping People

ITA brings animal resources to human needs. They specialize in providing animal-assisted therapy in the areas of physical, occupational, speech and psycho therapies, as well as special education. Their mission is "enhancing quality of life through the human-animal bond". Therapy dog teams are first registered with a national screening organization such as Delta Society (ITA, 2010).

Pet Partner Team

Delta Society's Pet Partners program trains volunteers and screens volunteers and their pets for visiting animal programs in hospitals, nursing homes, rehabilitation centers, schools and other facilities. The Pet Partners program was established in 1990 to ensure that "both ends of the leash," people as well as animals, were well-prepared to participate in animal-assisted activity and animal-assisted therapy programs. (Delta Society, 2010).

Reading Education Assistance Dogs (R.E.A.D.)

R.E.A.D. is a program of Intermountain Therapy Animals (ITA) and was created in 1999 as a way to improve children's reading skills through the assistance of certified therapy animal teams as literacy mentors (R.E.A.D., 2010). R.E.A.D. is the pioneering program that established the idea that animals can be used in a variety of ways to improve children's reading experience.

Therapy Dog

A therapy dog possesses the necessary skills and aptitude to facilitate therapy under the direction of health care or human services professional. Therapy animals are owned by individuals, not by the people or organizations they serve (R.E.AD., 2010).

BACKGROUND

Ever since dogs have been domesticated, they have been used in many different ways to help humans. Dogs have provided protection, as well as assistance with hunting and transportation. However, the most widespread use of dogs is in the role of companion and friend. Over the last half-century, professionals have begun to realize that bringing a dog into a therapeutic setting can improve outcomes in both mental and physical health. In the 1960's, a psychologist noticed that the presence of his pet dog improved therapy sessions for disturbed children. Around the same time, some of Sigmund Freud's old journals were published, and revealed that Freud had also written about the positive effect his pet dog had in therapy sessions. His conclusion was that the dog's presence gave the patient a sense of calm and reassurance (Fine, 2010).

Soon others began studying the use of animals in psychotherapy, and groundbreaking research emerged. The researchers demonstrated that the presence of a friendly dog during therapy sessions generates positive physiological changes in patients. Respiration and heart rate slowed, muscles relaxed, and stress responses were reduced. This study generated a huge increase in the acceptance and number of animal assisted therapy programs in the next twenty years. In addition, animals began to be used in a wide variety of settings, from nursing homes to hospitals, to schools (Fine, 2010).

Any adult who remembers confiding their deepest fears, sorrows, and secrets to their childhood pet already understands how a dog helps people cope with life. This phenomenon has been clinically researched for several decades and demonstrates benefits such as reduction in heart rate, lowered blood pressure, and increased social connectivity (Velde, 2005). The positive impact of a calm dog can be greater than the presence of an adult or even a friend (Jalongo, 2004). Studies have shown that interacting with a friendly pet almost doubles the flow of oxytocin, a brain chemical

that provides a feeling of calm even in stressful situations. Even looking at a pet will stimulate the release of calming oxytocin (Olmert, 2009). In addition, recent research shows early evidence that dogs possess an understanding of their own mental state and that of others (Arnold, 2010). This research suggests that canines do indeed possess empathy and provide comfort instinctively (Arnold, 2010).

College students who were studied while taking tests in a stressful situation again verified the theory that the presence of a dog can calm humans. Those in the group who were tested in the same room as a dog exhibited fewer nervous behaviors than the group with no dog. In addition, the students self-reported less anxiety (Velde, 2005).

According to the Center for the Human Animal Bond at Purdue University, children can become more nurturing by spending time with animals. In addition to improvement in physical health, pets can improve emotional health. Several researchers have shown that children who grow up in a household with pets show better self-esteem and self-concept (Mertz, 2009). Lori Friesen cites several studies that support the physiological, emotional, and social benefits for children of interacting with animals (2009). In the classroom, children were demonstrated to be more attentive, responsive, and cooperative with a dog present (Friesen, 2009). Studies show that more than seventy percent of children confide in, and talk to animals (Jalongo, 2004). Needless to say, endless anecdotes are available to lend intuitive verification that dogs help people to feel more positive, relaxed, and nurturing.

What does this have to do with public libraries? Most public librarians know only too well the impact of income and education on their communities. Low educational attainment and income has a negative impact on the entire community. Public library use is highly dependent on household income, as indicated by the Institute of Education Sciences' Library Statistics Program's survey of public library use. Only 38% of those below the poverty line used a public library in the past year, while 60% of those with incomes in the highest fifth used a library (Glander and Dam, 2002). Among those with less than a high school diploma, fewer than 21% used a library within the past year, while 66% of those with an advanced degree used a library. Each incremental increase in educational levels resulted in a proportional increase in library use (Glander and Dam, 2002).

It seems obvious then, that public libraries need to find ways to reach out to children in our communities, especially those who do not visit the library. We have plenty of motivation to assist in successful educational outcomes for all children. The question then is, how best to help? Outreach and partnerships are ways that libraries can help their community, and indirectly, the library itself. The Institute of Museum and Library Services report "Museums, Libraries and 21st Century Skills" addresses this topic, and describes the shift from a 20th to a 21st Century approach to library service (Semmel, 2009). Instead of acting independently, libraries need to participate in "highly collaborative partnerships," and instead of merely being located in communities, libraries need to be "(e)mbedded in community (and be aligned with and act as a leader on community needs/issues)" (Semmel, 2009, p. 7). Instead of focusing on just on presentation and display of materials, libraries need to collaborate with others to develop "audience engagement and experiences" (IMLS, 2009).

The use of dogs to provide assistance to children with reading is a new practice. The first formal program was pioneered in 1999 by Intermountain Therapy Animals (ITA), one of the larger nonprofits in the field. At that time, ITA was a program that was experiencing great success using volunteers and therapy dogs to visit hospitals, schools, detention, and care facilities. Concerned by the nationwide decrease in reading and reading skills, ITA member Sandi Martin wondered whether therapy dogs could help children read (R.E.A.D., 2010).

Reading aloud can be a very stressful experience for any child, and can increase blood pressure dramatically, regardless of the setting (Lynch, 2003). For children who are shy, lack confidence, or struggle with reading, that stress is more intense. Lynch suggests that unchecked, this response in children can lead to a lifetime stress response associated with the worrisome activity (reading aloud) (2003). However, even the presence of a dog in the room while the child read aloud resulted in lower blood pressure (Lynch, 2003). When the child stroked the dog, blood pressure could drop up to 50% within moments (Lynch, 2003). This physiological evidence provides a strong basis for pairing therapy dogs with young readers. Some of the most commonly expressed sentiments by children about therapy dogs are, "he's my friend" and "she didn't laugh at me". Research suggests that children see dogs as non-judgmental and likable, which helps build the child's self-confidence and social interactions (Friesen, 2009).

Naturally, children have read to family pets for years, but the creation of an organized program was a brainstorm. ITA created their Reading Education Assistance Dogs (R.E.A.D.) program to use therapy animals as mentors and helpers to help improve the literacy skills of children (R.E.A.D., 2010). What began as a pilot program in 2000 is now a quickly growing and widely accepted practice. In only a decade, over 2000 R.E.A.D. teams have begun working on literacy skills with children and young adults in schools, public libraries, and other environments. This is referred to as animal assisted therapy (AAT) by R.E.A.D (2010). In order to become a R.E.A.D. team, the human and animal pair undergo a variety of tests together, and are evaluated by a registering agency such as Delta Society. R.E.A.D then provides its own testing, training, and support. Therapy animal teams can act as individuals or as part of a larger local program.

Because this is not yet an established field, basic terminology is not standardized. Several terms are used interchangeably to describe a variety of animal assisted interventions, as described below. Similar programs may use the same terms in different ways to describe therapeutic activities. The most common and widespread term used to describe dogs in therapeutic use is therapy dog, as it is a descriptive and convenient term that is understood by the general public. Animals besides dogs are also utilized, and the term therapy animal is widely used; however, this chapter will discuss dogs only.

Two types of programs predominate: those in which a therapy dog team visits a school, and those that hold programs in the public library. In the school setting, the students are selected by the teacher for a variety of reasons. Reading time might take place during the school day or afterward. R.E.A.D. considers this type of program to be animal assisted therapy because specific goals are set for each child, documentation is kept, and progress is recorded. At the public library, the program is generally held after school or on the weekend, and is open to any grade school child. No plans, goals, or documentation is recorded; therefore this is considered animal assisted activity.

The R.E.A.D. program began with a program in a Utah public school with children who were reading below grade level. Teachers selected the children, who met weekly with volunteer teams to read one on one for about twenty minutes. The school's usual assessment tool was used to evaluate results. All of the children's reading scores improved markedly. However, improved reading was not the only benefit for these children. The teachers also described these children as more self-confident, more proud of their accomplishments, and more willing to become involved in other activities. These children also began to see reading as fun and checked out books from the library. These students began to volunteer to read in class and completed their homework more often. In addition, grades in other subjects improved, absenteeism decreased, personal hygiene was improved, and interactions with animals was more respectful (R.E.A.D., 2010).

A Chicago-based reading dog program called Sit Stay Read has been helping student readers since 2003. Sit Stay Read is one of the pioneering literacy organizations to use dogs as a tool to improve reading skills and foster the love of learning in at-risk children. Through a structured curriculum designed with the University of Illinois at Chicago Center for Literacy, Sit Stay Read's trained volunteers and certified dog teams improve reading fluency, make reading fun, and inspire children to become lifelong readers (http://www. sitstayread.org/).

The program provides data to show that the program is helping low income second and third grade students succeed. Test results show that the students' reading scores improved overall and their reading rate improved (Smith, 2009). In addition, teachers unanimously applaud this program for the positive behavioral changes in students, including motivating and engaging students in learning, and increasing calm behavior. Teachers also state that students find the dogs to be non-judgmental and good listeners (Smith, 2009).

Both the R.E.A.D. and the Sit Stay Read program reward students with a book at the end of their year to help students continue to embrace and value reading. There are many other smaller local programs popping up across the country, as awareness of the concept increases. The numbers of both school-based and library-based programs are quickly increasing. The vast majority of the programs employ volunteer therapy dog teams. As noted above, library-based programs provide anecdotal results of reading improvement but do not test for results. School-based programs use the school's data collection methods to document improvement in reading.

One goal of programs that focus on children reading to dogs is to create a motivation to read that would otherwise be lacking. For struggling readers, sitting down with a book is not a pleasurable activity. While most children enter first grade excited about learning, for some, the difficulties of learning remove the excitement. By the time a student leaves high school, the majority say that they will never read a book again on their own (Mertz, 2009). According to the National Education Association, having children read as much as possible is one of the vital parts of becoming a good reader (NEA, 2010). The U.S. Department of Education found that, generally, the more students read for fun on their own time, the higher their reading scores (NEA, 2010). A White House Early Childhood Cognitive Development Summit stated that children learn best when safe environments are provided and children feel emotionally secure and develop close relationships (R.E.A.D. 2010). Between 1984 and 1996, however, the percentage of 12th grade students reporting that they "never" or "hardly ever" read for fun increased from 9 percent to 16 percent (National Education Association, 2010).

The Bedford Public Library is a medium-size public library in south-central Indiana. The library serves approximately 34,000 people in Bedford and North Lawrence county with a staff of 30 (20 full-time equivalent). The library's collection contains 95,000 items and circulates about 425,000 items per year to approximately 21,000 registered borrowers. Bedford is a city of 14,000 in a largely rural and blue collar library district of 34,000. Of the area's adults, 81% have high school degrees, and 12% have a Bachelor's degree or higher (2005-2009 American Community Survey).

The area's jobs were largely manufacturing-related, until a few years ago when the majority of those jobs were lost. For the last several years, the double-digit unemployment rate in our county has surpassed the state average (which is above the national average) (Hoosiers by the Numbers, 2010). These job losses have upended the lives of many children. Foreclosures of homes have sent many families to live in apartments or with family members. In 2008, almost 20% of Lawrence county children were living in poverty, higher than both the state and national levels (Indiana Youth Institute, 2010). Sometimes family pets have lost their homes as well, adding to the stress felt

by children. As one child told me while hugging Bridget, "My dog was named Bongo, but we had to get rid of him when we moved to Grandma's."

Indiana's standardized test, the Indiana Statewide Testing for Educational Progress (ISTEP), is given to third through eighth grade students. These third grade results help illustrate the impact of loss of income. Of North Lawrence county students who were eligible for free or reduced price meals, only 53% passed both Math and Reading tests. Almost 76% of students with paid meals passed both Math and Reading tests, a difference of more than 20% (Indiana Department of Education, 2010). Similar were the findings of The Nation's Report Card, which showed statewide results for Indiana fourth grade public schools (Institute of Education Sciences, 2009). Among students not eligible for school meals assistance, 80% attained basic achievement. Among those eligible for assistance, only 57% attained basic achievement (Institute of Education Sciences, 2009).

Fortunately, the Bedford Public Library's Director and Board of Trustees value collaborative relationships with local organizations to be a priority for service. When our community was hit with job losses and the recession, Library administration and staff helped create programs and strategies to help residents cope. Library staff frequently cooperates with other organizations to plan local events, especially those for children.

As the Adult Services and Circulation Manager for the Library, I wear many hats each day. However, my personal volunteer activities have gradually added a dimension to my position. I am a volunteer puppyraiser and trainer of service dogs for people with disabilities. Since 1998 I have been working with various service dog programs to raise and train puppies and send them on to advanced training. Over the last several years, I have read with intense interest the articles describing new programs that use therapy dogs to encourage young readers. Since then, my goal has been to become part of a therapy dog team so that we could help children learn to enjoy reading. In 2009 a dog was placed with me that was a perfect fit for this kind of work. We successfully passed evaluations to become a Delta Society Pet Partner team in 2010, and began to plan for the most effective way to reach children who would most benefit.

One goal of programs that focus on children reading to dogs is to create a motivation to read that would otherwise be lacking. For struggling readers, sitting down with a book is not a pleasurable activity. While most children enter first grade excited about learning, for some, the difficulties of learning remove the excitement. By the time a student leaves high school, the majority say that they will never read a book again on their own (Mertz, 2009). According to the National Education Association, having children read as much as possible is one of the vital parts of becoming a good reader (NEA, 2010). The U.S. Department of Education found that, generally, the more students read for fun on their own time, the higher their reading scores (NEA, 2010). A White House Early Childhood Cognitive Development Summit stated that children learn best when safe environments are provided and children feel emotionally secure and develop close relationships (R.E.A.D. 2010). Between 1984 and 1996, however, the percentage of 12th grade students reporting that they "never" or "hardly ever" read for fun increased from 9 percent to 16 percent (National Education Association, 2010).

MAIN FOCUS

"I'm not a good reader," cautioned the blonde-haired boy as he sat down next to me on the classroom floor. "That's okay" I said, "I'm not a teacher, and neither is my dog." I introduced the third-grader to Bridget, whose feathery tail brushed the floor in welcome. Haltingly and barely audible, he began to read aloud, his hand drifting to stroke Bridget's silky head. And so began our reading dog program, a partnership between an elementary school and the Bedford Public library.

In 2009, a Golden Retriever named Bridget was placed with me for an extended period while she was in training. She is also a breeder for a service dog program. She quickly became a good will ambassador with customers and staff at the Library. Once we registered as a Pet Partners team with Delta Society, we were eligible to work in a variety of therapeutic activities. Our library administration knew from our experience in our local community that those who would most benefit from reading to a dog were those least likely to attend a library based program. Instead, we wanted to collaborate with the schools to take the program to the children.

Because of the value placed on partnerships by both the Bedford Public Library and our local school system, long-term relationships were already in place. The Library and the school system partner in many ways. The library Board and administration consider our library to be more than a building, and therefore the library staff and resources are actively involved throughout the community. For the past ten years, the Library's Outreach Services staff has taken literacy-based programming into the schools to provide approximately 600 programs each year for children up to 5th grade.

We contacted Dennis Turner, PhD., our school system's superintendent, to discuss the possibility of creating a therapy/reading dog program in a school. He embraced the concept immediately. While many school superintendents might not even discuss such an idea, he was immediately enthusiastic and supportive. He made it possible for us to work with an elementary school principal, who was also very supportive of any new method that might help his students succeed.

Knowing that 3rd grade is a critical year in attaining reading proficiency, we suggested working with 3rd grade students. Indiana's initiative to promote reading proficiency in third grade made this a perfect fit. The Indiana General Assembly has called on the Indiana Department of Education to develop a plan for improving third grade reading. The plan's first draft mandates increased reading time, using research based strategies for reading instruction, and includes a provision for additional help to struggling students (Stanczykie-wicz, 2010). Indiana third graders also take the ISTEP standardized test, which increases pressure on them. According to the Annie E. Casey Foundation report, students who are not able to read before entering fourth grade are likely to never achieve literacy skills. These students are more likely to drop out of high school, be unemployed, be unqualified for military service and live in poverty (Stanczykiewicz, 2010).

In the selected school, a majority of the students are on free or reduced price meals, which tends to predict lower standardized test score. Although Indiana students test slightly above the national proficiency average, the statistics are sobering. Among tested fourth graders, only thirty four percent are at or above Proficiency levels. Another thirty four percent of students tested below Basic levels (National Center for Education Statistics, 2009). Although these students are most in need of reading help, they are less likely to be receiving that help at home. In addition, they are less likely to be regular library users. Those children who would be most likely to visit the library to read to a dog are probably those who need it least. Low income library users are less likely to participate in library programs than middle income children, and to read less (Neuman, 2005).

To begin, we set up reading times with the four third grade teachers, who each selected two students. These students tended to have difficulty reading, but several were also children who were having a hard time for a variety of reasons. Some were going through difficult family situations and some were so shy that they tended to seem invisible among their peers. I met with each teacher to discuss the anticipated perception of the program with the children. The teachers were confident that reading to the dog would be perceived as a special treat, not as another remedial activity. Being the

'chosen' student meant an increase in esteem by classmates, not denigration.

PROGRAM GOALS

The school's teachers and staff have worked with me to learn about the school's reading assessment, and to help create documentation methods for this program. Also, as I have researched this topic, program goals are being developed, and include:

- Improvement of students' reading scores. Student reading proficiency will be assessed using a variety of methods already in use by the school.
- Work towards our Library's Vision: to be a highly valued resource that establishes and promotes long-term relationships with the community.
- Increase student awareness about the Library, and interest in visiting and using the Library.
- Increase student self-confidence in reading aloud, enjoyment of reading, and improvement in self-esteem and socialization skills overall.

Materials Selection

Each week I select a variety of books from the Children's section of our Library. I choose titles with each student in mind, searching for something appealing yet challenging. It is important for each child to be able to select a book of their own choosing. Being able to choose from a wide variety of books can be an empowering experience for a reluctant reader. I check to ensure that all of the books we take to the school are Accelerated Reader, so a student can gain points. In addition, I always remind students that they are from the public library and available for checkout. The R.E.A.D. program listserv provides a venue for finding and sharing appropriate book titles.

Book selection is an important part of this process. With each book the child reads, I am trying to help each student have a successful session that day, but beyond that, we are working toward the bigger picture. Our goal is to 'grow a reader' within these children – to create a successful relationship with books, reading, and the library that will continue throughout their lives. If the person in a therapy dog team is a volunteer visiting the school, unless they have a school or library background, book selection will be dependent upon others or rely on the use of pre-prepared booklists or on a classroom collection or school library. When volunteers visit public libraries with their dogs for animal assisted activities, books may be pre-selected by library staff, but without staff knowledge of the individuals who may be reading. Visiting children may also select books themselves from the library's collection to read to the dog, but may choose books that are too easy or too hard. Similarly, the child might select a familiar book that they know they can read, which ensures the visit will be pleasurably easy for the child, but it will not be challenging.

"Bridget! You're here!" The enthusiastic welcome may come from either a student or staff member as we enter the school for our weekly reading sessions. As I check in with the school secretary, Bridget enjoys her first of the many hugs and pats she will receive in the next two hours. The secretary calls up to our first class to tell the teacher, "Bridget's here." We make our way to the room where we will have our reading sessions. On the way, teachers or other staff members may rush up to greet Bridget and receive a quick dog therapy boost. A group of students may be lined up in the hallway on their way to class. I check with their teacher to see if the students may greet her, and if so, Bridget is soon hidden from view by eager students who take turns hugging her. Many will eagerly tell me about their own dogs, especially if there has been a traumatic event, such as the dog's injury or death. After a few moments, we pull away to go set up our reading area.

Each week, Bridget greets each student as they arrive. We all sit on a special reading blanket and Bridget snuggles up to each child while they read for their allotted twenty minutes. Sometimes the student will select two books and ask Bridget to pick which one she wants to hear. Some children will stroke the dog continuously while they are reading, and some unconsciously reach out to pet her when they come to a confusing word. I have learned that this is often a signal that help or encouragement is needed to tackle that word.

With these types of programs, what is especially difficult to quantify is the 'magic' that is created when children read to trained dogs. Statistics cannot demonstrate the warmth, acceptance, and lack of judgment that a child feels with a therapy dog. When we met one student, he announced solemnly that, "dogs don't like me." Four months later, that boy arrived each week with a huge grin on his face and an enthusiastic greeting for Bridget. Teachers assure me that besides viewing statistics, they see a tangible difference in students who read to Bridget. Self-confidence is improved and children who were 'invisible' are more involved. As one parent wrote on a survey, her son "never liked reading to anyone, but he loves reading to Bridget." Children are easily able to accept the idea that the reading dog is listening to them read and is enjoying the story. At our first session, a third grade girl stopped reading and said, "Can Bridget really read?"

Special Needs Class

We also meet weekly with the Special Needs class in the same elementary school, for animal assisted activities. The children greet and interact with Bridget, although they do not read. A school system therapist noted that she had never seen one student as verbal and interactive as during his visit with Bridget. A parent of another student said her son talks about Bridget all the time. These visits help to realize the library's vision by creating lifelong relationships with the community.

Unanticipated Benefits

Bridget forms and maintains individual relationships with each student. During her first semester at school, a very quiet boy read in a soft whisper without touching Bridget. Finally she sat up, put her chin on top of the book he was holding, and gazed at him lovingly. He smiled widely and began to pet her. After that day, he strode confidently into the room each time, and greeted Bridget as a friend. That summer I saw him at the Library with his family, and we visited Bridget in our office. His mother enthusiastically told me what a difference Bridget's visits had made in her son.

Bridget clearly provides therapy for some teachers and staff. Many of their students are facing economic, family, and personal difficulties every day, and staff members witness these children's painful struggles firsthand. During the school day, a furry hug with a therapy dog helps lighten their load. As we encounter both staff and students, I can see burdened faces lighten as they greet and pet Bridget.

This program has created and strengthened relationships between our library and students and their families. Additionally, our partnership with the local school system as a whole has grown. Our local school board has been listening with interest to the positive comments about the reading dog program. This school board appoints three of the seven members of our library's Board of Trustees, so this school board has an important role in our library's administration. Our relationship with the schools has a direct impact on future services and program for all citizens in our community.

Staff Involvement and Program Evaluation

With school staff assistance, we have begun using the school's assessment methods. This teacher and staff involvement makes this program a true partnership between the library and the school, and not merely a library outreach program. In their efforts to reach every student, the school uses a number of programs. In addition, teachers and staff members share with me their knowledge and anecdotal information about each child, to assist in goal setting.

The school's computer lab is used for periodic reading testing. The reports from these tests track reading levels over time. Again, the staff has been very helpful and involved in providing me with data. A baseline test has been set up with the group of eight readers. The test will be repeated after several weeks, with Bridget present, to assess any impact her presence might have.

Accelerated Reader test results, which school staff provides to me, can be used to assess both interest in reading, number of books the child has read, and the number of points earned. By reviewing students' test scores, I am able to gauge their comprehension of the books they read to Bridget. Right after her first reading session in 2010, a student took an AR test and scored her very first perfect score. After that, she was much more willing to participate, and she is reading near grade level in 2011. For this reason, at a staff member's suggestion, we are now examining data from Accelerated Reader tests to follow up on last year's readers. This will help us track any long term impact on students who participate in the program.

Obviously the data we are collecting is not scientific, and there is no formal study or control group. Data collected will reflect and include the results of all the tangible and intangible inputs. However, for the purposes of this program, this information will be sufficient to track outcomes. Because of the school's willingness to try new methods and track data in different ways, we will be able to continue finding better and more accurate ways to reflect growth.

Anecdotal Information

We use teacher and parent surveys to track anecdotal information. Comments about the students such as "showed more enthusiasm," "increased confidence in reading", and "could not wait for Reading Dog day to arrive" provide useful information. Survey results from 2010 show that 100% of the parent/guardian respondents felt their child's reading had improved since taking part in the program. They also all agreed that their child was exhibiting positive changes. One teacher stated that her students were very motivated to take Accelerated Reader tests after reading to Bridget.

Summer Reading

Summer reading loss is a real concern for American educators. Research consistently shows that struggling readers lose ground over the summer. Of even greater concern is the fact that these losses are cumulative, creating a wider gap each year between more proficient and less proficient students. A reader with difficulties can accumulate a two year lag in reading achievement before reaching middle school. In addition, this loss is magnified for students from lower income homes, and makes up a large part of the difference between high and low income students (Mraz, Rasinski, 2007). Children from low-income homes do not have the same access to books and other educational opportunities during the summer. This summer learning loss continues throughout the child's education (Gambrel, 2008). Children in families with incomes below the poverty line are less likely to be read to aloud everyday than are children in families with incomes at or above poverty (McGill-Franzen, A., Allington, R., 2003).

In 2010 we sought a way to continue the 'reading dog' program throughout the summer. Again, we wanted to take the program to children who might not visit the Library or participate in library programming. According to the American Library Association's website, "(d)ozens of research studies have shown that it is essential for children to read outside of the school environment. National research proves that reading over the summer is crucial to a child's success in school" (American Library Association, http://www.ala.org). Students who do more reading at home are better readers. Additionally, having children read as much as possible is one of the critical components of becoming a proficient reader, according to the National Education Association, 2010. Low-income children, who are the target group for summer meals, often don't have educational alternatives when school is not in session (Neuman, 2009).

To address this challenge, our Library has partnered with the schools in additional ways. Our community's schools serve as host sites for the U.S. Department of Agriculture's Summer Meals program. This program provides free breakfast and lunch for children throughout the summer at a local school cafeteria. During the school year, many children depend upon free and reduced-price breakfast and lunch through the School Breakfast and National School Lunch Programs. Lack of nutrition during the summer months may set up a cycle for poor performance once school begins again in the fall (http://www.summerfood.usda.gov/).

Again, when we inquired of the school system superintendent about partnering with the school for summer reading, the idea was enthusiastically received. Our library's Outreach Services holds very popular weekly programs there throughout the summer. Throughout the summer we set up a reading station in the school once each week, where school age children had the opportunity to read with Bridget. The school staff actively participated by promoting the program to everyone who arrived for meals. Because of their enthusiastic promotion, many children eagerly awaited 'Bridget's Day' each week. We set up a colorful divider between the waiting crowd and our reading area so that each child received a one on one experience with Bridget. We provide an assortment of library books from which to select, and many children read while they waited. We frequently remind the families that the books are available from the library, and encourage them to visit the library. However, due to the 'drop-in' aspect of the program, we are not able to follow up on any library visits that may have resulted from the program. Over twenty children generally read to Bridget each week during Summer Meals.

Books into the Home

Hoosier Uplands, a regional non-profit that administers Head Start and other programs, also partnered with us to support this summer reading effort. They provided funding for the summer program to give Bridget's readers their own book. After reading to Bridget, each child was invited to browse through a wide variety of new paperback books and select one to take home. Each book included a bookplate with a photograph of Bridget and an inscription reading, "I read to Bridget," with a line for the child to add their name. This provided a way to get books into the homes of children who are most likely low-income. According to the National Education Association, the more types of reading materials there are in the home, the higher students are in reading proficiency (2010).

This program proved to be not only a partnership, but a relationship-builder with the community at large. For months after the summer program, parents have greeted us at church and in the grocery store, saying "My children read to Bridget this summer, and it was wonderful. Thank you for providing this service! The kids talked about it all summer." In addition, when children see us out in the community, they rush over to talk about how they read to Bridget last summer. This program is helping to realize our library's Vision to be "a highly valued resource that establishes and promotes long-term relationships with the community" and helped us to reach non-library users (http://www.bedlib.org).

Program Expansion Difficulties

The biggest problem with our unique approach to animal assisted therapy is that we are only one team. Throughout the school year, we are meeting with the same eight students from third grade. During the summer, we see at least 20 children each week. Obviously, with more therapy dog teams we could impact many more children each year. Because our team consists of a therapy dog and a professional librarian representing our public library, the possibilities for replicating this exactly within our community are small. Now that our program is established, we hope to encourage volunteers to register as therapy dog teams. However, this is difficult to accomplish due to our rural population and the intensive nature and requirements of therapy dog work.

A volunteer must be extremely dedicated to commit to animal assisted therapy. A huge investment of time and resources is required. The first step is creating awareness of the concept and the program. Because the reading dog idea is still so new, many people are surprised when they hear about it. A common reaction from adults is still, "Read to a dog? Dogs can't read!" Media involvement has helped this lack of awareness tremendously, and television and print coverage make a 'feel good' story that sells itself.

Once a person is interested enough to investigate the program, owning an appropriate dog is required. In order to pass the evaluation with Delta Society or another organization, the team must meet a high standard. Delta Society states that dogs must meet many criteria to be successful, including behavior that is reliable, controllable, and predictable. The dog must enjoy being petted and hugged, remain calm even in chaotic environments such as fire drills, and must have obedience skills and good health. The human partner must be a confident experienced handler and pass a written test.

FUTURE PLANS

As mentioned above, the best way to be able to provide more therapy dog teams is through increased awareness among the general public. In 2011, we will develop publicity designed to interest potential therapy dog teams.

As the field of animal assisted therapy and animal assisted activities grows and develops, and awareness is increased, hopefully more professional librarians and teachers will create their own therapy dog teams. As more education professionals work directly to provide this kind of programming, benefits will be apparent. Ideally, if classroom teachers are part of a therapy dog teams, the dog could spend more time in the classroom. Teachers would be able to readily assess the students' response and improvement. In addition, having more professionals in the field would reduce the reliance on volunteers.

FUTURE RESEARCH DIRECTIONS

The use of Facility Dogs in schools is an increasing trend, and provides many benefits to students. Facility dogs are trained and placed by service dog organizations with a specific teacher or administrator as the dog's partner. The dog lives with its partner and attends school daily. This is an area for future research, which could help determine the benefits and pitfalls of having more dogs in schools.

The use of dogs to facilitate reading fluency and improved behavior is a brand-new field that is wide open to research possibilities. A new field of professional study is beginning to emerge, and this will increase the amount of research undertaken. Virtually every aspect of animal assisted therapy is a prime topic for research. Because reading to dogs is still a new concept, most of the research already conducted has been small in scale and limited to local programs for limited amounts of time. Important topics for research include determining how and why animal assisted therapy affects students, as well as developing and selecting the best settings, techniques, and delivery methods. Data collection and student assessment is already an important research topic in education. Studies that address assessment of the impact of reading dogs would be a valuable addition. Partnerships between public libraries and schools provide benefits for both organizations. Research that examines and develops best practices for these partnerships would increase their effectiveness.

CONCLUSION

Having children read to therapy dogs is proving to be a valuable educational experience. Studies completed to this point clearly demonstrate value with improved reading levels and test scores. Also of importance are the many positive behavioral changes that can take place in these children. Because of the partnership between our public library and school system, we have been able to develop a reading dog program that is helping to improve children's reading skills and their school experience. Additionally, the summer program will help to expand reading involvement to children who need it most. Now that the reading dog program is underway we will be able to continually refine the assessment tools we are using, and to create new ones. By creating this program, we have deepened the relationship between our public library, schools, and the community.

Many adults can point to a special person or event that helped make their elementary school years brighter. As a librarian, I am eager to help our community provide a positive educational start for our children. For some children whose school experience is difficult, being able to read to a special dog could be that special experience.

REFERENCES

American Library Association. (n.d.). *Website*. Retrieved February 10, 2011, from http://www.ala.org/

Arnold, J. (2010). *Through a dog's eyes*. New York, NY: Spiegel & Grau.

Census. (2010). *American community survey, 2005-2009*. Retrieved February 1, 2011 from http://factfinder.census.gov/

Delta Society. (n.d.). *Website*. Retrieved February 1, 2011, from http://www.deltasociety.org/

Fine, A. (Ed.). (2010). *Handbook on animal-assisted therapy: Theoretical foundations and guidelines for practice*. Burlington, MA: Elsevier Press.

Friesen, L. (2010). Exploring animal-assisted programs with children in school and therapeutic contexts. *Early Childhood Education Journal, 37*(4), 261–267. doi:10.1007/s10643-009-0349-5

Gambrell, L. (2008). Closing the summer reading gap. *Reading Today, 25*(5), 18.

Glander, M., & Dam, T. (2006). *Households' use of public and other types of libraries: 2002*. U.S. Department of Education. (2011). *Publications and product search*. Washington, DC: National Center for Education Statistics. Retrieved February 1, 2011, from http://nces.ed.gov/pubsearch

Indiana Department of Education. (2010). *Indiana's plan to ensure student literacy by the end of 3rd grade, 2010*. Retrieved January 15, 2011, from http://www.doe.in.gov/

Indiana Department of Education. (2011). *Office of student assessment*. Retrieved January 20, 2011, from http://www.doe.in.gov/

Indiana Department of Workforce Development. (2010). *Hoosiers by the numbers*. Retrieved February 13, 2011, from http://www.hoosierdata.in.gov/

Indiana Youth Institute. (2010). *Kids count in Indiana 2010 data book*. Retrieved February 1, 2011, from http://www.iyi.org/

Institute of Education Sciences. (2009). *The nation's report card*. U.S. Department of Education. Washington, DC: National Center for Education Statistics. Retrieved February 1, 2011, from http://nces.ed.gov/. Retrieved February 5, 2011 from http://nationsreportcard.gov/reading_2009/

Intermountain Therapy Dogs. (2010). *Reading education assistance dogs (R.E.A.D.) team training manual* (10th ed.). Salt Lake City, UT: Intermountain Therapy Dogs.

International Reading Association. (n.d.). *Website*. Retrieved February 10, 2011, from http://www.reading.org/

Jalongo, M. R. (2004). Canine visitors: The influence of therapy dogs on young children's learning and well-being in classrooms and hospitals. *Early Childhood Education, 32*(1), 9–16. doi:10.1023/B:ECEJ.0000039638.60714.5f

Kulpinski, D. (2009). *Partnership for a nation of learners: joining forces, creating value*. Institute of Museum and Library Services. Retrieved February 1, 2011 from http:// www.oclc.org/us/en/default.htm

Lynch, J. (2003). Developing a physiology of inclusion: Recognizing the health benefits of animal companions. In *Reading Education Assistance Dogs (R.E.A.D.) team training manual*. 10th ed. (2010). Salt Lake City, UT: Intermountain Therapy Animals.

McGill-Franzen, A., & Allington, R. (2003). Bridging the summer reading gap. *Instructor, 112*(8), 17.

Mertz, C. (2009). *A qualitative study examining the use of canine reading programs with young readers*. Unpublished doctoral dissertation, University of Wisconsin-Stout.

Mraz, M., & Rasinski, T. (2007). Summer reading loss. *The Reading Teacher, 60*(8), 784–789. doi:10.1598/RT.60.8.9

National Education Association. (2010). *Facts about children's literacy*. Retrieved February 12, 2011, from http://www.nea.org/

Neuman, S. (2009). *Income affects how kids use technology and access knowledge*. National Summer Learning Association. Retrieved January 30, 2011, from http://www.summerlearning.org/

Olmert, M. D. (2009). *Made for each other: The biology of the human-animal bond*. Cambridge, MA: Da Capo Press.

(2010). *Reading Education Assistance Dogs (R.E.A.D.) team training manual* (10th ed.). Salt Lake City, UT: Intermountain Therapy Animals.

Semmel, M. (2009). *Museums, libraries, and 21st century skills*. Institute of Museum and Library Services. Retrieved February 4, 2011, from http://www.oclc.org/us/en/default.htm

Smith, C. (2009). *An analysis and evaluation of Sit Stay Read: Is the program effective in improving student engagement and reading outcomes?* Unpublished doctoral dissertation, National-Louis University.

Stanczykiewicz, B. (2010). *Indiana's 3rd grade reading plan*. Indiana Youth Institute. Retrieved January 30, 2011, from http://www.iyi.org/

United States Department of Agriculture. (2009). *Summer food service program*. Retrieved February 12, 2011, from http://www.summerfood.usda.gov/

Velde, S. (2005). *The development and validation of a research evaluation instrument to assess the effectiveness of animal-assisted therapy*. Unpublished doctoral dissertation, Kennedy-Western Univrsity.

ADDITIONAL READING

All Ears Reading. http://arf.net/people-programs/all-ears-reading/index.php

Barrett, L. (2003). Paws to read @ your library. *Virginia Libraries, 49*(3), 7.

Biden, A. (2004). Who's the Four-Legged Librarian? *Children & Libraries: The Journal of the Association for Library Service to Children, 2*(2), 44–47.

Bittner, M. (2008). Nine to nineteen: youth in museums and libraries: engaging America's youth-a leadership initiative of the Institute of Museum and Library Services. Institute of Museum and Library Services. Retrieved February 4, 2011 from http:// www.oclc.org/us/en/default.htm.

Black, S. (2009). Sit, Stay, and Read. *The American School Board Journal, 196*(12), 36–37.

Butler, K. (2004). *Therapy dogs today: their gifts, our obligations*. New York, NY: Funpuddle press.

Canines will help with synthetic phonics, says charity. (2010). *Education, (413), 5*. Carolina Canines Paws for Reading http://www.carolina-canines.org/Paws_for_Reading.html

Corbet-Alderman, T. (2004). Kids reading-it's going to the dogs. *Behavior Analysis Digest., 16*(1), 1–2.

Debra, N. (2006, August 13). Literacy; at these reading, listeners growl for more. *New York Times,* p 5. Fidos for freedom DEAR program. http://www.fidosforfreedom.org/therapy-dogs/dear-teams/dear_program.php

Francis, A. (2009). Thursdays with MacGyver. *Children and Libraries, 7*(2), 50–53.

Going to the dogs. (2003) *Reading Today.* 20(4)46.

Griess, J. O. (2010). *A canine audience: The effect of animal-assisted therapy on reading progress among students identified with learning disabilities*. Unpublished doctoral dissertation, University of South Florida, Tampa.

Grover, S. (2010). *101 creative ideas for animal assisted therapy; interventions for AAT teams and working professionals.* New York, NY: Motivational Press.

Hughes, K. (2002). See Spot read. *Public Libraries., 41*(6), 328–330.

Implementing a reading education assistance dog program. (2005). *Childhood Education, 81*(3), 153-156.

International Reading Association. http://www.reading.org/General/Default.aspx

International Society for Animal Assisted Therapy. http://www.aat-isaat.org/

Jalongo, M. R. (2005). "What are all these dogs doing at school?": Using therapy dogs to promote children's reading practice. *Childhood Education, 81*(3), 152–159.

Kaymen, M. (2005). *Exploring animal-assisted therapy as a reading intervention strategy.* Unpublished master's thesis. Dominican University of California.

Kulpinski, D. (2009). *Partnership for a nation of learners: joining forces, creating value.* Institute of Museum and Library Services. Washington, D.C. Retrieved February 4, 2011 from http://www.oclc.org/us/en/default.htm.

Library Dogs. http://www.librarydogs.com

Margolis, R. (2000). Dog day afternoons. *School Library Journal, 46*(2), 26.

Newlin, R. (2003). Paws for reading. *School Library Journal, 49*(6), 43.

Paradise, J. (2007). *An analysis of improving student performance through the use of registered therapy dogs serving as motivators for reluctant readers.* Unpublished doctoral dissertation, University of Central Florida, Orlando.

Perkins, M. M. (2009). Tail Wagging Tutors Program at Kiln Public Library. *Mississippi Libraries, 73*(2), 42.

Prest, M. J. (2005). Dog days at the library. *Chronicle of Philanthropy, 17*(20), 4–5.

Reading program gets "Paws Up!". (2007). *Curriculum Review, 46*(5), 6-7. Reading with Rover http://www.readingwithrover.org/

Smith, K. (2010). *Impact of animal assisted therapy reading instruction on reading performance of homeschooled students.* Unpublished doctoral dissertation, Northcentral University.

Snider, B. (2007). Gone to the dogs: kids connect with canine classmates. Edutopia. Retrieved on 1/15/11 from http://www.edutopia.org/read-with-rover

Tales to Tails. (2010). *Unabashed Librarian, 15*(6), 25.

Chapter 14
A Tale of Two Schools

Karen Ellis
Taylor Public Library, USA

ABSTRACT

This case study illustrates two partnerships between the Taylor Public Library and two area schools, first with the Taylor Independent School District for facility use, and second with the Temple College satellite campus at Taylor for their use of the public library facilities in exchange for a free student worker. The partnership with the local school district was specifically during 2002 through 2006 to continue providing programming during the summer. The Taylor Public Library lost its old facility, and while temporarily located elsewhere, had no venue for summer programs. The library and the school district partnered to hold the summer events on local campuses until the new public library building opened in 2007. The partnership between the Taylor Public Library and Temple College consisted of use of library space to house the college's nursing and medical collections, allow access to these holdings to enrolled college students, and grant students public library cards. For this use, the Taylor Public Library acts as supervisor for a qualifying student worker, funded by Temple College.

INTRODUCTION

Schools and public library can share resources and collaborate to the benefit of both the students and the public. While often facility based partnerships involved a shared campus or shared library between the public and educational institutions, the partnerships illustrated here are not to that extent.

There is no melding of institutions; illustrated here are two much smaller collaborations. Still, both parties provide and both parties benefit in each of these partnerships—a fair exchange. These partnerships are stop-gap measures to meet specific needs with their partners. These partnerships also speak to the small town atmosphere, where community leaders are more apt to compromise and come together for solutions. It doesn't hurt

DOI: 10.4018/978-1-61350-387-4.ch014

BACKGROUND

The City of Taylor, located in east Williamson County, Texas, was incorporated in 1876. Taylor was very much a railroad town, built on land purchased by investors in advance of the construction of tracks through the new town. The small town grew up quickly, as the area's rich, black prairie soil made for favorable farming. Immigrants from Czechoslovakia and Germany were attracted to the fertile soil and small farming communities sprung up throughout the county. Cotton became the crop of choice. Local gins processed the cotton, which was then shipped off via the Taylor railroad depots. More recently, construction of instate highways better connected the western side of Williamson County to Austin. This slowed growth in Taylor. Williamson County, Texas, is one of the ten the fastest growing counties in the U.S. Taylor is still a rural, agricultural town of 15,191, self sufficient with slow growth.

Taylor Public Library

The Taylor Public Library (TPL) was first established in 1899 by a woman's study club called the Sesame Circle, one of their goals being the creation of a lending library. Club members served as librarians and a small charge was required for lending. Those fees went towards purchasing more materials and the book collection grew. The early charter for the library defined the primary populations served would be the residents of the City of Taylor and all students who attended school within the city. TPL had many homes throughout the last century, including a Quonset hut shared with the local Girl Scouts troop, a room in the Chamber of Commerce offices at City Hall, a small building on school land, etc. Despite the efforts of local groups and city management, no permanent home

or paid librarian could be secured. In the 1950's the push for a library building was energized, and a committee was established to raise funds. Donations from many community organizations and individuals resulted in a dedicated library building with furnishings, collections and head librarian in 1960. The library was independently governed for many years by a Library Board who raised funds and made operational decisions. There was an addition to the original building in 1970, and a second addition in 1990. This brought the size of the library up to 9,143 square feet. Unfortunately these additions were accompanied by roof leaks and ground seeps, a common problem due to the region's geology. By the late 1990's water leaks had taken their toll on the structure and the building was closed due to mold. Eventually the library was quartered in the Auditorium at Taylor City Hall for five years. A bond issue was approved by a narrow margin (2 votes) to construct a new library building which would be much larger at 20,000 square feet. Land was donated by the Taylor Independent School District, with extra property to expand the library to 35,000 square feet in the future. Ground was broken in 2006, and the new Taylor Public Library opened its doors in March 2007.

Taylor Independent School District

The Taylor Independent School District (TISD) began as a small three-room school in 1884. As the city grew, money was then raised to construct a three story brick school in 1890, which is coincidently where the new Taylor Public Library now sits. TISD continued to build more campuses and grow. It wasn't until 1950 that the school district pulled away from city control to create its own independent district, with a school board and taxes for operations. This gave TISD the ability to have control over operations and policies free from any city restrictions and gave the district the ability to deal directly with neighboring school districts. As the east part of Williamson County grew, so did

---

that everybody knows everybody, and personal connections ease the way for cooperation.

TISD. Many students came from unincorporated parts of the county. Today TISD has over 3,000 students enrolled at seven active campuses. The newest campus is a brand new high school which opened in August 2011.

TPL PARTNERSHIP WITH TISD

The Taylor Public Library has held annual summer programming since the 1960's and had typically used space in the original library building. Tables and chairs were pushed back to afford enough space for the children to sit on the floor and enjoy the programs. These programs were entertainment with a reading slant, to encourage area children to participate in the Texas State sponsored reading incentive program. The Friends of the Taylor Public Library raise money through events, grants and sponsors to pay for entertainers and components of the program. The local Taylor Kiwanis Club would sponsor the tee-shirts for youth participants. This was a very organized annual program with lots of community support and involvement. Even at the old library site space was getting very tight for this programming.

When the old library building closed due to mold and water damage in July 2002, some of the already planned summer programs took place in the old school auditorium on 7th Street. For the next summer, TPL Director Norma Patschke worked with the school district for use of facilities. Each year one of the two main elementary school campuses was open to hold summer school classes for elementary school students. An agreement was reached to allow TPL to hold the entertainment part of the summer programs in the cafeteria space of whichever elementary campus was open, either at Pasemann or T.H. Johnson Elementary School. Part of the agreement was that the library would provide a separate program on Wednesday morning just for the summer school students. While there was some extra performers costs on behalf of the library, the Friends of the Library stepped

up and funded these additional programs. The use of the school facilities extended into the month of July when summer school was out, so the school district absorbed the cost of keeping the school open, air conditioned, and maintained.

This partnership was of course to great benefit of the Taylor area youth. In June and July of 2003 TPL held the Summer Reading Program (SRP) events at Pasemann Elementary School cafeteria. The cafeterias at both elementary schools have large, elevated stages and integrated sound system, making them quite versatile for the library's events. Programs were held Monday nights and Wednesday mornings. Per the agreement, a separate Wednesday morning program was offered just for the elementary school students taking summer school classes. This nearly doubled the attendance to SRP events for the library. The size of the cafeteria space was very much larger than afforded in the old library building, and there was much better parking and access at the schools. It some coordination on the part of summer school administrators and teachers to allow students to attend the special Wednesday programs. All classes were ushered into the cafeteria and seated by instructors and aides. Audience sizes were approx. 240 for the school only programs, as opposed attendance by the public, which varied depending on the program, from 195 to 500 per performance. The SRP attendance for programs in subsequent years also fluctuated, partly because of the change from one campus one summer to another the next summer for the performances, a confusion also shared by the performers who would call library staff from the wrong campus, wondering where everybody was.

TPL has always supported summer reading, even through difficulties with location. The Texas State Library & Archives Commission has sponsored an annual theme for summer programming since 1958, providing manuals with programming ideas, reading forms and certificates to make providing a well rounded program easier for all public libraries in the state. The benefits of a youth summer reading program have been long touted by public libraries and have likewise been well documented in recent studies. Benefits of public library summer reading programs include the following:

- It is necessary for young students to continue reading through the summer or lose their reading skills
- Loss of reading skills can result in a 50-67% "achievement gap" especially for minority children or those living in poverty
- Summer reading enables struggling students to have positive reading experiences and develop good reading habits
- Fun, voluntary reading is important for students to become better readers, writers and spellers
- Students engaged in voluntary reading outperform students who do not. (American Library Association)

The bond-funded new TPL facility included a 2,000 square foot Meeting Room, with a small kitchen, surround sound, 12 foot screen, projector, and a occupancy limit of 286 people. Since TPL opened its new building in 2007, just in time for summer programming, TISD has not been able to regularly attend these programs. Problems with securing transportation and the demands of state testing are a direct cause. Summer school was now dedicated to those students who performed poorly on state required achievement tests. As there is a rating system for school districts pertaining to student scores on these tests, summer school became very tightly focused on raising the scores of lower performing students. As these are exactly the types of student who would also benefit from summer reading, this competition for student time is unfortunate. However, some of the federally funded programs for at risk-children were able to bring their students to the library during summer events. Consequently, TPL did not drop the non-public Wednesday morning program and instead

advertised this to special classes like Even Start and local day cares and private schools. Popularity for this time slot continues, as the day care teachers had better management of their classes when not competing for space with the general public audiences.

CONCLUSION AND FUTURE CONSIDERATIONS

There are many benefits to a school/public library partnership. Public libraries and schools hold similar missions to educate and improve youth, to engender a love of learning, and give students the tools to become successful in life. As the audience is the same, marketing and programming can be shared between public libraries and schools. Frequently it is the public library that makes the first contact to schools. With the right attitude, a multitude of possible opportunities for partnerships and collaborations exist between these two institutions. A school can certainly play a part in encouraging summer reading programs at public libraries, and students could be given recognition at school for their summer reading achievements (MacDonald, p. 11).

This facility-based partnership between TPL and TISD was successful because of its focus and the benefit to both partners. Since this was not an ongoing joint use project, there were no complications of access and hours. Both partners were able to maintain their own policies and programs without unduly infringing on each other. Because there was a pending solution to the library's facility problems with the construction of the new library building, the end was in sight and smaller issues could be overcome without hard feelings or other complications to the partnership. There was a clear beginning and end to this partnership. The ability to cooperate continues, as the City of Taylor, the Taylor Public Library and Taylor ISD have a very good working relationship. There is in fact an interagency agreement between the school district and the city pertaining to facility use. This agreement is also reflected in the TPL *Meeting Room Policy*, citing that while other entities are bound to certain use rules and fees for the meeting room, the school district is not. In recent years, the TPL Meeting Room has been utilized by the school district for meetings, workshops and graduation ceremonies. Conversely, when the City of Taylor needs to hold public hearings or meetings, TISD offers its facilities free of charge or restrictions for city use. This spirit of partnership is unique and staff in both City Administration and TISD work to maintain this relationship.

This relationship also opens up the possibility of future facility use between TISD and TPL. The TISD campuses still contain components not replicated in the new library facility—this includes larger parking, a theater style auditorium and stage at the older high school and athletic fields. Should TPL need to hold a much bigger program than can be handled by the library's current meeting room, the schools could meet that need. Since there are a number of schools in different parts of the city, library programs that target different neighborhoods could be coordinated from those campuses. In terms of venue and site, the use could be varied. This valued partnership has many future possibilities.

TPL PARTNERSHIP WITH TEMPLE COLLEGE

Background

Temple Junior College was established in 1926, but changed their name to Temple College in 1996 as its role had changed somewhat, offering nursing and allied medical programs and transferable credits for students moving on to four year colleges and universities. In addition to the main campus in Temple, Texas, there are three other campuses—the Taylor Campus, the Cameron Education Center in Milam County, and the Texas Bioscience Institute in Temple off the main campus. The Taylor campus is 37 miles away from the main campus, the Cameron center is 34 miles away. Primarily, the Temple College service area covers the City of Temple and the Temple Independent School District, communities and school districts of eastern Bell County, Texas, as well as selected school districts in Milam County, just to the southeast of Bell County, and many of the eastern school districts in Williamson County, just the county south of Bell County. This includes, among others, the Taylor Independent School District. Temple College is a two-year college, as defined by Texas Statute, to provide vocational, technical and academic courses for certification or associate degrees. College coursework from this junior college is transferable to four year universities in Texas, so many students find this an affordable step towards a four year degree. Temple College is a member of the Southern Association of Colleges and Schools.

Temple College at Taylor

A chance encounter at a 1996 Taylor Independent School Board meeting led to the establishment of Temple College at Taylor (TCAT). Taylor ISD Superintendent Herman Smith had promoted a school bond issue to build a new middle school on the north side of town and had created a citizen's advisory committee to help move the issue forward. Other concerns surrounding this possible bond issue was the potential demolition of the old historic school on 7th Street and some thought that a new football field was the true motivation for the bond issue. Some prominent citizens and local leaders were very much opposed the destruction of the old school building. This group of individuals came to the school board meeting to voice their objections to the possible bond issue.

Dr. Mark Nigliazzo, then President of Temple College, had been working on a plan to bring college coursework to the Taylor community. Dr. Nigliazzo brought his board members to the TISD

Board meeting to propose a partnership. While it appeared that this proposal met with lukewarm reception, it sparked quite a bit of interest with members of the public, namely the same group of individuals opposed to the middle school bond issue. John Nelson was a member of this group of concerned citizen, and was himself the President of the Taylor Economic Development Corporation (TEDC). Mr. Nelson and interested citizens and community leaders subsequently met with Dr. Nigliazzo. (J. Nelson, personal communication, March 15, 2011.)

A Temple College at Taylor (TCAT) Foundation was formed and set about to seek local support and funding. The TEDC was closely involved, seeing this as an opportunity to strengthen Taylor's appeal to business prospects. However, the local Taylor community would have to fund the facilities for a local campus. Under this stipulation, local taxes would not be required to fund the Taylor campus. The TCAT Foundation solicited local business, school districts, civic organizations and area governments in attempt to raise the estimated $1,577,869.00 required for facilities in Taylor and the required renovations and equipment. TISD enhanced their advance placement courses to better mesh with the college curriculum. HEB, a Texas based grocery chain, owned an old store on Main Street in downtown Taylor. With funds raised through donations and other contributions, the TCAT Foundation purchased the old HEB store, renovated it and made it available for use by Temple College in late 1996. This expansion of the Temple College system was heartily welcomed by enrolling students in Taylor and eastern Williamson and western Milam counties. In the fall of 1996 TCAT offered an initial eighteen courses to students. Further expansion of the building in 1997 allowed for a licensed vocational nursing program. A grand opening celebration in November 1997 featured then First Lady of Texas Laura Bush as keynote speaker.

TCAT Problems

However, even with the renovations and specialized labs for the LVN and EMT programs, the old HEB building was soon at capacity. TISD offered class space at some of their older facilities. The one thing lacking was any space for a library. The Temple College does have a campus library in Temple, the Hubert M. Dawson Library. Holdings of the Dawson Library include over 55,000 items, periodicals, microforms and online resources. These are available to all students at all campuses. In addition, the Dawson Library is a member of TexShare, a state-wide reciprocal borrowing system among participating libraries. The TexShare Card is a program promoted by the Texas State Library & Archives Commission. Public libraries who participate in this program qualified for grant funding. The TexShare Card program potentially opens up most public and academic library collections to Temple College students and staff. The Hubert M. Dawson Library would issue its TexShare Cards to faculty and registered students, who in turn could use that to gain access to other libraries, including TPL. Students still needed specific titles not owned by TPL, so they could request materials from the Dawson Library. Eventually a courier route was established to transport materials between the Temple and other campuses.

Joint Use Libraries: Issues

The typical model in use for combining library services between a public and academic library has been joint use facilities. Sometimes this arrangement succeeds, as in the case of St. Petersburg Junior College and Seminole Community Library, Florida. The City of Seminal needed a new library and St. Petersburg Junior College was building a new campus in town. The city and the college worked out a joint use agreement. This was a real bargain for the City of Seminole, with the college securing not only state construction funds, but also a match to the grant funds raised by the city for the library. The library was constructed on campus, with staffing to be provided by the city, with two additional staff hired by the college. The library hours were then increased from 52 hours to 62 hours a week, adding Sunday hours with some additional hours during college exam periods. This 20 year agreement also included collections funding from both partners. This agreement had major cost-savings for the City of Seminole, and officials from both institutions seemed quite pleased with the arrangement. The joint use library continues in operation today. (Norton, 2000, April 28).

Sometimes the political climate or ownership issues can torpedo a joint use facility. The City of Clearwater, Florida, had quite a different take on a joint use library with St. Petersburg Junior College. City commissioners did not support the idea of giving up the existing East Library location of the city library system for an addition onto the college library. The entire idea of a shared library was unattractive to the city commissioners; one member cited that such a facility would not be family friendly. There were concerns about funding sources, sales of the old city library and commissioners could not support a request for $8 million state fund to be used in the project. (*City rejects idea of sharing library*, 1998, November 7).

If issues can be overcome, there are many benefits of joint use facilities for the local community. These benefits include better facilities that are either bigger or newer than the community could fund on its own. This would also include advantages in access to library services with potentially expanded hours. Another benefit would be access to a more diverse educational collection in addition to a popular public collection. This gives access for citizens for learning opportunities not otherwise afforded in a smaller public library. The staffing would typically be a melded of public, academic and student employees and librarians. This diverse staffing would enhance services to both the student and public populations. As students

and the general public come together there is the potential for interaction between many walks of life and generations. Think of the programming possibilities using expertise of college faculty or more popular entertainment and enrichment programming that public libraries do so well.

The drawbacks of joint use libraries between academic and public include possible alienation of either of the service populations. College students may be less than happy to engage in research and study when there are groups of small children or noisier public patrons about. Likewise, it may be off-putting to a citizen to enter a campus or school facility. Campus layouts themselves favor access to students and faculty. Also, the collections can be tipped to the academic side, since research and curriculum support is the college library's purpose. There may be less space or visibility for popular materials that citizens would wish to use. College or other academic libraries have a different degree of campus security that might make a public user apprehensive. Likewise, the service philosophies of public librarians and academic librarians are different and could become an issue. Likewise, as seen above, funding is always a sticky problem—how much, from which partner, etc. (McNicol, 2006).

For Taylor, a joint use facility was never really an option. The City of Taylor had passed a bond issue for $3.4 million in 2003 to construct a new library building. The site of the new building was never in question, as TISD had given the city a tract of land adjoining the old 1960 library site. There were no funds for purchase of any different property, and Temple College was not interested in a joint venture.

TCAT Library Requirements

To maintain accreditation in the Southern Association of Colleges and Schools, American Dental Association, and nursing and allied health agencies, library services are required:

The institution, through ownership or formal arrangements or agreements, provides and supports student and faculty access and user privileges to adequate library collections and services and to other learning/information resources consistent with the degrees offered. Collections, resources, and services are sufficient to support all its educational, research, and public service programs. (Temple College, sec. 2.9)

To meet that specific requirement, the following is described in the narrative section of Temple College's accreditation report:

Temple College provides and supports student, faculty, and staff access and user privileges to adequate library collections as well as to other learning and information resources consistent with the degrees offered by the College. Through ownership and formal agreements, sufficient information resources are available for educational programs.

Temple College maintains a library in the Hubert M. Dawson Library building on the main campus in Temple, a reference library at the Texas Bioscience Institute, and has a Library Use Agreement with the Taylor Public Library for students at the Temple College at Taylor Center. (Temple College, sec. 2.9 Narrative)

Students at both the Cameron Educational Center and TCAT could make use of the collection at the Dawson Library, by either actually going there in person or by requesting materials through the Dawson's online catalog. Originally, those reserved Dawson Library materials would be delivered to the main offices at the satellite campuses. While this is still the case for Cameron, and further agreement was reached at between Temple College and TPL. The Temple College courier now makes a stop at the Taylor Public Library, delivering and picking up materials at least twice a week. The Dawson Library charges the materials to the student's library account, so no further handling by TPL staff. TPL is open much longer hours than the front office at TCAT. TPL also has an afterhours book drop, making it easy for student to return items at any time. This is reiterated in the Library and Other Learning Researches section of the Temple College's accreditation compliance reports, affirming that appropriate library and research services were available for all students and facility.

The Taylor Public Library and Temple College have a formal agreement whereby Taylor Public Library helps supply library services, including checkout privileges, to Temple College students. In addition, Taylor Public Library houses Temple College's collection of nursing and general medical books and journals which helps support the LVN and EMS programs offered in Taylor.

A new instructional building in Taylor currently in the planning stage includes space for a library. This new library area should make it possible to offer a broader selection of materials and services directly to students at Taylor, while still providing access to the Dawson Library's collection via courier service. (Temple College, sec. 3.8.1)

The mentioned new instructional building for Taylor never quite materialized, due to funding issues. However, the nursing program is still held at the TCAT campus on Main Street in Taylor, though this could change in the future, should funding become available. However, to date, the agreement between TCAT and TPL continues, as long as the nursing program remains in town.

Another aspect of the requirements for Temple College's accreditation also includes library instruction:

The institution ensures that users have access to regular and timely instruction in the use of the library and other learning/information resources. (Temple College, sec 3.8.2)

This library instruction is also provided by the staff of TPL when tours and library instruction are requested by TCAT faculty. This covers general tours of the public library and use of the catalog up to specific uses of online resources and databases. When classes are in session at TCAT, the public library sees frequent student study groups using the reading tables or the study rooms available at TPL for anyone to use.

Student Workers

According to Kim Townsend, Admissions & Records at Temple College, Taylor Center, there are currently three student workers at TCAT, though this can change from semester to semester. Temple College, like most such institutions, offers student employment through the work-study program. Students qualify by completing a Free Application for Federal Student Aid (FAFSA) for each academic year. After meeting required deadlines, the Temple College Financial Aid Office determines qualification for work-study, also considering each student's financial needs and academic performance. Other qualifications include hours of enrollment and citizenship. The student's qualification for work-study also includes scholarships, state grants, sponsorships and other loans that may be awarded to the student. With limited funds and only so many job openings not all students who qualify may actually get a job. The TCAT student workers typically assist with office operations, proctoring tests, or assist students with special needs. Students who qualify for the work-study program must abide to confidentiality agreements and complete sexual harassment training that is required for all Temple College office staff. Neither is employment guaranteed, as student workers are expected to perform their assigned functions and meet other work standards. For many students, work study might be their first paid employment, and not all have developed good work habits. Student workers are paid minimum wage and duties are

scheduled around their class schedules. According to Ms. Townsend, student workers are invaluable at TCAT—they help at the front desk and answer phones, freeing up the full time staff for their other duties. (K. Townsend, personal communication, February 25, 2011)

Establishment of a Partnership

The Taylor Public Library's Mission Statement reads:

The mission of the Taylor Public Library is to promote a lifelong love of reading and to provide educational, informational, and recreational resources to patrons of all ages, cultural and economic backgrounds. (Approved by the Taylor Public Library Advisory Board, February 18, 1997)

This statement echoes the earliest charter of the Library to service city residents and students in Taylor schools, public or private. By extension, the Taylor Public Library also serves students of Temple College at Taylor, or any future educational institutions that are established within city limits.

Library use Agreement

Temple College and their extended campuses had certain criteria to comply to accreditation standards. Without their own library space in the Taylor facility, the Taylor Public Library was asked to provide library services for the Temple College students. Since the library's policies already stipulate library services to students going to school in Taylor, it wasn't a stretch to allow TCAT students borrowing privileges. Since the Temple College had no space for the TCAT book collection, the Taylor Public Library did allow shelf space to hold these materials, and then also cataloged and circulated these materials to TCAT students.

When the TCAT campus opened up in 1996, the Director of Library Services for Temple College, Walter Harrison, signed a library use agreement with the Taylor Public Library. That agreement was as follows:

1. The Taylor Public Library will allow all students enrolled at the TCAT center a free library card and access to all eligible library materials. These students would still be required to meet all the normal Taylor Public Library rules and policies.

2. TCAT students must present a valid Temple College student identification card to verify that they are indeed currently enrolled. They then can check out Taylor Public Library materials as well as the Temple College materials housed at the library.

3. If a TCAT student fails to follow library policies, fails to return materials and accrues fines, Taylor Public Library staff will report these issues and the delinquent student will have their transcripts and records on hold until all transgressions are rectified and all financial aid would be suspended.

4. Temple College will provide the library materials needed by the students, but the Taylor Public Library will manage the materials without undue hardship on the library. The Temple College materials are primarily for access for TCAT students. The library will circulate materials and if needed, employ normal process to retrieve overdue materials.

5. The Temple College library materials remain the property of Temple College and may as needed be replaced, removed or updated.

While this agreement asks for Taylor Public Library to act as college library for TCAT students, there are a couple of benefits: Temple College materials are still available to Taylor residents as reference materials, and Temple College had much better leverage in securing the return of overdue library materials, both those owned by

the public library and college library, and payment of fines by withhold transcripts, records and financial aid. The Taylor Public Library also provided research instruction to TCAT classes, which it continues to do.

This agreement was in effect while the Taylor Public Library was still in the 1960 building at 721 Vance Street. When the library closed due to mold, the library eventually set up in the City Hall Auditorium at 400 Porter Street, in the downtown Taylor. This was a squeeze, from the old library space of 9,143 square feet into a 4,000 square foot space—less than half the size as the old library building. Consequently, TPL had much less shelf space to offer to house TCAT materials. In addition, since auditorium was a squeeze, the library transferred its computer lab into the old 7th Street school building. As mentioned above, TISD had always been a great partner with the library, and allowed the library to use it without charge. However, that meant that the library staff had to cover two locations without any staffing increases, and maintain the same public service hours.

Due to the physical limitations of the Taylor Public Library and the unexpected demand on staffing, the Temple College H.M. Dawson Library altered the Library Use agreement in 2006. The Director of Library Services for Temple College Kathy Fulton and newly hired Taylor Public Library Director Karen Ellis met to discuss the best way for TCAT students to still access library resources. It is at this point in time that a real partnership was forged between both institutions.

The revised Library Use Agreement between Temple College and Taylor Public Library covered the following points:

1. This agreement was between the City of Taylor and Temple College. At this point in time the Taylor Public Library had been clearly defined as a city department, with a regular budget from the city. Since all policy and agreements with any city department

needed to be approved by the Taylor City Council, the wording reflected this.

2. Although Temple College could not itself construct a library, accreditation required provision of library services and materials. With this agreement, the college was indeed providing those library services to their students.

3. As in the old agreement, only currently registered TCAT students could check out Taylor Public Library materials or Temple College materials held at the library.

4. If a TCAT student had outstanding fines, delinquent materials or other outstanding issues, Temple College would put a hold on the student's records. This means that not only would Temple College withhold the student's records and transcripts, the student would also be barred from future registration.

5. The City of Taylor had no obligation to purchase materials solely for the use of TCAT students. That was solely the responsibility of Temple College. Restrictions on the use of the Temple College materials housed at the Taylor Public Library would be defined by the library or the college.

6. The space to be used for Temple College library materials was defined to be no more than 24 linear feet.

7. The Library would make sure that only TCAT students could check out Temple College materials.

8. In consideration for use of library space to house Temple College materials and allow TCAT students borrowing privileges, Temple College would provide, if available, at least one student worker without charge to the City of Taylor. The Library Director would approve any student worker prior to assignment to the Taylor Public Library.

Many considerations of the previous agreement exist in this revision. The access to Temple College materials was more tightly defined, but the materials were still accessible to in-house use by any library user. Best of all for TPL, there was an exchange of services—a student worker, especially valuable for the library.

Since that agreement was approved by the Temple College administrators and the Taylor City Council, the new Taylor Public Library building opened, affording much more space for the Temple College nursing & health sciences collection. The new building, with 20,000 square feet, offers more seating, tables, two study rooms, wi-fi throughout and the library's computer lab of 15 computers. This new and enhanced facility was a great asset to all the library users, including TCAT students. The Taylor Public Library staff continues to work well with local TCAT instructors and classes, providing materials, class tours and research instruction.

Enrollment at the Taylor Campus has continued to grow and expand. Over the last year student enrollment has increased 7% from 795 students to 850 students. Unfortunately, the growth has outstripped existing space at the TCAT facility. Some classes have moved to the old 7th Street school. This is an old and outdated structure, but has been the only alternative. A new addition to the TCAT campus has included an advanced mini high school, named Legacy High School. This is dual credit coursework, with students from Taylor ISD and Hutto ISD, a neighboring city in Williamson County about eight miles west of Taylor. Due to space requirements and state regulations, Legacy High School has overflowed into portable classrooms in the side street next to the TCAT campus, using the City Hall Auditorium for a lunch room. This is far from favorable for any of the partners.

BENEFITS

Even student workers have needs that can be satisfied in a library job. Everheart (1994) suggested that needs such as belonging and self-worth are met in a library work environment. Due to the layout of TPL to allow staff their own workspace and break room with private bathroom, a TCAT student worker also has the benefit of accessing this more private space, complete with a working kitchen. Some TCAT student workers live in more rural areas and bring their meals with them to the library and having access to the kitchen and break room make coming to work at the library much more attractive. Student workers have access to the "behind the scenes" areas of the Library. Work at the library can be much more enjoyable than other hourly wage jobs that are typically available in the region. Working on crafts for story time, assisting with publicity and displays, helping with movie programs or children's events are quite a departure from most fast food or service industry jobs. Shelving duties allow the student workers to understand library organization, enabling them more confidence when they have to do research and locate resources. Previous teen volunteers and temporary summer workers have come back to TPL and relayed how much more confident they are in their college or university libraries. Student workers learn how to use the library's databases and other online resources that they may not have otherwise been exposed to. Student workers are certainly exposed to a wide variety of customers with an equally diverse skill set. From assisting a patron to set up an e-mail account to helping a neighborhood boy find all the books on dinosaurs, library work is generally very satisfying. There are some staff privileges afforded to student workers, such as some free photocopies, first picks on new library books and AV, and first chance to purchase donations or weeded materials destined for the Friends of the Library book sale. For some of these TCAT student workers, this may be their first paying job, and the library can be an excellent training ground for customer service, taking responsibility for assignments and even initiating projects. On top of that, full time TPL employees

have great pride in the library and won't let any student worker produce shabby or poor work.

CONCLUSION AND FUTURE CONSIDERATIONS

Despite the best efforts of Taylor City Administration, the new campus for Temple College in east Williamson County will be built in Hutto, the city just eight miles to the west of Taylor. And really, it just boiled down to money. Dr. Glenda Barron replaced Dr. Mark Nigliazzo as Temple College President in 2008. The timing of this administrative change coincided with the beginning of the economic downturn in the US. Despite the fact that the City of Taylor and the Taylor Independent School District had collaborated with Temple College for new campus to be built in Taylor, Dr. Barron and the Temple College Board took the campus a different direction. Called the East Williamson County Higher Education Center (EWCHEC), this was originally proposed to be on land located adjacent to the new Taylor High School on the south side of town. The City of Taylor contributed to the construction of water lines and utilities to this proposed site. Likewise, some building costs would be absorbed by TISD as part of their new campus construction. However, the TCAT Foundation was finding it difficult to raise all funding to build the new campus and Temple College would have to fund a chunk of the construction costs. Hutto had also proposed that the EWCHEC campus to be built there, but had been initially passed over. With the new Temple College President and the dismal economic climate, the game changed. The Temple College Board declared that they would only consider a location that would be completely funding by the community. This sent Taylor officials scrambling, but Hutto officials offered a 5 cent tax to be approved by voters. This tax, with other donations of land and utilities, would cover construction and operations of a Hutto campus completely. So, Temple College committed to the Hutto site.

This draws into question the continuing partnership of TCAT and TPL. For the next few years, there are no plans to move the nursing program from TCAT. Since that is the crux of the agreement between TCAT and TPL, the nursing collection will remain on TPL shelves and a student worker will be provided by TCAT for now. However, as college students currently enrolled at TCAT move over for non-nursing coursework, these Hutto campus students will no longer qualify for TPL library cards. It also seems unlikely that Temple College will want to retain two campuses in east Williamson County indefinitely. While the TPL staff has a great relationship with TCAT staff and staff at the Dawson Library in Temple, those individuals do not control the continuation of the TCAT campus. With current City of Taylor budget and staffing cuts, TCAT student workers have been needed at TPL to cover evening and Saturday shifts. So despite the desires of TPL and the willingness of TCAT campus administrators, this partnership has an uncertain future.

Even so, this unique partnership has been quite specific in meeting the needs of each partner. The TCAT campus needed a proxy library location; TPL needed more staff members. Cooperation between the directors of TPL and the Dawson Library at Temple College made this partnership work. It also speaks to the need for a public library to not be shy to ask for something valuable from a partner. Too often public libraries absorb costs and staff time to provide more and more. A fair exchange should be the foundation for any good partnership.

REFERENCES

American Library Association. (2011). *ALA library fact sheet 17*. Library Summer Reading Programs. Retrieved from http://www.ala.org/ala/professionalresources/libfactsheets/alalibrary-factsheet17.cfm

Everhart, N. (1994). Library aides: If you fulfill their needs, they will come (and work!). *Book Report, 13*(1), 12.

Gillham, V., Newman, W., Bury, S., & Madden, A. (2003). Wilfrid Laurier University and the Brantford Public Library: A unique exercise in joint service provision. *Feliciter, 49*(6), 298–301.

MacDonald, C. (2007). Public libraries + School libraries = Smart partnerships. *CSLA Journal, 30*(2), 11–12.

McNicol, S. (2006). What makes a joint use library a community library? *Library Trends, 54*(4), 519–534. doi:10.1353/lib.2006.0041

Norton, W. (2000, April 28). Joint-use library accord reached. *St. Petersburg Times*, p. 1. Retrieved from http://go.galegroup.com/ps/i.do?&id=GALE%7CA61977660&v=2.1&u=txshrpub100370&it=r&p=STND&sw=w

Tampa Tribune. (1998, November 7). City rejects idea of sharing library. *Tampa Tribune*, p. 11. Retrieved from http://go.galegroup.com/ps/i.do?&id=GALE%7CA66059695&v=2.1&u=txshrpub100370&it=r&p=STND&sw=w

Temple College. (2010). *Reaffirmation of accreditation, compliance reports*. Retrieved from http://www.templejc.edu/SACS2010/ComplianceRpt.htm

Compilation of References

(2010). IFLA public library guidelines. InKoontz, C., & Gubbin, B. (Eds.), *The Management of public libraries* (pp. 95–108). New York, NY: Grutyer Saur.

(2010). *Reading Education Assistance Dogs (R.E.A.D.) team training manual* (10th ed.). Salt Lake City, UT: Intermountain Therapy Animals.

Adeyemi, T. O. (2001). The school library and students learning outcomes in secondary schools in Ekiti State, Nigeria. *Asian Journal of Business Management, 2*(1), 1–8. Retrieved February 26, 2011

Age Action Ireland. (n.d.). *Home page*. Retrieved February 26, 2011, from http://www.ageaction.ie/

Aguolu, C. C. (1975). The school library as an instrument of education in Nigeria. *Integrated Library Review*, 46-50.

Akpovwa, D. (2010). FG step-up action to curb boy-child drop out in South East. *The Abuja Inquirer.* Retrieved February 10, 2011, from www.abujainquireronline.com/fetcher.php?fid=2812.

Akpunonu, C. (2010). 60% Imo boys drop out of school yearly. *Oriental Life News.* Retrieved February 10, 2011, from www.orientallifenewsonline.com/news/general/269.html

American Association of School Librarians (AASL). (2011). *The school library center: Quotable facts*. AASL website. Retrieved April 2, 2011, from http://www.ala.org/ala/mgrps/divs/aasl/aaslissues/toolkits/schoollibraryfacts.cfm

American Library Association (ALA). *About Smart Investing @ your library*. Retrieved February 3, 2011, from http://smartinvesting.ala.org/about/

American Library Association. (2011). *ALA library fact sheet 17.* Library Summer Reading Programs. Retrieved from http://www.ala.org/ala/professionalresources/libfactsheets/alalibraryfactsheet17.cfm

American Library Association. (n.d.). *Website*. Retrieved February 10, 2011, from http://www.ala.org/

Applied Research & Consulting LLC. (2009, December 1). *Financial capability in the United States: Initial report of research findings from the 2009 national survey* (A component of the national financial capability study). Retrieved from http://www.finrafoundation.org/web/groups/foundation/@foundation/documents/foundation/p120536.pdf

Arnold, J. (2010). *Through a dog's eyes*. New York, NY: Spiegel & Grau.

Ayorinde, S. (2009, March 22). Libraries not antiquity please. *Lagos: The Punch*, p. 3.

Baribeau, S., & McGrail, B. (2010, September 10). Florida issuers sell $442 million with debt cost at record high. *Bloomberg Businessweek*. Retrieved February 6, 2011, from http://www.businessweek.com/news/2010-09-10/florida-issuers-sell-442-million-with-debt-cost-at-record-high.html

Burnett, R. (2010, May 13). Orlando ranks 10th with average consumer debt of $25,316. *Orlando Sentinel.* Retrieved February 6, 2011, from http://articles.orlandosentinel.com/2010-05-13/business/os-orlando-ranks-consumer-debt-20100513_1_credit-card-debt-personal-debt-consumer-debt-counselors

Busayo Oluwadare, I. (2010). The role of libraries in the unified Tertiary Matriculation examination. *PNLA Quarterly*. Retrieved February 24, 2011, from unllib.unl.edu/LPP/PNLA%20Quarterly/busayo74-4htm

Canlas, H. L. (2009). *Study tips for parents: How to motivate your children to read.* Retrieved November 11, 2010, from www.associatedcontent.com

Celano, D., & Neuman, S. B. (2001). *The role of public libraries in children's literacy development: An evaluation report.* Pennsylvania Dept of education, Office of Commonwealth Libraries. Retrieved February 10, 2011, from www.childcareresearch.org/location/ccrca5613

Census. (2010). *American community survey, 2005-2009.* Retrieved February 1, 2011 from http://factfinder.census.gov/

Census2006. (2006). *Beyond 2020.* Retrieved February 26, 2011, from http://beyond2020.cso.ie/Census/TableViewer/tableView.aspx?ReportId=76524

Census2011. (2011). *CDP01: Population and actual and percentage change 2006 and 2011 by sex, province county or city, year and statistic.* Retrieved September 7th, 2011, from http://www.cso.ie/px/pxeirestat/Statire/SelectVarVal/Define.asp?maintable=CDP01&PLanguage=0

Chartered Institute of Library and Information Professionals (CILIP). (2002). *Start with the child: A report of the CILIP working group on library provision for children and young people.* Retrieved January 13, 2011, from www.cilip.org.uk/get-involved/.../children/start/...full

Chew, I. (2005). *Parents' role in nurturing the child's reading habit.* Retrieved September 13, 2010, from ramblinglibrarian.blogspot.com

City-Data. (2009). *81435 zip code detailed profile* [Data file]. Retrieved from http://www.city-data.com/zips/81435.html.

Citylink, U. S. A. (2000). *Telluride demographics* [DataFile]. Retrieved from http://tellurideco.usl.myareaguide.com/demographics.html.

Clay, S. E. (2009). The partnership between public libraries and public education. *Virginia Libraries, 55*(2). Retrieved February 26, 2011, from http://scholar.lib.vt.edu/ejournals/VAlib/v55_n2

Clay, E. (2009). The partnership between public libraries and public education. *Virginia Libraries, 55*(2), 11–14.

Colorado State Library. (2010). *Public library annual statistics* [Data file]. Retrieved from http://www.lrs.org.

Cox, J. (2010). Academic libraries in challenging times. *An Leabharlann: The Irish Library, 19*(2), 7–13.

Cullinan, B. E. (2000). Independent reading and school achievement. *School Library Reading Research, 3.* Retrieved January 12, 2011, from http://www.alia.org.au/groups/aliaschool/lamarca.ppt.

Czopek, V. (1995). Extending public resources into the classroom. *Emergency Librarian, 5*(22), 23–27.

Davies, J. (December, 2008). *Intel, Microsoft and a post join forces to Promote "Log On 'Learn".* Retrieved February 26, 2011, from http://www.logonlearn.ie/News.aspx

Davis, C. (2008, June). Librarianship in the 21st century – Crisis or transformation? *Public Library Quarterly, 27*(1), 53–83. doi:10.1080/01616840802122401

De, R. C., Johnson, J., & OCLC. (2008). *From awareness to funding: A study of library support in America: A report to the OCLC membership.* Dublin, OH: OCLC Press.

Del Vecchio, S. (1993). Connecting libraries and schools with CLASP. *Wilson Library Bulletin, 68*, 38–40.

DelGuidice, M. (2009). Are you overlooking a valuable resource? A practical guide to collaborating with your greatest ally: The public library. *Library Media Connection, 27*(6), 38–39.

Delta Society. (n.d.). *Website.* Retrieved February 1, 2011, from http://www.deltasociety.org/

Department of Education. (1993). *Transition Year programmes guidelines for schools.* Dublin, Ireland: The Stationery Office. Retrieved February 26, 2011, from http://www.education.ie/servlet/blobservlet/pp_transition_year_guidelines_school.doc

Doust, R. W. (1998). *Provision of school library services by means of mobile libraries- The Zimbabwe experience.* Paper presented at the 64th IFLA General Conference, Amsterdam. Retrieved February 2, 2011, from http://archive.ifla.org

Dublin, Ireland. Retrieved February 26, 2011, from http://www.fingalcoco.ie/Publications/Council/Corporate%20Plan%202010-2014.pdf: Fingal County Council. (n.d.). *Website*. Retrieved February 26, 2011, from www.fingalcoco.ie

Everhart, N. (1994). Library aides: If you fulfill their needs, they will come (and work!). *Book Report, 13*(1), 12.

Fajt, M. (2009, November). How to reach Hispanics: Give them credit. *US Banker, 119*(11), 28-29. Retrieved February 6, 2011, from http://www.americanbanker.com/usb_issues/119_11/how-to-reach-hispanics-give-them-credit-1003190-1.html

Fajt, M. (2009, September 21). A twist on reaching out to unbanked Hispanics. *American Banker*. Retrieved February 6, 2011, from http://www.progressfin.com/A_Twist_on_Reaching_Out_to_Unbanked_Hispanics.pdf

Fakoya, A. (2002, October 18). Bastardization of English language. *Lagos: The Punch*, p. 39.

Federal Deposit Insurance Corporation (FDIC). (2009, December). *FDIC national survey of unbanked and underbanked households: Executive summary*. Retrieved February 6, 2011, from http://www.fdic.gov/householdsurvey/executive_summary.pdf

Federal Deposit Insurance Corporation (FDIC). (2010, September). *Addendum to the 2009 FDIC national survey of unbanked and underbanked households: Use of alternative financial services*. Retrieved February 6, 2011, from http://www.fdic.gov/householdsurvey/AFS_Addendum.pdf

Federal Republic of Nigeria. (1998). *National policy on education (Revised)*. Lagos, Nigeria: NERDC Press.

Fenwick, S. (1966). *School and children's libraries in Australia: A report to the Children's Libraries section of the Library Association of Australia Cheshire, Melbourne*. Retrieved February 24, 2011, from alianet.alia.org.au/publishing/alj/5.1/full text

Festival, B. (2011). *An Irish festival celebrating the older person*. Retrieved from http://bealtaine.com/

Figueroa, C. (2009, February 4). Enseñan ahorro a estudiantes hispanos. *La Prensa*, p. 3.

Figueroa, C. (2009, January 8). Charlas en Español orientan a ahorrar. *La Prensa*, p 3.

Financial Industry Regulatory Authority (FINRA) Investor Education Foundation. (2009, December). *Financial capability in the United States: National Survey—Executive Summary*. Retrieved from http://www.finrafoundation.org/web/groups/foundation/@foundation/documents/foundation/p120535.pdf

Fine, A. (Ed.). (2010). *Handbook on animal-assisted therapy: Theoretical foundations and guidelines for practice*. Burlington, MA: Elsevier Press.

Fingal County Council. (2010). *Fingal County council corporate plan 2010–2014*.

Fingal Libraries Department. (n.d.). *Website*. Retrieved February 26, 2011, from www.fingalcoco.ie/libaries

Fishkind., & Associates. Inc. (2007). *Hispanic communities of Central Florida: Economic contributions to the region. Executive Summary*. Orlando, FL: Orlando Regional Chamber of Commerce.

Fitzgibbons, S. A. (2000). *School and public library relationships: Essential ingredients in implementing educational reforms and improving student learning*. Retrieved February 5, 2011, from www.ala.org/aasl/

Fitzgibbons, S. (2001). School and public library relationships: Déjà vu or new beginnings? *Journal of Youth Services in Libraries, 14*(3), 3–7.

Fitzgibbons, S. A. (1983). Reference and Information services for children and young adults: Definitions, services and issues. In Katz, W. A., & Forley, R. A. (Eds.), *Reference services for children and young adults* (pp. 1–30). New York, NY: Hawthorn Press.

Friedrich, A., & Rodriguez, E. (2001). *Financial insecurity amid growing wealth: Why healthier savings is essential to Latino prosperity*. National Council of La Raza, Issue Brief, No. 5, August.

Friesen, L. (2010). Exploring animal-assisted programs with children in school and therapeutic contexts. *Early Childhood Education Journal, 37*(4), 261–267. doi:10.1007/s10643-009-0349-5

Gambrell, L. (2008). Closing the summer reading gap. *Reading Today, 25*(5), 18.

Gillham, V., Newman, W., Bury, S., & Madden, A. (2003). Wilfrid Laurier University and the Brantford Public Library: A unique exercise in joint service provision. *Feliciter, 49*(6), 298–301.

Glander, M., & Dam, T. (2006). *Households' use of public and other types of libraries: 2002*. U.S. Department of Education. (2011). *Publications and product search*. Washington, DC: National Center for Education Statistics. Retrieved February 1, 2011, from http://nces.ed.gov/pubsearch

Gundersen, B. (2009). The DIGIKOMBI project library initiative for a national model to improve digital competence. *Scandinavian Public Library Quarterly, 42*(3), 8-9. Retrieved February 26, 2011, from http://splq.info/issues/vol42_3/04.htm

Gutter, M. S., & Mountain, T. P. (2007). *Understanding minority preferences for investor education: Results from African-American and Hispanic focus groups*. Accepted for presentation at 2007 Academy of Financial Services.

Hampstead Public Library. (2011). *Easy to take the Carbon Challenge*. Retrieved from http://www.hampsteadlibrary.org/easychallenge.asp

Hampstead Public Library. (2011). *Green websites*. Retrieved from http://www.hampsteadlibrary.org/green-websites.asp

Hampstead Public Library. (2011). *Hampstead Carbon Challenge*. Retrieved from http://www.hampsteadlibrary.org/carbonchallenge.asp

Hampstead Public Library. (2011). *Hampstead Public Library*. Retrieved from http://www.HampsteadLibrary.org

Hispanic Business Initiative Fund (HBIF). (n.d.). *Website*. Retrieved from http://www.hbifflorida.org/

Hovius, B. (2005). *Public libraries which add value to the community. The Hamilton Public Library experience*. Retrieved January 17, 2011, from archive.ifla.org/iv/ifla 71/papers/041 e-Hovius.pdf

Hovius, B. (2005, August). *Public library partnerships which add value to the community: The Hamilton Public Library Experience* (041-E). Paper presented at the World Library and Information Congress: 71th IFLA General Conference and Council, Oslo, Norway.

Ihanamäki, S. (2010). Partnerships in the North Calotte area. *Scandinavian Public Library Quarterly, 43*(3), 18-19. Retrieved February 26, 2011, from http://splq.info/issues/vol43_3/09.htm

Indiana Department of Education. (2010). *Indiana's plan to ensure student literacy by the end of 3rd grade, 2010*. Retrieved January 15, 2011, from http://www.doe.in.gov/

Indiana Department of Education. (2011). *Office of student assessment*. Retrieved January 20, 2011, from http://www.doe.in.gov/

Indiana Department of Workforce Development. (2010). *Hoosiers by the numbers*. Retrieved February 13, 2011, from http://www.hoosierdata.in.gov/

Indiana Youth Institute. (2010). *Kids count in Indiana 2010 data book*. Retrieved February 1, 2011, from http://www.iyi.org/

Institute of Education Sciences. (2009). *The nation's report card*. U.S. Department of Education. Washington, DC: National Center for Education Statistics. Retrieved February 1, 2011, from http://nces.ed.gov/. Retrieved February 5, 2011 from http://nationsreportcard.gov/reading_2009/

Intermountain Therapy Dogs. (2010). *Reading education assistance dogs (R.E.A.D.) team training manual* (10th ed.). Salt Lake City, UT: Intermountain Therapy Dogs.

International Reading Association. (n.d.). *Website*. Retrieved February 10, 2011, from http://www.reading.org/

Jackson, M. D. (1999, Fall). Forging partnerships: Schools, school libraries and communities. *Teacher Education Quarterly, •••*, 99–122.

Jalongo, M. R. (2004). Canine visitors: The influence of therapy dogs on young children's learning and well-being in classrooms and hospitals. *Early Childhood Education, 32*(1), 9–16. doi:10.1023/B:ECEJ.0000039638.60714.5f

Jeffers, G. (2004). Implementing the Transition Year Programme in the Republic of Ireland. In A. Burke (Ed.), *Teacher education in the Republic of Ireland: Retrospect and prospect* (pp.54-61). Armagh, Northern Ireland: The Centre for Cross Border Studies.

Jeffers, G. (2007). *Attitudes to Transition Year: A report to the Department of Education and Science.* Maynooth, Ireland: Education Department, National University of Ireland. Retrieved February 26, 2011, from http://eprints.nuim.ie/1228/

Jeffers, G. (2008). *Innovation and resistance in Irish schooling: The case of Transition Year.* Unpublished doctoral dissertation, University of Limerick, Co. Limerick, Ireland

Koontz, C., & Gubbin, B. (Eds.). (2010). *IFLA public library service guidelines.* New York, NY: Saur, IFLA.

Kulpinski, D. (2009). *Partnership for a nation of learners: joining forces, creating value.* Institute of Museum and Library Services. Retrieved February 1, 2011 from http:// www.oclc.org/us/en/default.htm

LaMaster, J. (2005). Collaboration of Indiana Public and school media center services: A survey of current practices. *Indiana Libraries, 24*(1), 38–41.

Lance, K. C. (2001). *Proof of power: Quality library media programs affect academic achievement.* Retrieved January 21, 2011, from www.infotoday.com/MMSchools/sep01/lance.htm

Lovatt, S. (2010). Making connections: The library and the community. *An Leabharlann: The Irish Library, 19*(1), 22–27.

Lynch, J. (2003). Developing a physiology of inclusion: Recognizing the health benefits of animal companions. In *Reading Education Assistance Dogs (R.E.A.D.) team training manual.* 10th ed. (2010). Salt Lake City, UT: Intermountain Therapy Animals.

MacDonald, C. (2007). Public libraries + School libraries = Smart partnerships. *CSLA Journal, 30*(2), 11–12.

Maduekwe, A. N., & Oyenike, A. (2010). *Parental involvement in children's literacy development in Nigeria: Empirical findings and improvement strategies.* Retrieved December 21, 2010, from http://www.linguist.org

Malahide Community School. (2010). *Website.* Retrieved February 26, 2011, from https://sites.google.com/a/malahidecs.ie/malahide-community-school/

Malahide Library. (n.d.). *Website.* Retrieved 7th September 2011, from http://www.librarybuildings.ie/library.aspx?ID=72

Mathews, V., Flum, J., & Whitney, K. (1990). Kids need libraries! Schools and public libraries preparing the youth today for the world of tomorrow. *Youth Services in Libraries, 30,* 197–207.

Matthews, V. (1991). Kids need libraries: School and public libraries preparing the youth of today for the world of tomorrow. *School Library Media Annual, 9,* 201.

McGill-Franzen, A., & Allington, R. (2003). Bridging the summer reading gap. *Instructor, 112*(8), 17.

McKenzie Mohr, D. (1999). *Fostering sustainable behavior: An introduction to community-based social marketing.* Gabriola Island, Canada: New Society Publishers.

McNicol, S. (2006). What makes a joint use library a community library? *Library Trends, 54*(4), 519–534. doi:10.1353/lib.2006.0041

Mertz, C. (2009). *A qualitative study examining the use of canine reading programs with young readers.* Unpublished doctoral dissertation, University of Wisconsin-Stout.

Metro Orlando Economic Development Commission. (2011, January 21). *Employment by industry: Metro Orlando.* Retrieved February 6, 2011, from http://www.orlandoedc.com/core/file.php?loc=/Solodev/clients/solodev/Enterprise%20Main/Documents/EDC%20Documents/Data%20Center/workforce/Workforce_EmpbyInd_1210.pdf

Millar, D., & Kelly, D. (1999). *From junior to leaving certificate: A longitudinal study of 1994 junior certificate candidates who took the leaving certificate examination in 1997 (Final Report).* Dublin, Ireland: Educational Research Centre & National Council for Curriculum and Assessment.

Mordern, S. (2003). *Cooperation between public libraries and schools in Canada.* CELPLO report. Retrieved January 15, 2011, from www.sols.org/.../CELPLO.pdf

Mraz, M., & Rasinski, T. (2007). Summer reading loss. *The Reading Teacher, 60*(8), 784–789. doi:10.1598/RT.60.8.9

Murray, S. (2004). *Library collaboration, what makes it work?* Retrieved January 15, 2011, from http://www.iatul.org/doclibrary/public/conf_Proceedings/2004/Murray 20 Shepherd.pdf

National Education Association. (2010). *Facts about children's literacy.* Retrieved February 12, 2011, from http://www.nea.org/

Neuman, S. (2009). *Income affects how kids use technology and access knowledge.* National Summer Learning Association. Retrieved January 30, 2011, from http://www.summerlearning.org/

Norton, W. (2000, April 28). Joint-use library accord reached. *St. Petersburg Times*, p. 1. Retrieved from http://go.galegroup.com/ps/i.do?&id=GALE%7CA61977660&v=2.1&u=txshrpub100370&it=r&p=STND&sw=w

OECD. (2009). *PISA 2009 assessment framework - Key competencies in reading, mathematics and science.* Paris, France: OECD. Retrieved February 26, 2011, from http://www.oecd.org/dataoecd/11/40/44455820.pdf

Ogbonna, I. M. (2010). *Compendium of public library laws in Nigeria.* Enugu, Nigeria: His Glory Publishers.

Okoye Obi, C. (2000). The role of the library in the promotion of book readership: A Nigerian view. In Chukwuemeka, I. (Ed.), *Creating and sustaining a reading culture* (pp. 121–131). Awka, Nigeria: Nigerian Book Foundation.

Olalokun, S. O. (1996). Education and libraries in Nigerian schools. *International Library Review*, 476–481.

Olmert, M. D. (2009). *Made for each other: The biology of the human-animal bond.* Cambridge, MA: Da Capo Press.

On, L. Learn. (2008). *Press release.* Retrieved from http://www.dohc.ie/press/releases/2008/20081001b.html

Otti, S. (2011). Mass failures worries stakeholders. *NBF News.* Retrieved February 23, 2011 from www.nigerianbestforum.com/blog/?p=78374

Packaged Facts. (2005, July 1). *Market trends: Opportunities in the "unbanked" consumer market.* Retrieved from http://www.packagedfacts.com/Trends-Opportunities-Unbanked-1079258/

Personal Finance Employee Education Foundation. (2000, May 5). *Workers with financial stress are less productive.* (Press Releases). Retrieved February 6, 2011, from http://pfeef.org/press/press-releases/Workers-with-Financial-Stress-Less-Productive.html

Ratcliffe, R. G. (2007, April 29). *TYC abuse claims poured in amid debate.* Retrieved from http://www.chron.com/disp/story.mpl/metropolitan/4758560.html

Ray, K. (2001, March). *The postmodern library in an age of assessment: Crossing the divide.* Paper presented at the National Conference of the College and Research libraries. Retrieved February 23rd, 2011, from http://www.ala.org/ala/acri/acrievents/kray.pdf

Rødevand, A. M. (2009). Learn computer technology in your library. *Scandinavian Public Library Quarterly, 42*(3), 13. Retrieved February 26, 2011, from http://splq.info/issues/vol42_3/08.htm

Scordato, J. (2004). School and public librarians working together. *Library Media Connection, 22*(7), 32–33.

Semmel, M. (2009). *Museums, libraries, and 21st century skills.* Institute of Museum and Library Services. Retrieved February 4, 2011, from http:// www.oclc.org/us/en/default.htm

Shannon, D. M. (1991). Cooperation between school and public libraries: A study of one North Carolina county. *North Carolina Libraries, 49*, 67–70.

Small, R. V., Synder, J., & Parker, K. (2008). *New York State's school media and library media specialists: An impact study.* Preliminary report. Syracuse NY: Center for Digital Literacy, Syracuse University. Retrieved January 8, 2011, from fromwww.ciplc.net/attachments/179_Do%20School%20Libraris%20

Smith, C. (2009). *An analysis and evaluation of Sit Stay Read: Is the program effective in improving student engagement and reading outcomes?* Unpublished doctoral dissertation, National-Louis University.

Smith, K. (2010), Multi-faceted, cross-generational learning teams for the 21st century. *MASCD Perspectives,* Spring, 10-12. Retrieved February 26, 2011, from www.nctaf.org/.../KarenSmith-Multi-facetedCross-genLTs-for21C-MASCDPerspectives-Spring2010.pdf

Smith, M. (2004, January-February). California DREA-Min'. A model for school-public library cooperation to improve student achievement. *Public Libraries, 43*, 47–51.

Stanczykiewicz, B. (2010). *Indiana's 3rd grade reading plan.* Indiana Youth Institute. Retrieved January 30, 2011, from http://www.iyi.org/

Sullivan, M. (2011). Hampstead library accepts carbon challenge. *Eagle Tribune.* Retrieved from http://www.eagletribune.com/newhampshire/x1876451833/Hampstead-library-accepts-carbon-challenge

Tampa Tribune. (1998, November 7). City rejects idea of sharing library. *Tampa Tribune,* p. 11. Retrieved from http://go.galegroup.com/ps/i.do?&id=GALE%7CA66059695&v=2.1&u=txshrpub100370&it=r&p=STND&sw=w

Telluride Film Festival. (2011). *Purchase passes.* Retrieved from http://telluridefilmfestival.org/passes.html.

Temple College. (2010). *Reaffirmation of accreditation, compliance reports.* Retrieved from http://www.templejc.edu/SACS2010/ComplianceRpt.htm

Thomas, D. A., & Gabarro, J. J. (1999). *Breaking through: The making of minority executives in corporate America.* Boston, MA: Harvard Business School Press.

Toussaint-Comeau, M. (2003, August) *Changing Hispanic demographics: Opportunities and constraints in the financial market.* Chicago, IL: Chicago Fed Letter. Retrieved February 12, 2011 from http://www.chicagofed.org/digital_assets/publications/chicago_fed_letter/2003/cflaug2003_192.pdf

Transition Year Support Service. (n.d.). *Website.* Retrieved 8 September, 2011, from http://ty.slss.ie/ UNESCO/IFLA. (2011). *Public libraries manifesto.* Retrieved 26 February, 2011, from http://www.unesco.org/webworld/libraries/manifestos/index_manifestos.html

U.S. Census Bureau. (2009). *2005-2009 American community survey.* Retrieved from http://factfinder.census.gov/servlet/ACSSAFFFacts?_event=Search&geo_id=&_geoContext=&_street=&_county=hampstead&_cityTown=hampstead&_state=04000US33&_zip=&_lang=en&_sse=on&pctxt=fph&pgsl=010

U.S. Census Bureau. (2009). *S0201: Selected population profile in the United States, Hispanic or Latino (of any race). Orange County, Florida* [Data file]. American FactFinder: American community survey 1-year estimates. Retrieved from http://factfinder.census.gov

U.S. Environmental Protection Agency. (2008). *Inventory of U.S. greenhouse gas emissions and sinks: 1990-2006* (pp. ES-8). Retrieved from http://www.epa.gov/climatechange/emissions/downloads/08_CR.pdf

UNESCO. (2000). *UNESCO public library guidelines.* Retrieved January 12, 2010, from www.unesco.org/.../ev.php-URL_ID=4638&url-do=do-topic&url_section=201.html-

United States Department of Agriculture. (2009). *Summer food service program.* Retrieved February 12, 2011, from http://www.summerfood.usda.gov/

University of New Hampshire. (2009). *UNH University events & programs: Notable events & programs: UNH speakers bureau.* Retrieved from http://www.unh.edu/universityevents/speakersbureau

Velde, S. (2005). *The development and validation of a research evaluation instrument to assess the effectiveness of animal-assisted therapy.* Unpublished doctoral dissertation, Kennedy-Western University.

Wenger, E. (June, 2006). *Communities of practice: A brief introduction.* Retrieved 26 February 2011, from http://www.ewenger.com/theory/index.htm

William, S., & LaGrange, J. (1989, Spring, Fall). Resource sharing between schools and public libraries in Texas. *Current Studies in Librarianship,* 28-34.

Zobec, H. (1990). Cooperation between schools and public libraries. *Australian Public Libraries and information Services, 3*(4), 245.

Related References

To continue our tradition of advancing information science and technology research, we have compiled a list of recommended IGI Global readings. These references will provide additional information and guidance to further enrich your knowledge and assist you with your own research and future publications.

Abbas, J. (2010). Social software use in public libraries. In Dumova, T., & Fiordo, R. (Eds.), *Handbook of research on social interaction technologies and collaboration software: Concepts and trends* (pp. 451–461).

Abresch, J., Hanson, A., Heron, S. J., & Reehling, P. J. (2008). Geography and librarianship. In Abresch, J., Hanson, A., Heron, S., & Reehling, P. J. (Eds.), *Integrating geographic information systems into library services: A guide for academic libraries* (pp. 1–21).

Afifi, M. (2008). Process mapping for electronic resources: A lesson from business models. In Yu, H., & Breivold, S. (Eds.), *Electronic resource management in libraries: Research and practice* (pp. 90–104).

Agarwal, N. K., & Poo, D. C. (2008). Collaborating to search effectively in different searcher modes through cues and specialty search. In Goh, D., & Foo, S. (Eds.), *Social information retrieval systems: emerging technologies and applications for searching the web effectively* (pp. 1–30).

Ahmand, K., & Al-Sayed, R. (2006). Community of practice and the special language "Ground". In Coakes, E., & Clarke, S. (Eds.), *Encyclopedia of communities of practice in information and knowledge management* (pp. 77–88).

Akporhonor, B. A. (2010). Library photocopy policies. In Adomi, E. (Ed.), *Handbook of research on Information Communication Technology policy: Trends, issues and advancements* (pp. 520–526).

Albert, S., Flournoy, D., & LeBrasseur, R. (2009). Creating applications and a culture of using. In Albert, S., Flournoy, D., & LeBrasseur, R. (Eds.), *Networked communities: Strategies for digital collaboration* (pp. 129–169).

Albert, S., Flournoy, D., & LeBrasseur, R. (2009). The network society. In Albert, S., Flournoy, D., & LeBrasseur, R. (Eds.), *Networked communities: Strategies for digital collaboration* (pp. 1–34).

Albuquerque, M. D., Siqueira, S. W., & Braz, M. H. (2011). Cataloguing and searching musical sound recordings in an ontology-based Information System. [IJKSR]. *International Journal of Knowledge Society Research*, 2(4), 18–34. doi:doi:10.4018/jksr.2011100102

Alfano, C. S., & Henderson, S. L. (2007). Repositories. In Taylor Northrup, P. (Ed.), *Learning objects for instruction: Design and evaluation* (pp. 16–28).

Allan, M. B., Korolis, A. A., & Griffith, T. L. (2009). Reaching for the moon: Expanding transactive memory's reach with Wikis and tagging. [IJKM]. *International Journal of Knowledge Management*, 5(2), 51–63. doi:doi:10.4018/jkm.2009040104

Allen, B., Juillet, L., Paquet, G., & Roy, J. (2005). E-government and private-public partnerships: Relational challenges and strategic directions. In Khosrow-Pour, M. (Ed.), *Practicing e-government: A global perspective* (pp. 364–382).

Andoh-Baidoo, F. K., Baker, E. W., Susarapu, S. R., & Kasper, G. M. (2007). A review of IS research activities and outputs using pro forma abstracts. [IRMJ]. *Information Resources Management Journal, 20*(4), 65–79. doi:doi:10.4018/irmj.2007100105

Ani, O. E., & Edem, M. (2010). Framework for effective development of information and communication technology (ICT) policy in university libraries in Nigeria. In Adomi, E. (Ed.), *Frameworks for ICT policy: Government, social and legal issues* (pp. 148–163).

Ansari, M. A. (2012). Modernization of a traditional library. In Tella, A., & Issa, A. (Eds.), *Library and information science in developing countries: Contemporary issues* (pp. 32–44).

Arkyhypska, O., Bilous, S., & Yarinich, V. (2006). Civic space portal. In Marshall, S., Taylor, W., & Yu, X. (Eds.), *Encyclopedia of developing regional communities with information and communication technology* (pp. 103-106). doi:10.4018/978-1-59140-575-7.ch017

Arora, J. (2010). Digitisation: Methods, tools and technology. In Ashraf, T., Sharma, J., & Gulati, P. A. (Eds.), *Developing sustainable digital libraries: Socio-technical perspectives* (pp. 40–63).

Ashraf, D., & Gulati, M. A. (2010). Digital libraries: A sustainable approach. In Ashraf, T., Sharma, J., & Gulati, P. A. (Eds.), *Developing sustainable digital libraries: Socio-technical perspectives* (pp. 1–18).

Axup, J. (2009). Building a path for future communities. In Whitworth, B., & de Moor, A. (Eds.), *Handbook of research on socio-technical design and social networking systems: (2-volumes)* (pp. 313–332).

Baer, L. L., & Duin, A. H. (2009). Partnerships. In Rogers, P. L., Berg, G. A., Boettcher, J. V., Howard, C., Justice, L., & Schenk, K. D. (Eds.), *Encyclopedia of distance learning* (2nd ed., pp. 1597–1604).

Bakelli, Y. (2012). Public access ICT in Algeria. In Gomez, R. (Ed.), *Libraries, telecentres, cybercafes and public access to ICT: International comparisons* (pp. 490–509).

Baker, P. M., Bell, A., & Moon, N. W. (2009). Accessibility issues in municipal wireless networks. In Reddick, C. (Ed.), *Handbook of research on strategies for local e-government adoption and implementation: Comparative studies* (pp. 569–588).

Banks, W. P., & Van Sickle, T. (2011). Digital partnerships for professional development: Rethinking university–public school collaborations. In Bowdon, M., & Carpenter, R. G. (Eds.), *Higher education, emerging technologies, and community partnerships: Concepts, models and practices* (pp. 153–163).

Barón, L. F., & Valdés, M. (2012). Public access ICT in Colombia. In Gomez, R. (Ed.), *Libraries, telecentres, cybercafes and public access to ICT: International comparisons* (pp. 169–183).

Bartsch, R. A. (2008). Misuse of online databases for literature searches. In Kidd, T. T., & Song, H. (Eds.), *Handbook of research on instructional systems and technology* (pp. 373–380).

Bashirullah, A. K. (2006). Library networking of the Universidad de Oriente: A case study of introduction of Information Technology. In Khosrow-Pour, M. (Ed.), *Cases on Information Technology and organizational politics & culture* (pp. 399–405).

Baum, J., & Lyons, K. (2012). Librarianship presence in virtual worlds. In Yang, H. H., & Yuen, S. C. (Eds.), *Handbook of research on practices and outcomes in virtual worlds and environments* (pp. 384-399). doi:10.4018/978-1-60960-762-3.ch020

Béjar, R., Nogueras-Iso, J., Latre, M. Á., Muro-Medrano, P. R., & Zarazaga-Soria, F. J. (2009). Digital libraries as a foundation of spatial data infrastructures. In Theng, Y., Foo, S., Goh, D., & Na, J. (Eds.), *Handbook of research on digital libraries: Design, development, and impact* (pp. 382–389).

Blair, K. (2011). Preparing 21st-century faculty to engage 21st-century learners: The incentives and rewards for online pedagogies. In Bowdon, M., & Carpenter, R. G. (Eds.), *Higher education, emerging technologies, and community partnerships: Concepts, models and practices* (pp. 141–152).

Bodea, C., Mogos, R., & Dascalu, M. (2012). How e-learning experience enhances the social presence in community of practice: An empirical analysis. In El Morr, C., & Maret, P. (Eds.), *Virtual community building and the information society: Current and future directions* (pp. 75–120).

Bodomo, A. B. (2010). Digital literacy: Reading in the age of ICT. In Bodomo, A. B. (Ed.), *Computer-mediated communication for linguistics and literacy: Technology and natural language education* (pp. 17–35).

Bond, H. (2010). Digitizing our common memory. In Blanchard, E. G., & Allard, D. (Eds.), *Handbook of research on culturally-aware Information Technology: Perspectives and models* (pp. 520–542).

Boston, G., & Gedeon, R. J. (2008). Beyond OpenURL: Technologies for linking library resources. In Yu, H., & Breivold, S. (Eds.), *Electronic resource management in libraries: Research and practice* (pp. 235–249).

Bower, E., & Brodsky, K. (2008). Teaching credibility of sources in an age of CMC. In Kelsey, S., & St.Amant, K. (Eds.), *Handbook of research on computer mediated communication* (pp. 196–206).

Bozzon, A., Comai, S., Fraternali, P., & Carughi, G. T. (2010). Towards Web 2.0 applications: A Conceptual model for rich Internet applications. In Murugesan, S. (Ed.), *Handbook of research on Web 2.0, 3.0, and X.0: Technologies, business, and social applications* (pp. 75–95).

Brambilla, M., Fraternali, P., & Molteni, E. (2010). A tool for model-driven design of rich internet applications based on AJAX. In Murugesan, S. (Ed.), *Handbook of research on Web 2.0, 3.0, and X.0: Technologies, business, and social applications* (pp. 96–118).

Bramble, W., & Pachman, M. (2008). Costs and sustainability of learning object repositories. In Lockyer, L., Bennett, S., Agostinho, S., & Harper, B. (Eds.), *Handbook of research on learning design and learning objects: Issues, applications, and technologies* (pp. 629–650).

Brown, K. C. (2008). Tactics and terms in the negotiation of electronic resource licenses. In Yu, H., & Breivold, S. (Eds.), *Electronic resource management in libraries: Research and practice* (pp. 174–192).

Bui, A. (2012). The challenges of discovering online research/reference content: An introduction to the end user's perspective. In Polanka, S. (Ed.), *E-reference context and discoverability in libraries: Issues and concepts* (pp. 19–33).

Burk, D. L. (2007). Privacy and property in the global datasphere. In Hongladarom, S., & Ess, C. (Eds.), *Information Technology ethics: Cultural perspectives* (pp. 94–107).

Byrne, P., & McIlrath, L. (2011). Tightrope walking: Balancing IT within service-learning in Ireland. In Bowdon, M., & Carpenter, R. G. (Eds.), *Higher education, emerging technologies, and community partnerships: Concepts, models and practices* (pp. 77–87).

Calzonetti, J. A., & de Chambeau, A. (2006). Telework and the academic librarian. In Dasgupta, S. (Ed.), *Encyclopedia of virtual communities and technologies* (pp. 439–442).

Candela, L., Castelli, D., & Pagano, P. (2009). OpenDLib: A digital library service system. In Theng, Y., Foo, S., Goh, D., & Na, J. (Eds.), *Handbook of research on digital libraries: Design, development, and impact* (pp. 1–7).

Candela, L., Castelli, D., & Pagano, P. (2009). OpenDLib: A digital library service system. In Theng, Y., Foo, S., Goh, D., & Na, J. (Eds.), *Handbook of research on digital libraries: Design, development, and impact* (pp. 1–7).

Candela, L., Castelli, D., & Pagano, P. (2011). History, evolution, and impact of digital libraries. In Iglezakis, I., Synodinou, T., & Kapidakis, S. (Eds.), *E-publishing and digital libraries: Legal and organizational issues* (pp. 1–30).

Cantoni, L., & Tardini, S. (2008). Communicating in the information society: New tools for new practices. In Rivoltella, P. (Ed.), *Digital literacy: Tools and methodologies for information society* (pp. 26–44).

Carpenter, R. G. (2011). Conclusion - Remediating the community-university partnership: The multiliteracy space as a model for collaboration. In Bowdon, M., & Carpenter, R. G. (Eds.), *Higher education, emerging technologies, and community partnerships: Concepts, models and practices* (pp. 387–401).

Carroll, J. M. (2009). Introducing digital case library. In Pagani, M. (Ed.), *Encyclopedia of multimedia technology and networking* (2nd ed., pp. 782–788).

Carroll, J. M., Rosson, M. B., Farooq, U., & Burge, J. D. (2009). Community collective efficacy. In Whitworth, B., & de Moor, A. (Eds.), *Handbook of research on socio-technical design and social networking systems: (2-volumes)* (pp. 608–619).

Casbas, O. C., Nogueras-Iso, J., & Zarazaga-Soria, F. J. (2009). DL and GIS: Path to a new collaboration paradigm. In Theng, Y., Foo, S., Goh, D., & Na, J. (Eds.), *Handbook of research on digital libraries: Design, development, and impact* (pp. 390–399).

Cervi, L. M., Paredes, O., & Tornero, J. (2010). Current trends of media literacy in Europe: An overview. [IJDLDC]. *International Journal of Digital Literacy and Digital Competence*, *1*(4), 1–9. doi:doi:10.4018/jdldc.2010100101

Chan, T. S. (2009). A digital rights management system for educational content distribution. In Drossos, L., Tsolis, D., Sioutas, S., & Papatheodorou, T. (Eds.), *Digital rights management for e-commerce systems* (pp. 196–213).

Chías, P., Abad, T., & Rivera, E. (2010). The project of the ancient Spanish cartography e-library: Main targets and legal challenges. In Portela, I. M., & Cruz-Cunha, M. M. (Eds.), *Information communication technology law, protection and access rights: Global approaches and issues* (pp. 384–396).

Childs, M., & Wagner, R. (2012). Beyond the look: Viral learning spaces as contemporary learning environments. In Keppell, M., Souter, K., & Riddle, M. (Eds.), *Physical and virtual learning spaces in higher education: Concepts for the modern learning environment* (pp. 33–50).

Choudhary, P. K. (2010). Tools and techniques for digital conversion. In Ashraf, T., Sharma, J., & Gulati, P. A. (Eds.), *Developing sustainable digital libraries: Socio-technical perspectives* (pp. 64–89).

Chudamani, K. S., & Nagarathna, H. C. (2009). Metadata interoperability. In Theng, Y., Foo, S., Goh, D., & Na, J. (Eds.), *Handbook of research on digital libraries: Design, development, and impact* (pp. 122–130).

Clark, M., & Gomez, R. (2012). "Free" service or "good" service: What attracts users to public access computing venues? In Gomez, R. (Ed.), *Libraries, telecentres, cybercafes and public access to ICT: International comparisons* (pp. 43–50).

Clark, M., & Gomez, R. (2012). Libraries, telecenters and cybercafés: A comparison of different types of public access venues. In Gomez, R. (Ed.), *Libraries, telecentres, cybercafes and public access to ICT: International comparisons* (pp. 1–10).

Collins, C., Vásquez, O. A., & Bliesner, J. (2011). Bridging the gaps: Community-university partnerships as a new form of social policy. In Bowdon, M., & Carpenter, R. G. (Eds.), *Higher education, emerging technologies, and community partnerships: Concepts, models and practices* (pp. 319–328).

Conrad, L. Y. (2012). Discovering authoritative reference material: It's all about "location. location. Location.". In Polanka, S. (Ed.), *E-reference context and discoverability in libraries: Issues and concepts* (pp. 137–147).

Corazza, L. (2009). ICT and interculture opportunities offered by the Web. In Cartelli, A., & Palma, M. (Eds.), *Encyclopedia of information communication technology* (pp. 357-364). doi:10.4018/978-1-59904-845-1.ch047

Corradini, E. (2009). Enhancing collective memory with a community repository. In Salmons, J., & Wilson, L. (Eds.), *Handbook of research on electronic collaboration and organizational synergy* (pp. 637–650).

Coutinho, C. P. (2011). Mobile Web 2.0: New spaces for learning. In Chao, L. (Ed.), *Open source mobile learning: Mobile Linux applications* (pp. 180–195).

da Silva, H. P., & da Silva, L. (2010). Digital inclusion and electronic government: Looking for convergence in the decade 1997-2008. In Rahman, H. (Ed.), *Handbook of research on e-government readiness for information and service exchange: Utilizing progressive information communication technologies* (pp. 21–47).

Daly, A. (2007). The diffusion of new technologies: Community online access centre in indigenous communities in Australia. In Dyson, L. E., Hendriks, M., & Grant, S. (Eds.), *Information Technology and indigenous people* (pp. 272–285).

Damiani, E., Mezey, P. G., Pumilia, P. M., & Tammaro, A. M. (2007). Open culture for education and research environment. In Lytras, M. D., & Naeve, A. (Eds.), *Open source for knowledge and learning management: Strategies beyond tools* (pp. 219–244).

Das, A. K., Sen, B. K., & Dutta, C. (2010). Collaborative digital library development in India: A network analysis. In Ashraf, T., Sharma, J., & Gulati, P. A. (Eds.), *Developing sustainable digital libraries: Socio-Technical perspectives* (pp. 206–222).

de Campos, L. M. (2009). Thesaurus-based automatic indexing. In Song, M., & Brook Wu, Y. (Eds.), *Handbook of research on text and Web mining technologies* (pp. 331–345).

de Vos, H., & Verwijs, C. (2006). Business advantage of community knowledge. In Dasgupta, S. (Ed.), *Encyclopedia of virtual communities and technologies* (pp. 10–12).

De Weaver, L. (2008). Delivering more effective community consultation and support for regional ICT programs. In Rahman, H. (Ed.), *Developing successful ICT strategies: Competitive advantages in a global knowledge-driven society* (pp. 298–312).

DeBerg, C. L. (2011). SAGE: An international partnership linking high school students, universities and the private sector through social enterprise. In Bowdon, M., & Carpenter, R. G. (Eds.), *Higher education, emerging technologies, and community partnerships: Concepts, models and practices* (pp. 15–28).

Deng, H. (2009). An empirical analysis of the utilization of university digital library resources. In Theng, Y., Foo, S., Goh, D., & Na, J. (Eds.), *Handbook of research on digital libraries: Design, development, and impact* (pp. 344–351).

Denison, T. (2009). Support networks for rural and regional communities. In Lytras, M. D., & Ordóñez de Pablos, P. (Eds.), *Social Web evolution: Integrating semantic applications and Web 2.0 technologies* (pp. 216–232).

Dikkers, A. G., & Whiteside, A. L. (2011). Leveraging the technology-enhanced community (TEC) partnership model to enrich higher education. In Bowdon, M., & Carpenter, R. G. (Eds.), *Higher education, emerging technologies, and community partnerships: Concepts, models and practices* (pp. 191–203).

Dolson, T. (2011). "How do we know what they need?": An analysis of how ConnectRichmond changed service-learning at the University of Richmond. In Bowdon, M., & Carpenter, R. G. (Eds.), *Higher education, emerging technologies, and community partnerships: Concepts, models and practices* (pp. 124–128).

Dotsika, F. (2006). IT perspective on supporting communities of practice. In Coakes, E., & Clarke, S. (Eds.), *Encyclopedia of communities of practice in information and knowledge management* (pp. 257–263).

Elizabeth, L. S., Ismail, N., & Tun, M. S. (2012). The future of the printed book. In Sharma, R. S., Tan, M., & Pereira, F. (Eds.), *Understanding the interactive digital media marketplace: Frameworks, platforms, communities and issues* (pp. 416–429).

Ellaway, R., & Tworek, J. (2012). The net generation illusion: Challenging conformance to social expectations. In Ferris, S. P. (Ed.), *Teaching, learning and the net generation: Concepts and tools for reaching digital learners* (pp. 324–339).

Elwood, S. (2006). Participatory GIS and community planning: Restructuring technologies, social processes, and future research in PPGIS. In Balram, S., & Dragicevic, S. (Eds.), *Collaborative Geographic Information Systems* (pp. 66–84).

Engel, D., & Robbins, S. (2008). Evolving roles for electronic resources librarians. In Yu, H., & Breivold, S. (Eds.), *Electronic resource management in libraries: Research and practice* (pp. 105–120).

Eom, S. (2009). The impact of the ISI convention of relying on only the name of the first author on ACA results: An empirical investigation. In Eom, S. (Ed.), *Author cocitation analysis: Quantitative methods for mapping the intellectual structure of an academic discipline* (pp. 62–90).

Eshet-Alkalai, Y. (2009). A holistic model of thinking skills in the digital era. In Rogers, P. L., Berg, G. A., Boettcher, J. V., Howard, C., Justice, L., & Schenk, K. D. (Eds.), *Encyclopedia of distance learning* (2nd ed., pp. 1088–1093).

Ewing, R. L. (2009). Document delivery. In Rogers, P. L., Berg, G. A., Boettcher, J. V., Howard, C., Justice, L., & Schenk, K. D. (Eds.), *Encyclopedia of distance learning* (2nd ed., pp. 734–735).

Fabbro, E. (2009). Information literacy. In Rogers, P. L., Berg, G. A., Boettcher, J. V., Howard, C., Justice, L., & Schenk, K. D. (Eds.), *Encyclopedia of Distance Learning* (2nd ed., pp. 1178–1182).

Fantin, M. (2011). Beyond Babel: Multiliteracies in digital culture. [IJDLDC]. *International Journal of Digital Literacy and Digital Competence, 2*(1), 1–6. doi:doi:10.4018/jdldc.2011010101

Farmer, L. (2009). Using real case studies to teach ethics collaboratively to library media teachers. In Demiray, U., & Sharma, R. (Eds.), *Ethical practices and implications in distance learning* (pp. 268–283).

Farmer, L. S., & Murphy, N. G. (2010). eGaming and girls: Optimizing use in school libraries. In Van Eck, R. (Ed.), *Interdisciplinary models and tools for serious games: Emerging concepts and future directions* (pp. 306-332). doi:10.4018/978-1-61520-719-0.ch013

Farooq, U., Carroll, J. M., & Canoe, C. H. (2008). Designing for creativity in computer-supported cooperative work. [IJeC]. *International Journal of e-Collaboration, 4*(4), 51–75. doi:doi:10.4018/jec.2008100104

Farrell, R., Danis, C., Erickson, T., Ellis, J., Christensen, J., Bailey, M., & Kellogg, W. A. (2010). A picture and a thousand words: Visual scaffolding for mobile communication in developing regions. [IJHCR]. *International Journal of Handheld Computing Research, 1*(4), 81–95. doi:doi:10.4018/jhcr.2010100105

Fehring, H. (2010). Multiple literacies in the ICT age: Implications for teachers and teacher educators, an Australian perspective. In Rodrigues, S. (Ed.), *Multiple literacy and science education: ICTs in formal and informal learning environments* (pp. 180–206).

Ferri, P. (2010). Digital and inter-generational divide. [IJDLDC]. *International Journal of Digital Literacy and Digital Competence, 1*(1), 1–23. doi:doi:10.4018/jdldc.2010101901

Ferro, N. (2011). Quality and interoperability: The quest for the optimal balance. In Iglezakis, I., Synodinou, T., & Kapidakis, S. (Eds.), *E-publishing and digital libraries: Legal and organizational issues* (pp. 48–68).

Foley, K. (2011). Using the XO laptop to build a digital bridge between primary schools and universities. In Bowdon, M., & Carpenter, R. G. (Eds.), *Higher education, emerging technologies, and community partnerships: Concepts, models and practices* (pp. 40–50).

Fons, T. (2008). The future of electronic resource management systems: Inside and out. In Yu, H., & Breivold, S. (Eds.), *Electronic resource management in libraries: Research and practice* (pp. 363–373).

Foo, S., Theng, Y., Goh, D. H., & Na, J. (2009). From digital archives to virtual exhibitions. In Theng, Y., Foo, S., Goh, D., & Na, J. (Eds.), *Handbook of research on digital libraries: Design, development, and impact* (pp. 88–100).

Ford, N. (2008). ICT developments: Resource discovery. In Ford, N. (Ed.), *Web-based learning through educational informatics: Information science meets educational computing* (pp. 145–190).

Ford, N. (2008). Library and information science. In Ford, N. (Ed.), *Web-based learning through educational informatics: Information science meets educational computing* (pp. 110–144).

Fortuna, C., Henderson, S., McLuckie, J., Rodrigues, S., Syme-Smith, L., Taylor, N., & Williamson, G. (2010). A conversation between colleagues: Defining multiple literacy in science education. In Rodrigues, S. (Ed.), *Multiple literacy and science education: ICTs in formal and informal learning environments* (pp. 1–10).

Fox, E. A., Suleman, H., Gaur, R. C., & Madalli, D. P. (2005). Design architecture: An introduction and overview. In Theng, Y., & Foo, S. (Eds.), *Design and usability of digital libraries: Case studies in the Asia Pacific* (pp. 22–37).

Fredericka, T. M., & Schwelik, J. (2012). INFOhio transforms content delivery for PreK-12 students: From physical classrooms to virtual schoolrooms. In Polanka, S. (Ed.), *E-reference context and discoverability in libraries: Issues and concepts* (pp. 126–135).

Fry, M. L., & Ensminger, D. C. (2008). Integration of digital primary sources. In Tomei, L. A. (Ed.), *Encyclopedia of Information Technology curriculum integration* (pp. 441–448).

Fudzee, M. F., & Abawajy, J. (2010). Request-driven cross-media content adaptation technique. In Ragab, K., Helmy, T., & Hassanien, A. (Eds.), *Developing advanced Web services through P2P computing and autonomous agents: Trends and innovations* (pp. 91-113). doi:10.4018/978-1-61520-973-6.ch006

Fujima, J., Yoshihara, S., & Tanaka, Y. (2011). Spreadsheet-based orchestration for describing and automating Web information access processes. In Kreuzberger, G., Lunzer, A., & Kaschek, R. (Eds.), *Interdisciplinary advances in adaptive and intelligent assistant systems: Concepts, techniques, applications, and use* (pp. 40–62).

Galvez, C. (2009). Standardization of terms applying finite-state transducers (FST). In Theng, Y., Foo, S., Goh, D., & Na, J. (Eds.), *Handbook of research on digital libraries: Design, development, and impact* (pp. 102–112).

Gander, L., & Rhyason, D. (2011). Community-university engagement in an electronically-defined era. In Bowdon, M., & Carpenter, R. G. (Eds.), *Higher education, emerging technologies, and community partnerships: Concepts, models and practices* (pp. 365–373).

Ganguly, S., & Pandey, S. (2010). Managing change in reference and information services in digital environment. In Ashraf, T., Sharma, J., & Gulati, P. A. (Eds.), *Developing sustainable digital libraries: Socio-technical perspectives* (pp. 160–183).

Garofalakis, J., & Koskeris, A. (2010). Digital divide and rural communities: Practical solutions and policies. In Ferro, E., Dwivedi, Y. K., Gil-Garcia, J., & Williams, M. D. (Eds.), *Handbook of research on overcoming digital divides: Constructing an equitable and competitive information society* (pp. 386–408).

Gaur, R. C. (2010). Facilitating access to Indian cultural heritage: Copyright, permission rights and ownership issues vis-à-vis IGNCA collections. In Ashraf, T., Sharma, J., & Gulati, P. A. (Eds.), *Developing sustainable digital libraries: Socio-technical perspectives* (pp. 235–251).

Gavgani, V. Z. (2011). Ubiquitous information therapy service through social networking libraries: An operational Web 2.0 service model. In Biswas, R., & Martin, C. M. (Eds.), *User-driven healthcare and narrative medicine: Utilizing collaborative social networks and technologies* (pp. 446–461).

Geiger, C. (2011). Copyright and digital libraries: Securing access to information in the digital age. In Iglezakis, I., Synodinou, T., & Kapidakis, S. (Eds.), *E-publishing and digital libraries: Legal and organizational issues* (pp. 257–272).

Gemmill, L., & Wildermuth, J. (2012). Hooligans in the archives: Easing restrictions and partnering with the users. In Polanka, S. (Ed.), *E-reference context and discoverability in libraries: Issues and concepts* (pp. 209–218).

Gibson, J., Lloyd, B., & Richmond, C. (2011). Localisation of indigenous content: Libraries and knowledge centres and the our story database in the Northern Territory. In Steyn, J., Van Belle, J., & Mansilla, E. V. (Eds.), *ICTs for global development and sustainability: Practice and applications* (pp. 151–175).

Ginsburg, M. (2006). Unified citation management and visualization using open standards: The open citation system. In Jakobs, K. (Ed.), *Advanced topics in Information Technology standards and standardization research* (*Vol. 1*, pp. 230–250).

Goetzfridt, N. J. (2007). "Life in the round" and the history of libraries in Micronesia. In Inoue, Y. (Ed.), *Online education for lifelong learning* (pp. 253–270).

Goh, D. H. (2009). Learning geography with the G-Portal Digital Library. In Rees, P., MacKay, L., Martin, D., & Durham, H. (Eds.), *E-learning for geographers: Online materials, resources, and repositories* (pp. 260-269). doi:10.4018/978-1-59904-980-9.ch016

Gomez, R. (2012). Success factors for public access computing: Beyond anecdotes of success. In Gomez, R. (Ed.), *Libraries, telecentres, cybercafes and public access to ICT: International comparisons* (pp. 82–94).

Gomez, R., & Camacho, K. (2011). Users of ICT at public access centers: Age, education, gender, and income differences in users. [IJICTHD]. *International Journal of Information Communication Technologies and Human Development, 3*(1), 1–20. doi:doi:10.4018/jicthd.2011010101

Gomez, R., & Camacho, K. (2012). Who uses public access venues? In Gomez, R. (Ed.), *Libraries, telecentres, cybercafes and public access to ICT: International comparisons* (pp. 11–23).

Gomez, R., & Gould, E. (2012). Perceptions of trust: Safety, credibility, and "cool". In Gomez, R. (Ed.), *Libraries, telecentres, cybercafes and public access to ICT: International comparisons* (pp. 32–42).

Goodrum, A. A. (2008). Watching what we read: Implications of law enforcement activity in libraries since 9/11. In Loendorf, T., & Garson, G. D. (Eds.), *Patriotic Information Systems* (pp. 91–127).

Gould, E., & Gomez, R. (2012). Infomediaries and community engagement are key. In Gomez, R. (Ed.), *Libraries, telecentres, cybercafes and public access to ICT: International comparisons* (pp. 24–31).

Griffin, M., Saitta, E., Bowdon, M., & Walters, L. J. (2011). Engaging STEM: Service-learning, technology, science education and community partnerships. In Bowdon, M., & Carpenter, R. G. (Eds.), *Higher education, emerging technologies, and community partnerships: Concepts, models and practices* (pp. 51–56).

Gunjal, B., Gaitanou, P., & Yasin, S. (2012). Social networks and knowledge management: An explorative study in library systems. In Boughzala, I., & Dudezert, A. (Eds.), *Knowledge management 2.0: Organizational models and enterprise strategies* (pp. 64–83).

Gunn, M., & Kraemer, E. W. (2012). The agile teaching library: Models for integrating information literacy in online learning experiences. In Kelsey, S., & St. Amant, K. (Eds.), *Computer-mediated communication: Issues and approaches in education* (pp. 191–206).

Hadzilias, E. A., & Carugati, A. (2009). Bridging user requirements and cultural objects: A process-oriented framework for cultural e-services. In Zaphiris, P., & Ang, C. (Eds.), *Cross-disciplinary advances in human computer interaction: User modeling, social computing, and adaptive interfaces* (pp. 12–36).

Hagenhoff, S., Ortelbach, B., & Seidenfaden, L. (2009). A classification scheme for innovative types in scholarly communication. In Theng, Y., Foo, S., Goh, D., & Na, J. (Eds.), *Handbook of research on digital libraries: Design, development, and impact* (pp. 216–226).

Hai-Jew, S. (2010). Maximizing collaborative learning and work in digital libraries and repositories: A Conceptual meta-case. In Russell, D. (Ed.), *Cases on collaboration in virtual learning environments: Processes and interactions* (pp. 169–192).

Hamilton, B. J. (2012). Embedded librarianship: A high school case study. In Polanka, S. (Ed.), *E-reference context and discoverability in libraries: Issues and concepts* (pp. 237–253).

Hanson, A. (2008). Accessibility: Critical GIS, ontologies, and semantics. In Abresch, J., Hanson, A., Heron, S., & Reehling, P. J. (Eds.), *Integrating geographic information systems into library services: A guide for academic libraries* (pp. 151–174).

Hanson, A. (2008). Reference services. In Abresch, J., Hanson, A., Heron, S., & Reehling, P. J. (Eds.), *Integrating geographic information systems into library services: A guide for academic libraries* (pp. 175–201).

Hart, D., & Warne, L. (2008). A dialectic on the cultural and political aspects of information and knowledge sharing in organizations. In Jennex, M. E. (Ed.), *Current issues in knowledge management* (pp. 104–118).

Hatzimihail, N. (2011). Copyright infringement of digital libraries and private international law: Jurisdiction issues. In Iglezakis, I., Synodinou, T., & Kapidakis, S. (Eds.), *E-publishing and digital libraries: Legal and organizational issues* (pp. 447–460).

Hea, A. C. (2011). Rearticulating Web 2.0 technologies: Strategies to redefine social media in community projects. In Bowdon, M., & Carpenter, R. G. (Eds.), *Higher education, emerging technologies, and community partnerships: Concepts, models and practices* (pp. 235–244).

Helling, K., & Ertl, B. (2011). Fostering collaborative problem solving by content schemes. In Pozzi, F., & Persico, D. (Eds.), *Techniques for fostering collaboration in online learning communities: Theoretical and practical perspectives* (pp. 33–48).

Henry, J. (2011). Hybridizing F2F and virtual collaboration between a government agency and service-learning technical writing students. In Bowdon, M., & Carpenter, R. G. (Eds.), *Higher education, emerging technologies, and community partnerships: Concepts, models and practices* (pp. 58–67).

Holloway, K. (2012). Fair use, copyright, and academic integrity in an online academic environment. In Wang, V. C. (Ed.), *Encyclopedia of e-leadership, counseling and training* (pp. 298–309).

Holt, J., Unruh, L., & Dougherty, A. M. (2011). Enhancing a rural school-university teacher education partnership through an e-mentoring program for beginning teachers. In Bowdon, M., & Carpenter, R. G. (Eds.), *Higher education, emerging technologies, and community partnerships: Concepts, models and practices* (pp. 212–220).

Honkaranta, A., Salminen, A., & Peltola, T. (2005). Challenges in the redesign of content management: A case of FCP. [IJCEC]. *International Journal of Cases on Electronic Commerce, 1*(1), 53–69. doi:doi:10.4018/jcec.2005010104

Hornett, A. (2004). Varieties of virtual organizations and their knowledge sharing systems. In Pauleen, D. (Ed.), *Virtual teams: Projects, protocols and processes* (pp. 186–119).

Hsu, I., & Wang, Y. (2008). A model of intraorganizational knowledge sharing: Development and initial test. [JGIM]. *Journal of Global Information Management, 16*(3), 45–73. doi:doi:10.4018/jgim.2008070103

Huerta-Canepa, G., & Lee, D. (2010). A multi-user ad-hoc resource manager for public urban areas. [IJARAS]. *International Journal of Adaptive, Resilient and Autonomic Systems, 1*(4), 26–45. doi:doi:10.4018/jaras.2010100103

Ing Tiong, C., Cater-Steel, A., & Tan, W. (2009). Measuring return on investment from implementing ITIL: A review of the literature. In Cater-Steel, A. (Ed.), *Information Technology governance and service management: Frameworks and adaptations* (pp. 408–422).

Inoue, Y., & Bell, S. (2006). Technology, educational media, and e-resources. In Inoue, Y., & Bell, S. (Eds.), *Teaching with educational technology in the 21st century: The case of the Asia-Pacific region* (pp. 24–49).

Ivanova, M., & Popova, A. (2011). Formal and informal learning flows cohesion in Web 2.0 environment. [IJISSC]. *International Journal of Information Systems and Social Change, 2*(1), 1–15. doi:doi:10.4018/jissc.2011010101

Jaeger, P. T. (2009). Public libraries and local e-government. In Reddick, C. (Ed.), *Handbook of research on strategies for local e-government adoption and implementation: Comparative studies* (pp. 647–660).

Jahnke, I. (2010). A way out of the information jungle: A longitudinal study about a socio-technical community and informal learning in higher education. [IJSKD]. *International Journal of Sociotechnology and Knowledge Development, 2*(4), 18–38. doi:doi:10.4018/jskd.2010100102

James, T., Finlay, A., Jensen, M., Neville, M., & Pillay, R. (2012). Public access ICT in South Africa. In Gomez, R. (Ed.), *Libraries, telecentres, cybercafes and public access to ICT: International comparisons* (pp. 429–451).

Jameson, J. (2010). An e-learning metaphor: The CAMEL nomadic community of practice. In Mukerji, S., & Tripathi, P. (Eds.), *Cases on technology enhanced learning through collaborative opportunities* (pp. 1–27).

Jansen, B. J. (2009). The methodology of search log analysis. In Jansen, B., Spink, A., & Taksa, I. (Eds.), *Handbook of research on Web log analysis* (pp. 100–123).

Jiang, H., Carroll, J. M., & Ganoe, C. (2010). Managing case-based learning with interactive case study libraries. In Kats, Y. (Ed.), *Learning management system technologies and software solutions for online teaching: Tools and applications* (pp. 351–371).

Jindal, S. C. (2010). Digital libraries and scholarly communication: A perspective. In Ashraf, T., Sharma, J., & Gulati, P. A. (Eds.), *Developing sustainable digital libraries: Socio-technical perspectives* (pp. 19–39).

Johannesson, P., Andersson, B., & Weigand, H. (2010). Resource analysis and classification for purpose driven value model design. [IJISMD]. *International Journal of Information System Modeling and Design, 1*(1), 56–78. doi:doi:10.4018/jismd.2010092303

Johnson, K. T., & Smith-Jackson, T. L. (2010). A human factors view of the digital divide. In Ferro, E., Dwivedi, Y. K., Gil-Garcia, J., & Williams, M. D. (Eds.), *Handbook of research on overcoming digital divides: Constructing an equitable and competitive information society* (pp. 606–629).

Jones, M. G., Schwilk, C. L., & Bateman, D. F. (2012). Reading by listening: Access to books in audio format for college students with print disabilities. In Aitken, J. E., Fairley, J. P., & Carlson, J. K. (Eds.), *Communication technology for students in special education and gifted programs* (pp. 249–272).

Joshipura, S. (2008). Selecting, acquiring, and renewing electronic resources. In Yu, H., & Breivold, S. (Eds.), *Electronic resource management in libraries: Research and practice* (pp. 48–70).

Jovanovic, J., Gasevic, D., & Devedzic, V. (2006). Ontology-based automatic annotation of learning content. [IJSWIS]. *International Journal on Semantic Web and Information Systems*, *2*(2), 91–119. doi:doi:10.4018/jswis.2006040103

Kamthan, P. (2007). Accessibility of mobile applications. In Taniar, D. (Ed.), *Encyclopedia of mobile computing and commerce* (pp. 9–14).

Kani-Zabihi, E., Ghinea, G., & Chen, S. Y. (2010). Experiences with developing a user-centered digital library. [IJDLS]. *International Journal of Digital Library Systems*, *1*(1), 1–23. doi:doi:10.4018/jdls.2010102701

Kanyengo, C. W. (2012). Fostering and developing leadership amongst library staff at the University of Zambia library. In Tella, A., & Issa, A. (Eds.), *Library and information science in developing countries: Contemporary issues* (pp. 1–10).

Kennedy, D. M. (2008). Digital literacy research. In L. A. Tomei (Ed.), *Encyclopedia of Information Technology curriculum integration* (pp. 228-234). doi:10.4018/978-1-59904-881-9.ch037

Kennedy, M. R. (2008). The impact of locally developed electronic resource management systems. In Yu, H., & Breivold, S. (Eds.), *Electronic resource management in libraries: Research and practice* (pp. 350-362). doi:10.4018/978-1-59904-891-8.ch019

Kettunen, J. (2009). The strategic plan of digital libraries. In Theng, Y., Foo, S., Goh, D., & Na, J. (Eds.), *Handbook of research on digital libraries: Design, development, and impact* (pp. 457–464).

Kettunen, J., Hautala, J., & Kantola, M. (2009). Knowledge management with partners in a dynamic information environment. In Cartelli, A., & Palma, M. (Eds.), *Encyclopedia of information communication technology* (pp. 503-509). doi:10.4018/978-1-59904-845-1.ch066

Kheng Grace, S. W. (2009). Digital libraries overview and globalization. In Theng, Y., Foo, S., Goh, D., & Na, J. (Eds.), *Handbook of research on digital libraries: Design, development, and impact* (pp. 562–573).

Kiau, B. W. (2007). DRM practices in the e-publication industry. In Quigley, M. (Ed.), *Encyclopedia of information ethics and security* (pp. 157–163).

Kichuk, D. (2008). Using consistent naming conventions for library electronic resources. In Yu, H., & Breivold, S. (Eds.), *Electronic resource management in libraries: Research and practice* (pp. 275–293).

Kimani, S., Panizzi, E., Catarci, T., & Antona, M. (2009). Digital library requirements: A questionnaire-based study. In Theng, Y., Foo, S., Goh, D., & Na, J. (Eds.), *Handbook of research on digital libraries: Design, development, and impact* (pp. 287–297).

Kirk, M. (2009). Partnership language and media: Creating a new IT culture. In Kirk, M. (Ed.), *Gender and Information Technology: Moving beyond access to co-create global partnership* (pp. 193–211).

Kirk, M. (2009). Partnership science and technology education. In Kirk, M. (Ed.), *Gender and Information Technology: Moving beyond access to co-create global partnership* (pp. 212–238).

Kitalong, K. S. (2011). From collision to collaboration: An expanded role for project evaluators in the development of interactive media. In Bowdon, M., & Carpenter, R. G. (Eds.), *Higher education, emerging technologies, and community partnerships: Concepts, models and practices* (pp. 278–285).

Klempa, M., & Wegner, L. (1997). *USCInfo: A high volume, integrated online library resources automation project* (pp. 132-155). doi:10.4018/978-1-87828-937-7.ch012

Kock, N. (2008). Global funding of e-collaboration research. In Kock, N. (Ed.), *Encyclopedia of e-collaboration* (pp. 314–318).

Kock, N., & Antunes, P. (2009). A comparative analysis of e-collaboration research funding in the European Union and the United States. In Kock, N. (Ed.), *Virtual team leadership and collaborative engineering advancements: Contemporary issues and implications* (pp. 40–48).

Koppel, T. (2008). In the eye of the storm: ERM systems are guiding libraries' future. In Yu, H., & Breivold, S. (Eds.), *Electronic resource management in libraries: Research and practice* (pp. 374–382).

Koppel, T. (2008). Standards, the structural underpinnings of electronic resource management systems. In Yu, H., & Breivold, S. (Eds.), *Electronic resource management in libraries: Research and practice* (pp. 295–305).

Koumpis, A. (2010). Services and the humans. In Koumpis, A. (Ed.), *Service science for socio-economical and Information Systems advancement: Holistic methodologies* (pp. 86–140).

Koutsomitropoulos, D. A., Solomou, G. D., Alexopoulos, A. D., & Papatheodorou, T. S. (2009). Semantic metadata interoperability and inference-based querying in digital repositories. [JITR]. *Journal of Information Technology Research, 2*(4), 36–52. doi:doi:10.4018/jitr.2009062903

Kovacevic, A., & Devedzic, V. (2009). Duplicate journal title detection in references. In Theng, Y., Foo, S., Goh, D., & Na, J. (Eds.), *Handbook of research on digital libraries: Design, development, and impact* (pp. 235–242).

Kowalczyk, S. (2008). Digital preservation by design. In Raisinghani, M. S. (Ed.), *Handbook of research on global Information Technology management in the digital economy* (pp. 406–431).

Kurubacak, G. (2007). Building online knowledge societies for lifelong learning: The democratic university-community partnerships in Turkey. In Inoue, Y. (Ed.), *Online education for lifelong learning* (pp. 208–227).

Kushchu, I. (2012). Public access ICT in Indonesia. In Gomez, R. (Ed.), *Libraries, telecentres, cybercafes and public access to ICT: International comparisons* (pp. 315–329).

Kushchu, I. (2012). Public access ICT in Turkey. In Gomez, R. (Ed.), *Libraries, telecentres, cybercafes and public access to ICT: International comparisons* (pp. 534–553).

Kwon, N., & Gregory, V. L. (2010). Using transaction logs to study the effectiveness of librarian behaviors on user satisfaction in a virtual setting: A Mixed-method approach. [IJDSST]. *International Journal of Decision Support System Technology, 2*(2), 36–41. doi:doi:10.4018/jdsst.2010040104

Lamantia, J. (2009). Creating successful portals with a design framework. [IJWP]. *International Journal of Web Portals, 1*(4), 63–75. doi:doi:10.4018/jwp.2009071305

Lamp, J. (2007). The portal as information broker. In Tatnall, A. (Ed.), *Encyclopedia of portal technologies and applications* (pp. 705–711).

Landoni, M. (2011). E-books in digital libraries. In Iglezakis, I., Synodinou, T., & Kapidakis, S. (Eds.), *E-publishing and digital libraries: Legal and organizational issues* (pp. 131–140).

Langer, G. R. (2009). 21st century e-student services. In Rogers, P. L., Berg, G. A., Boettcher, J. V., Howard, C., Justice, L., & Schenk, K. D. (Eds.), *Encyclopedia of distance learning* (2nd ed., pp. 2160–2167).

Larson, D. (2011). Inter-organization partnership and collaborative work tools. In Milhauser, K. L. (Ed.), *Distributed team collaboration in organizations: Emerging tools and practices* (pp. 212–223).

Lastrucci, E., & Pascale, A. (2010). Cooperative learning through communities of practice. [IJDLDC]. *International Journal of Digital Literacy and Digital Competence, 1*(2), 11–21. doi:doi:10.4018/jdldc.2010040102

Lavariega, J. C., Gomez, L. G., Sordia-Salinas, M., & Garza-Salazar, D. A. (2009). Personal digital libraries. In Theng, Y., Foo, S., Goh, D., & Na, J. (Eds.), *Handbook of research on digital libraries: Design, development, and impact* (pp. 41–50).

Lawler, J. (2011). Critical success factors for partnering with nonprofit organizations on digital technology service-learning projects: A case study. In Bowdon, M., & Carpenter, R. G. (Eds.), *Higher education, emerging technologies, and community partnerships: Concepts, models and practices* (pp. 106–123).

Lekoko, R., Modise-Jankie, J., & Busang, C. (2012). Libraries as portal for knowledge driven rural community development cases from Botswana. In Lekoko, R. N., & Semali, L. M. (Eds.), *Cases on developing countries and ICT integration: Rural community development* (pp. 34–41).

Letic-Gavrilovic, A. (2009). Digital library for dental biomaterials. In Daskalaki, A. (Ed.), *Dental computing and applications: Advanced techniques for clinical dentistry* (pp. 232–272).

Leung, S., Martin, D., Treves, R., & Duke-Williams, O. (2009). Exchanging e-learning materials, modules, and students. In Rees, P., MacKay, L., Martin, D., & Durham, H. (Eds.), *E-learning for geographers: Online materials, resources, and repositories* (pp. 20-37). doi:10.4018/978-1-59904-980-9.ch002

Lichtenstein, S., & Hunter, A. (2006). Toward a receiver-based theory of knowledge sharing. [IJKM]. *International Journal of Knowledge Management, 2*(1), 24–40. doi:doi:10.4018/jkm.2006010103

Loh, S., Lichtnow, D., Borges, T., & Piltcher, G. (2008). Evaluating the construction of domain ontologies for recommender systems based on texts. In Nigro, H. O., Gonzalez Cisaro, S. E., & Xodo, D. H. (Eds.), *Data mining with ontologies: Implementations, findings, and frameworks* (pp. 145–158).

Longo, B. (2011). Mobile phones and cultural connections: Designing a mutual world between the DR Congo and United States. In Bowdon, M., & Carpenter, R. G. (Eds.), *Higher education, emerging technologies, and community partnerships: Concepts, models and practices* (pp. 245–257).

Lopes, R., & Carriço, L. (2009). Querying Web accessibility knowledge from Web graphs. In Cruz-M. M. Cunha, E. Oliveira, A. Tavares, & L. Ferreira (Eds.), *Handbook of research on social dimensions of semantic technologies and Web services* (pp. 88-112). doi:10.4018/978-1-60566-650-1.ch005

Love, E. W., Cushing, D. F., Sullivan, M., & Brexa, J. (2011). Digital storytelling within a service-learning partnership: Technology as product and process for university students and culturally and linguistically diverse high school youth. In Bowdon, M., & Carpenter, R. G. (Eds.), *Higher education, emerging technologies, and community partnerships: Concepts, models and practices* (pp. 88–105).

Loving, K., Stoecker, R., & Reddy, M. (2011). Service-learning, technology, nonprofits, and institutional limitations. In Bowdon, M., & Carpenter, R. G. (Eds.), *Higher education, emerging technologies, and community partnerships: Concepts, models and practices* (pp. 129–139).

Lu, Y., & Thai, K. V. (2012). Information management for public budget decision making: Insights from organization and budget theories. In Vaidya, K. (Ed.), *Inter-organizational information systems and business management: Theories for researchers* (pp. 206–228).

Lucas-Schloetter, A. (2011). Digital libraries and copyright issues: Digitization of contents and the economic rights of the authors. In Iglezakis, I., Synodinou, T., & Kapidakis, S. (Eds.), *E-publishing and digital libraries: Legal and organizational issues* (pp. 159–179).

Lucey, T. A., & Grant, M. (2008). Considering dimensions of the digital divide. In Kidd, T. T., & Song, H. (Eds.), *Handbook of research on instructional systems and technology* (pp. 869–883).

Lucke, J. V. (2007). Portals for the Public Sector. In Anttiroiko, A., & Malkia, M. (Eds.), *Encyclopedia of digital government* (pp. 1328–1333).

Luppicini, R., & Bratanek, L. (2010). A conversation approach to electronic collections development within university libraries. In Luppicini, R., & Haghi, A. (Eds.), *Cases on digital technologies in higher education: Issues and challenges* (pp. 34–49).

Ma, Y., Clegg, W., & O'Brien, A. (2009). A review of progress in digital library education. In Theng, Y., Foo, S., Goh, D., & Na, J. (Eds.), *Handbook of research on digital libraries: Design, development, and impact* (pp. 533–542).

Mairn, C. (2012). Acquiring, promoting, and using mobile-optimized library resources and services. In Polanka, S. (Ed.), *E-reference context and discoverability in libraries: Issues and concepts* (pp. 178–198).

Manouselis, N., Kastrantas, K., Sanchez-Alonso, S., Caceres, J., Ebner, H., & Palmer, M. (2009). Architecture of the organic.edunet Web portal. [IJWP]. *International Journal of Web Portals*, *1*(1), 71–91. doi:doi:10.4018/jwp.2009092105

Markgren, S., Eastman, C., & Bloom, L. M. (2010). Librarian as collaborator: Bringing e-learning 2.0 into the classroom by way of the library. In Yang, H. H., & Yuen, S. C. (Eds.), *Handbook of research on practices and outcomes in e-learning: Issues and trends* (pp. 260-277). doi:10.4018/978-1-60566-788-1.ch016

Martin, H., & Hesseldenz, P. (2012). Library resources and services in 21st century online education. In Kelsey, S., & St. Amant, K. (Eds.), *Computer-mediated communication: Issues and approaches in education* (pp. 33–49).

Maskey, M., Conover, H., Keiser, K., Bermudez, L., & Graves, S. (2011). OOSTethys/Oceans IE service registry based on catalog service for Web. In Zhao, P., & Di, L. (Eds.), *Geospatial Web services: Advances in information interoperability* (pp. 97–117).

Matei, S. A., & Bruno, R. J. (2012). Individualist motivators and community functional constraints in social media: The case of Wikis and Wikipedia. In Comunello, F. (Ed.), *Networked sociability and individualism: Technology for personal and professional relationships* (pp. 1–23).

Matzen, N. J., Ochoa, L., & Purpur, G. (2011). At the intersection of learning: The role of the academic library in 3D environments. In Cheney, A., & Sanders, R. L. (Eds.), *Teaching and learning in 3D immersive worlds: Pedagogical models and constructivist approaches* (pp. 99–111).

Mayol, E. (2011). An adaptative user interface for genealogical document transcription. In Styliaras, G., Koukopoulos, D., & Lazarinis, F. (Eds.), *Handbook of research on technologies and cultural heritage: Applications and environments* (pp. 306–324).

McCarthy, C. (2006). Digital library structure and software. In Marshall, S., Taylor, W., & Yu, X. (Eds.), *Encyclopedia of developing regional communities with information and communication technology* (pp. 193-198). doi:10.4018/978-1-59140-575-7.ch034

McCarthy, C. (2006). Promoting the culture and development of regional communities with digital libraries. In Marshall, S., Taylor, W., & Yu, X. (Eds.), *Encyclopedia of developing regional communities with information and communication technology* (pp. 593-597). doi:10.4018/978-1-59140-575-7.ch105

McCarthy, C. (2007). Portal features of major digital libraries. In Tatnall, A. (Ed.), *Encyclopedia of portal technologies and applications* (pp. 724–736).

McClure, R. (2011). The digital information divide. In D'Agustino, S. (Ed.), *Adaptation, resistance and access to instructional technologies: Assessing future trends in education* (pp. 1–18).

McLachlan, R., & Sullivan, K. (2012). E-reference in public libraries: Phoenix Public Library case study, our website is your 24/7 reference librarian. In Polanka, S. (Ed.), *E-reference context and discoverability in libraries: Issues and concepts* (pp. 220–229).

McLean, J. E., & Dail, A. R. (2012). Changing the grant culture of a college. In Burley, H. (Ed.), *Cases on institutional research systems* (pp. 22–38).

McNaught, C. (2008). Information literacy in the 21st century. In Tomei, L. A. (Ed.), *Encyclopedia of Information Technology curriculum integration* (pp. 406–412).

Medina-Garrido, J. A., & Ramos-Rodriguesz, A. R. (2006). Intellectual basis of research on alliances: A bibliomatic study. In Martínez-Fierro, S., Medina-Garrido, J., & Ruiz-Navarro, J. (Eds.), *Utilizing Information Technology in developing strategic alliances among organizations* (pp. 40–58).

Meletiou, A. (2010). The evaluation of library services methods: Cost per use and users' satisfaction. [IJDSST]. *International Journal of Decision Support System Technology, 2*(2), 10–23. doi:doi:10.4018/jdsst.2010040102

Menchaca, F. (2012). Hidden Greenlands: Learning, libraries, and literacy in the information age. In Polanka, S. (Ed.), *E-Reference context and discoverability in libraries: Issues and concepts* (pp. 61–73).

Menzin, M. (2008). Resources on Web-centric computing. In Brandon, D. M. (Ed.), *Software engineering for modern Web applications: Methodologies and technologies* (pp. 292–353).

Merchant, G. (2009). Learning for the future: Emerging technologies and social participation. In Tan Wee Hin, L., & Subramaniam, R. (Eds.), *Handbook of research on new media literacy at the K-12 level: Issues and challenges* (pp. 1–13).

Mescan, S. (2010). Putting their heads together virtually: Case studies on collaboration using content management technology. In Hewett, B. L., & Robidoux, C. (Eds.), *Virtual collaborative writing in the workplace: Computer-mediated communication technologies and processes* (pp. 158–173).

Molodtsov, O. (2006). Establishing a "knowledge network" of local and regional development subjects. In Marshall, S., Taylor, W., & Yu, X. (Eds.), *Encyclopedia of developing regional communities with information and communication technology* (pp. 289-294). doi:10.4018/978-1-59140-575-7.ch050

Morales-del-Castillo, J. M., Peis, E., & Herrera-Viedma, E. (2011). An approach to a semantic recommender system for digital libraries. In Lytras, M., de Pablos, P. O., & Damiani, E. (Eds.), *Semantic Web personalization and context awareness: Management of personal identities and social networking* (pp. 55–68).

Moreno-Clari, P., & Sanchis-Kilders, E. (2010). Integrating new open source assessment tools into dotLearn LMS. In Kats, Y. (Ed.), *Learning management system technologies and software solutions for online teaching: Tools and applications* (pp. 219–238).

Mummery, J., & Rodan, D. (2011). Chewing the communal cud: Community deliberation in broadsheet letters and political blogs. In Yearwood, J., & Stranieri, A. (Eds.), *Technologies for supporting reasoning communities and collaborative decision making: Cooperative approaches* (pp. 296–318).

Munkvold, B. E., & Zigurs, I. (2007). Research challenges for integration of e-collaboration technologies. In Kock, N. (Ed.), *Emerging e-collaboration concepts and applications* (pp. 41–69).

Mussi, C., Angeloni, M., & Serra, F. (2007). Knowledge sharing in the context of information technology projects: The case of a higher education institution. In Joia, L. A. (Ed.), *Strategies for information technology and intellectual capital: Challenges and opportunities* (pp. 188–200).

Na, J., Thet, T. T., Goh, D. H., Theng, Y., & Foo, S. (2009). Word segmentation in Indo-China languages for digital libraries. In Theng, Y., Foo, S., Goh, D., & Na, J. (Eds.), *Handbook of research on digital libraries: Design, development, and impact* (pp. 243–250).

Naughton, T., & Ariunaa, L. (2012). Public access ICT in Kyrgyzstan. In Gomez, R. (Ed.), *Libraries, telecentres, cybercafes and public access to ICT: International comparisons* (pp. 344–355).

Nepali, R. K., & Bista, B. (2012). Public access ICT in Nepal. In Gomez, R. (Ed.), *Libraries, telecentres, cybercafes and public access to ICT: International comparisons* (pp. 267–282).

Nicholas, A. J., & Lewis, J. K. (2011). The Net generation and e-textbooks. [IJCEE]. *International Journal of Cyber Ethics in Education, 1*(3), 70–77. doi:doi:10.4018/ijcee.2011070107

Nichols, D. M., Bainbridge, D., Marsden, G., Patel, D., Cunningham, S. J., Thompson, J., & Boddie, S. J. (2005). Evolving tool support for digital librarians. In Theng, Y., & Foo, S. (Eds.), *Design and usability of digital libraries: Case studies in the Asia Pacific* (pp. 171–190).

Njenga, J. K., & Fourie, L. C. (2011). Here and now or coming in the future? E-learning in higher education in Africa. In Bowdon, M., & Carpenter, R. G. (Eds.), *Higher education, emerging technologies, and community partnerships: Concepts, models and practices* (pp. 286–298).

Northrop, A. (2007). Lip service? How PA journals and textbooks view Information Technology. In Garson, G. D. (Ed.), *Modern public Information Technology systems: Issues and challenges* (pp. 1–16).

O'Gorman, J. (2012). Reference products and services: Historical overview and paradigm shift. In Polanka, S. (Ed.), *E-reference context and discoverability in libraries: Issues and concepts* (pp. 1–10).

O'Kane, T. (2007). Industry-university collaborations in research for information systems: An exploratory study of a management model. In Lowry, G. R., & Turner, R. L. (Eds.), *Information Systems and technology education: From the university to the workplace* (pp. 279–298).

Ofua, O. J., & Emiri, O. T. (2011). Perceptions and attitude of students in relation to vandalism in university libraries in South-South Zone of Nigeria. [IJDLS]. *International Journal of Digital Library Systems, 2*(3), 23–28. doi:doi:10.4018/jdls.2011070103

Ogbomo, M. O. (2012). The significance of marketing in library and information science. In Tella, A., & Issa, A. (Eds.), *Library and information science in developing countries: Contemporary issues* (pp. 70–81).

Onohwakpor, J. E., & Adogbeji, B. O. (2010). The implications of Alireza Noruzi's Laws of the Web for library Web-based services. In Adomi, E. (Ed.), *Handbook of research on information communication technology policy: Trends, issues and advancements* (pp. 724–733).

Orosbullard, D. D. (2009). Future trends: Global projects & virtual teaming. In Kidd, T. T. (Ed.), *Handbook of research on technology project management, planning, and operations* (pp. 480–493).

Osondu, M. C., & Solomon-Uwakwe, B. (2010). Positioning library and information services for user satisfaction through ICT policy formulation in Nigeria. In Adomi, E. (Ed.), *Handbook of research on information communication technology policy: Trends, issues and advancements* (pp. 581–589).

Otokunefor, H. O., & Kari, H. K. (2008). Issues, controversies, and problems of cybercafés located in a university campus. In Adomi, E. (Ed.), *Security and software for cybercafes* (pp. 62–83).

Ou, S., Khoo, C. S., & Goh, D. H. (2009). Automatic text summarization in digital libraries. In Theng, Y., Foo, S., Goh, D., & Na, J. (Eds.), *Handbook of research on digital libraries: Design, development, and impact* (pp. 159–172).

Paberza, K. (2010). Towards an assessment of public library value: Statistics on the policy makers' agenda. [IJDSST]. *International Journal of Decision Support System Technology, 2*(2), 42–51. doi:doi:10.4018/jdsst.2010040105

Paganelis, G. I. (2010). Recruitment experiences in area studies library organizations: The case of ACRL's Western European Studies Section (WESS). In Pankl, E., Theiss-White, D., & Bushing, M. C. (Eds.), *Recruitment, development, and retention of information professionals: Trends in human resources and knowledge management* (pp. 112–138).

Paganelli, F., Pettenati, M. C., & Giuli, D. (2006). A metadata-based approach for unstructured document management in organizations. [IRMJ]. *Information Resources Management Journal, 19*(1), 1–22. doi:doi:10.4018/irmj.2006010101

Pang, N. (2008). Cultivating communities through the knowledge commons: The case of open content licenses. In Sasaki, H. (Ed.), *Intellectual property protection for multimedia Information Technology* (pp. 260–277).

Pang, N. (2009). Digital libraries as centres of knowledge: Historical perspectives from European ancient libraries. In Theng, Y., Foo, S., Goh, D., & Na, J. (Eds.), *Handbook of research on digital libraries: Design, development, and impact* (pp. 506–513).

Paolozzi, S., Ferri, F., & Grifoni, P. (2009). Improving multimedia digital libraries usability applying NLP sentence similarity to multimodal sentences. In Theng, Y., Foo, S., Goh, D., & Na, J. (Eds.), *Handbook of research on digital libraries: Design, development, and impact* (pp. 227–234).

Papadopoulou, A. (2011). The digitization of contents in digital libraries: Moral right and limits. In Iglezakis, I., Synodinou, T., & Kapidakis, S. (Eds.), *E-publishing and digital libraries: Legal and organizational issues* (pp. 180–197).

Papastavrou, S., Samaras, G., Evripidou, P., & Chrysanthis, P. K. (2007). Dynamically generated Web content: Research and technology practices. In Vakali, A., & Pallis, G. (Eds.), *Web data management practices: Emerging techniques and technologies* (pp. 104–123).

Papoutsakis, H. (2009). Organizational knowledge sharing networks. In Girard, J. (Ed.), *Building organizational memories: Will you know what you knew?* (pp. 81–96).

Parkinson, C. M., & Olphert, C. W. (2010). Website accessibility and the role of accessibility statements. In Spiliotopoulos, T., Papadopoulou, P., Martakos, D., & Kouroupetroglou, G. (Eds.), *Integrating usability engineering for designing the Web experience: Methodologies and principles* (pp. 166–190).

Partarakis, N. (2007). Portals for development and use of guidelines and standards. In Tatnall, A. (Ed.), *Encyclopedia of portal technologies and applications* (pp. 782–787).

Patrick, K., Cox, A., & Abdullah, R. (2006). Exploring the selection of technology for enabling communities. In Coakes, E., & Clarke, S. (Eds.), *Encyclopedia of communities of practice in information and knowledge management* (pp. 166–176).

Phillips, J. B. (2012). Undergraduate information seeking behavior, e-reference and information literacy in the social sciences. In Polanka, S. (Ed.), *E-reference context and discoverability in libraries: Issues and concepts* (pp. 83–88).

Poda, I., & Brescia, W. F. (2006). Improving electronic information literacy in West African higher education. In Marshall, S., Taylor, W., & Yu, X. (Eds.), *Encyclopedia of developing regional communities with information and communication technology* (pp. 427-432). doi:10.4018/978-1-59140-575-7.ch074

Poe, J., Bevis, M., Graham, J., Latham, B., & Stevens, K. W. (2008). Sharing the albatross of e-resources management workflow. In Yu, H., & Breivold, S. (Eds.), *Electronic resource management in libraries: Research and practice* (pp. 71–89).

Poletti, G. (2006). Semantic Web and digital libraries. In Cartelli, A. (Ed.), *Teaching in the knowledge society: New skills and instruments for teachers* (pp. 271–285).

Power, C., Freire, A. P., & Petrie, H. (2009). Integrating accessibility evaluation into Web engineering processes. [IJITWE]. *International Journal of Information Technology and Web Engineering, 4*(4), 54–77. doi:doi:10.4018/jitwe.2009100104

Prakash, K. (2011). Library support to distance learners: Case of a university's distance library services in India. In Huffman, S., Albritton, S., Wilmes, B., & Rickman, W. (Eds.), *Cases on building quality distance delivery programs: Strategies and experiences* (pp. 122-134). doi:10.4018/978-1-60960-111-9.ch009

Prakash, K., Pannone, J. A., & Swarup, K. S. (2010). Building digital libraries: Role of social (open source) software. In Ashraf, T., Sharma, J., & Gulati, P. A. (Eds.), *Developing sustainable digital libraries: Socio-technical perspectives* (pp. 90–107).

Qayyum, M. A. (2008). Using annotations for information sharing in a networked community. In Putnik, G. D., & Cruz-Cunha, M. M. (Eds.), *Encyclopedia of networked and virtual organizations* (pp. 1722–1729).

Rahman, H. (2006). Empowerment of marginal communities through information-driven learning. In Rahman, H. (Ed.), *Empowering marginal communities with information networking* (pp. 16–43).

Rahman, H. (2009). Knowledge management portals for empowering citizens and societies. In Rahman, H. (Ed.), *Social and political implications of data mining: Knowledge management in e-government* (pp. 42–63).

Raihan, A. (2012). Public Access ICT in Bangladesh. In Gomez, R. (Ed.), *Libraries, telecentres, cybercafes and public access to ICT: International comparisons* (pp. 249–266).

Raisinghani, M. S., & Hohertz, C. (2009). Integrating library services into the Web-based learning curriculum. In Rogers, P. L., Berg, G. A., Boettcher, J. V., Howard, C., Justice, L., & Schenk, K. D. (Eds.), *Encyclopedia of distance learning* (2nd ed., pp. 1222–1227).

Ramachandra, M. (2010). Information archiving. In Ramachandra, M. (Ed.), *Web-based supply chain management and digital signal processing: Methods for effective information administration and transmission* (pp. 152–165).

Ramos, M. (2005). Sharing digital knowledge with end-users: Case study of the international rise research institute library and documentation service in the Philippines. In Theng, Y., & Foo, S. (Eds.), *Design and usability of digital libraries: Case studies in the Asia Pacific* (pp. 216–237).

Ramos, M. M., Alvaré, L. M., Ferreyra, C., & Shelton, P. (2009). The CGIAR virtual library bridging the gap between agricultural research and worldwide users. In Theng, Y., Foo, S., Goh, D., & Na, J. (Eds.), *Handbook of research on digital libraries: Design, development, and impact* (pp. 308–320).

Rennard, J. (2006). Producing and sharing free advanced scientific and technological knowledge using the Internet. In Marshall, S., Taylor, W., & Yu, X. (Eds.), *Encyclopedia of developing regional communities with information and communication technology* (pp. 587-592). doi:10.4018/978-1-59140-575-7.ch104

Rennard, J. (2008). Open access to scholarly publications and public policies. In Garson, G. D., & Khosrow-Pour, M. (Eds.), *Handbook of research on public Information Technology* (pp. 284–293).

Ribble, M. (2009). Becoming a digital citizen in a technological world. In Luppicini, R., & Adell, R. (Eds.), *Handbook of research on technoethics* (pp. 250–262).

Robbins, S., & Engel, D. (2005). Developing committees to create a Web content management system. In Yu, H. (Ed.), *Content and workflow management for library websites: Case studies* (pp. 216–236).

Robins, D. (2008). Accessible design for communication on the web. In Kelsey, S., & St.Amant, K. (Eds.), *Handbook of research on computer mediated communication* (pp. 527–540).

Rocheleau, B. (2006). Information management and ethical issues in government. In Rocheleau, B. (Ed.), *Public management information systems* (pp. 236-273). doi:10.4018/978-1-59140-807-9.ch008

Rocheleau, B. (2006). Public and private Information Systems: How are they similar? How are they different? In Rocheleau, B. (Ed.), *Public management Information Systems* (pp. 1-22). doi:10.4018/978-1-59140-807-9.ch001

Rodriguez, J. C., & Zhang, B. (2008). Authentication and access management of electronic resources. In Yu, H., & Breivold, S. (Eds.), *Electronic resource management in libraries: Research and practice* (pp. 250-274). doi:10.4018/978-1-59904-891-8.ch014

Romary, L., & Armbruster, C. (2010). Beyond institutional repositories. [IJDLS]. *International Journal of Digital Library Systems, 1*(1), 44–61. doi:doi:10.4018/jdls.2010102703

Romero, N. L., Cabrera Méndez, M., Carot, A. S., & Aquino, L. F. (2009). BIVALDI the digital library of the Valencian bibliographic inheritance. In Theng, Y., Foo, S., Goh, D., & Na, J. (Eds.), *Handbook of research on digital libraries: Design, development, and impact* (pp. 371–381).

Rousseau, R. (2008). Publication and citation analysis as a tool for information retrieval. In Goh, D., & Foo, S. (Eds.), *Social information retrieval systems: Emerging technologies and applications for searching the Web effectively* (pp. 252–269).

Rozengardt, A., & Finquelievich, S. (2012). Public access ICT in Argentina. In Gomez, R. (Ed.), *Libraries, telecentres, cybercafes and public access to ICT: International comparisons* (pp. 114–133).

Rubens, N., Kaplan, D., & Okamoto, T. (2011). ELIxIR: Expertise learning and identification x information retrieval. [IJISSC]. *International Journal of Information Systems and Social Change, 2*(1), 48–63. doi:doi:10.4018/jissc.2011010104

Russell, J., Glum, K., Licata, J., Russell, D., & Wohlfarth, J. (2011). Birds, bands and beyond. In Bowdon, M., & Carpenter, R. G. (Eds.), *Higher education, emerging technologies, and community partnerships: Concepts, models and practices* (pp. 29–39).

Ryan, J. (2012). Meeting them halfway: Using social networking to connect with students. In Kelsey, S., & St. Amant, K. (Eds.), *Computer-mediated communication: Issues and approaches in education* (pp. 1-14). doi:10.4018/978-1-61350-077-4.ch001

Sáenz, J., Aramburu, N., & Rivera, O. (2010). Exploring the links between structural capital, knowledge sharing, innovation capability and business competitiveness: An empirical study. In Harorimana, D. (Ed.), *cultural implications of knowledge sharing, management and transfer: Identifying competitive advantage* (pp. 321–354).

Sánchez, A., & Camacho, K. (2012). Public access ICT in Costa Rica. In Gomez, R. (Ed.), *Libraries, telecentres, cybercafes and public access to ICT: International comparisons* (pp. 150–168).

Santos, N., Campos, F. C., & Braga Villela, R. M. (2009). Digital libraries and ontology. In Theng, Y., Foo, S., Goh, D., & Na, J. (Eds.), *Handbook of research on digital libraries: Design, development, and impact* (pp. 206–215).

Saravani, S. (2009). Access and control; digital libraries; information ethics; privacy; security. In Theng, Y., Foo, S., Goh, D., & Na, J. (Eds.), *Handbook of research on digital libraries: Design, development, and impact* (pp. 16–26).

Sasaki, H., & Kiyoki, Y. (2007). Adaptive metadata generation for integration of visual and semantic information. In Zhang, Y. (Ed.), *Semantic-based visual information retrieval* (pp. 135–159).

Scarnò, M. (2010). User's behaviour inside a digital library. [IJDSST]. *International Journal of Decision Support System Technology, 2*(2), 52–59. doi:doi:10.4018/jdsst.2010040106

Schisa, K., McKinney, A., Faires, D., Kingma, B., Montague, R. A., Smith, L. C., & Sterna, M. (2011). Web-Based information science education: Leveraging the power of the network to re-define the global classroom. In Bowdon, M., & Carpenter, R. G. (Eds.), *Higher education, emerging technologies, and community partnerships: Concepts, models and practice* (pp. 164–181).

Schweibenz, W., & Sieglerschmidt, J. (2011). BAM: A German portal to libraries, archives, museums. In Styliaras, G., Koukopoulos, D., & Lazarinis, F. (Eds.), *Handbook of research on technologies and cultural heritage: Applications and environments* (pp. 68–84).

Schweibenz, W., & Sieglerschmidt, J. (2011). BAM: A German portal to libraries, archives, museums. In Styliaras, G., Koukopoulos, D., & Lazarinis, F. (Eds.), *Handbook of research on technologies and cultural heritage: Applications and environments* (pp. 68–84).

Scupola, A. (2009). E-Services in Danish research libraries: Issues and challenges at Roskilde University Library. In Scupola, A. (Ed.), *Cases on managing e-services* (pp. 204–217).

Segal, J., & Morris, C. (2012). Developing software for a scientific community: Some challenges and solutions. In Leng, J., & Sharrock, W. (Eds.), *Handbook of research on computational science and engineering: Theory and practice (2 vol.)* (pp. 177-196). doi:10.4018/978-1-61350-116-0.ch008

Seok, S. (2008). Maximizing Web accessibility through user-centered interface design. In Calero, C., Angeles Moraga, M., & Piattini, M. (Eds.), *Handbook of research on Web Information Systems quality* (pp. 206–219).

Shea, T., & Lewis, D. (2007). Cultural impact on global knowledge sharing. In Law, W. K. (Ed.), *Information resources management: Global challenges* (pp. 262–281).

Shewbridge, W. (2011). Partners in storytelling: UMBC, retirement living TV and the Charlestown Digital Story Project. In Bowdon, M., & Carpenter, R. G. (Eds.), *Higher education, emerging technologies, and community partnerships: Concepts, models and practices* (pp. 314–318).

Siachou, E., & Ioannidis, A. (2008). The centrality of team leaders in knowledge-sharing activities: Their dual role as knowledge processors. In Bolisani, E. (Ed.), *Building the knowledge society on the internet: sharing and exchanging knowledge in networked environments* (pp. 24–44).

Siakas, K., & Georgiadou, E. (2008). Knowledge sharing in virtual and networked organisations in different organisational and national cultures. In Bolisani, E. (Ed.), *Building the knowledge society on the internet: Sharing and exchanging knowledge in networked environments* (pp. 45–64).

Siqueira, S. W., Braz, M. H., & Melo, R. N. (2008). Accessibility, digital libraries and Semantic Web standards in an e-learning architecture. In Pahl, C. (Ed.), *Architecture solutions for e-learning systems* (pp. 137–153).

Sloan, D., Gibson, L., Milne, S., & Gregor, P. (2003). Ensuring optimal accessibility of online learning resources. In Ghaoui, C. (Ed.), *Usability evaluation of online learning programs* (pp. 371–386).

Smith, P. J., Stacey, E., & Ha, T. S. (2009). Blending collaborative online learning with workplace and community contexts. In Stacey, E., & Gerbic, P. (Eds.), *Effective blended learning practices: Evidence-based perspectives in ICT-facilitated education* (pp. 125–143).

Solomon, D. J. (2007). The role of open source software in open access publishing. In St. Amant, K., & Still, B. (Eds.), *Handbook of research on open source software: Technological, economic, and social perspectives* (pp. 649–658).

Soules, A., & Ferullo, D. L. (2008). Copyright implications for electronic resources. In Yu, H., & Breivold, S. (Eds.), *Electronic resource management in libraries: Research and practice* (pp. 145–173).

Sousa, J. B. (2012). The effect of google data centers on city competitiveness. In Bulu, M. (Ed.), *City competitiveness and improving urban subsystems: Technologies and applications* (pp. 233–242).

Stary, C. (2009). Ubiquitous access to adaptive hypermedia. In Khalil, I. (Ed.), *Handbook of research on mobile multimedia* (2nd ed., pp. 347–363).

Stefl-Mabry, J., Doane, W. E., & Radlick, M. S. (2011). Bringing the village to the university classroom: Uncertainty and confusion in teaching school library media students in the design of technology enhanced instruction. In D'Agustino, S. (Ed.), *Adaptation, resistance and access to instructional technologies: Assessing future trends in education* (pp. 381–394).

Stelmaszewska, H., Blandford, A., & Buchanan, G. (2005). Designing to change users' information seeking behaviour. In Chen, S. Y., & Magoulas, G. D. (Eds.), *Adaptable and adaptive hypermedia systems* (pp. 1–18).

Stewart, T., Hines, R. A., & Kinney, M. (2011). Teachers in action: High-tech, high-touch service-learning with special populations. In Bowdon, M., & Carpenter, R. G. (Eds.), *Higher education, emerging technologies, and community partnerships: Concepts, models and practices* (pp. 182–190).

Sticklen, D. J., & Issa, T. (2011). An initial examination of free and proprietary software-selection in organizations. [IJWP]. *International Journal of Web Portals*, *3*(4), 27–43. doi:doi:10.4018/jwp.2011100103

Stielow, F. (2007). Library portals and an evolving information legacy. In Tatnall, A. (Ed.), *Encyclopedia of portal technologies and applications* (pp. 554–558).

Strader, T. J. (2011). Digital convergence and horizontal integration strategies. In Strader, T. (Ed.), *Digital product management, technology and practice: Interdisciplinary perspectives* (pp. 113–141).

Straub, D. W., & Loch, K. D. (2007). Global programs of research: Maintenance and extensibility. In Hunter, M., & Tan, F. B. (Eds.), *Strategic use of Information Technology for global organizations* (pp. 33–58).

Stvilia, B., Gasser, L., & Twidale, M. B. (2007). Metadata quality problems in federated collections. In Al-Hakim, L. (Ed.), *Challenges of managing information quality in service organizations* (pp. 154–186).

Sulah, N. (2012). Public access ICT in Uganda. In Gomez, R. (Ed.), *Libraries, telecentres, cybercafes and public access to ICT: International comparisons* (pp. 466–489).

Suleman, H. (2011). Interoperability in digital libraries. In Iglezakis, I., Synodinou, T., & Kapidakis, S. (Eds.), *E-publishing and digital libraries: Legal and organizational issues* (pp. 31–47).

Swaminathan, N. (2012). Digital libraries: Their challenges and issues in the perspectives of developing countries like India. In Tella, A., & Issa, A. (Eds.), *Library and information science in developing countries: Contemporary issues* (pp. 222–232).

Synodinou, T. (2011). The protection of digital libraries as databases: An ideal choice or a paradox? In Iglezakis, I., Synodinou, T., & Kapidakis, S. (Eds.), *E-publishing and digital libraries: Legal and organizational issues* (pp. 232–256).

Székely, I. (2010). The four paradigms of archival history. [JITR]. *Journal of Information Technology Research*, *3*(4), 51–82. doi:doi:10.4018/jitr.2010100104

Tatnall, A. (2006). Web portal gateways. In Khosrow-Pour, M. (Ed.), *Encyclopedia of e-commerce, e-government, and mobile commerce* (pp. 1217–1221).

Taylor, V. (2005). Online group projects: Preparing the instructors to prepare the students. In Roberts, T. S. (Ed.), *Computer-supported collaborative learning in higher education* (pp. 19–50).

Taylor, V. A., & Coughlin, C. M. (2006). A case study of one IT regional library consortium: VALE - Virtual academic library environment. In Khosrow-Pour, M. (Ed.), *Cases on database technologies and applications* (pp. 244–266).

Taylor, W., & Wright, G. (2004). Organizational readiness for successful knowledge sharing: Challenges for public sector managers. [IRMJ]. *Information Resources Management Journal, 17*(2), 22–37. doi:doi:10.4018/irmj.2004040102

Teffeau, L., Mustafoff, M., & Estabrook, L. (2008). Access to information and the freedom to access: The intersection of public libraries and the USA Patriot Act. In Loendorf, T., & Garson, G. D. (Eds.), *Patriotic Information Systems* (pp. 57–90).

Tella, A., & Ojo, R. R. (2012). Marketing library and information services for effective utilization of available resources: The 21st century librarians and information professionals - Which ways and what works? In Tella, A., & Issa, A. (Eds.), *Library and information science in developing countries: Contemporary issues* (pp. 45–60).

Terry, A., & Gomez, R. (2012). Gender and public access ICT. In Gomez, R. (Ed.), *Libraries, telecentres, cybercafes and public access to ICT: International comparisons* (pp. 51–64).

Teusner, P. E. (2012). Networked individualism, constructions of community and religious identity: The Case of emerging church bloggers in Australia. In Comunello, F. (Ed.), *Networked sociability and individualism: Technology for personal and professional relationships* (pp. 264–288).

Theng, Y., Khoo, A., & Chan, M. (2007). Understanding usability issues in a public digital library. In Anttiroiko, A., & Malkia, M. (Eds.), *Encyclopedia of digital government* (pp. 1577–1581).

Theng, Y., Luo, Y., & Sau-Mei, G. T. (2010). QiVMDL - Towards a socially constructed virtual museum and digital library for the preservation of cultural heritage: A case of the Chinese "Qipao". [IJDLS]. *International Journal of Digital Library Systems, 1*(4), 43–60. doi:doi:10.4018/jdls.2010100103

Theng, Y., Lwin Lwin, N. C., Na, J., Foo, S., & Goh, D. H. (2009). Design and development of a taxonomy generator: A case example for Greenstone. In Theng, Y., Foo, S., Goh, D., & Na, J. (Eds.), *Handbook of research on digital libraries: Design, development, and impact* (pp. 73–84).

Tian, Q., Moghaddam, B., Lesh, N., Shen, C., & Huang, T. S. (2005). Visualization, estimation and user modeling for interactive browsing of personal photo libraries. In Srinivasan, U., & Nepal, S. (Eds.), *Managing multimedia semantics* (pp. 193-222). doi:10.4018/978-1-59140-569-6.ch009

Tobey, P. (2012). The impact of electronic reference content and discovery on publishers. In Polanka, S. (Ed.), *E-reference context and discoverability in libraries: Issues and concepts* (pp. 11–18).

Trujillo, M. F. (2006). Digital libraries and development for the illiterate. In Marshall, S., Taylor, W., & Yu, X. (Eds.), *Encyclopedia of developing regional communities with information and communication technology* (pp. 188-192). doi:10.4018/978-1-59140-575-7.ch033

Trusler, J., & Van Belle, J. (2006). A rural multi-purpose community centre in South Africa. In Marshall, S., Taylor, W., & Yu, X. (Eds.), *Encyclopedia of developing regional communities with information and communication technology* (pp. 618-623). doi:10.4018/978-1-59140-575-7.ch110

Tsingos, T. K. (2011). Liability of hosting provider with regard to open libraries. In Iglezakis, I., Synodinou, T., & Kapidakis, S. (Eds.), *E-publishing and digital libraries: Legal and organizational issues* (pp. 430–446).

Turner, M. W., Benfield, M. P., Utley, D. R., & McPherson, C. A. (2011). Integrated product teams at The University of Alabama in Huntsville. In Bowdon, M., & Carpenter, R. G. (Eds.), *Higher education, emerging technologies, and community partnerships: Concepts, models and practices* (pp. 68–76).

Upadhyay, P. K., & Moni, M. (2010). Digital library and e-governance: Moving towards sustainable rural livelihoods. In Ashraf, T., Sharma, J., & Gulati, P. A. (Eds.), *Developing sustainable digital libraries: socio-technical perspectives* (pp. 265–285).

van Dijk, J., & van Deursen, A. (2010). Inequalities of digital skills and how to overcome them. In Ferro, E., Dwivedi, Y. K., Gil-Garcia, J., & Williams, M. D. (Eds.), *Handbook of research on overcoming digital divides: Constructing an equitable and competitive information society* (pp. 278–291).

Vanin, B. (2009). Online catalogue of manuscripts conserved in libraries in the Veneto region. In Cartelli, A., & Palma, M. (Eds.), *Encyclopedia of information communication technology* (pp. 631-636). doi:10.4018/978-1-59904-845-1.ch083

Villazón-Terrazas, B. C., Suárez-Figueroa, M., & Gómez-Pérez, A. (2010). A pattern-based method for re-engineering non-ontological resources into ontologies. [IJSWIS]. *International Journal on Semantic Web and Information Systems*, 6(4), 27–63. doi:doi:10.4018/jswis.2010100102

Voelcker, M., & Novais, G. (2012). Public Access ICT in Brazil. In Gomez, R. (Ed.), *Libraries, telecentres, cybercafes and public access to ICT: International comparisons* (pp. 134–149).

Wallace, J. (2007). Surveying online scholarship. In Reynolds, R. A., Woods, R., & Baker, J. D. (Eds.), *Handbook of research on electronic surveys and measurements* (pp. 195–206).

Wanasundera, L. (2012). Public access ICT in Sri Lanka. In Gomez, R. (Ed.), *Libraries, telecentres, cybercafes and public access to ICT: International comparisons* (pp. 406–428).

Wang, S., & Song, H. (2008). Learning community and networked learning community. In Tomei, L. A. (Ed.), *Encyclopedia of Information Technology curriculum integration* (pp. 511–517).

Webb, M. A. (2009). Federal funding for career and technical education. In Wang, V. C. (Ed.), *Handbook of research on e-learning applications for career and technical education: Technologies for vocational training* (pp. 214–224).

Wendler, R., Altuna, A., Crain, T., Perez, O., Sanchez, S., & Vidotto, J. (2011). An architecture of participation: Working with Web 2.0 and High school student researchers to improve a service-learning partnership. In Bowdon, M., & Carpenter, R. G. (Eds.), *Higher education, emerging technologies, and community partnerships: Concepts, models and practices* (pp. 1–14).

Westermann, U., Zillner, S., Schellner, K., & Klaus, W. (2005). EMMO: Tradable units of knowledge-enriched multimedia content. In Srinivasan, U., & Nepal, S. (Eds.), *Managing multimedia semantics* (pp. 305-332). doi:10.4018/978-1-59140-569-6.ch013

Widén-Wulff, G. (2009). Library 2.0 as a new participatory context. In Pagani, M. (Ed.), *Encyclopedia of multimedia technology and networking,* 2nd ed., (pp. 842-848). doi:10.4018/978-1-60566-014-1.ch115

Widén-Wulff, G., & Suomi, R. (2009). The knowledge sharing model: Stressing the importance of social ties and capital. In Khosrow-Pour, M. (Ed.), *Best practices and conceptual innovations in information resources management: Utilizing technologies to enable global progressions* (pp. 146–168).

Wilson, L., & Salmons, J. (2009). Online collaborative integration and recommendations for future research. In Salmons, J., & Wilson, L. (Eds.), *Handbook of research on electronic collaboration and organizational synergy* (pp. 757–767).

Winkler, S. E. (2011). Opening the content pipeline for OpenSim-based virtual worlds. In Ciaramitaro, B. (Ed.), *Virtual worlds and e-commerce: Technologies and applications for building customer relationships* (pp. 231–243).

Witten, I. H., & Bainbridge, D. (2009). The Greenstone digital library software. In Theng, Y., Foo, S., Goh, D., & Na, J. (Eds.), *Handbook of research on digital libraries: Design, development, and impact* (pp. 61–72).

Woods, S., Poteet, S. R., Kao, A., & Quach, L. (2006). Dissemination in portals. In Schwartz, D. (Ed.), *Encyclopedia of knowledge management* (pp. 115–121).

Wu, S., & Witten, I. H. (2010). First person singular: A digital library collection that helps second language learners express themselves. [IJDLS]. *International Journal of Digital Library Systems*, 1(1), 24–43. doi:doi:10.4018/jdls.2010102702

Wu, Y. D., Cabrera, P., & Paul, J. (2010). Librarians for tomorrow at the San José Dr. Martin Luther King Jr. joint library. In Pankl, E., Theiss-White, D., & Bushing, M. C. (Eds.), *Recruitment, development, and retention of information professionals: Trends in Human resources and knowledge management* (pp. 62–82).

Xie, I. (2008). Interactive IR in digital library environments. In Xie, I. (Ed.), *Interactive information retrieval in digital environments* (pp. 116–152).

Xing, C., Zeng, C., Zhang, Z., & Zhou, L. (2005). Information filtering and personalization services. In Theng, Y., & Foo, S. (Eds.), *Design and usability of digital libraries: Case studies in the Asia Pacific* (pp. 76–96).

Yang, S., Wildemuth, B. M., Pomerantz, J. P., & Oh, S. (2009). Core Topics in Digital Library Education. In Theng, Y., Foo, S., Goh, D., & Na, J. (Eds.), *Handbook of Research on Digital Libraries: Design* (pp. 493–505). Development, and Impact.

Yang, S. Q., & Xu, A. (2012). Applying Semantic Web technologies to meet the relevant challenge of customer relationship management for the U.S. academic libraries in the 21st century using 121 e-Agent Framework. In Colomo-Palacios, R., Varajão, J., & Soto-Acosta, P. (Eds.), *Customer relationship management and the social and Semantic Web: Enabling Cliens Conexus* (pp. 284–311).

Yen, G. G. (2009). Information fusion for scientific literature classification. In Wang, J. (Ed.), *Encyclopedia of data warehousing and mining* (2nd ed., pp. 1023–1033).

Yilmaz, L. (2008). Collaborative technology: Improving team cooperation and awareness in distance learning for IT education. In Negash, S., Whitman, M., Woszczynski, A., Hoganson, K., & Mattord, H. (Eds.), *Handbook of distance learning for real-time and asynchronous information technology education* (pp. 157–169).

Yilmaz, L. (2011). Simulation-based study of community governance and conflict management in emerging global participatory science communities. In Koch, S. (Ed.), *Multi-disciplinary advancement in open source software and processes* (pp. 167–194).

Yu, H. (2005). Library Web content management: Needs and challenges. In Yu, H. (Ed.), *Content and workflow management for library websites: Case studies* (pp. 1–21).

Zanghi-LaPlaca, J. (2012). Online research without e-reference: What is missing from digital libraries? In Polanka, S. (Ed.), *E-reference context and discoverability in libraries: Issues and concepts* (pp. 74–82).

Zipperer, L. (2009). Knowledge workers, librarians, and safety: Opportunities for partnership. In Dwivedi, A. N. (Ed.), *Handbook of research on Information Technology management and clinical data administration in healthcare* (pp. 495–506).

Abresch, J., Hanson, A., Heron, S., & Reehling, P. J. (2008). *Integrating Geographic Information Systems into library services: A guide for academic libraries* (pp. 1-318). doi:10.4018/978-1-59904-726-3

Al-Mutairi, M. S., & Mohammed, L. A. (2011). *Cases on ICT utilization, practice and solutions: Tools for managing day-to-day issues* (pp. 1-346). doi:10.4018/978-1-60960-015-0

Al-Shammari, M. (2011). *Knowledge management in emerging economies: Social, organizational and cultural implementation* (pp. 1-424). doi:10.4018/978-1-61692-886-5

Ashraf, T., Sharma, J., & Gulati, P. A. (2010). *Developing sustainable digital libraries: Socio-technical perspectives* (pp. 1-378). doi:10.4018/978-1-61520-767-1

Bertot, J. C., & Fletcher, P. D. (2000). *World libraries on the information superhighway: Preparing for the challenges of the new millennium* (pp. 1-313). doi:10.4018/978-1-87828-966-7

Boughzala, I., & Dudezert, A. (2012). *Knowledge management 2.0: Organizational models and enterprise strategies* (pp. 1-282). doi:10.4018/978-1-61350-195-5

Eardley, A., & Uden, L. (2011). *Innovative knowledge management: Concepts for organizational creativity and collaborative design* (pp. 1-422). doi:10.4018/978-1-60566-701-0

Eom, S. (2009). *Author cocitation analysis: Quantitative methods for mapping the intellectual structure of an academic discipline* (pp. 1-368). doi:10.4018/978-1-59904-738-6

Fulkerson, D. M. (2012). *Remote access technologies for library collections: Tools for library users and managers* (pp. 1-487). doi:10.4018/978-1-46660-234-2

Hanson, A., & Levin, B. L. (2003). *Building a virtual library* (pp. 1–256).

Iglezakis, I., Synodinou, T., & Kapidakis, S. (2011). *E-publishing and digital libraries: Legal and organizational issues* (pp. 1-552). doi:10.4018/978-1-60960-031-0

Jennex, M. E. (2011). *Global aspects and cultural perspectives on knowledge management: Emerging dimensions* (pp. 1-464). doi:10.4018/978-1-60960-555-1

Jennex, M. E. (2012). *Conceptual models and outcomes of advancing knowledge management: New technologies* (pp. 1-510). doi:10.4018/978-1-46660-035-5

Jennex, M. E., & Smolnik, S. (2011). *Strategies for knowledge management success: Exploring organizational efficacy* (pp. 1-350). doi:10.4018/978-1-60566-709-6

López Sáez, P., Castro, G., Navas López, J., & Delgado Verde, M. (2010). *Intellectual capital and technological innovation: Knowledge-based theory and practice* (pp. 1-398). doi:10.4018/978-1-61520-875-3

Morais da Costa, G. (2011). *Ethical issues and social dilemmas in knowledge management: Organizational innovation* (pp. 1-358). doi:10.4018/978-1-61520-873-9

O'Brien, E., Clifford, S., & Southern, M. (2011). *Knowledge management for process, organizational and marketing innovation: Tools and methods* (pp. 1-308). doi:10.4018/978-1-61520-829-6

Polanka, S. (2012). *E-reference context and discoverability in libraries: Issues and concepts* (pp. 1-294). doi:10.4018/978-1-61350-308-9

Rivoltella, P. (2008). *Digital literacy: Tools and methodologies for information society* (pp. 1-368). doi:10.4018/978-1-59904-798-0

Roberts, T. S. (2008). *Student plagiarism in an online world: Problems and solutions* (pp. 1-320). doi:10.4018/978-1-59904-801-7

Tella, A., & Issa, A. (2012). *Library and information science in developing countries: Contemporary issues* (pp. 1-335). doi:10.4018/978-1-61350-335-5

Theng, Y., & Foo, S. (2005). *Design and usability of digital libraries: Case studies in the Asia Pacific* (pp. 1-395). doi:10.4018/978-1-59140-441-5

Theng, Y., Foo, S., Goh, D., & Na, J. (2009). *Handbook of research on digital Libraries: Design, development, and impact* (pp. 1-690). doi:10.4018/978-1-59904-879-6

Vallejo-Alonso, B., Rodriguez-Castellanos, A., & Arregui-Ayastuy, G. (2011). *Identifying, measuring, and valuing knowledge-based intangible assets: New perspectives* (pp. 1-438). doi:10.4018/978-1-60960-054-9

Yu, H. (2005). *Content and workflow management for library websites: Case studies* (pp. 1-282). doi:10.4018/978-1-59140-533-7

Yu, H., & Breivold, S. (2008). *Electronic resource management in libraries: Research and practice* (pp. 1-440). doi:10.4018/978-1-59904-891-8

About the Contributors

Karen Ellis has been Director of the Taylor Public Library (TPL), TX, since 2004. She received her B.A. in English (1984) and Master's in Library Science (1985) from Brigham Young University and has been working in public libraries in Texas since 1985. Karen started her professional career at the Victoria Public Library in south Texas, became a branch manager for the Harris County Public Library System in Houston, then Assistant Director for Public Services for the Nicholson Memorial Library System in the Dallas area, and finally Director of TPL (located northeast of Austin). She has reviewed books for *Kliatt* from 1986 to 2000 and for *Library Journal* since 1991.

* * *

Susan Bach (Ph.D., Rollins College Crummer Graduate School of Business) is Executive Director of the Center for Leadership Development, which under her leadership is ranked 24th nationally and #1 in Florida for leadership education by *Leadership Excellence* magazine. In 2011, she spearheaded a community engagement initiative, which earned the Rollins MBA the Graduate Management Admissions Council Institutional Award for support and commitment to community service. Her professional focus is in organizational effectiveness and leadership development, and she is a certified leadership coach. Leadership and leadership development is the field in which she currently teaches and speaks. In addition, she also has a strong track record in higher education administration. Her background also includes the corporate, entrepreneurial, and consulting sectors with an emphasis on the hotel industry. She taught hospitality management, and published in the areas of guest service and hotel crime prevention.

Barbara Brattin is Director of the Wilkinson Public Library in Telluride, Colorado. Before coming to Telluride in 2005, she worked in five libraries in Ohio and the suburbs of Chicago managing reference, technology, facilities, and security. Barbara serves on numerous boards and task forces and is currently involved in planning the Risk and Reward Conference for innovative library thinkers to be held in Telluride in 2012.

Carolyn Brooks (MLIS, San Jose State University) is the Branch Manager of the El Dorado Hills Library (El Dorado County Library system, California). A Youth Services Librarian for four years, she is also a credentialed teacher who has taught all grade levels (Preschool through College) and is an Educational Consultant. Early literacy and brain development in young children is her area of expertise, and it is through her extensive collaborative relationships with First 5 El Dorado and varied educational agencies that she is able to effect positive growth in the lives of families with young children. Carolyn has presented on these topics for the CAEYC (California Association for the Education of Young Children) and CLA (California Librarian's Association), as well as the El Dorado County Office of Education. She has been a Mentor Teacher in the areas of Literature, Storytelling, and Thematic Instruction. San Jose State University recognized her with a Research Award for her research on societal attitudes as reflected through children's literature.

Hillary Dodge obtained her MLS from Emporia State University in 2010. With twelve years of experience in libraries, she is currently the Head of Youth Services at the Clearview Library District and is an active member of several professional organizations including the Colorado Association of Libraries and Colorado Libraries for Early Literacy. Hillary has previously published Through the Eyes of Bay-Staters: A Teacher's Guide to Using Primary Sources to Understand the Civil War (Secretary of the State of Massachusetts, 2001).

Mary L. Hall (MLS, Indiana University) is the Adult Services Manager at the Bedford Public Library. She has been involved in raising and training dogs for service dog programs since 2000. She lives in Bedford, Indiana with her family (including assorted animals), and competes in triathlons.

Catherine Hakala-Ausperk is currently the Executive Director of the Northeast Ohio Regional Library System (NEO-RLS). A frequent speaker at national and state conferences, staff days, and workshops, she has a passion for supporting, coaching, and developing successful libraries, staff members, and leaders. A 27-year public library veteran and an adjunct faculty member of Kent State University's School of Library and Information Science, she has been a contributor and guest editor for ALA-APA's *Library Worklife* and her book, "Be a Great Boss: One Year to Success" was published in January, 2011, by ALA Editions. Hakala-Ausperk is an Ohio Certified Public Librarian and an American Library Association Certified Public Library Administrator (CPLA.)

Sol M. Hirsch recently retired as Director of the Alachua County (Florida) Library District. For the past several years he has been positioning his public library to provide essential services that enhance a community's quality of life rather than focus solely on improving traditional library services. This has been accomplished through partnerships with other agencies, defining library service delivery in 21st century terms, and transitioning the library's workforce to have the necessary skills to provide these new services. The challenge continues to be maintaining quality traditional services valued by many current supporters while introducing services that appeal especially to youth and non-users to grow new, future library advocates.

Kathleen Houlihan is the Youth Program Librarian for the Austin Public Library, which has been a dream job for her, tapping into many of her professional interests, like leadership, advocacy, marketing, and outreach. Kathleen has also been a leader in increasing library services to incarcerated youth. She has presented on working with at-risk youth at the city-, state-, and (in 2012) national-level, and has also been instrumental in the creation of a new ALA (ASCLA) Interest Group for those serving incarcerated youth. She's a voluminous contributor to the Library Services for Incarcerated Youth Wiki, and regularly shares her successes and struggles with the YALSA-Lockdown listserv. Her greatest ambition is to improve the quality and quantity of library services available to incarcerated youth throughout the

U.S. By empowering librarians with the resources and knowledge needed to work with the correctional facilities in their community, they can be a touchstone for youth who are struggling in their communities. By empowering these youth through literacy, a thirst for knowledge, and a connection to the community, she believes that libraries can create positive change in the world.

Susan Lovatt, BA, DipLIS is a Public Librarian working for Libraries Department of Fingal County Council (Ireland). She is currently reading for an MSc. in Leadership through Education and Training at Dublin City University. Her area of research is looking at the role public libraries can provide as educational partners to the Irish Educational Curriculum and the skills needed of librarians to fulfil these roles. She is especially interested in the teaching role of librarians. She has presented at the Irish Public Library Conference and published an article based on the work her library has done in making connections with the local community to enhance and sustain a high level of service delivery to the public. She is an active member of the Library Association of Ireland (LAI).

Paolo Melillo has over seventeen years experience working in public libraries at various librarian and managerial roles. He is currently a Branch Manager with the Orange County Library System in Orlando, Florida. He is a native of Montréal, Canada and holds an MLIS from McGill University. Paolo has coordinated several grant projects and presented programs on Smart Investing for the Florida Library Association Conference in 2009 and at the Public Library Association National Conference in March 2010. He also wrote an article on "Transforming ESOL-Learning Opportunities through Technology" for *Florida Libraries Magazine* in 2007. In 2003, he was named a Mover and Shaker for the profession by *Library Journal*.

Nkem Ekene Osuigwe (MLS) is the Director Anambra State Library Board. She is also the Chairperson, Nigerian Library Association Anambra State Chapter and the National Secretary, Public Library Section of the Nigerian Library Association. She is a doctoral student at the Department of Library and Information Science, Abia State University Uturu and is presently conducting a study on Information Technology skills of librarians in Nigerian public libraries.

Robert K. Prescott, SPHR has spent twenty years in industry and fifteen years in teaching and consulting roles. He is currently Graduate Faculty of Management at the Crummer Graduate School of Business at Rollins College in Winter Park, Florida, U.S.A. In this role, Bob is responsible for teaching graduate level courses in both the MBA and Master's of Human Resources (MHR) programs. He is a native of Birmingham, Alabama, holds a B.S. in Marketing from the University of Alabam,a and a Ph.D. in Workforce Education and Development from The Pennsylvania State University. Bob co-authored the books The Strategic Human Resource Leader: How to Prepare Your Organization for the 6 Key Trends Shaping the Future (Davies-Black, 1998) and HR Transformation: Demonstrating Leadership in the Face of Future Trends (Davies-Black/SHRM, 2009).

Erica Rose is the Head of Outreach Services for the Clearview Library District (Windsor, CO). She has over eleven years of library experience and has dedicated her work in libraries to studying and promoting outreach services. Formerly the Director of After School Programming for Omaha Public Library, she has spent years examining the relationship between schools and public libraries-searching for and creating opportunities for partnership. Erica is an active member of the American Library Association, Colorado Association of Libraries, and the Association of Bookmobile and Outreach Services. The authors conducted a workshop at the 2010 Colorado Association of Libraries annual conference on the topic of outreach in the school district. The workshop session was entitled "I Hate Reading Book Clubs" and presented a dynamic approach to working with schools and reluctant readers.

Erica Segraves is a Young Adult Librarian at the Mamie Doud Eisenhower Public Library in Broomfield, CO. Erica works extensively with professional members of the scientific community to foster lasting relationships that promote the relevance of scientific thinking and the scientific method for elementary and middle school students. She received her Master's of Library Science from Emporia State University with an emphasis on Information Management.

Lindsy Serrano (MLS, Indiana University) is a Senior Librarian for the New York Public Library (NYPL), specializing in Young Adult Services. She has served on the board of Literacy for Incarcerated Teens, a non-profit group that funds libraries and literacy programming in New York City's juvenile detention centers and is currently a contributor for Stuff for the Teenage, NYPL's blog for YA readers. In her free time, Lindsy develops the library's zine and independent press collection and films videos that highlight NYPL's arts and crafts collection.

J. Clay Singleton is the George and Harriet Cornell Professor of Finance at the Crummer Graduate School of Business at Rollins College. At Rollins Professor Singleton has been recognized with the Crummer Distinguished Faculty Award in 2004 and with the Rollins College Cornell Distinguished Teaching Award in 2009. Before joining the Crummer faculty in 2002 he was Vice President of Ibbotson Associates (now a division of Morningstar) where he was responsible for the firm's consulting, training, and research activities. Before Ibbotson Associates he was Senior Vice President for Curriculum and Examinations at the CFA Institute. In this capacity he was responsible for the CFA program's job analysis, candidate curriculum, and certification examinations. Dr. Singleton holds the Chartered Financial Analyst (CFA) designation. Dr. Singleton's research in investments and finance has been widely published in both practitioner and academic journals. He has written two books, Core-Satellite Portfolio Management: A Modern Approach to Professionally Managed Funds, and Survey Research in Finance, co-authored with H. Kent Baker and Ted Veit. Dr. Singleton earned his BAS in Political Science from Washington University in St. Louis in 1969 and his MBA and his PhD in Business from the University of Missouri-Columbia in 1972 and 1979, respectively.

Peggy Thrasher (MLIS, San Jose State University) is the Systems and Technology Librarian at the Dover Public Library in Dover, NH. She believes that public libraries can be a coalescing force in a community, and that the future of libraries lies in both the physical and virtual communities that they create. She has recently reduced her carbon footprint by purchasing a hybrid car, and now gets 60 MPG.

Index

CPSIA information can be obtained at www.ICGtesting.com
Printed in the USA
BVOW052348291211

279376BV00003B/3/P